Social Stratification of the Jewish Population of Roman Palestine in the Period of the Mishnah, 70–250 CE

The Brill Reference Library of Judaism

Editors

Alan J. Avery-Peck (*College of the Holy Cross*)
William Scott Green (*University of Miami*)

Editorial Board

Herbert Basser (*Queen's University*)
Bruce D. Chilton (*Bard College*)
José Faur (*Netanya College*)
Neil Gillman Z"l (*Jewish Theological Seminary of America*)
Mayer I. Gruber (*Ben-Gurion University of the Negev*)
Ithamar Gruenwald (*Tel Aviv University*)
Arkady Kovelman (*Moscow State University*)
Baruch A. Levine (*New York University*)
Allan Nadler (*Drew University*)
Jacob Neusner Z"l (*Bard College*)
Maren Niehoff (*Hebrew University of Jerusalem*)
Gary G. Porton (*University of Illinois*)
Aviezer Ravitzky (*Hebrew University of Jerusalem*)
Dov Schwartz (*Bar Ilan University*)
Güenter Stemberger (*University of Vienna*)
Michael E. Stone (*Hebrew University of Jerusalem*)
Elliot R. Wolfson (*University of California, Santa Barbara*)

VOLUME 59

The titles published in this series are listed at *brill.com/brlj*

Social Stratification of the Jewish Population of Roman Palestine in the Period of the Mishnah, 70–250 CE

By

Ben Zion Rosenfeld
Haim Perlmutter

BRILL

LEIDEN | BOSTON

Cover image courtesy of R&B Potchebutzky (2019).

Library of Congress Cataloging-in-Publication Data

Names: Rosenfeld, Ben Zion, author. | Perlmutter, Haim, author.
Title: Social stratification of the Jewish population of Roman Palestine in the period of the Mishnah, 70–250 CE / by Ben Zion Rosenfeld, Haim Perlmutter.
Description: Leiden ; Boston : Brill, [2020] | Series: The Brill Reference Library to Judaism, 1571-5000 ; vol. 59 | Includes bibliographical references.
Identifiers: LCCN 2020002407 (print) | LCCN 2020002408 (ebook) | ISBN 9789004422131 (hardback) | ISBN 9789004418936 (ebook)
Subjects: LCSH: Jews—History—70-638. | Jews—Palestine—Economic conditions. | Palestine—History—70-638. | Palestine—Economic conditions. | Palestine—Social conditions. | Palestine—Antiquities.
Classification: LCC DS123.5 .R69 2020 (print) | LCC DS123.5 (ebook) | DDC 305.5095694/09015—dc23
LC record available at https://lccn.loc.gov/2020002407
LC ebook record available at https://lccn.loc.gov/2020002408

Typeface for the Latin, Greek, and Cyrillic scripts: "Brill". See and download: brill.com/brill-typeface.

ISSN 1571-5000
ISBN 978-90-04-42213-1 (hardback)
ISBN 978-90-04-41893-6 (e-book)

Copyright 2020 by Koninklijke Brill NV, Leiden, The Netherlands.
Koninklijke Brill NV incorporates the imprints Brill, Brill Hes & De Graaf, Brill Nijhoff, Brill Rodopi, Brill Sense, Hotei Publishing, mentis Verlag, Verlag Ferdinand Schöningh and Wilhelm Fink Verlag.
All rights reserved. No part of this publication may be reproduced, translated, stored in a retrieval system, or transmitted in any form or by any means, electronic, mechanical, photocopying, recording or otherwise, without prior written permission from the publisher.
Authorization to photocopy items for internal or personal use is granted by Koninklijke Brill NV provided that the appropriate fees are paid directly to The Copyright Clearance Center, 222 Rosewood Drive, Suite 910, Danvers, MA 01923, USA. Fees are subject to change.

This book is printed on acid-free paper and produced in a sustainable manner.

Contents

Abbreviations IX
Preface X

1 **Introduction** 1
   1   Methodology 6
   2   Sources of the Study: Literature and Archeology 7
   3   Historical Background and Chronology 11
   4   The Roman Economy 13
   5   Structure and Stratification in Roman Society 16
   6   Outline and Structure 21
   7   Sources and Translations 23

2 **Dissecting the Poor Strata of Jewish Society in Roman Palestine, 70–250 CE** 25
   1   The Poor and Poverty in the Old Testament 27
   2   The Poor in Non-Biblical Second Temple Literature 29
   3   The Poor in the New Testament 33
   4   Summary 37
   5   The Poor and Poverty in Rabbinic Sources 37
   6   Borderline Poor 42
   7   "Poor" Can Be a Relative Term 45
   8   Historical Background for the Spread of Poverty in Jewish Society 48
   9   Summary 49
   10   Substratification of the Poor in the Roman World 50
   11   Rabbinic Attitudes toward the Poor after the Destruction of the Temple 54
       11.1 *Interest in the Poor and Poverty* 54
       11.2 *Encouraging Charity for the Poor* 57
       11.3 *Assuming Community Responsibility for the Poor* 60
       11.4 *Recommended Strategy to Avoid Poverty* 62
       11.5 *Rabbinic Theological Approach to Poverty* 63
       11.6 *Summary* 66

3 **The Laborer (*Po'el*): On Both Sides of the Poverty Line** 67
   1   The Use of the Word *Po'el* from the Bible to Second Temple Literature 68

	2	The Laborer in Josephus and the New Testament 68
	3	The Laborer in Rabbinic Sources 71
		3.1 *The Laborer and His Working Conditions* 71
	4	The Laborer's Economic Situation 82
	5	Summary 87
	6	Laborers in the Roman World 88

4 Craftsmen and Artisans: the Low Middle Class 91
 1. Crafts in the Roman Empire 95
 2. The Craftsman in Archeological Finds in Roman Palestine 98
 3. The Literary Sources 99
 4. The Craftsman in the Old Testament 100
 5. The Craftsmen in Non-Biblical Second Temple Literature 101
 6. The Craftsmen in the New Testament 104
 7. The Craftsmen in Rabbinic Literature 106
 8. Further Development of Terminology of Craftsmen 109
   8.1 Ba'alei Umanuyot 109
   8.2 Beit Ha'uman: *the Workshop of the Craftsman* 109
   8.3 *The Expert:* Tsaba Uman, Rofeh Uman 110
 9. Historical Background 112
 10. Rabbinic Endorsement of Craftsmanship 113
 11. Summary 115

5 The Independent Farmer (*Ba'al Habayit*) 116
 1. The Term "*Ba'al Habayit*" ("Homeowner") from Biblical Times until the First Century CE 117
 2. New Testament: Home and Landowner 118
 3. Development of *Dominus* in Roman Legal Vocabulary 120
 4. *Ba'al Habayit* in Tannaitic Sources 123
 5. Landowners Representing Members of a Social Group 125
 6. The Economic Status of the *Ba'al Habayit* 125
 7. Was the Landowner, *Ba'al Habayit*, Rich? 129
 8. The "House" of the "Householder" (*Ba'al Habayit*) in Archeological Findings 130
 9. Historical Background 135
 10. The Small Landowner in the Roman Empire 136
 11. Conclusion 139

6 The "Rich" 141
 1. The "Rich" in the Old Testament and Second Temple Literature 142
 2. The "Rich" in the New Testament 144
 3. The Attitude toward the Rich in the New Testament 145
 4. Summary 153
 5. The Term "Wealthy" in Early Rabbinic Literature 154
 6. Terminology for Wealth 156
 7. Rabbinic Attitudes toward the Rich and Powerful 158
 8. Summary 161
 9. Subdivision of the Wealthy Stratum 161
 10. The Wealthy in Rabbinic Narrative 163
 11. Rich Individuals in Roman Palestine 164
 12. Archeology of Wealth 166
 13. Dwellings in the Vicinity of Roman Palestine: Southern Syria 178
 14. Conclusion 179

Epilogue 181

Bibliography 185
Index of Modern Authors 230
General Index 232

Abbreviations

AJA	*American Journal of Archeology*
AJS	*Association for Jewish Studies* (Review)
ASBS	*The Aramaic Scriptures Research Society in Israel*
BAR	*Biblical Archaeology Review*
BJS	*British Journal of Sociology*
CAH	*The Cambridge Ancient History*
CHC	*The Cambridge History of Christianity*
CHJ	*The Cambridge History of Judaism*
CPJ	*Corpus Papyrorum Judaicarum*
DJD	*Discoveries in the Judaean Desert*
DSD	*Dead Sea Discoveries*
HGV	*Heidelberger Gesamtverzeichnis der Griechischen Papyrusurkunden Ägyptens*
IEJ	*Israel Exploration Journal*
JAJ	*Journal of Ancient Judaism*
JEP	*The Journal of Economic Perspectives*
JBL	*Journal of Biblical Literature*
JESHO	*Journal of Economic and Social History of the Orient*
JJS	*Journal of Jewish Studies*
JNES	*Journal of Near Eastern Studies*
JRA	*Journal of Roman Archaeology*
JRS	*Journal of Roman Studies*
JSNT	*Journal for the Study of the New Testament*
JSQ	*Jewish Studies Quarterly*
JTS	*Journal of Theological Studies*
MBAH	*Münstersche beiträge z. antiken Handelsgeschichte*
NEAEHL	*The New Encyclopedia of Archaeological Excavations in the Holy Land*
NP	Brill's *New Pauly*
OCD	*The Oxford Classical Dictionary*
PEQ	*Palestine Exploration Quarterly*
PBSR	*Papers of the British School at Rome*
SCI	*Scripta Classica Israelica*
SLR	*Stanford Law Review*
TDNT	*Theological Dictionary of the New Testament*
ZPE	*Zeitschrift für Papyrologie und Epigraphik*

Preface

This book deals with a unique aspect of the social and cultural history of Jewish society in Roman and early Byzantine Palestine. The time period is that of the Mishnah, 70–250 C.E. The book identifies describes and dissects the varied social strata in Jewish society Using the rabbinic literature as its primary source, as well as Roman and Christian sources adding archaeologic and anthropologic findings. In addition to defining the poor and wealthy groups, it uncovers the middling groups that were previously overlooked, innovatively using the terminology of professional endeavor as an indication of economic status. It also describes sub stratification within the poor, middle and wealthy elements of society. It shows the criteria contemporary sources used to differentiate the socio economic groups and the legal and ethical ramification of these distinctions. This book also contributes to the scholarly research of social stratification in the Roman World, establishing interdisciplinary and philological terminology representing social stratification. It paves new pathways to analyses of social and economic status in all groups of society enriching the arsenal of approaches toward this complex and dynamic topic.

Special thanks to the following individuals that significantly contributed to this volume. Ms. Rebecca Potchebutzky, and her daughter Bella, who creatively designed the cover for this book. Ms. Leah Namdar, senior librarian of the Central Library at Bar Ilan University, whose wisdom was an invaluable asset to us in this research; the librarians at the Library of Jewish Studies, who enabled us to benefit from their extensive knowledge; the anonymous reviewers who commented on the manuscript, as well as the editor of this series and editorial staff at Brill publications. Last but not least, my wife, Rivka Rosenfeld, who assisted much in the writing and editing of this volume.

CHAPTER 1

Introduction

This volume is a result of the study of social stratification in Roman Palestine in the better part of the first three centuries of the common era as it is depicted in contemporaneous literary (especially rabbinic) sources and as it can be reconstructed from various archeological sources. It explores the orderly economic hierarchy of Jewish society under Roman rule, paying specific attention to the nature and semantic range of the various terms that the sources used to paint the picture. It shows that the rabbis, for their own legal purposes, had clear definitions for the term "poverty," conceived of various levels of poverty according to a gradated scale, actually defined a poverty line, and had a unique use for the term "rich." In addition, the rabbis defined middling groups of people according to their various vocations: day laborers, craftsmen, homeowners, etc. The present research is a culmination of separate but related inquiries into each term that together can provide the reader with an overview of the social structure of Jewish society in Roman Palestine during the period under discussion. It provides philological insight into various social and economic terms, looking not just at their denotative meanings but also at their connotative meanings in order to shed light on the nature of a specific provincial economy.

In the past, research on the Greco-Roman world tended to focus exclusively on the political and religious leaders who shaped the policies, laws, and overall direction of their societies. During the twentieth century, the spectrum of research widened to include social and material history, with an emphasis on the day-to-day life of average people, the phenomenon of social stratification, and the nature of the relationships between social groups. Much research, of course, has been conducted regarding Roman society in the heart of the Empire,[1] and our research pertains to the social structure of Roman Palestine,

---

1 On Roman society, see Christ, "Roman Social"; Alföldy, *Roman Society*; MacMullen, *Social Relations*; John, *Social Standing*, Saller, *Patronage* and "Status and Patronage"; Dyson, *Community and Society*; Joshel, *Work Identity*; Aubert, "Conclusion" and "Workshop Managers"; Purcell, "Plebs Urbana," 644–688; Hopkins, *Conquerors and Slaves*, "Economic Growth," 35–77, and "Rome Taxes," 190–230; Veyne, *Bread and Circuses*; Anderson, *Architecture and Society*; Hope, "Roman Identity," 103–121; Prell, *Sozialökonomische*; Horrell, *Social*; Erdkamp, *Grain Market*; Garnsey, "Introduction," *Famine*, "Peasants," "Mass Diet," and "The Land"; Brown, *Poverty and Leadership*; Wood, "Class Relations," 17–69; Oakes, "Constructing Poverty," 367–371; Scheidel, "Human Mobility," 1–25, "Stratification," 40–59, "Economic Growth," 46–71;

a small province in the Roman Empire.[2] However, understanding the way in which social groups were organized in this province can be leveraged by researchers looking to understand the socioeconomic realities of other Roman provinces.

Furthermore, in the past, socioeconomic research into the Roman world tended to use the Roman government as an interpretive key for understanding the status of Roman subjects. The legal system, for example, divided the population according to the areas in which the government interacted with the Roman people: eligibility for military service, taxation, and jurisprudence.[3] In Roman law, the upper classes were treated preferentially, enjoying rights that included eligibility for various government positions; the lower classes, however, did not enjoy those privileges and were judged harshly when they transgressed the law (from the second half of the second century CE, these classes were known as *honestiores* and *humiliores*, respectively). Therefore, society was divided into two parts: the elite and the common people.[4] The literature of the period, which was created by and for the privileged strata, often followed this division as well.[5] Roman high society saw the lower classes as a single mass of individuals that, at best, could be used to create client–patron relationships that would give the former honor, popularity, and political support and power.[6]

Osborne, *Roman Society*; Kenny, "Past Poor," 275–306; Parkin and Pomeroy, *Social History*; Verboven, "Associative Order," 861–893; Winterling, *Politics*; Fagan, "Social Structure"; and Rawson, "Family and Society."

2 Regarding the historical geography of Roman Palestine, see, for example, Smallwood, *The Jews*, esp. 331–545; Avi-Yonah, "Jews under Roman," 1–157; Millar, *Near East*, 337–386; Butcher, *Roman Syria*, 35–64; and Sartre, *Middle East*, 54–150, 319–342.

3 Scheidel, "Stratification," points out that the Roman law did not differentiate between levels of poverty and wealth within the population and that it only distinguished members of the upper classes, *honestiores*, from members of the lower classes, the *humiliores*. This division was prevalent in the research on Roman society for many years. See Christ, "Roman Social"; and Alföldy, *Roman Society*, 78–81. See also Nicolet, "The Citizen," 20–21, on the development of the above distinction between the *honestiores* and *humiliores*.

4 Alföldy, *Roman Society*, 1–30.

5 See ibid., 125. For a summary of classical Roman literature on this topic, see Morgan, *Morality*, 90–94.

6 See Brunt, *Italian Manpower*, 383; Garnsey and Saller, *Economy and Society*; Kloft, *Wirtschaft*, 203; Purcell, "Plebs Urbana," 656–657; Jongman, "Hunger and Power," 271; Toner, *Rethinking Roman*, 50–53; and Drexhage, Konen, and Ruffing, *Wirtschaft*, 76–173. Jongman establishes that the majority of the population lived on the bare necessities. Toner maintained that 99 percent of the population merely subsisted and that 1 percent of the population comprised the upper classes that lived in luxury. See also Welborn, "The Polis and the Poor."

Social stratification traditionally relates to the economic levels of various groups in society and to the relationship between them. In the ancient world, the literary sources, including contemporaneous rabbinic literature, have only two ways of relating to types of economic groups—that is, as either being rich or poor. This dichotomy seems to indicate that society was polarized and that there were few members of society that were situated in the middle, who were neither rich nor poor. However, archeological and epigraphic finds have proven that there was a gradation and that individuals existed at many points along the economic spectrum, that is, from the extremely wealthy down to the extremely poor. This raises a question about the literature, which seems not to depict things as they were.[7] One of the objectives of our research was to address this question.

The period examined in this volume (70–250 CE) is a cohesive unit in Jewish history in Roman Palestine. It starts from the destruction of the Second Temple in 70 CE and ends in the middle of the great economic crisis in the Roman Empire (approx. 235–284 CE). It also corresponds with the period in which the earliest rabbinic literature—the Mishnah, Tosefta, and halakhic exegetical texts—were edited. The opinions quoted in this literature, which is collectively referred to as "Tannaitic literature," were attributed to sages who were called "Tannaim" (70–c. 220 CE). This research is focused on the Tannaitic period because it produced a great deal of contemporaneous literature reflecting the people and events of the time. This literature also contains remnants from earlier periods, which is material that can also be analyzed thoroughly.[8]

The research in this book analyzes society as portrayed in Tannaitic literature. It distinguishes between the various groups and classes that are mentioned, portrays the inner divisions within the latter (substratification), and describes additional important characteristics of group and class stratification. It will identify the terms used by contemporaneous sages and other authors to describe the various socioeconomic groups and their situation in society, and will show that contemporaneous literature had intentional and unintentional definitions for the various groups and social strata of society. It is the first study of its kind exploring all strata and substrata of Jewish society

---

[7] On the dichotomy between "rich" and "poor" in ancient society, see MacMullen, *Social Relations*, 88ff.; and Gibson, *Social Stratification*, 50–75, who present Roman society in that way. However, the following researchers object to this argument and claim that a middling group exists as well as a continuum of socioeconomic statuses from rich to poor. See Wallace-Hadrill, "Roman Luxury," 156–161; Longenecker, "Economic Middle," 243–278; Mayer, "Lower Middle Class," 409–436, *Middle Classes*; and Scheidel and Friesen, "Size Economy," 61–62, take a middle approach and limit the middling population to 6–10 percent.

[8] On the redaction of Tannaitic texts, see below.

in Roman Palestine in the first centuries CE.[9] It incorporates socioeconomic criteria and terminology, with a philological examination of the ample literary sources from the period, and utilizes archeological findings, including those from recent excavations, to help expose the stratification of the Jewish population.

We employ stratification terminology in this study not only because of its archeological resonance, but because of the layered way in which social groupings are presented in the textual sources from the period under discussion. The most common economic terms used in the sources are "rich" and "poor," but we intend to show below that in the contemporaneous rabbinic literature "rich" often meant that a person was simply "not poor." We will also examine the semantic range of a variety of additional terms that we uncovered as a result of a close reading of the texts within their economic contexts. These terms have two levels of meaning: the first identifies an aspect of a social group such as occupation, trade, or profession, while the other denotes a person's economic situation. Thus, the sources define different groups that belong to the categories in between "rich" and "poor." For practical reasons, we will refer to these groups as "middling groups."[10] The reason for this choice is so that we can avoid the use of the terms "middle" and "class." We want to preclude readers from identifying these groups with what we today would call the "middle class," which describes a certain phenomenon that evolved during the Industrial Revolution in Europe in the nineteenth century and that was not found in the ancient world.[11] Indeed, this study will use elements from modern research on social stratification, including those mentioned above, in order to contextualize our findings, but it will primarily focus on the terms actually used by the rabbinic sages themselves and then explain their meanings.[12]

---

9   Fiensy, *Social History*, researched stratification prior to the destruction of the Temple. The current research focuses on the period after the destruction in 70 CE. There has been research on the poor in Jewish society. See Hamel, *Poverty*.

10 Knapp, *Invisible*, 5–10; termed the middling groups "ordinary Romans" or "invisible Romans." However, he describes mainly the people who were on the fringes of society, not the merchants or craftsmen that were the largest groups in this category.

11 This term has been used to refer to ancient middle classes by a number of researchers. See Wallace-Hadrill, "Roman Luxury," esp. 146, "Trying"; and Scheidel and Friesen, "Size Economy," 63. However, Mayer, *Middle Classes*, calls them "middle classes."

12 For some contemporary theories of middle class research, see Morazé, *Middle Classes*; O'Boyle, "Middle Class," 826–845; Cole, "Conception Middle Class," 165–185; Stearns, "Middle Class," 377–396; Foster, "Relative Poverty," 335–341; Beechey, "Rethinking Work," 45–62; Grusky, "Social Stratification," 1–18; Lee, "Class Theories," 245–253; Birkelund, "Class Future," 217–221; Edgell, *Class*, esp. 44–53; Costin, "Craft and Social," 1–13; Banerjee and Duflo, "Middle Class," 3–28; Dahms, "Weberian Marxism," 182–217; Birdsall, "Middle Class,"

Modern literature primarily uses the terms "rich" to refer to the top echelons of society, "poor" to refer to those who lack money, and "middle class" to refer to those who are located somewhere in between—those who are neither "rich" nor "poor." The line between the poor and middle class is defined as the "poverty line" in many societies, but there is usually no clear line between the middle and upper classes.[13] The concept of "middle class" has been used in modern times primarily for the purposes of both understanding and describing economic and social stratification.[14] Historians often use the term, but do not define what it means.[15] Defining the in-between groups is essential because it also defines the lower and upper classes on either side of them. It is also important to identify hierarchies within the middling groups. The headings of the chapters to come will follow the authentic terms used in the rabbinic sources. And these terms will be elucidated for the modern reader in the body of each respective chapter.

The research presented in this study also deals with the issue of the attitude(s) that the literary sources present vis-à-vis the various socioeconomic strata of society. Did the authors of these sources (collectively and individually) see the poor, for example, as "others"—outcasts of society—or as part of society? When, how, and why did Jewish society organize community assistance for the poor? What were the criteria for public assistance and what were the goals of that assistance? What is known about the middling groups

---

157–188; Milanovic and Yitzhaki, "Middle Class," 155–178; Daly and Wilson, "Keeping Up," 1–41; Devine, *Social Class*, esp. 18–45; Kharas and Gertz, "New Global Middle Class," 32–51; Ravallion, "Middle Class," 445–454; Gane, "Weber," 211–226; Crompton, *Class*, esp. 103–109; Cashell, "Middle Class"; Cain, "Marxian Economic"; Kerbo, *Social Stratification*, 202–236; and Giddens et al., *Introduction*, 170–176.

13   See López-Calva and Ortiz-Juarez, "Vulnerability," 24.

14   Blau, *Approaches*, 222. On the various approaches to measuring the economic capabilities of the middle classes, see Cashell, "Middle Class," 2–3. He measures according to household income. See also Milanovic and Yitzhaki, "Middle Class," 155–178; Kharas and Gertz, "New Global Middle Class," 32–51; Birdsall, "Middle Class," 157–188; Banerjee and Duflo, "Middle Class," 3–28; and Ravallion, "Middle Class," 445–454. All these researchers follow family or per capita income in comparison to the average household income, but argue about what the calculation should be to consider households as belonging to the middle class. Another way of defining middle class is according to the subjective question of whether groups see themselves as poor, middle class, or rich. On this approach, see Cole, "Conception Middle Class," 275–280; Cashell, "Middle Class," 3. López-Calva and Ortiz-Juarez, "Vulnerability," 30–35, focus on the potential dangers of a family sinking below the poverty line.

15   On the use of stratification terms by historians, see Stearns, "Middle Class," 377. On the differences between modern stratification and ancient stratification, see Nolte, "Social Inequality"; and Kerbo, *Social Stratification*, 51–82, esp. 69–77.

in society? How can they be identified and placed on an economic spectrum? Were they critical of the rich or did they see the rich in a positive light? Did the authors of rabbinic literature come from the social milieu of the rich, the poor, or from somewhere in between?

In order to accurately answer these questions and to understand the social stratification of the Jews in Roman Palestine, it is necessary to compare the knowledge gleaned from local sources to that which can be found in sources from other parts of the Roman Empire. It is also helpful to understand what wealth meant in Rome and how wealth in metropolitan Rome differed from wealth in the provinces or the smaller towns of Italy. The conclusions that we reach in this study will supply tools with which scholars can accurately analyze ancient societies and thus overcome methodological obstacles that currently hinder modern research. They will present new inroads to discovering and defining groups of various socioeconomic statuses and capabilities and find the social and economic meaning of terms that are not primarily socioeconomic.

1   Methodology

Social and economic history investigates the history of societies, their leadership, their technology, and their culture.[16] Research into the stratification of society is a method of understanding society from the point of view of the average person who dealt with issues of social and economic survival alongside political, religious, and ideological challenges. Much research has been devoted to ideological and political history, but there is a need for more research devoted to social and economic history, especially research that investigates the history of the subdivision of societies into various groups or strata.[17] The present research uses an interdisciplinary approach, incorporating social and economic history, literary texts, archeology, and epigraphy (i.e., inscriptional evidence).

This study proposes economic criteria for defining the various strata of society that come from contemporaneous literature and provide a glimpse into how the authors gradated the population economically, determining the level of financial capability that in their eyes would be considered basic and

---

16   Burke, *History and Social*, 13–21. On class research in social history, see ibid., 60–70.
17   Goodman, *Roman Galilee*, 3–5, points out the lack of socioeconomic studies of Roman Palestine. Regarding the study of the lower classes of ancient society in general, see Lenski, *Power and Privilege*. See also Loewe, "Structure and Practice," 485–486; and Nishijima, "Han History," 552–553. Garnsey, *Food*, 113–127, shows the varied diets of various strata of ancient Greco-Roman society.

minimal. This is accomplished by analyzing the legal legislation of the ancient sources regarding the financial obligations and rights of the various groups in society, and by conducting a philological analysis to understand the precise meaning of words and terms used in these sources. Using the criteria of contemporaneous authors prevents problems of anachronism when applying modern social concepts to the ancient texts.[18]

The findings from Roman Palestine are compared to findings from other parts of the Roman world. The Roman economy was not a monolithic system, and each locale and province had their own unique conditions and characteristics, which is not, of course, to say that there were not any similarities. And one must keep in mind that the Roman civil and military administrative apparatus and the Roman military itself were similarly organized throughout the Empire, and that these were strong unifying factors that affected a *somewhat* uniform legal and economic policy throughout the Empire, as baseline if you will. Therefore, it is logical to assume that existing similarities between regions and provinces increased as time passed. Ancient society was, for the most part, extremely traditional and conservative in nature, and it did not tend to see dramatic changes unless it they were absolutely necessary (revolutions, natural disasters). This is a factor that suggests that we can make the educated assumption that there was a basic similarity of institutions and social practices as long as there is no evidence of disparity or change over time. This is why socioeconomic history can cover longer periods of time than political history.[19]

2   Sources of the Study: Literature and Archeology

Most of the literary sources consulted are gleaned from rabbinic literature. Data was also obtained from sources from the Roman-Byzantine world and ancient Christian sources, as well as from archeological and epigraphic finds.

The earliest layer of material found in rabbinic literature is that of the Tannaim—Jewish sages who were active between 70 and 220 CE. This material was gathered, compiled, and edited in later times. The Mishnah was created around 200 CE, and the Tosefta and halakhic Midrash (*midreshei halakha*)

---

18   On the phenomenon of historical events and processes that influence the meaning of words in the Mishnah from a philological perspective, see Fraade, "Innovation," 129–148. He concludes that the "lexical-conceptual innovations and transformations were as much responses to history as propellants of history."

19   De Ligt, "Peasantry," 25–26.

around the year 250 CE.[20] The period under discussion here is close to the time that these sources were compiled.[21]

From a geographic perspective, Tannaitic sources were compiled primarily in rabbinic centers after the destruction of the Second Temple (70–250 CE), first in Yavneh (Jamnia) and Lydda (Diospolis) in the Judean Plain (Shfela) and to a lesser degree in the Sepphoris (Diocaesarea) area in the Galilee. At a later period, after the Bar Kokhba Revolt (132–135 CE), the literary work was conducted primarily in Lower Galilee, in centers like Usha, Beit Shea'rim, Sepphoris, and others, and sporadically in Lydda in Judea. Finally, the Mishnah was edited in Sepphoris by Rabbi Judah the Prince. The Tosefta and halakhic Midrash were also compiled in the Galilee. Since the Mishnah and Tosefta were compiled in the Galilee, it is possible that the agricultural, economic, and social conditions described primarily reflect Jewish society in the Galilee in the second and third centuries CE with some information that originated in the southern centers of Lydda and Yavneh.[22]

Researchers today dispute the possibility of extracting accurate historical information from rabbinic sources. Neusner and others maintain that the rabbis who produced this literature lived in intellectual isolation and did not have influence over the legal and religious conduct of the masses that they ascribed to themselves.[23] The opposite approach is that of the "historical nucleus" view. This view maintains that it is in fact possible to extract valuable historical knowledge from rabbinic literature through careful analysis. The rabbis wrote for religious and legal purposes and not for the sake of recording history, and may not always depict reality exactly the way it was. However, this issue can be

---

20   On the redaction of the literature of the Tannaim, see Strack-Stemberger, *Introduction*, 149–156, 169–177, 269–273; Neusner, *Introduction*, 97–98, 124–128, 130–131, 249–250, 271–272, 305–306, 328–329; Goldberg, "Mishnah," "Tosefta"; Kahana, "Hallakhic Midrashim," esp. 60–64; Kraemer, "Mishnah"; Mandel, "Tosefta"; and Harris, "Midrash Halakhah."

21   On the advantage of the early sources over information found in the Babylonian Talmud (BT) and Aggadic Midrash, there is much literature. For a recent discussion and additional sources, see Garrison, *Redemptive Almsgiving*.

22   See Rosenfeld, "Galilean Valleys," 66–86, *Torah Centers*, esp. 82–114, 173–202; and Schwartz, "Political Geography."

23   Neusner, *Economics*, 13, *Introduction*, xix–xxxi, 1, 28–29, 97–98, 129–131, 153–155, 182–189; Neusner, "Rabbinic Sources"; Strack-Stemberger, *Introduction*, 50–68. It seems that they did not take into account the research on the archeological findings in Roman Palestine that show that the sages accurately described the material culture, the agricultural practices, and the economic and scientific reality of their times. For example, Neusner, "Aristotle," 41–45, states that the Mishnah addresses the wealthy. In contrast to this, see Levine, *Rabbinic Class*, 3–4. See also the debate between Safrai and Neusner in Neusner, "Rabbinic Sources," esp. 123; Safrai, "Rabbinic Sources," 167; and Stemberger, "Rabbinic Sources," 186.

overcome if scholars examine each source in the same way they evaluate historical narratives. The text must be checked for variations in its manuscripts, parallel texts should be seen in context, and the text's frame of reference should be determined.[24]

A compromise opinion maintains that, although one must be aware of bias and selective accounts in rabbinic literature, the sources are not reliable when relating to the status and influence of the rabbis. Nevertheless it is possible, with careful scrutiny, to study the history of the day from their writings, since the objective historical information portrayed what they experienced and witnessed day in and day out.[25] Research that primarily discusses the economic and social environments of the rabbis suggests that what can be inferred from these dicta is indeed valid. Recent archeological and material finds show in many places that rabbinic descriptions of the material culture of the time is accurate.[26] Hezser, for example, has pointed out that this kind of information can be derived from rabbinic sources since this information is candidly included in the dicta and legal rulings and is not subject to manipulation by interested parties; thus, it can be accepted by all researchers.[27]

Conclusions from the sources can only be cautiously derived after a comprehensive study of all relevant contemporaneous texts and the conversion of ancient concepts to contemporary concepts due to their incommensurability.[28] The use of a wide spectrum of sources, which would assist converting conditions in the Roman Empire and archeological data to modern measures and understandings, helps bridge the gap between the present perspective and ancient reality, confirms the part of the rabbinic corpus that reflects reality,

---

24 See Levine, *Rabbinic Class*, 13–22, 66–69; Lieberman, *Studies*, 12–23; Safrai, *Economy*, 3–16, "Rabbinic Sources," "Judaean Desert," 213–214; Gafni, "Rabbinic Historiography"; Elman, "Response," "Orality"; Schiffman, "Scrolls and Rabbinic"; Sivan, *Palestine Late Antiquity*, 262–265; as well as the different articles in Safrai, *The Literature*, 1–2. For Talmud scholars who have a similar approach, see Friedman, "Yevamot," 275–280; Halivni, "Methods"; and Milikowsky, "Status." The opposing view is maintained by Schäfer, "Rabbinic Literature." The discussion continues in Schäfer and Milikowsky, "Current Views"; and Fine, "Reading Sources," *Art and Judaism*, 97–124.

25 Goodblatt, "Rehabilitation"; Lapin, *Law and History*, 19–32 and n. 83; Hezser, *Social Structure*, 1–44, with summary of all opinions; Goodblatt, "History"; Cohen, "Rabbi," 958–970; Kalmin, "Problems Talmud," 165–183; Boyarin, *Carnal Israel*; Stern, *Jewish Identity*, xxii–xxxix, "Attribution and Authorship," "Authorship"; Mattila, "Inner Village," esp. 313. The approach of the latter three is fairly close to the approach that ascribes historical reliability to the rabbinic literature.

26 See Miller, *Texts and Material*.

27 Hezser, *Social Structure*, 40–44.

28 Pennycook, "Incommensurable Discourses." See the summary of approaches to the problem by Ling, *Poor*, 1–7.

and determines whether there are misrepresentations in rabbinic texts when compared to other sources.

It must be emphasized that the measurement of social strata by the rabbis was done first and foremost for a practical reason: the allocation of public funds for the poor and the regulation of begging. On the other hand, they needed to determine the ability of the individual to assume responsibility for religious obligations that had a financial commitment attached to them. In some cases, this information came as a result of the rabbis' interest in making order in society and in carrying out intellectual exercises. Nevertheless, it is unlikely that such measurement of social strata was pure literary fiction. The rabbis used what they saw and experienced using the names of the currencies of their time and knowing the relative value of the currency as well as its buying power in the commodity market. Inventing such information is more difficult than observing and recording it.

It should be noted that this problem of using ancient texts for the purpose of studying history is not limited to rabbinic literature. It applies also to other texts from Roman times. One important source is Roman law, which is used as an additional source for the current research.[29] The records of Roman law were not written for the sake of recording history. They present cases and rulings of the judges according to the law of the time. Researchers ask: Do the rules reflect the reality? Do the cases mentioned represent real events or are they merely hypothetical?[30] In any case, historians use Roman law as a source for historical information, assuming that to some degree the source reflects real-life situations, even if the specific cases discussed were invented by the legislators.[31]

Archeological surveys conducted in Roman Palestine in recent decades have supplied much knowledge concerning the geography of the cities, towns, villages, and farms of the area.[32] Archeological digs have enabled scholars to make the distinction between cities and villages and to carry out more detailed analyses of houses and various kinds of material findings (i.e., tools,

---

29   On Roman commercial law, see recently Sirks, "Law."
30   Alexander, "Rabbinic Literature," briefly mentioned this point. The same problems of using rabbinic sources apply to using Roman law.
31   See Watson, *Spirit*; D'Arms, *Commerce Standing*, 97–120; Robinson, *Roman Law*, 102–130; Johnston, *Roman Law*, 8–11, 131–136; Kehoe, *Profit Tenancy*, Chaps. 3–4, *Law Rural Economy*, 12–13, 19–23, 44–45, 142–148; Aubert, "Conclusion," 182–188; and Luhmann, *Law*, esp. 236–243; followed by Verhagen, "Pignus." Regarding the methodological approach to understanding the place of Roman law, see Frier and Kehoe, "Law and Institutions," 113–114; Aubert and Sirks, *Roman Law*; and Safrai, "Judaean Desert," 120. On the formation of Roman law and its use, see, for example, Wieacker, *Römische Rechtsgeschichte*, 3–200.
32   Miller, *Commoners*, 178–185.

containers, coins). There are unique methods of identifying Jewish remains in contrast to Roman, Samaritan, or other remains.[33] At some sites, there is a still a question about whether the findings belong to the Roman period or to the Byzantine period.[34] In the present study, archeological information that can be meaningfully applied to the issue of socioeconomic stratification research has been gathered. Examples include home design and size, income-generating property, vessels and movable objects, quality and décor, numismatic findings, and burials.[35] In addition, the interdisciplinary approach used here, which incorporates social, geographical, and anthropological methods into the analysis of historical and archeological sources, produces in-depth conclusions.

3 Historical Background and Chronology

A brief survey of the economic changes that Jewish society underwent during the period under discussion will help us better contextualize the various sources that we will analyze below. The Roman conquest in 63 BCE brought to Palestine a ruling power that had very different policies and a different sociopolitical culture than the previous rulers, who belonged to the Hasmonean dynasty (167–63 BCE). The Jewish population lost its independence and had to get used to the massive presence of the Roman army and administration, and to the fact that the Greek-speaking population and their Greco-Roman cultural norms began to gain increasing influence over daily life.[36] Gradually,

---

33 See Fine, *Art and Judaism*, 1–5. He relates to these findings as "Jewish archeology," defining its unique attributes and findings. See also Meyers, "Sepphoris Pools," 46–60; Levine, *The Ancient Synagogue*, 3–15; Schwartz, "Economic Life," 23–28; and Aviam, "Socio-Economic," 29–38.

34 Regarding issues of dating, see Tsafrir, "Synagogues," 151–161; Magness, "Synagogues," 507–525; and Sivan, *Palestine Late Antiquity*, 6. However, since economic factors remained stable in the ancient world for hundreds of years, later and earlier findings can help test the criteria developed from contemporary findings.

35 On the use of archeology for stratification studies, see Dark, *Theoretical Archeology*, 88–133. On home and field size and quality, see Yeivin, *Survey Settlements*, xi, 186–189; Samson, *Social Houses*, 3–15; Fiensy, *Social History*, 124; Dark, *Theoretical Archeology*, 99; Ellis, *Roman Housing*, 3–12; Meyers, "Sepphoris Pools," 46–60, "Gendered Space," 44–69; 2007; Aviam, "Socio-Economic," 29–38; and Galor, "Domestic Architecture," 420–439. On the geographical aspects of rabbinic activity, see Dar, *Landscape and Pattern* and *Sumaqa*, fig. 43. On the archeology of the poor, see Bouquet, *Everyday Life*, 27; and Sodini, "Archaeology," 43–44.

36 Although for a time Herod, who was technically Jewish, was king—not to mention his son Archelaus—he too administered his domain according to the Roman style. See Shatzman, *The Armies*, 129–216; Fiensy, *Social History*, 50–191; Butcher, *Roman Syria*, 32–121; Sartre,

friction between the Jewish population and the yoke of Roman rule, combined with an animosity between the Jewish and Gentile Greek population of the cities of Palestine that had heterogeneous populations, brought about the Great Revolt of 66–73 CE that essentially ended with the destruction of the Temple in Jerusalem in 70 CE; the Roman victory was punctuated with the capture of the fortress of Masada in 73 CE.[37]

The failure of the revolt accelerated changes in the economy related to the amount of land available to Jewish farmers. They had a lot less land to work, and this hindered their ability to sustain themselves. Though Jewish society started to recover, the Great Revolt was followed only three generations later, in 132 CE, by the Bar Kokhba Revolt, which caused even more devastation and loss of land, and caused the economic situation to become extremely difficult. Many Jews were forced to leave farming altogether and enter into commercial trade or to practice crafts in workshops. The Jewish population in Judea was practically annihilated. Some Jews remained in southern Judea from the Beit Guvrin (Eleutheropolis) area to the Lydda area, but the bulk of the Jewish population was concentrated in the Galilee and the Golan Heights in the north.[38]

During the second half of the second century, there was a certain degree of economic stability in Palestine. In the third century (235–284 CE), however, a massive political crisis in the Roman Empire affected Palestine as well, creating a difficult economic situation.[39] When the Roman Empire embraced

Middle East; Udoh, *Taxes Palestine*. On the impact of the Roman conquest on Jewish society, see Schalit, *König Herodes*, 483–562; Stern, "Herod," 239–243, 268–271; Butcher, *Roman Syria*, 275–289, 371–426; and Galinsky, "Augustan Programme," esp. 38–40. See also a number of studies on the subject in Jacobson and Kokkinos, *Herod and Augustus*. On the Roman army presence in Palestine, see Chancey, *Culture, Galilee*, 47–50, 116–117, index, s.v. Roman army; and Saddington, "Armies under Augustus."

37 On the causes of the Great Revolt, see Stern, "Herod," 296–299; Schürer, *History*, 1:484–508; Smallwood, *The Jews*, 293–327; and Goodman, *Ruling Class*, 1–93. Goodman posits that the revolt was also a social struggle of the poor against the wealthy landowners. See also Horbury, *Trajan and Hadrian*, 100–115. On the importance of the Temple to Jewish society, see Schiffman, "Temple." The destruction of the Temple had theological ramifications as well. See Najman, *Losing the Temple*, esp. 66–67, 123–125. For other aspects of the destruction, see articles in Tomson and Schwartz, *Jews and Christians*. On the development of Jewish life after the destruction, see Schwartz, "Yavne Revisited"; and Cohen, *Yavneh*.

38 See Urbach, "Idolatry." For a survey of this period, see Kasher, *Cities*; Schürer, *History*, vols. 1–2; Smallwood, *The Jews*, 441–478; Avi-Yonah, *Rome and Byzantium*; Stern, *Greek and Latin Authors*, 2: no. 391–405; Sperber, *Land*, esp. 160–176; Schwartz, *Judaea*; Eshel, "Bar Kochba"; Mor, "Bar Kokhba Revolt" and *Bar Kokhba*; Horbury, *Trajan and Hadrian*, 339–352, 401–409; and Udoh, *Taxes Palestine*, 279–287. On Roman policy toward its provinces, see Bang, *Roman Markets*, 173–190, 212–282.

39 On the crisis in the Roman Empire in the third century and its influence on Roman Palestine, see Alon, *The Jews*, 2:746–748; Avi-Yonah, *Political History*, 89–136; Urbach,

Christianity in the fourth century, living conditions for the Jews in the Land of Israel became increasingly difficult. This is also the period with which we end this study because it opens a new era in the history of the Roman Empire and because Tannaitic Jewish literature had been mostly compiled by the year 250 CE.[40]

4 The Roman Economy

In this study, we argue that social stratification derives, at least in part, from the economic conditions under which a society exists. The "form" of the economy shapes the society and vice versa. There was a great controversy among historians of the Roman Empire on this very issue between so-called "maximalists" and "minimalists." Rostovtzeff maintained that the Roman economy was more advanced than those that had preceded it. It had large-scale production as well as a considerable volume of imports and exports. In this scenario, there is room not only for a landed middling group but also for entrepreneurs and merchants. Finley, and researchers who followed his approach, posited that the Roman economy was primitive, limited, and did not have large-scale production, investment, or commerce. In a society that was so local and backward, there would be little room for middling groups of merchants or entrepreneurs, although there was still the possibility that a landed middle class existed.[41]

In the years since this well-known debate, modern researchers have uncovered much epigraphic and archeological information that has caused theorists to portray the Roman economy as indeed sophisticated and complex. Finley's claim that ancient economies were primitive in comparison with the modern industrial world and that they lacked long-term planning and large-scale factory manufacture and commerce is still valid. However, recent archeological, epigraphic, and papyrological findings have shown that Rome had many products that were made in large quantities and extensive commercial networks

---

"Idolatry," "Slavery," esp. 56–95; Levine, "The Third Century"; and Sperber, *Money and Prices*, 128–131, "The Third Century," and *Land*, Ch. 1–5. Another approach minimizes the crises: see Bar, "Third Century," esp. 169–170. On the crises in the Empire in general, see Alon, *The Jews*, 2:159–181; Philipson, "Securities," 1243–1246; Howgego, "Use of Money," 9; Van Minnen, "Money and Credit," 227–228; Avi-Yonah, *Rome and Byzantium*, 74–97; and Southern, *Roman Empire*, 50–133, 257–268.

40 This is also the starting point chosen by A.H.M. Jones to open his well-known book describing the decline and fall of the Roman Empire. See Jones, *Later Empire*.

41 See Rostovtzeff, *Roman Empire*, esp. 1276–1288; and Finley, *Ancient Economy*, esp. 150–208.

that brought these products to markets that were geographically far away from the place of manufacture—and this evidence aligns well with Rostovtzeff's opinion.[42] There are many examples of these kinds of economic activities in various areas of the Roman Empire. One important case is the ancient papyri discovered in Egypt that contained various contracts and economic correspondence. When translated, they revealed how complex and sophisticated the Roman economy was in comparison to the ancient economies that preceded it.[43] In addition, advanced research on Roman cities shows that there was much economic activity in the markets, institutions existed that financed commercial endeavors, and the technology in use was more sophisticated than ever before. Expert craftsmen perfected manufacturing methods, left their insignia on their products, organized themselves into associations or *collegia*, and left behind inscriptions describing their endeavors.[44]

---

42   Love, *Antiquity Capitalism*, primarily 93–98, 110–153; Corbier, "Coinage"; Temin, "Market Economy," "Economy"; Scheidel and Von Reden, *Economy*; Meikle, "Modernism"; Saller, "Ancient Economy"; Aarts, "Coins and Money," 2–4; Bang, *Roman Markets*, 17–36 (follows Finley); Silver, "Roman Bazaar" (a review of Bang), "Roman Economic Growth"; Scheidel, "Roman Economy" and the sources he cites in nn. 1, 15, 16, 27; Morley, *Antiquity*, 21–47; Erdkamp, "Economic Growth," esp. 1–4, 17n. 17. For other aspects concerning the commerce in Rome, see Frier and Kehoe, "Law and Institutions"; and Sneider, "Technology." This debate relates to the question of economic growth in the Roman Empire as well. See Scheidel, "Economic Growth," who posits that during the era of the Roman Empire there were periods of economic growth and expansion, and who tries to suggest ways to measure that growth. On the other hand, Wilson, "Growth Indicators," claims that it is not possible to measure growth of an ancient economy today. On the controversy concerning the Greek and Hellenistic economies, see Millett, *Lending in Athens*, 15–18; and Cohen, *Economy*, 3–25.

43   See, for example, Van Minnen, "Agriculture," 205–220. Among the 55,000 papyri that are recorded in the HGV, there are about 2,000 that relate primarily to loans. See Palme, "Texts," 388, and n. 28; Knapp, *Invisible*, 22–23; and Kelly, *Petitions*, 123–127.

44   Hopkins, "City Region"; Loane, *Industry*; Hopkins; "Economic Growth," 35–77, *Conquerors and Slaves*, "Taxes," 101–125, "Rome Taxes," 190–230; Mackensy, "Pay Differentials," 267–273; A.M.H. Jones, *Cities Eastern, Later Empire*; Jones, *Bankers*; De Ligt, *Markets, Peasants*; Greene, *Archaeology*, "Technological Innovation," 29–50; Temin, "Market Economy," 169–181, "Economy," 133–151; Kehoe, *Economy Agriculture, Profit Tenancy*; *Law Rural Economy*, "State and Production," 33–54; Howgego, "Use of Money," 1–31; Garnsey and Saller, *Economy and Society*; Garnsey, *Famine*; Saller, "Ancient Economy," 251–269; Erdkamp, *Grain Market*; Jongman, "Hunger and Power," 259–284; Hales, *House and Social*; Frier, "Subsistence Anuities," 222–230; Morley, *Antiquity*; Bang, "Trade and Economy"; Scheidel and Von Reden, *Economy*; Scheidel, "Roman Economy," 1–23; Harris, *Imperial Economy*; Wilson, "Growth Indicators," 71–82; Bintliff, "Protocapitalist," 285–292; Flohr and Wilson, "Craftsmen," 29–40; Wilson and Bowman, "Introduction," 1–26, esp. 3–7, summarize recent findings and research that side with the maximalistic view and disagree with Finley and his followers.

From the second part of the second century CE, the economic strata of Roman society were referred to in legal and literary documents as *honestiores* and *humiliores*, meaning the "honest" class and the "humble" class. This was one among other distinctions that were made between the common people and the elite. Roman literature does not recognize a third category of people who are in between the two extremes of rich and poor.[45] However, between the lines of the literature and from archeological evidence, it is clear that there was a continuum of economic status from the absolutely destitute through numerous interim levels up to the wealthy senators and the Emperor himself.

Examples for known groups in Roman society that were located in the middle of the economic spectrum were the many *collegia* that provided a social home for people in the same trade. These groups of people were not connected to each other and did not have social awareness. However, some of these organizations had membership fees that meant that the members had to have some level of economic means.

As we have mentioned above, the term "middle class" was not invented until the eighteenth century in Europe. Marx, considered the father of stratification theory, still refers in most of his writings to the rich versus the poor and only vaguely mentions a third group.[46] Weber, Marx's main ideological opponent, did in fact refer to the middle groups. However, there still seems to be little research on the middling groups in ancient societies in general and in Roman society in particular.[47]

---

[45] See Garnsey, "Legal Privilege"; Rilinger, *Humiliores–Honestiores*. On the structure of ancient society there is much literature. See Lenski and Lenski, *Human Societies*, 166–213; Wallace-Hadrill, "Roman Luxury"; and Erdkamp, "Economic Growth."

[46] See a few recent contributions on Marxian class theory: Giddens, *Class Structure*, 23–41; Wolf, "Europe"; Resnick and Wolff, *Marxian Critique*; Giddens and Held, "Introduction"; Miliband, *Class Struggle*, esp. 1–24; Crompton, *Class*, 28–32; and Kolakowski, *Currents of Marxism*. For general information about Marxist stratification theory, see Fine, "Marxist Social"; and Cain, "Marxian Economic." Indeed, this was one of Weber's prime criticisms of Marxian theory. See Giddens, *Class Structure*, 41–52; Giddens and Held, "Introduction"; Edgell, *Class*, 1–15, Hall, "Reworking," 10–20; and Crompton, *Class*, 33–35. For contemporary approaches to class theory, see Miliband, *Class Struggle*, esp. 1–24; Goldthorpe and Marshall, "Promising Future," 391–395; Clement and Myles, *Class and Gender*; Lee, "Class Theories"; Manza and Brooks, "Class Analysis"; Wright, "Continuing Relevance"; Devine, *Social Class*, 1–45; Marshall, *Repositioning*, 49–65; Portes, "Resilient Class"; Sørensen, "Sounder Basis"; Birkelund, "Class Future"; Therborn, "Class Perspectives"; Crompton, *Class*; and Wright, *Classes*.

[47] There are a number of researchers that have pointed out the common denominators of Marxist and Weberian social structures. See Wright, "Rethinking," 269–279; Edgell, *Class*, 16–37; and Hall, "Reworking," 1–15. There is also a school of thought called "Weberian Marxism" that advocates for this combination of research into modern society. Lukács is

It is also necessary to understand the difference between the rural and urban context in the history of society in the Roman Empire. In the previous generation, research on this issue had expanded and developed through discussions surrounding cities and the villages that surrounded them and by examining the relationship between the villages and the towns that governed them.[48] In the Roman world, two-thirds to three-quarters of society lived in villages. Between the second and fourth centuries CE, many people migrated from villages to cities at the encouragement of the Roman authorities.[49] This process of urbanization existed in Roman Palestine as well, where some Jews moved to the larger cities that were predominantly (culturally) Roman, while the core of Jewish society remained in villages and small towns that developed in the Galilee at the beginning of the second century. This latter population is the principal society that is described by the Tannaitic literature.[50]

5 Structure and Stratification in Roman Society

Since Palestine was part of the Roman Empire, it is necessary to know how Roman society in general was economically and socially stratified in order for us to be able to more clearly understand the structure of Jewish-Palestinian society. Alföldy was the first modern researcher to map Roman stratification. He accompanied his description with a detailed diagram (see Figure 1.1).[51]

The solid line in the top third of the pyramid divides Roman society into the upper class or *honestiores*, and the lower class plebeians, the *humiliores*, who were mostly poor. This diagram shows that, numerically speaking, many more people belonged to the lower class than to the upper class and that

---

commonly considered the founder of Weberian Marxism, and *History and Class* (Lukács, HCC) is considered to be its founding text. See Dahms, "Weberian Marxism," 182–193.

48   For various aspects of this issue, see Jones, *Cities Eastern*, 59–84, and s.v. land, villages. See also Owens, *The City*, 149–163; De Ligt, *Markets*, 106–154, 199–240, *Peasants*, 230–233, 246, and s.v. growth, urbanization; Goodman, *Roman Galilee*, 1–78, esp. 1–38; Adams, *Rome, Elite, and Suburbs*, esp. 1–24, 63–70, 83–116; and Kehoe, "State and Production." On Roman Palestine, see, for example, Schürer, *History*, 2:3–198, esp. 85–97, 184–198; Hopkins, "City Region"; Dan, *The City*, esp. 68–85, 184–226; Safrai, *Economy*, esp. 17–103, 352–404; and Sperber, *The City*, 3–7, 18–19.

49   On the difference between the city and country with regard to social stratification, see Cole, "Conception Middle Class," 284–285, who discusses the issue in feudal and modern times. However, his analysis, *mutatis mutandis*, could be relevant for ancient times as well.

50   See Yeivin, "Towns"; Levine, *Rabbinic Class*; Millar, "Near East," 347–386 and map VI; Rosenfeld, "Galilean Valleys," *Torah Centers*, 115–202, esp. 188–202; Fiensy, "Villages"; and Choi, "Interaction."

51   Alföldy, *Roman Society*, Figure 1.

INTRODUCTION

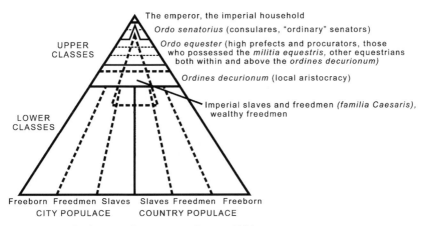

FIGURE 1.1   The division of society according to Alföldy

there is economic gradation in both groups as the pyramid becomes narrower. However, in the wording that defines the groups, Alföldy does not have a horizontal line in the pyramid to separate the middling groups from the poor. This indicates that the middle was negligible in comparison to both extremes—the rich and the poor.

On the other hand, there is differentiation of various groups within the thin stratum of rich that controlled the powerful positions in society, the ownership of land, and the conduct of trade. Winterling points out that, among the plebeians, Alföldy differentiates between slaves, freedmen, and freeborn based on status and not on economic capability. An emancipated slave could be wealthier than a freeborn plebeian. Sometimes a plebeian could be wealthier than a member of aristocratic origin who was for whatever reason(s) impoverished.[52]

When it comes to the poor, Alföldy draws a line between city and country people: the *plebs urbana* and *plebs rustica*. In comparison to city people, the people in the villages and countryside led a simpler life, had less financial opportunities, had less education, and were provided fewer services. Also, from a cultural point of view, the rustic and pastoral people had less knowledge and cultural exposure than city people did.[53]

A number of researchers have criticized Alföldy's description and have suggested alternative depictions of Roman society.[54] Regarding the upper echelons

---

52   Winterling, *Politics*, 20–21.
53   See Alföldy, *Roman Society*. See also Zanker, *Images*, 5–33; and Fiensy, *Social History*, 155–176.
54   See, for example, Vittinghoff, "Gesellschaft," "Social Structure"; Rilinger, *Humiliores–Honestiores*, 3–133, "Collegia," "Ordo"; Longenecker, "Economic Middle," 268–269; and Winterling, *Politics*, 17–25. Kron, "Housing and Distribution," 123–146, is much more optimistic about the standard of living in the Roman Empire than his predecessors.

of society, Alföldy's critics add number of important points. Stratification was gradated *within* the social groups themselves. The wealthy upper classes showed off their wealth by hosting public events, wearing expensive clothing, and adorning themselves with expensive jewelry.[55] An extremely wealthy man did not work for a living; he spent his time practicing law or politics.[56] The rich of Rome enjoyed an annual income that was unimaginable outside Rome and a lifestyle beyond the reach of the provincial upper classes. This category of wealthy Romans included the Caesar, or Emperor, and his family, the senatorial families, and some high-ranking officials. Below them was the equestrian order, which consisted of retired generals, provincial governors, and some decurions (high-ranking local officials).[57]

Some researchers have criticized Alföldy because he omits the middling groups. Freyne, for example, identifies a group of people that he calls the "*plebs media*," who lived in towns, provided services, and were not poor.[58] Verboven calls them the "Associative Order" and defines them as "able to support themselves and to devote money to social life, but not wealthy enough for luxuries."[59] Cole suggests tripartite structure of an upper, middle, and lower class that fits (among other societies) "a rural structure based on a mingling of landlordism with large and small scale farming" and "a free city at the height of medieval development."[60] The urban setting, though ancient not medieval, still fits the conditions in flourishing Roman cities in the east and the west. According to this approach, there was room in the Roman social structure for a wide stratum of "middling groups" between the rich and the poor. This coincides with the findings that we have gleaned from rabbinic literature and from the archeology of Roman Palestine, which we will demonstrate in the following chapters.

Regarding the poor, Alföldy did not distinguish between levels of poverty, putting all the poor in one stratum whether they were destitute and starving, whether they had their basic needs met, or whether they were close to the poverty line. In addition, he did not attempt to explain the nature of poverty or the reasons for it; he only distinguished between the freeborn poor and former

---

55 Saller, "Status and Patronage," 828–831.
56 Applebaum, *Work*, 71.
57 Rilinger, "Collegia," 171; Winterling, *Politics*, 24–25; Katsari, *Monetary System*, 169–185. See also Tchernia, *The Romans*, 32–42, on Roman wealth.
58 Freyne, *Jesus Galilee*, 9–97. See also Prell, *Sozialökonomische*, 10–55; and Longenecker, "Economic Middle," 243–250.
59 Verboven, "Associative Order," 861–870. He bases this definition on the *collegia* that organized the Roman professionals. These organizations had a membership fee, and a destitute person could not afford to pay them (Gibbs, "Collegia"). There is no distinct evidence for the existence of *collegia* in Roman Palestine. See Rosenfeld and Menirav, "Synagogue."
60 See Cole, "Conception Middle Class," 278.

slaves, a division that is compatible with the legal approach, but that does not deeply analyze the social picture.

There is also research on the Roman world regarding the quantities and representation of the various economic groups in society. Many researchers posit that the wealthy stratum that Alföldy wrote about was no more than 1 percent of the population.[61] Meggitt, for example, posits that 99 percent of the population was poor and struggling to achieve subsistence. However, he differentiates between the "poor," who struggled, and the "destitute," who had absolutely nothing.[62] Indeed, the definition of "poverty" in the ancient world is highly disputed, and the estimate is that the percentage of poor people varied from 5 percent of society to 33 percent depending on the location, time, and precise definition of poverty that is applied.[63] However, most researchers posit that the poor consisted of a smaller segment of society than can be seen in Alföldy's proposed structure. Friesen suggests dividing the plebeian strata of society according to income levels. In his view, the relationship of income to subsistence level determined the situation of that group in society.[64] This approach is further developed by Longenecker, who claims that there was an even larger middling class than suggested by Friesen. The following table shows the class distribution of Roman society according to the approaches of Friesen and Longenecker:

---

61   MacMullen, *Social Relations*, 89; Alföldy, *Roman Society*, 130; Rilinger, *Collegia*, 302; Scheidel, "Economy and Quality." Jones, *Bankers*, 172, calculates a much smaller percentage for the smaller cities such as Puteoli, as most of the wealthy Romans resided in the area of Rome. Scheidel and Friesen, "Size Economy," consider the elite to have comprised 1.5 percent of the general population.

62   Meggitt, *Poverty*, 1–20. His definition of poverty is a lack of basic necessities that include food, clothing, and a bed. It does not include a home, which shows why the homeowner was not poor. The Roman jurist Gaius (234.2, 50.16) is the source for this definition.

63   On the definition of poverty, see Hamel, *Poverty*, 3–15, "Poverty and Charity," 308–324; and Meggitt, *Poverty*, 4–5. Lenski defined poor people as the "expendable that are unemployed" (Lenski, *Power and Privilege*, 111–112). On the other hand, Woolf defined poverty as "people who have to devote all of their energy for survival" (Woolf, "Food Poverty," 153). Similarly, MacMullen defines the poor as "people who devote all their income to their immediate needs and do not save money" (MacMullen, *Social Relations*, 89). He estimates that about a third of ancient society fit that definition. Fiensy, who investigated Jewish society in Palestine during the Herodian period, places the sharecroppers and day laborers with the poor (Fiensy, *Social History*, 155, and chart c). He divides the independent farmers into two levels of wealth according to the amount of land they owned.

64   See Friesen, "Poverty Pauline," 131. In a later publication, Scheidel and Friesen, "Size Economy," esp. 85–88, present a similar scale placing middling groups at 6–10 percent of society, the elite at 1.5 percent, and the rest as poor. However, in a society that numbered many millions, 10 percent is a significant number. Katsari, *Monetary System*, 167–178, wrote that more than 2 percent of the population consisted of wealthy provincials (and that this figure was in addition to the Roman elite).

TABLE 1.1   Class distribution of Roman society according to Friesen and Longenecker

Sign	Description	Details of stratum	Friesen	Longenecker
PS1	Caesarian elite	The Caesar and family, senatorial families, high-ranking officials	0.04%	N/A
PS2	Provincial or local elite	equestrian families, governors of provinces, Decurions, retired army generals	1%	N/A
PS3	City elite	Most families of Decurions, independently wealthy, successful emancipated slaves, released officers, successful managers of estates, wealthy merchants	1.76%	N/A
PS4	Moderately wealthy[a] modest surplus	Some merchants, some workshop owners, soldiers, wealthy freedmen	7%	17%[b]
PS5	stable, close to subsistence	Many merchants, salary earners, craftsmen, large store owners, some freedmen, some farmers	22%	25%[c]
PS6	On the subsistence line and often beneath[d]	Small farmers, day laborers (skilled and non-skilled), some salary earners, most merchants, small storekeepers, innkeepers	40%	30%[e]
PS7	Below subsistence[f]	Some farmers, widows and orphans, beggars, non-professional day laborers, former prisoners	28%	25%

a   This is Friesen's terminology and division; see Friesen, "Poverty Pauline," 132–134. Longenecker, "Economic Middle," 267, prefers to divide this group into the rich that had surplus and the upper middling class that had moderate surplus. For an additional approach, see Oakes, "Constructing Poverty," 370–371.
b   Scheidel, "Stratification," posits that this group had 20–25 percent of the population. Longenecker, "Economic Middle," 261, maintains that Scheidel is being too generous with this figure.
c   Knapp, *Invisible*, considers this stratum as "middle class" and agrees with Longnecker's 25 percent estimate.
d   Knapp, *Invisible*, 97, 103, includes both of the lower strata in the term "poor," stating that they were 65 percent of Roman society.
e   In these two lowest strata, Longenecker is following Whittaker, "The Poor," 4–8, in accepting the lower of the two figures.
f   Whittaker, "The Poor," 4–8, divides this group into two segments: 20 percent who were in constant economic crisis and 4 percent who were expendable and who had nothing.

INTRODUCTION 21

It needs to be emphasized that in a society as vast as the Roman Empire—where some estimate the peak population in the second century CE to have been between 50 and 70 million people, even a group measuring 1–10 percent of society consisted of a large number of people and is therefore worthy, especially on statistical grounds, of research and description.[65]

Another aspect of stratification theory is the determination of the criteria that one ought to employ in the categorization of society into socioeconomic groups. The above model uses income and vocation as basic criteria. However, both MacMullen and Saller refer to the amount of property and production facilities owned by the subject as being important criteria, while for Oakes it is the ability of the individual to provide for his needs.[66] Friesen and Scheidel use income translated into kilograms of grain for their assessment.[67] Similar criteria were used in Tannaitic literature as well, and we will explore this issue in further detail in the following chapters.

This study contributes new insights to ancient social stratification that will hopefully enrich current academic methods of social inquiry. The thorough examination of all the existing information yielded a more complex internal division of Jewish society in the Roman period than was previously thought. It offers new ways in which to analyze ancient texts, a method that allows one to see the socio-structural information that is otherwise hidden in their subtexts.

6 Outline and Structure

The chapters of this study are arranged in order from lower to higher social strata. The rationale for this division is that the definition for destitute people in a given community is clear: those who have no food in the house. The levels of wealth, though finite, can at times seem endless, and their delineation involves a much higher degree of judgment. Furthermore, as will be shown below, the wealthiest Jewish residents in Roman Palestine would have been considered "comfortable" middling people in the city of Rome at most. Palestine, maybe more than other Roman provinces, was much poorer than Rome itself. The

---

65   The estimate of 70 million in the second century is from Scheidel and Friesen, "Size Economy," 66. See the sources for this estimate in n. 21. See also Scheidel, "Population." Even according to minimalizing estimates, the Roman Empire had many millions of people, and therefore a small percentage of society was still a significant portion of it.
66   MacMullen, *Social Relations*, 89; Saller, "Status and Patronage," 823–824; Oakes, "Constructing Poverty," 370–371.
67   Scheidel and Friesen, "Size Economy," 61–64.

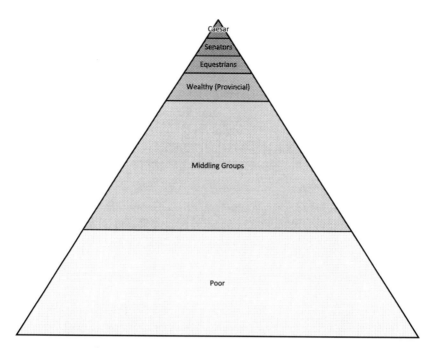

FIGURE 1.2   Social stratification in Roman Palestine (excluding the last three levels) and the Roman Empire

following diagram shows the relationship between the two societies, though the proportions are not exact: Jewish society had wealthy up to the provincial level. Perhaps the Herodian family was higher than that. Therefore, the term "rich," when used in the context of Jewish society, would not be compatible with that term used in the context of Roman society. On the other hand, the poverty levels were compatible. Therefore, this work starts from the bottom and works its way up.

Chapter 2 deals with the "poor." It shows that "poor" is a relative term in the sense that there are different levels of the absence of wealth. The lowest were the destitute, who had no money and no regular income. Above them were several groups of people who lacked wealth, as described by the sources. The sources also draw a "poverty line."

Chapter 3 proceeds to groups of people who were "not poor." The lowest groups of the "not poor" were on the border between the poor and middling groups: working as a laborer, especially as a day-laborer, was a common form of employment in the period discussed.

Chapter 4 deals with groups that were slightly better off—craftsmen of various kinds and sharecroppers. People in these groups could be poor, middling, or even moderately rich, but were usually not destitute.

Chapter 5 discusses landowners, most of whom were small landowners who worked their own land and belonged to the middling groups. This category contains various levels depending on the size of the holdings and whether the farmer worked the land himself, used workers, or involved sharecroppers.

Chapter 6 addresses the rich, the very rich, and princes. It shows that the term "rich" in literary sources is relative and often means simply "not poor." This definition includes the middling groups. When the rabbis want to talk about the upper classes, they use additional adjectives to show that "rich" means "very rich."

The stratification described in the progressive chapters of the book, from poor to rich, exposes many segments of society that together compose a complex structure. They therefore help map Roman society in Palestine and provide us with a better understanding of it.

7   Sources and Translations

For English texts of the Old Testament (OT), we primarily used the New Revised Standard Version (NRSV) and compared it to the Oxford Jewish Study Bible. For rabbinic texts, scientific editions were used whenever available and we were sure to pay attention to possible variations between manuscripts. Our Mishnah citations follow the Albeck edition, our Tosefta citations follow the Lieberman or Zuckermandel editions, and our halakhic Midrash citations will use a variety of sources: we will list the particular source or sources in the notes. Word searches were executed utilizing the database of the Responsa Project of Bar-Ilan University.[68] The English translations of the rabbinic texts appearing in this study are the standard scholarly translations. For the most part, the Neusner editions were cited. Where a different translation is used, we are sure to cite it in the notes. Occasionally, we found that it was necessary to make minor modifications in the English translations in order to make our understandings of them clearer or to make their general meaning clearer. In these cases, we note that the translation is "based on" the particular edition used.

The non-Jewish citations, such as those from the Roman world or the Church Fathers, are taken from the original sources using a scholarly English translation if one exists, such as that of the Loeb Classical Library, or, for New Testament (NT) quotes, the New International Version (NIV). In these instances as well, modifications were sometimes made due to a different interpretation of the text.

---

68   https://www.responsa.co.il/home.en-US.aspx.

Words from both Jewish and non-Jewish sources are sometimes cited. They are presented in the original language and translated into English. However, there are some words whose translation is problematic, and in these cases the word is transliterated into English from the source language (e.g., the Hebrew terms *"ashir"* = *"rich,"* *"ani"* = *"poor"*).

Earlier versions of Chapters 2 through 5 were published as separate articles and have been expanded, changed, and adapted for the present study. Much bibliography and research that appeared after the publication of these articles was added and the conclusions were clarified and modified in light of the new information. The chapter about day laborers is completely new. This text analyzes all the components of society and is not limited to a group or a social class, which was the case in the previous articles. It should be noted that little attention was paid to the various commercial occupations because this issue was addressed in a previous work.[69]

---

[69] Rosenfeld and Menirav, *Markets and Marketing*.

CHAPTER 2

Dissecting the Poor Strata of Jewish Society in Roman Palestine, 70–250 CE

In 1989, Whittaker wrote: "There are no studies specifically on poverty in ancient Rome."[1] Today, there is a lot more interest in this topic.[2] The work of numerous social scientists has focused on going beyond the legal divisions of society to distinguish the various socioeconomic subgroups within the "masses" and to analyze their various characteristics.[3] Research on poverty in the Roman world has led researchers to conclude that in late antiquity Roman society itself began to realize that poverty was a social problem and not merely the existence of a collection of individuals who did not succeed in life.[4]

The state of research, when it comes to the specific "poor" socioeconomic strata of Roman Palestine in the first centuries CE, is quite similar. Therefore, it is not surprising that in contemporaneous Palestinian sources there was a similar social division between עשיר (*ashir*), "rich," and עני (*ani*), "poor," and that there were no distinctions made between different levels of poverty.[5] Indeed, researchers have found that it is especially difficult to identify and measure the poor strata of ancient society because the latter had little property and their voice was not heard in the political realm or in the civic realm. There were also

---

1 See Whittaker, "The Poor," 3, 4, 25; and Welborn, "The Polis and the Poor," 189–190.
2 See: Veyne, *Bread and Circuses*; Garnsey, "Veyne"; Prell, *Sozialökonomische*; and Brown, *Poverty and Leadership*.
3 See Nishijima, "Han History," 552–553; Loewe, "Structure and Practice," 485–486; Garnsey, *Food*, 113–127, considering diet; and Morley, "Poor Rome," 29–30. Nishijima points out that in the Han Dynasty in China that ruled at the same time as the Roman Empire, the rulers divided society into 20 different levels. There were criteria for climbing the social ladder from level to level. Anyone who managed to rise a level was awarded with a lower rate of taxation, eligibility for land ownership, and even the right to be appointed to public office. The prospect and ability to move between levels created the interest in dividing society into so many groups.
4 Prell, *Sozialökonomische*, Chapter 3.
5 On the rich and the poor in the time of the Mishnah, see Rosenfeld, "Rich"; Hamel, *Poverty*, 5–76; and "Poverty and Charity," 308–324. In "Poverty and Charity," Hamel adjusts his analysis of Judean society, acknowledging the existence of groups that were not totally poor. See, in this regard, Fiensy, *Social History*, 165–168; and, recently, Gray, "Formally Wealthy," 101–103; and Drexhage, Konen, and Ruffing, *Wirtschaft*, 161–191.

very few authors among the poor.[6] Uyterhoeven sums it up well: "Of all social groups in late Antiquity, the poor have left the weakest imprint upon the archaeological record."[7]

In ancient economic research as well there is debate about how to define the term "poor." As it stands, most scholars tend to identify "the poor" with those people who do not earn enough for basic sustenance. However, the latter term too needs to be defined: what do we mean by the term "sustenance"? Knapp, for example, states that 65 percent of the population in the Roman Empire was poor, and the poor included "the beggar on the street, the peasant, tenant farmer and day laborer."[8] Jewish sources seem to have a different perspective on the matter. There are people defined as "poor," but with certain other criteria in mind. We will show below that not all the individuals in Knapp's definition would be considered by the rabbis as "poor."

Naturally, this limitation applies to Jewish society in Palestine as well. However, contemporaneous literary sources did in fact recognize and distinguish various kinds of "poor" and used this differentiation for socio-organizational purposes.[9] This caused greater social awareness among the Jewish leadership in Roman Palestine of the various poor strata of society.[10]

Our discussion begins with the OT and various Jewish non-biblical sources from the Second Temple period, both of which provide important background information. It then moves on to the NT, which describes the complex social situation of Palestinian Jewry around the time of the destruction of the Temple (60/70–90 CE). Finally, our discussion will shift to ancient rabbinic literature, especially the Tannaitic literature—the Mishnah, which was compiled in the

---

6   On the definition of poverty in the ancient world, see Alcock, *Understanding Poverty*, 3; Whittaker, "The Poor," 2–7; and Morley, "Poor Rome." On the meaning of "poor" and "poverty" in Roman literature, see Woolf, "Writing Poverty."

7   From Uytterhoeven, "Housing in Late Antiquity," 48. The reason is that the vast majority of archeological finds are attributed to the wealthy strata of society. Sometimes this attribution can go as low as to the middling groups. The assumption of archeologists is that material remains of the poor will be of low quality and will not last. Also, archeological digs are interested in and attracted to sites that suggest wealth and that are full of artifacts, coins, and elaborate structures. See Hirschfeld, *Dwelling*, 24.

8   See Knapp, *Invisible*, 97–103.

9   This indicates that poverty was a relative as well as an absolute situation. The same individual may belong to different categories of poverty at different stages of his life. Relative and absolute poverty is also a topic of discussion in contemporary sociology. See, for example, Foster, "Relative Poverty."

10   See Hamel, *Poverty*, 1–33, claiming that there is no known parallel in the Roman world for community-organized relief for the poor. See also Hamel, "Poverty and Charity"; and Satlow, "Charity," 244–277.

first decades of third century CE, and the Tosefta and halakhic Midrash, which were compiled a generation or two later.

1 The Poor and Poverty in the Old Testament

In order to understand the attitude of Palestinian-Jewish sources toward poverty, it is necessary to understand the biblical basis that influenced the sources of the Roman era. The Bible very much related to the poor, making it easier for them to fulfill their obligations toward the Temple.[11] It warns the people against taking advantage of the poor or doing them injustice.[12] In addition, the Bible instructs the people to give special consideration to the poor with regard to monetary assistance, charity, loans, and tithes from the fields—such as wheat, grapes, and olives, which constituted the staple crops in Palestine at the time.[13] The method of allocation to the poor commanded by the Bible was unique. A farmer was obligated to leave an unharvested corner of his field to the poor. He was to leave for the poor individual stalks of wheat that fell to the ground from a bunch cut by a sickle. Also, if the owner of the field forgot a sheaf of wheat in the field, he was to leave it for the poor.[14] An additional tithe for the poor was a tenth of all produce that was to be given to them every third and sixth year in the debt cycle of seven years.[15] During the seventh year, known as the Sabbatical year, when farmers did not plant crops the poor and the rich ate equally from the wild produce of the fields and orchards.[16] During this seventh year, there was also to be an absolution of debts as commanded in Deut. 15:9.

The Torah describes different levels of poverty using various terms such as *ani, eviyon, rash, dach,* and *miskhen*. It is not always clear what the difference

---

[11] See Exod. 30:15. The poor are not exempt from payment of the annual half shekel to the Temple. However, in Lev. 5 there are two levels of poor concerning the offering of *asham*, and in Lev. 14:21 there is consideration for the poor regarding the sacrifices of a leper who was cured of his ailment. The poor bring a cheaper offering. Lev. 27:8 concerns dedications to the Temple.

[12] See Exod. 23:3; Lev. 19:15; and Deut. 24:12, 14–15.

[13] Regarding lending without interest, see Exod. 22:25; Lev. 25:37; and Deut. 15:8. Regarding tithes from the vineyard and field, see Lev. 19:10 and 23:22. For financial assistance to avoid economic collapse, see Lev. 25:35.

[14] These tithes are discussed in the mishnaic tractate *Pe'ah*. The corner is discussed in 1–4, 9; the fallen stalks in 4:9–10, 5:1, 8:1; the forgotten sheaf in 5:7–8, 6, 7:1–2; and the tithes from the vineyard in 7:3–8.

[15] Lev. 25:6–7 and *M. Pe'ah* 8:2, 5.

[16] Exod. 23:11 and Lev. 25:4 (according to Oxford ed., 258).

between these terms is, though it seems that *eviyon* refers to the destitute compared to *ani*, which describes those with little to their name. In the Torah, the burden of assisting the poor rests with the individual who leaves tithes in his field, gives charity to a poor man who comes to his door, or lends money to a distressed Jew. However, it does not order consistent care for the poor, and does not require that society set up assistance funds or organizations for the relief of the poor.[17]

There is also a clear social message in the Torah concerning the poor. The poor person is "your kinsman."[18] You are supposed to open your hand and give to him generously.[19] God's attitude toward you will be affected by your attitude toward the poor.[20] And this idea influenced the entirety of later Jewish literature.[21] There is information in the Book of Ruth, for example, that indicates that the Jewish people actually fulfilled the commandments concerning the giving of tithes to the poor from the produce of their fields.[22]

On the other hand, a lack of an organized support system for the poor and leaving the acts of charity to the discretion of the individual opens the door for neglect, and this was later depicted by the prophets, who criticized the lack of care for the poor in society. There is also some indication that the poor were not generally seen as "kinsmen" and were not treated with the compassion that the Torah advocated.[23]

The Prophets and Wisdom sections of the Bible emphasized sympathy for the poor and scolded the Jewish people for violating the rulings of the Torah concerning the poor. God is described as the protector of the poor.[24] However,

---

17 Deut. 15:4.
18 Lev. 25:25, 39, 46, 47; Deut. 15:12; and Deut. 23:20 concern lending money to the poor without interest.
19 Deut. 15:8–11.
20 Lev. 25:38, 55; Deut. 15:9.
21 For a summary of the biblical attitude toward the poor, see Hauck, "πένης," 6, 37–40; Bammel, "πτωχός"; Loewenstamm, "Neshech ve'Tarbit"; Domeris, "ebion," "dk'," "mwk," "misken," "rws"; Rodas, "dal II"; Dumbrell, "anaw, ani"; and Rodd, *Old Testament Ethics*, 161–184. On the poor in Qumran, see Charlesworth, "Suffering," and s.v. "poor," "poverty"; Barton, *Ethics*, s.v. "poor," and 179–181.
22 Ruth 2:2–3, 8–10, 15–18, 23.
23 See, for example, 2 Kgs 4:1–4; the widow owed money and her children were to be taken as slaves. She is saved by the prophet.
24 Examples are 1 Sam. 2:8; 2 Sam. 12:1–4; Isa. 14:30, 25:4, 29:19, 32:7, 41:17; Jer. 2:34, 5:28, 22:16, 26:13; Amos 2:6, 4:1, 5:12, 8:4–6; and Ez. 16:49, 18:2, 22:29. It is especially common to relate to the poor and their problems in the Wisdom section of the Bible. See Ps. 9:19, 12:8, 28:27, 35:19, 37:14, 69:34, 72:4, 12–13, 82:3–4, 107: 41, 109:16, 31, 140:13, 112:9, 132:15; Prov. 13:8, 17:5, 22:2, 7, 22, 14:31, 18:23, 19:1, 22, 28:6, 29:13, 31:9, 20; Job 5:15, 24:4, 14, 29:16, 30:25, 31:19, 30:14; and Ecc. 5:7.

there is some criticism of the poor as well. For example, in Proverbs a connection is made between a lack of food and laziness: "Laziness induces sleep and a negligent person will go hungry."[25] And it goes on to say that "in winter the lazy man does not plow; at harvest time he seeks and finds nothing."[26]

In the Second Temple period, it is found that Mordechai and Esther instituted "presents to the poor" as part of the Purim festival and that Nehemiah ordered the rich to forfeit the debts of the poor, release all Jewish slaves, and return all land confiscated due to a lack of payment.[27] The Book of Nehemiah reports the eponymous leader's concern for the poor and his legislation on their behalf, which consisted of a land reform that gave the poor fields to tend and that canceled their debts.[28]

2 The Poor in Non-Biblical Second Temple Literature

Sources composed during the Second Temple period apart from the OT usually describe the poor in biblical terms. This is true for the Apocrypha as well as for other kinds of Jewish literature from the Second Temple period.

Ben Sira is the first Jewish writer to pay a significant amount of attention to the poor and to the gap between the rich and poor.[29] He presents poverty as a difficult situation and describes the plight of the poor rather vividly: "The poor [man] toils for a meager subsistence, and if he resists he finds himself in want" (Sir. 31:4).[30] He goes on: "The poor abhors lowliness, so does the rich abhor the poor. When the rich stumbles, he is supported by a friend; when the poor trips, he is repulsed by a friend" (13:20–21).[31] He also describes the poor asking for alms at the door, and discourages wandering and eating at others' houses (40:28–29).[32] The rich take advantage of the poor and use them for their needs, but when the rich are needed they neglect their duties (13:4). One should generously give alms to the poor (4:1–6), and God listens to the poor person when

---

25 Prov. 19:15.
26 Ibid., 20:4.
27 Esth. 9:22; Neh. 8:10, 12. This event is known in research as "the debt bondage mechanism," which was prevalent in the ancient world. See Brabec, "Laborers–Citizens," 158.
28 Neh. 5:9–13.
29 Skehan and Di Lella, *Ben Sira* (hereafter, Sir.) 4:1–9, 7:32–33, 10:23, 30–31, 11:1–6, 13:3–4, 19–21, 22–24; 21:5, 29:8–9, 12, 30:14, 31:4, 35:16–18, 38:19, 40:28–29.
30 Sir. 13:3–4.
31 See also Sir. 10:30–31, which talks about honor for the rich at the expense of the poor.
32 See also Wright and Camp, "Ben Sira's Discourse," 153–174; and Adams, "Poverty and Otherness," esp. 189–195. Later, Adams points out a change in 4QInstruction that sees poverty in a different light than Ben Sira (195–203).

he calls out in pain (21:5; 35:16–18). Poverty derives from God and is a trial given by God to test those close to him (11:14). Ben Sira emphasizes that rich and poor should be treated equally (10:30–31; 11:1, 4). He states that wealth is not something that is eternal; one can be rich and then become poor (18:25; 22:23). After death, the rich man's wealth is left to others (14:15). If one spends his money on luxuries, he could end up borrowing money with interest and end up becoming poor (18:32–19:1).

Regarding charity, Ben Sira states that charity atones for sin and that he who is benevolent to others will be supported when he is in trouble (3:30–31). He calls on his readers not to evade the poor and destitute or to detest the hungry. One should not cause sorrow to the poor or add emotional crisis to the afflicted (4:1–6). He advocates that charity be given with soft words and not criticism or scolding (18:15–17). He reiterates the demand to financially support the poor throughout the book.[33] And despite much of the above, it is still better to be a healthy poor man than to be rich and sick (30:14).

Ben Sira, who relates to the plight of the poor and the obligation of the rich, has a dilemma. Wright clarifies the dire situation: on the one hand, the Torah obligates that the rich care for the poor, and this may lead to conflict between the former and the latter; on the other hand, the rich are higher than the poor on the social scale and they will be able to inflict harm on the poor if the poor should rise up against them.[34] Wright articulates Ben Sira's advice on this issue: "For his budding scribes he makes it clear that if they find themselves in position of rendering judgments they must be fair and not prefer the case of the rich because of their influence."[35]

In the Qumran literature, poverty is usually not an economic condition but rather an attribute of humility, a confession of one's own futility and powerlessness as an attribute of faith, and the eschatological hope for salvation plays a very important role in all Qumran texts.[36] However, in the *Damascus Document* there is a criticism of society that it allows injustice to be committed against the poor.[37] In the *Hodayot Scroll*, the term relates to God helping the poor against the rich and powerful.[38] The Book of Instruction was found among the scrolls of the Qumran sect in the Judean Desert. It contains a substantial

---

33 Sir. 4:31, 7:32–33, 22:23, 25, 29:8–13, 31:23, 40:24.
34 See Wright, "Rich and Poor," 102 and n. 6.
35 See Ibid., 102 and n. 45. This idea is seen at length in an earlier work of his, Wright and Camp, "Ben Sira's Discourse."
36 See below for an elaborate discussion of the poor in Ro, "Piety," esp. 65. See also on this topic Wright, "Rich and Poor."
37 CD MS A 6.16, 21; 13:14. There is the giving of charity through the communal authorities.
38 *Hodayot* 2:34; 5:13.

amount of material concerning the poor and poverty.[39] However, in this work the term "poor," which is frequently found in the Wisdom section of the Bible, is rarely found. On the other hand, the work employs other economic terms such as *dal, evyon, rash,* and *makhsor*.[40]

These terms often refer to a lack of spirituality and the connection between this lack and poverty.[41] The Book of Instruction claims that the plight of the poor is that they are humiliated in society, and it advocates that the wealthy should support them, indicating that, if they do not support them, God may not bestow life upon them.[42] The Book of Instruction contains advice for the poor on how to conduct their lives, and promises a better future and a future reward for living according to this advice.[43] The author does not see poverty as an ideal situation that creates a better person; rather, it is an unfortunate circumstance that will eventually change for the better if one lives his life in a pious manner.[44]

In The Thanksgiving Scroll (*hodayot* = thanksgiving hymns), which was found at Qumran and which belonged to the Dead Sea sect, there is material that identifies with the plight of the poor. The poor are oppressed by the rich; they are currently humiliated and dependent on others, but this strengthens their sacrifice for God, and in the future they will not want for anything.[45] The first-century CE Alexandrian Jewish philosopher Philo and the historian Josephus, Philo's younger Palestinian contemporary, describe the Essenes as a society that despises wealth and rank and that sees poverty as a virtue. However, the writings found in the caves of Qumran only allude to that and do not state it so explicitly.[46]

---

39 See Strugnell et al., *Qumran Cave 4*; and Collins, "Wisdom, Apocalypticism," and "Wisdom."
40 As will be shown below, rabbinic literature uses the term "poor" (*ani*) and avoids the other terms used in biblical literature.
41 See, for example, 4QInstruction^b 1:1–7 and 4QInstruction^d 1:1–4. See also Adams, "Poverty and Otherness," esp. 195–203.
42 For a harsh warning to those who close their hand and do not give charity, see 4QInstruction^b 2 I 22 2 ii 4; 4QInstruction^c 2 ii 2–5; 4QInstruction^d 7 12:8 1–3; and 4QInstruction^e 8 I 7.
43 Murphy, *Wealth*, 163–180, 184–198, 207–208.
44 4QInstruction^b 2 ii, 20–21. However, Wright, "Rich and Poor," 121–123 posits that this does not relate to a wealthy person. The wise man is satisfied that he is not destitute and sees himself as being "rich" because of that.
45 These books were found in Caves 1 and 4 of Qumran. See Murphy, *Wealth*, 242–246. The idea of the rich mocking the poor is also found in 4QApocrLam B: 1–4.
46 Philo, *That Every Good Person Is Free*, 12.79, *Hypothetica* (Praep. Ev. 8.11.2); Josephus, *War* 2:122–124. An extensive analysis of the above sources is found in Murphy, *Wealth*, 415, 429–430, 450.

There are a few statements attributed to sages by rabbinic literature that date to before the destruction of the Second Temple. First, there is Simeon the Righteous, who states three cornerstones of Jewish belief, one of which is doing acts of benevolence that include charity. One of the more remarkable sayings is attributed to Yossi ben Yohanan, who, according to the sources, was active in the second century BCE during the Hasmonean Revolt. He is reported as saying "And seat the poor at your table," which means that one should share his food with the poor. This shows that there was some identification with the plight of the poor. However, this statement seems to indicate that the method recommended by Yossi ben Yohanan for the support of the poor is through hospitality—hosting the poor for meals. This is help on an individual basis and is far from recommending a society-wide organization for the relief of the poor.[47]

In another source, special attention is given to wealthy people who become poor (for whatever reason); it mentions a fund that the priests in the Temple maintained—"the discrete fund" (*lishkat hashain*) that God-fearing Jews would put money into so that poor people from good families would come and take from it discreetly.[48] It seems that it became a policy in the Temple to care for the newly poor separately from poor people who grew up in poverty.[49] The people who contributed to this fund are defined as "God-fearing," which indicates that these were voluntary donations that supported the Temple fund and that there was no attempt to collect this money from everyone. There is a parallel source that adds that this kind of fund existed not only in the Temple but also and in each and every city.[50] The sage Hillel was said to supply a poor man, a "son of the good," with a horse to ride because that is what he was used to before he lost his money.[51] This term, "son of the good" (*ben tovim*), appears independently in the two sources attributed to the beginning of the Roman conquest—the text about Hillel the Elder, who was active in the time of King Herod, and text about the fund in the Temple.[52] In addition, the Tosefta tells us

---

47   M. Avot 1:5.
48   M. Shekalim 5:6; Sifre Deuteronomy, 117 (Finkelstein ed., 176).
49   The term "*ben tovim*" appears also in Mekhilta de-Rabbi Shimeon bar Yohai, 23:3 (Epstein-Melamed ed., 214–215) in the context of poverty that the judge may favor a *ben tovim* and not the plaintive, who deserves justice. In Sifre Deuteronomy, 38, (Finkelstein ed., 74), the term appears as well, but in this case the *ben tovim* is not poor.
50   T. Shekalim 2:16.
51   T. Pe'ah 4:10 (Lieberman ed., 58).
52   There, the term "*ben tovim*" appears independently of the term "poor," but it is implied that the person is poor but "one of ours."

of a family that lost its fortune but was able to stay in Jerusalem and stay afloat because several rabbis collected a large sum of money for it.[53] It cannot be verified that the events described actually happened; it is possibly a mere glorification of the past. However, the element of a special attitude to the formerly wealthy is unique in the sources attributed to this period. It shows that the identification with the poor was restricted primarily to those who had previously been financially secure. As we will show below, the sages that are quoted from after the destruction of the Temple do not emphasize the previous state of the poor, because they consider instead the fact that one had the right to support from the community.

There is no information attributed to this period concerning the support of the people who were always poor, and it seems that the expectation was that they would survive by collecting the tithes in the field and from begging at doorsteps or in the street, while the previously rich were too proud to go to the fields or to collect door to door. This indicates some degree of neglect for and suspicion of the ordinary poor, as the special-purpose Temple fund was only for "poor people from good families."[54]

3   The Poor in the New Testament

The books of the NT, primarily the Synoptic Gospels (Mark, Matthew, and Luke), relate to Jewish-Palestinian society during the second half of the first century CE.[55] Careful analysis can utilize this source, which devotes much attention to the poor and destitute in Palestinian-Jewish society in that era. In the NT, there are many references to supporting the poor, sick, and destitute, but little description of the poor themselves and their lives.[56]

The authors, who were critical of the Jewish society of their time, provide information concerning the attitude of contemporary society to the poor. The relevant passages describe people who were completely destitute and who were considered outcasts. Among the most desolate persons, we find Lazarus, a "beggar":

---

53   *T. Pe'ah* 4:11 (Lieberman ed., 58).
54   It is possible that this is the background for the criticism voiced in the NT that the Pharisees "loved wealth" and neglected the poor. See Luke 16:14 and see below concerning the NT.
55   On the editing of the NT works, see Chapter 1.
56   See Danker, *Dictionary*, 896, s.v. "πτωχός"; and Bammel, "πτωχός," 902–907.

> At his door squatted a beggar named Lazarus covered with sores and longing to be fed if only with the scraps that dropped from the rich man's table.[57]

Lazarus was definitely someone who had absolutely nothing of his own.[58] The dog is the only creature that takes interest in his plight. He is to be rewarded by heaven, and those who did not pay attention to him will be punished. Another episode considering the poor is the following:

> And there came a certain poor widow, and she threw in two mites, which make a farthing.[59]

This woman was "poor," but had coins to put into the "treasury," and it is likely that she also had a meal in her home as well.[60] These two examples, Lazarus and the widow, showcase two kinds of "poor" people: the needy and the destitute. The destitute are helpless and rely entirely on the generosity of others for their very survival, while the needy are trying to work and struggling to make ends meet, but are not able to earn enough to sustain themselves. This differentiation between the two types of "poor"—πτωχός and πένης—is found in the writings of Greek authors who lived long before the Roman Empire came into being.[61] Nevertheless, scholars have shown that the authors of NT and other later Greek texts tended to use the two terms freely, and did not restrict them to the respective meanings described above.[62] The vast majority of "poor" mentioned in the NT belong to the πτωχός category. The other category, πένης, is rarely found. The NT is interested in showing that God prefers the offering of the poor person who gives from the little he has. And this is in contrast to the general public, which attributes more importance to the rich.

---

57 Luke 16:21–16:22 (Fitzmyer, *Luke I–IX*, 1124). See also Bauckham, "Lazarus," 97–118; and Derret, *Law*, 78–79.
58 See Matt. 12:42–43; and Luke 16:19–21. Lazarus is a poor man full of aches and pains and eats from the remnants of the rich man's food. See also Hamel, *Poverty*, 167–168; and Balch, "Rich and Poor," 216–218, who discusses the tension between rich and poor in Luke.
59 Mark 12:42; Luke 21:2. Note that Lazarus is not only poor but also "covered in sores" and that the widow is poor because she is a widow.
60 See Finley, *Ancient Economy*, 41; Danker, *Dictionary*, 220, 695, 795, 896; and Louw and Nida, *Lexicon*, 50, 57.
61 See Aristophanes, *Plutus*, 553. The life of a poor person (πένης) is to live, having nothing at all, whereas the life of a needy person (πτωχός) is to live sparingly and depend on toil.
62 See Longenecker, "Economic Middle," 245–246; and Osborne, "Roman Poverty," 11.

The NT contains much criticism of the Pharisees, a Jewish group that supposedly "loved money" and did not help the poor.[63] In the NT, Jesus cares for the poor; he instructs his disciples to divide all their belongings among the poor and recommends inviting the poor to communal meals, rather than inviting the rich.[64] On the other hand, there is a stark difference between his attitude toward illness and disability, which he promises to cure, and his attitude toward the poor, to whom he offers a portion in the "Kingdom of God" but whose economic plight he does not offer to alleviate.[65] According to NT sources, money is not important and therefore Jesus does not propose a better social system that will solve the poor's immediate need for sustenance.[66] He demanded total devotion to the poor and sick and to transfer all one's money to them rather than accumulating wealth.[67] Indeed, Jesus does all this on an individual level, and he instructs his disciples to do the same. He does not preach the establishment of a relief organization for helping the poor. Some say that giving the money to the poor was a constructive way of not having wealth rather than a way to support the poor.[68]

Nevertheless, Jesus's disciples create public relief and care for the poor. Approximately three generations after the beginning of Christianity, at the beginning of the second century CE, there were budding public relief organizations for the poor in Egypt and in Asia Minor. This phenomenon quickly expanded and encompassed Christian communities throughout the world. This development began outside Palestine and therefore does not affect the present inquiry.[69]

---

63 Luke 16:14. On Jesus's criticism of the Pharisees on socioeconomic grounds, see Mark 12:38–40; Matt. 23:13, 23, 25, 28; Luke 11:39–41, 20:47. For research on the subject, see Kittel, *TDNT*, 9:11–48; Chilton, "James"; Friedrichsen, "The Temple"; and Neudecker, *Moses Interpreted*, esp. 20–23.

64 Matt. 11:5; Luke 4:18, 6:20, 7:22.

65 Matt. 22:1–11.

66 Fitzmyer, *Luke I–IX*, 1322.

67 Matt. 19:21, 21:10; Luke 18:22. In Matt. 5:11; and Luke 4:18, 7:22, 20:6, we see the assistance that Jesus and his disciples extended to the poor and destitute, helping them with bare necessities. Regarding the sick, see Luke 14:13.

68 See Davies, "Work and Slavery," 323–324. She emphasizes that the story in Mark 10:17–31 describes Jesus telling people to give their wealth to the poor. It does not describe the actual giving. The abandonment of wealth was merely a preparation to enter the "Kingdom of God" and not a way to help the poor. See also Matt. 26:9–11 and Mark 14:5 concerning the woman who poured expensive oil on Jesus's head. When his disciples said the oil could be traded for 300 *denar* to the poor, Jesus answered that the poor will always be there, but he himself would not always be around. On Jesus's relation to the rich in the NT, see Marcus, *Mark 8–16*, 735–737.

69 Meeks, "Social," 1:156–159; Cardman, "Early Christian," 941–943.

The Synoptic Gospels may be the first sources that related to the complicated situation of the poor person in Jewish society in Roman Palestine to make a distinction between poverty types. These sources contain two descriptions of poor individuals who are in effect prototypes. One is of a "beggar" who is penniless. The other is of a poor person, but a person who is nevertheless able to function economically and even help others financially. In other contexts, the poor are mentioned side by side with the sick and afflicted or are mentioned in the abstract as a concept. Jesus preaches that "The Kingdom of Heaven" belongs primarily to the poor. In practice, Jesus is surrounded by people who, having chosen to become beggars, leave everything they own and join him. The destitute poor are of more interest to the authors of the Gospels, as they are freer and therefore more likely to follow Jesus.

In the background of the main plot in the NT, it is possible to see that society was more complex. In his travels, Jesus encounters fishermen, shepherds, and farmers. He himself grew up as the son of a carpenter, and in the Temple he confronts merchants and moneychangers. He relates parables about sharecroppers, superintendents of estates, construction workers, and day laborers. He champions the virtues of tax collectors and other "sinners."[70] Mention of these professionals in the NT tells us that they existed, but does not tell us anything about their economic status.[71] The variety of professionals mentioned show us that despite the focus of the narrative on the desperate poor, there were in society people who worked and seem to have been supporting themselves at various levels of income.[72] In addition to those who leave everything and follow Jesus, we find poor people who stay in their homes and struggle to survive.[73] The information in the NT about the life and challenges of this kind of poor person is slight, because his interaction with Jesus and his disciples would naturally be very limited. More information about the situation of this

---

70 Fishermen are described in Luke 5:1–8; and Matt. 1:16–17. John and James, Jesus's disciples, had been fishermen. Their father employed workers as fishermen as well. See Mark 3:5, which states that Jesus himself was a carpenter. Merchants are mentioned in Mark 11:15. A superintendent is mentioned in Mark 16:1–2. Builders are mentioned in Mark 16:10. Farmers are mentioned in Luke 8:4, 9:62: he who places his hand on the plow and looks back is not capable of service in the "Kingdom of God." Tax collectors are mentioned in a number of contexts. See Luke 5:27 for a tax collector whose name was Levi—Jewish—who made a large banquet.
71 Interestingly, in the beginning of the story we find Jesus encountering various professionals. As the story moves toward the climax, people are mentioned by name without mentioning their vocation.
72 Davies, "Work and Slavery," 323. See there the sources from the NT.
73 Ibid., 315–327.

category of poor is found in contemporaneous legal sources, which discuss them with relative frequency and elaboration.

4 Summary

The Synoptic Gospels may be the first sources relevant to our discussion of Roman Palestine to actually distinguish between poverty types. These sources describe to prototypical types of poor. There is the "beggar," who is penniless, and then there is the poor person, who is still able to function in society. In other contexts, the poor are mentioned side by side with the sick and afflicted or mentioned as a concept. Jesus preaches that kingdom to come belongs primarily to the poor. In practice, Jesus is surrounded by people who leave everything they own in order to join him. It therefore seems that the destitute are of more interest to the authors of the Synoptics, as they are freer and therefore more likely to join Jesus. Nevertheless, outside the limelight, we see in the NT people engaged in various forms of labor, skilled and unskilled, hired or independent, or involved in commerce. These people were of various economic levels, from poor to rich.[74]

5 The Poor and Poverty in Rabbinic Sources

Rabbinic literature shows significant expansion of the biblical laws concerning the poor.[75] There is a process of gaining an awareness of the responsibility of the leadership toward the poor. In statements attributed to sages from before the destruction of the Temple, there is a more proactive attitude toward taking care of the poor, though there is still no systematic organization designed to do just that. After the destruction, it seems that the rabbis describe the existence of a system of care for the poor. This indicates a change in the attitude toward the common poor by including them in society and addressing their needs systematically.

As a byproduct of meeting the various needs of the poor, ancient rabbinic literature from Roman Palestine contains a precise "poverty line" and a differentiation between various levels and forms of poverty; it undoubtedly supplies

---

74 Matt. 19:23–24: "It is easier for a camel to go through the eye of a needle than for a rich man to enter into the Kingdom of God."

75 On the relationship between the scriptures and the rabbinic interpretation of the obligation to separate tithes for the poor, see Avery-Peck, "Agriculture."

a more detailed picture of Palestinian-Jewish poverty. The presentation is included in legal legislation concerning the allocation of funds from the community to support and sustain the poor.[76] It provides a clearer definition of the poor and of poverty than we can glean from other contemporaneous sources.

In the Mishnah, for example, we see legislation concerning the implementation of the biblical instructions about care for the poor.[77] The Mishnah deals with the amounts one is to give for charity, tithes, and other forms of financial assistance.[78] It determines the boundaries on the prohibition of usury, the enforcement of which was important for the relief of the poor, for it prevented them from falling into complete financial ruin.[79] The following excerpt from the Mishnah instructs a farmer on how to distribute the tithe and give one-tenth of his produce in the third and sixth years of the Sabbatical cycle:

> [When dispensing the poor man's tithe], they must give to the poor at the threshing floor no less than one half *qab* of wheat, one *qab* of barley. Rabbi Meir says one half *qab* of barley. One and a half *qab* of spelt, one *qab* of dried figs, one *maneh* of fresh figs, R. Akiba says one half. One half *log* of wine, R. Akiba says one quarter. A quarter [*log*] of oil, Rabbi Akiba says: an eighth. And all other types of produce—said Abba Saul: enough so that they [the poor] may sell it and buy sufficient food for two meals.[80]

The above allocation to the poor constitutes regulation of the main food sources of the time: grain—including primarily wheat and barley—figs, dates, wine, and olive oil. We can learn from the words of Abba Saul concerning other fruits that the intent was to provide the poor man a daily amount of the staple from one source that did not combine various foods. The explanation for this can be that each species was harvested at different times and that it is therefore likely that each one would be given out to the poor at a different time of year. Therefore, when the poor person came to the threshing floor or warehouse to collect tithes, the rabbis wanted him to receive sustenance at least for that day. The main staple of produce was grain. Therefore, the Mishnah mentions the

---

76 There is a debate as to when the organized assistance for the poor began. See a summary of the various opinions in Loewenberg, *Charity*, 116–118.
77 See *M.* and *T. Pe'ah*.
78 This is elaborated in tractate *Pe'ah*, which is devoted to formulating and implementing the biblical instructions concerning the poor.
79 *M. Bava Metzia* 5 deals with this issue.
80 *M. Pe'ah* 8:5 (based on Neusner ed.).

threshing floor and does not mention the home or warehouse that would be the distribution place for the other species.[81]

In addition, it is important to emphasize that the Mishnah represents a new stage in the development of *halakha* (rabbinic law) concerning the assistance extended to the poor in relation to the Jewish religious literature that preceded it.[82] Biblical law had granted the poor certain parts of agricultural produce, and seems to leave the distribution to the various kinds of poor to the judgment of the individual giver.[83] The Mishnah takes into account that there would be many poor and that each one may receive very little. It stipulates that each one should be given enough for the day possibly assuming that the poor that have enough will go home and leave those that did not receive an allocation to go to a more distant farmer. This would preclude the possibility of all the poor running from farm to farm and receiving little in each place.

Thus, immediately after the above source, concerning the method of distribution of a biblical tithe aiding the poor, and in a natural transition, the Mishnah proceeds to describe the "new" aid for the poor organized by the communities and the regulation of its implementation. The public fund would give a wandering poor man a portion of bread that was carefully measured and carefully regulated:

> They give to a poor man traveling from place to place no less than a loaf [of bread] worth a *pondion*[84] [made from wheat that costs at least] one *sela* for four *sea'h*.[85]

The loaf was a half of a *qab* large—about 900 ml.[86] In the threshing house, the poor man receives a half a *qab* of wheat. The cost for grinding and baking the wheat was evaluated at a third of the price of bread. It seems that the village

---

81   M. Shabbat 1:1 mentions the homeowner giving something to the poor from his house. The poor are standing outside empty-handed in the beginning and are receiving a present. There is no mention of a common example for a present given from the house to the poor. See also *T. Sabbath* 1:6 (Lieberman ed., 2).

82   In *T. Shabbat* 16: 22, Beit Shammai are quoted as prohibiting the promise of funds for the poor on the Sabbath in the synagogue. This indicates that the tradition in the time that this was written was that Beit Shammai prohibited stating contributions for the poor on the Sabbath. Beit Shammai ceased to exist after the destruction of the Temple. See Ben Shalom, *Beit Shammai*, 273–276.

83   Regarding previous practice of benevolence, compare *M. Shabbat* 1:1.

84   Neusner (35) translates *dupondion*, but Danby, *The Mishnah*, 20, translates *pundion* as is stated in the text.

85   M. Pe'ah 8:7 (based on Neusner ed.).

86   A *kav* was approximately 1.8 liters.

poor man would not spend on grinding and baking bread but would instead do it himself primitively or eat it as porridge.[87]

The second public charity mentioned in the Mishnah, in tractate *Pe'ah*, is the *tamhui*. One source tells us that this form of charity was meant for the support of the wandering poor, while the *kupa* mentioned below was primarily for the local population.[88] The *tamhui* was a large, deep serving dish that was used for preparation of food, or that was used as a central dish for serving food to the table.[89] The dish would be brought to the houses in the city, and every household would contribute a food item or a portion thereof. Then the full plate would be distributed to the poor on a daily basis.[90]

The mentioning of this type of organization indicates the existence of more fortunate members of society who supported the poor—the middling groups. There were very few wealthy people in Roman society (and even fewer in Jewish society).[91] It seems that the method for supporting the poor was collection from the entire community, indicating that the philanthropic enterprise relied on small contributions of many people rather than on large contributions from the rich (as was practiced in Roman society).[92] The definition of a poor man who was entitled to receive help from the *tamhui* was he who did not have food for two meals or the equivalent of one day. This level of poverty is what we call "borderline hunger."[93]

---

87   See Albeck, *Mishnah, Pe'ah* 8:7 (Vol. 1, 65) in his commentary to the above mishnah. See also Sperber, *Money and Prices*, 113–114; Lieberman, *Tosefta Kifshuta*, Zeraim 183, concerning the relative value of wheat and bread, and production costs.

88   See *T. Pe'ah* 4:9 (Lieberman ed., 57). Indeed, it will be seen that the Mishnah differentiates, based the level of desolation that they are in, between those who receive the *tamhui* and those who receive the *kupa*. This indicates that the plight of the wandering poor was worse than that of those who stayed home.

89   See *M. Maasrot* 1:7, *Sabbath* 3:5, *Beitza* 1:8, *Nedarim* 4:4, *Kelim* 16:1, 30:2.

90   *T. Pe'ah* 4:9 (Lieberman ed., 57). See also *M. Pesahim* 10:1, which states that the *tamhui* supplied the poor with the four cups of wine for use at the Passover meal. It could be that the bread allocated to the poor in the previous quote was provided from the *tamhui*. Alternatively, a different form of collection that preceded it could have supplied it.

91   See Rodewald, *Money Tiberius*, 7–15, 27; and Friesen, "Poverty Pauline." He estimates that the elites are 1.23 percent of Roman society, leaving 90 percent of society "poor" (339–341). See also Scheidel, "Human Mobility," "Stratification"; and Parkin and Pomeroy, *Social History*, 357.

92   On philanthropy in Roman Society, see Veyne, *Bread and Circuses*, 253; Parkin and Pomeroy, *Social History*, 28, 30–31, 205, 229–230, 245; and Brown, *Poverty and Leadership*, 25.

93   See *M. Eruvin* 4:9, which discusses a poor man who cannot muster two meals of food to place outside the city so he may venture in that direction further than 2,000 cubits (around half a kilometer) restricted to him on the Sabbath. The rabbis said that he may use his "feet" to sit at the edge of the border of the town in the direction he wants to go

There was a third organized method to support the poor. The above mishnah (the small "m" referring to the actual passage) mentions: "[Whoever has sufficient] food for 14 meals may not take [money] from the *kupa*."[94] The *kupa* was a "box" or tin into which people placed money intended for charity. It seems that money was collected in this box and not merchandise, as the Tosefta mentions a poor man who gave a penny for the "box" or a piece of bread for the *tamhui*.[95] A person was entitled to financial support if he did not have in his house food for 14 meals or the equivalent of two meals a day for the next week. He may have food for a day or two but not for the week. This is a different level of poverty. This man would not be entitled to eat from the *tamhui* as long as he has food for the day, but he would be able to be assisted from the *kupa*. Two collectors and three distributors administered the *kupa*, indicating that it was a larger enterprise than the *tamhui*. We do not know historically how and why two separate establishments were set up.

Both of these support systems are geared toward supplying the poor man with his most basic necessities on a daily or weekly basis. We see, however, in the above sources that, according to rabbinic law, society related to two kinds of poor. One kind was completely destitute and did not have any food in the house, and the other might be day laborers who had enough money to buy food from their daily salary but who did not have food for the week. It is possible that the money given to a poor man in this latter category was meant to supplement his food needs, to provide him with additional food for the Sabbath, or to make up for his inability to work on that day and therefore make up for a lack of income.

It should be noted that the rabbinic measure for poor was reckoned in "real time." It could be that on any given day a man would be defined as "poor" and would therefore be entitled to financial help, but that on another day would have food in his house and would therefore not be considered "poor" (or in the same category of "poor"). This is a functional definition of poverty. It does not attribute other cultural or psychological connotations to poverty and therefore does not label the person. In the conception of the law, a person who is poor is different than other Jews only in his economic capability and nothing else.

---

and it is considered as if he left food there. It is impressive that alms distributors were expected to supply wine to the poor to fulfill the rabbinic instruction to drink four cups of wine during the banquet on the night of Passover. See *M. Pesahim* 10:1.

94 *M. Pe'ah* 8:7 based on Neusner. He translates *kupa* as "communal fund." On the social significance of the *kupa*, see Gardner, *Organized Charity*, 111–138.

95 *T. Pe'ah* 4:10 (Lieberman ed., 58). See also Lieberman, *Tosefta Kifshuta*, Zeraim, Pe'ah 4:10, 84.

6 Borderline Poor

There is an alternative definition for "poor" that concerns the collecting of poor tithes from the fields. The Mishnah states: "Whoever has 200 *zuz* [in liquid assets] may not collect gleanings, forgotten sheaves, *pe'ah*, or a poor man's tithe."[96] The definition here for the poverty line is 200 *zuz*.[97] The measure is money, not food, as was the measurement for the *tamhui* and the *kupa*. Practically speaking, the possessor of 200 *zuz* may not collect the tithes from the fields left for the poor. There is a very large gap between this poor man and the poor man that does not have 14 meals. Two hundred *zuz* was close to an average person's salary for a year! The difference is in the source of the support. The support left in the fields was a biblical decree that every landowner complied with whether or not the poor needed it. It took effort to go out to the field and collect it. The sages were therefore liberal in allocating it not only to the poorest elements of society, but also to individuals or families who were economically insecure. The *tamhui* and *kupa* were collected door to door and were therefore a large expenditure on the part of the community. These resources were relatively small, and the sages allocated them only to the poor who were on the brink of hunger.

It is unknown why the sum of 200 *zuz* was precisely the sum stated. However, it was probably not chosen randomly. People saw that sum as a minimal requirement to be considered "not poor." We see it used in other contexts to define economic status. The Mishnah used this sum as a measurement concerning conditions made when a man wishes to marry a woman:

> Behold you are betrothed to me on condition that I pay you 200 *zuz* … On condition that I have 200 *zuz*, this woman is betrothed if he has that sum. On condition that I shall show you 200 *zuz*, lo, this woman is betrothed and he will show her that sum. But if he showed her the money on the table of a moneychanger she is not betrothed.[98]

The possession of 200 *zuz* was a sign that one was not poor. The Mishnah emphasizes that even if all he said is that he will show her 200 *zuz*, the condition is

---

[96] *M. Pe'ah* 8:8 based on Neusner. Notice that the translator in Neusner's edition added in brackets the comment "liquid assets." The 200 *zuz* do not include his house and personal clothing and dishes.

[97] Knapp, *Invisible*, 98, sets the poverty line of the Roman economy at 300 *denar* a year of expenses based on the source from Matt. 21:33–41. He excludes the big cities, in which the cost of living would be higher.

[98] *M. Kiddushin* 3:2 based on Neusner.

fulfilled only if he shows her 200 *zuz* that belong to him. If he shows her on the table of the banker, the condition has not been fulfilled. A *zuz* was the equivalent of a Roman *denarius* (= *denar*). A worker could earn approximately one *denar* per day of work.[99] It is possible that 200 *zuz* represented a year's income (subtracting Sabbath days, festivals, and rainy days).

This sum 200 *denar* to determine the poverty line is found also in a source from the classical Greek period. There, it states that a resident of Athens appealed to the authorities that had refrained from giving him public support because he had 200 *drachma* (rough Greek equivalent to the *denar*), which equaled the salary of 200 workdays.[100]

The sum of 200 *zuz* is also the amount of money mentioned when a husband writes his wife a *ketubba*.[101] The husband is required to pay his wife this sum if he should divorce her or he should die and leave her a widow.[102] The use of this precise sum for giving the widow or divorced woman indicates that this was considered a sum that gave the person holding it an economic basis with which to continue their life. This sum is also used in other contexts, on which is when one brother takes 200 *zuz* from the inheritance in order to study Torah or a profession.[103] Interestingly, many farmers did not own an ox and a plow,

---

[99] See *Avoth De-Rabbi Nathan*, Schechter, 2nd ed., 27b; Matt. 20:2; and Cato, *De afr.* 22,3. Regarding salaries in Rome, see Duncan-Jones, *Economy*, 54; Mackensy, "Pay Differentials," 267–268; Curchin, "Labour," 179; Sperber, *Money and Prices*, 101–102, 122–125; and Scheidel and Friesen, "Size Economy," 67 and sources cited there. However, Erdkamp, "Economic Growth," 6, points out that "we have few data on wages and everyday market prices (rather than famine prices or prices given in a context of measures taken by the authorities)," and he also says that (23) "we have no evidence on the number of workdays, the contribution of women and children, and the proportion of wage-labor in Roman society."

[100] Lysias "For the Disabled Man," 24:6 (400 BCE), cited by Finley, *Ancient Economy*, 79. Indeed, he must have translated the paragraph differently because in Todd, *Lysias*, 255, the translation does not include the sum of 200 *drachma*. However, in his introduction to the speech Todd mentions that the law determined that a man who did not have capital of three *mina*, which equaled 300 drachma, and who was disabled was entitled to communal support (from *Ath. Pol.* 49.4). In the Roman army, the annual salary of a private was 225 *zuz*. Domitian raised it to 300 *zuz*. See Lo Cascio, "Roman State." This puts the Roman soldiers in the bottom of the middling group.

[101] The *ketubba* was written before the marriage of a couple. See *M. Ketubbot* 1:2 and 2:1. See Friedman, *Marriage*, 450–453 and n. 6; and Jackson, "Ketubah," 209–215.

[102] This sum of 200 *zuz* is also used as an example for a present toward betrothal or a condition for divorce in *M. Gittin* 7:5; and *T. Gittin* 4:9 (Lieberman ed., 262); 5:5 (Lieberman ed., 265), and 5:10 (Lieberman ed., 267). For additional uses of the example of 200 *zuz* as a standard sum of money, see also *M. Sanhedrin* 3:6; *M. Makkot* 1:2–3; *T. Makkot* 1:2; *M. Shevuot* 4:8 and 7:5; *T. Shevuot* 2:12–14; and *T. Gittin* 2:13 (Lieberman ed., 253).

[103] *T. Bava Batra* 10:4. This sum is also used as an example for damage payments in *T. Bava Kamma* 3:5. It is also used as an example for payment of taxes to the authorities in

and hired someone to plow the field or hired the ox. Two hundred *zuz* could buy two oxen and a yoke to plow the fields.[104]

In the same tractate that set 200 *zuz* as the "poverty line," the Mishnah states: "Whoever has only 50 *zuz* yet conducts business with them, this man may not collect [produce designated for the poor]."[105] The Mishnah considers 50 *zuz* invested in commerce to be a significant amount of money. There is a need to understand how the investment in commerce adds so much to the value of money. Theoretically speaking, one who has even 199 *zuz* can take 50 and invest that sum in commerce instead of taking charity. Obviously, the 200 *zuz* discussed is not available for investment in commerce. Plausible explanations can be that the person involved is a laborer who does not have time to go to the market, or, that the money is invested in his field, in his animals, and/or in tools.[106] The initial sum of 50 *zuz* invested in merchandise could provide a person with the income that he needs for a year. The market took place twice a week, on Mondays and Thursdays.[107] Average income from a deal was a profit of one-sixth. Fifty *zuz* equaled 50 multiplied by 48 *pundion* or 2,400 *pundion*. The profit from selling out even once a week (half the potential) would be 400 *pundion*. One *pundion*, to give some reference, could buy a loaf of bread. This left a merchant plenty of income to live on (deducting travel expenses, taxation, labor, etc.). Dealing in commerce could be much more lucrative than being a laborer (and maybe even an independent farmer). This definition of poverty is another measurement for the use of the shapers of policy of the community relief fund to determine how to allocate funds for the poor, as well as for the use of the individual in determining whether he is entitled to go to the fields to take the portion allocated by the Bible to the poor.

An example for a member of the class of borderline poor is the day laborer: *po'el* (פועל). The term "*po'el*" regarding day laborers is not found in the Bible or in earlier sources of the Mishnah. The earlier term for hired work was *sakhir* (שכיר). It seems that the term was created in response to the need to define the large segment of the workforce that was hired on a daily basis,

---

T. Demai 6:4 (Lieberman ed., 94). It appears as a sum used for bribery in *T. Rosh Hashanah* 1:15 (Lieberman ed., 309). In addition, the sum is referred to in Sifre Deuteronomy, 322, (Finkelstein ed., 338–339). See esp. Midrash Tannaim, Devarim 32:2 (Hoffman ed., 185), and sources mentioned in the previous note.

104 *M. Bava Batra* 5:1 has the price of the oxen and yoke. *M. Bava Metzia* 8:1 discusses the laws of borrowing oxen with their owner to plow the field. See also *M. Bava Metzia* 6:4.

105 *M. Pe'ah* 8:9 based on Neusner.

106 It is impossible to say that the 200 *zuz* are his personal or family belongings—bed, clothing, or kitchenware—as the Mishnah tells us that he is not required to sell those things to avoid taking charity. See *M. Pe'ah* 8:8.

107 See *M. Ketubbot* 1:1; and *M. Megillah* 1:3.

leaving the term שכיר principally for people that were hired for a longer period of time. The hired worker and the day laborer were worse off economically than the landowners, and many of them were close to or below subsistence level.[108]

7 "Poor" Can Be a Relative Term

Another contemporaneous view of the term "poor" appears concerning obligations of a husband to support his wife when he is living elsewhere and sending her necessities through a third party. The Mishnah states:

> He who maintains his wife by a third party may not provide for her less than two *qabs* of wheat or four *qabs* of barley [per week]. Said R. Yose: Only R. Ishmael ruled that barley may be given to her for he was near Edom. And one pays over to her half a *qab* of pulse, a half *log* of oil, and a *qab* of dried figs or a *maneh* of fig cake. And if he does not have it, he provides instead fruit of some other type. And he gives her a bed, a cover and a mat. And he gives her a cap for her head and a girdle for her loins and shoes from one season to the next, and clothing worth 50 *zuz* from one year to the next…. He gives her in addition a silver *maah* [a sixth of a *denar*] for her needs [per week].[109]
>
> Under what circumstances? In the case of the poor man in Israel; but in the case of a wealthier person all follows the extent of his capacity [to support his wife].[110]

---

[108] On the reason for the phenomenon of the day laborer versus the long-term employee in the ancient world, see Cohen, *Athenian Nation*, 132 and n. 79, and "Unprofitable Masculinity," 100. Silver, "Hired Workers," 258. Their research applies to classical Greece, but the phenomenon of the day laborer in Roman times can assume the same explanations. However, there is a view that the laborer in the Roman world belonged to the middling groups and not to the lower class. See Allen, "Prosperous Romans," 344, who concludes that "the Roman worker in Diocletian's time was doing about as well as most workers in eighteenth century Europe or Asia." His assessment relates to the period of Diocletian, which was a period of crisis in the Empire. Scheidel, "Real Wages," 425–462, argues with this assumption and claims that the worker was close to subsistence level. However, this statement applies to non-skilled workers, not to skilled workers. See also Freu, "Labour Status," esp. 161–162.

[109] *M. Ketubbot* 5:8–9 (based on Neusner).

[110] Neusner (390) translates it as: "In the case of the most poverty-stricken man in Israel." This translation does not seem accurate because, as seen earlier, if the most poverty-stricken did not have two meals in his house, then he certainly could not provide all the above!

Hamel compared the amounts mentioned here and concluded that they are minimal but sufficient for sustenance.[111] However, it is unlikely that a "poor man" who requires community support, whose income is below 200 *zuz*, can be expected to supply the above list of commodities to his wife. It seems that even a man above the poverty line would not be able to supply his wife with wheat or barley, legumes, oil, dried figs or dates, or other fruit. In addition, the husband is expected to supply his wife with a bed, bedding, clothing, a hat, belt, shoes, and 50 *zuz* per year for other equipment. It seems that this mishnah is using a different term "poor in Israel," which is someone who is part of respected society "in Israel" but who is relatively poor when compared to other, external groups.

The above mishnah states later that the wife and husband eat together on Friday nights. This indicates that the source is talking about someone who is away during the week but comes home on the Sabbath. This indicates that the reason for the separation is not marital strife. It could be that the husband is an agricultural worker who needs to travel in order to find work. It could be that he lives by collecting the tithes left in the fields. He could be a peddler who wanders the countryside all week, or perhaps he is the owner of a small plot of land far away from his home. It could be that the husband sends money and the third party who is a farmer gives it to the woman in kind.[112]

Indeed, when we compare the two tractates we see that the person receives more wheat in the former. It could be that this mishnah is supplementing the wheat for other products.[113] However, it could be that it is representing a different policy of food distribution to the poor resulting from different estimates as to the amount of food that is necessary for sustenance. Another possibility is that the amount allocated to the woman by the third party is small because it does not include the weekend food that the husband supplies because he is home on those days.[114]

---

111 Hamel, *Poverty*, 40–42, 65–66, mentions that in Rome they gave more wheat to the poor man than to the poor woman and that in Islamic tradition they gave more to a male orphan. The male required more calories than a female. Also, these measurements are adequate if the woman is supporting herself and not her children.

112 The money is not given directly to the woman to avoid the risk of it being stolen in the absence of the husband, or he does not trust her with the money, or he does not want to burden her to go out of the house and purchase the food.

113 M. Pe'ah 8:7 mentions only the bread given to the poor and his bedding. T. Pe'ah 4:8 (Lieberman ed., 57) mentions that he is also given wine, legumes, and fruit. Lieberman, *Tosefta Kifshuta*, Zeraim 183, says that the Tosefta is explaining the Mishnah, not disagreeing with it. See also Broshi, "Diet," 50–54, who states that scholars disagree as to how to translate the Mishnah's measurements. In any case, he maintains that the amounts allocated in *Pe'ah* are sufficient even with today's standards for caloric intake.

114 See Broshi, *Bread, Wine, Scrolls*, 121–143, 252–258.

The poor man in *Ketubbot* is called עני שבישראל (the "poor man in Israel"). It is possible that this terminology is used specifically because he is not a poor man living off the people of Israel (מוטל על הציבור) but a man living with the people. In this way, the sources wish to give him dignity. We find this language also with regard to funeral arrangements, where the tractate says that even a "poor man in Israel" should do no less for his wife's funeral than hire two flutes and one eulogizer.[115] Someone who can hire two flutes and a eulogizer to lament at his wife's funeral is far from destitute. If that was the case, the mishnah could have said that the public supplies the flutes and eulogizer.

In this light, it is possible to explain the use of this term in the Mishnah in *Pesahim*:

> And even a poor Israelite should not eat until he reclines at his table.[116] And they should provide him with no fewer than four cups of wine and even if [the funds] come from the *tamhui*.[117]

This source seems to refer to two types of poor. One type has the necessary food and wine but is told that he must recline. The other needs to be supplied the four cups of wine from the public fund. The first is termed "poor in Israel," which can be explained as a working man who is self-sufficient but relatively poor. He is commanded to recline on the Passover night.[118] The destitute who cannot supply his own food and beverages receives the four cups of wine for the festival from the public fund.[119]

The tosefta that is parallel to the above mishnah dealing with an absent husband providing for his wife through an arbitrator adds additional details that help to fully describe what makes a household "poor":

---

115   *M. Ketubbot* 4:6.
116   Neusner translates עני שבישראל "the poorest of Israel." Here, the translation was changed and based on Albeck, *Mishnah, Pesahim* 8:1 (Vol. 2, 176). He comments that the "poor in Israel" is not identical to the "poor" of the next stanza relating to he who receives his wine from the charity.
117   From *M. Pesahim* 10:1; the translation is based on Neusner. Regarding the relationship between this mishnah and the parallel tosefta, see Friedman, *Tosefta Atiqta*, 405–412.
118   See Schwartz, "Material Culture," 204–209, which shows that even the "poor" had beds while the destitute did not. The early Christian monks learned from the destitute to sleep on a mat on the floor and not on a bed, while even the "poor" woman sleeps on a bed.
119   See Albeck, *Mishnah, Pesahim* 10:1 (Vol. 2, 176), which states that the phrase "to him" could refer to the poor man or to the person attending the *seder* in general. It is not attached to the previous sentence concerning the obligation of the poor man to be reclining.

She has no claim for wine, for the wives of the poor do not drink wine. She has no claim for a pillow for the wives of the poor do not sleep on pillows.[120]

The mishnah related to the basic foods. The tosefta mentions additional "luxuries" to which a wife of a "poor" man is not entitled. She did not sleep with a pillow nor drink wine.[121]

8 Historical Background for the Spread of Poverty in Jewish Society

Tannaitic sources devote much attention to the poor and the problem of poverty, which seems to indicate that the phenomenon was widespread at the time. The background for this phenomenon can possibly be the continued erosion of the economic status of many Jews throughout the long Roman occupation, a point that was elaborated above in Chapter 1. As a result of the many wars of revolt against the Romans that shook the society of Palestine, especially the revolt that led to the destruction of the Second Temple in 70 CE (also known as the Great Revolt) and the later Bar Kokhba Revolt of 132–135/6 CE, tens of thousands were killed, captured, or wounded, and families and individuals fled or were exiled. Jewish land and money was lost in the revolts and in the confiscations that followed. Many small farmers found it impossible to survive. They had to sell their farms to big landowners and make a living from sharecropping on their own land or from becoming day laborers (*poel*) without permanent employment.[122]

This economic pressure coincided with the gradual process of the breaking down of the paternal social structure of the extended family that was prevalent during the Persian and Hellenistic periods. This breakdown led to the development of a social structure consisting of nuclear families with no familial ties between them. This change to nuclear families created a situation in which the

---

120 See *T. Ketubbot* 5:8–9 based on Neusner. See also Lieberman ed., 74.
121 Some commentators translate "mattress" instead of "pillow." Regarding the popular definition of "rich" and "poor," see also *M. Kiddushin* 2:2 and *T. Kiddushin* 3:8. See also Mekhilta de-Rabbi Yishmael, Beshalach (Horowitz ed., 167), where the midrash contrasts the functioning of the poor and that of the rich. The "rich" is described as a person who can rally his family to be efficient at collecting the *manna* bread, which came down from heaven when the Jews wandered in the desert after the exodus from Egypt.
122 Rubin, "Mourning," esp. 93–102, *Time*, esp. 93–94; Dar, *Landscape and Pattern*, 85; Safrai, "Family Structure," *Economy*, s.v. *Hamula*; Pastor, *Land and Economy*, 87–170; Bar Ilan, "Patrimonial Burial"; Rosenfeld, "Innkeeping," 145–148; Satlow, "Rabbinic Views," 620–622, "Charity," 244–277. On similar trends in non-Jewish populations in the Roman Empire, see Brown, *Poverty and Leadership*, 75–76.

welfare of the family lay entirely on the fortune of the breadwinner—usually the male in the household, but also the mother. When the source of income faltered, there was no extended family safety net. When there was not enough work, or the laborer became aged or sick, the seeds for poverty and destitution were sown.[123]

This applies, of course, to the rabbinic awareness of and care for the poor. The poor and destitute existed long before the destruction of the Temple. Interestingly, though the poor rarely leave an archeological imprint, there is a finding from the excavations of the Temple Mount that seem to belong to a destitute individual. There is an ostracon that reads as follows: "Unfortunate (and) poor, that something bad, in all A ... D ... H, Mattathias, not sword, Peace, in Peace." This seems to have been written by a poor individual named Mattathias who wished, on himself, that he would not die by the sword and who mentioned that he had no belongings.[124]

9   Summary

Contemporaneous rabbinic literature defines four types of "poor." Three kinds of poor are defined primarily because of the help that they are entitled to from society. The destitute that do not have the bare necessities were entitled to a daily dole from the community-collected *tamhui*. Slightly better than the destitute person was a poor person who was not starving, but who was lacking basic needs. This person was entitled to community support from the *kupa*—charity collected and distributed by the community. One step higher is the person who "does not have 200 *zuz*" or "does not have 50 *zuz* to purchase merchandise—if he is a merchant." This person is too wealthy to enjoy help from the community, but may partake in the tithes allocated to the poor in the field. The fourth category—that is, he who may be considered the "wealthiest" poor person—is a man who is expected to eulogize his wife at her funeral and support her on a weekly basis with necessary goods even if it is through a third party, and who must recline during the Passover meal even though during the year he never reclines during a meal. This man could be a day laborer (*po'el*) or one who travels to the fields to collect tithes left in the fields.[125] The following table illustrates the substratification of the poor:

---

123   On the importance of land ownership in the ancient world, see Watson, *Roman Law*, 139–141; Osborne, "Roman Poverty," 4–5; and Kehoe, *Law Rural Economy*, 5–9.
124   Eshel, "Aramaic Ostraca."
125   There are of course other possibilities. The two that we mentioned emerge from our previous discussion.

TABLE 2.1 Levels of "poor"

Level #	Definition	Characteristics	Rights
1	Destitute	Does not have food for two meals in the house.	May receive food from the *tamhui*.
2	Poor	Does not have 14 meals or equivalent in the house.	May receive assistance from the *kupa*.
3	Poor	Does not have 200 *zuz*, or a merchant who does not have 50 *zuz*.	May collect tithes allocated to the poor from agricultural fields.
4	"Poor in Israel"	Does not normally recline when he eats. His wife does not drink wine.	Undefined. His responsibilities are defined: to support his wife, to eulogize her properly, to purchase four cups of wine for the Passover feast.

The destitute were entitled to the rights of the poor but not vice versa.

10 Substratification of the Poor in the Roman World

The substratification described above fits a society that contains gradations of economic levels and situations starting from the destitute that have nothing, through the poor struggling to subsist, and ending at the poverty line. This description could indeed portray the structure of society in the Roman world as a whole. The following section will analyze sources from the Roman Empire that indicate that poverty in the Empire was a gradated phenomenon creating different types of poor.

Contemporaneous Roman literature contains various definitions for poverty that are extremely different from one another. For example, the satirist Juvenal considers someone poor because he does not have slaves.[126] Historian Valerius Maximus mentions the fact that the poor man must work his land himself and lacks money for a proper dowry for his daughter.[127] On the other hand, there

---

126   Juvenal, *Satires* 3.147–3.151. He considers the poor who try to mix with "polite" society "ridiculous" (3.153–154). See Morley, "Poor Rome," 35.
127   Valerius Maximus, *De Paupertate* 4.4.

are descriptions of poverty that involve a real lack of basic needs and food.[128] The combination of their accounts points to a society containing both types of poor, meaning that there are various kinds of poverty. Accordingly, Garnsey constructs the subgroups found in Roman literature from poor workers, to those who have the necessities for day-to-day existence but who lack extra money for a dowry, to a higher level of poverty in which a person can meet his needs but cannot afford a slave.[129] In a different article, he adds clearer definitions of the above categories: "Most Romans ... were poor, but there were different levels of poverty." He distinguishes between permanent and temporary poor, and between the "very poor" (destitute) and the "ordinary poor" at the edge of subsistence.[130]

Woolf explains the peculiarity of the definitions of "poor" in Roman literature in a different way. He shows that the Roman rich rarely came into contact with the poor and destitute, and dealt with them through agents, bailiffs, and slaves.[131] Therefore, when writing literature, they are not aware of the very existence of the destitute, hungry individual who has nothing. When they write of "poor," they are referring to the kind of poor people they know. The beggar in the street exists and is seen, but he is not part of society. This attitude is seen in records of money distributions to people in the community.

Another indication of different subgroups within Roman society comes from the well-known fact of the "grain dole" (*frumentatio*), as it is often referred to in scholarship that gave a minimum handout of grain to the desolate citizens of Rome for their sustenance.[132] Brown shows that records of government distribution of free wheat to the poor reveal that the Caesars of Rome doled out relief only to Roman citizens. This creates two kinds of poor: those who can rely on the grain dole and those who cannot. While the former group will have something to eat despite unemployment, the latter will not. This creates strata of poor that are not hungry and can rise economically because their food expenses are partially covered.[133] This analysis applies, of course, only to Rome and not to the rest of the Empire. The grain dole existed on a permanent

---

128 D7.91, cited by Morgan, *Morality*, 48. See also sources cited by Knapp, *Invisible*, 97.
129 Garnsey, *Famine*, 176–178.
130 Garnsey, "Mass Diet," 226–235.
131 See Woolf, "Writing Poverty," 85.
132 Balch, "Rich and Poor," 222–224, believed that Roman society cared for the poor. On the other hand, Hands, *Charities*, and Davies, "Work and Slavery," 313–320, claim that Roman society did not care for the poor at all. It is notable that the poor are absent from recorded economic activity in the Roman Empire during the Principate. See Wiedemann, "Patron."
133 See Brown, *Poverty and Leadership*, 4. See also Garnsey, *Food*, 82–86. Furthermore, it is pointed out that the *tessera*—tokens indicating eligibility to benefit from the "grain dole"—were given to people who were poor and hungry, as well as to people who did

basis only in the city of Rome itself. In other places, it is known that when there was a crisis, rich people would give wheat to the poor. Herod the Great imported wheat from Egypt in 30 BCE when there was a drought in Palestine, and he gave it to the poor.[134] In most of the Empire, the destitute had no source for food that they could rely on.

Subdivision of the poor strata of society is found in empirical social research of Roman society as well. Alföldy divides social relations in Roman society in the first two centuries CE into many substrata. His primary division is between the "upper strata" and "lower strata," but within the lower strata of society he distinguishes various subgroups. He argues that the majority of Roman society that was non-elite must have been divided into subgroups and was not one mass of humanity.[135] Since Alföldy's important analysis, research has become more specific and substratification of the various levels of society has developed. Friesen suggested a more detailed division of Roman society into seven socioeconomic strata. He maintains that about 68 percent of society belonged to the lowest two strata, making the poor a majority of society.[136] The two lowest strata in Friesen's schema are parallel to the "poor" and "destitute" recognized generations earlier in classical Greek literature. Oakes criticizes Friesen's structure but accepts the principle that there were three types of poor: two below sustenance level and one on the border.[137] Longenecker agrees with Friesen's categories in principle but wishes to alter the numbers. Nevertheless, he attributes 55 percent of the population to the two lower strata that include the poor and the destitute.[138] All the researchers mentioned thus far agree that the poor strata of Roman society were a significant part of the social fabric and that within these strata were inner divisions. Given that more than half of

---

not need it. See Virlouvet, *Tessera*, 243–262. See also Woolf, "Food Poverty," 197–228; and Scheidel, "Libertina," 151–160.

134   *Ant.* 15:299–316.

135   Alföldy, *Roman Society*, Figure 1. Later, Woolf, "Writing Poverty," 94, discussed "the gradations of poverty" indicating that the poor were not one mass of destitute people but were rather groups of people that constituted a gradual and gradated scale of poverty.

136   See Friesen, "Poverty," 341, 343–344. He figures the level of annual income needed to subsist in the country at 250 to 300 *denar*. That figure is very close to the figure of 200 that appears in Jewish literature and may be a basis on which to interpret the use of the figure as what was assumed by the legislators of the time to be sufficient sustenance for a year. On page 347, he estimates the lowest strata—the "poor"—at 28 percent of society and those living "at subsistence" who would occasionally qualify as "poor" at 40 percent. This picture is plausible with what we saw above. See also Barclay, "Poverty Pauline," 363–366, who claims that Friesen's assumptions of the diversity of society and existence of many levels of "poor" are agreed upon by many researchers not mentioned by Friesen.

137   See Oakes, "Constructing Poverty."

138   Longenecker, "Economic Middle," 262–264.

society was considered "poor," it is reasonable to divide society more specifically, beyond the two or three levels just mentioned.

Archeological analyses of dwellings discovered in the Roman Empire support the assumption that society was gradated and that there were people living at various levels of poverty. Researchers of Roman Syria mention that there have been various types of houses discovered there including "small farms and humble shanties."[139] Jongkind writes that in Roman Corinth the types of houses discovered indicate that there were destitute poor and also other kinds of poor.[140] Andrew Wallace-Hadrill, who has carried out research on Roman Pompeii, comments, in one of his volumes on the city, on "the strikingly mixed distribution of houses" and on the "jigsaw of large, medium and small houses that repeats itself constantly throughout the city."[141] And Richardson summarizes home gradation in "the Levant" in the eastern part of the Roman Empire. He identifies numerous types of humble abodes that would suit various kinds of poor families.[142]

It is further possible to see a distinction, in Garnsey's research on the philanthropy of Opramoas of Lycia in Asia Minor, between the poor, who were part of society, and the destitute who were not. There is an inscription stating that Opramoas donated money to the "poor" and "needy" as recipients of "education and nourishment, funeral funds and dowries."[143]

The New Testament, as we have mentioned above, devotes much attention to the issue of the poor and compassionately describes two kinds of poor: those who are destitute and completely without funds, who are completely dependent on others for their bare necessities, and poor people who have modest economic means but who are not completely self-sufficient. These two kinds of "poor" coincide with the two kinds of poor found in Greek literature. Rabbinic sources compiled since the destruction of the Second Temple (70 CE) elaborate and enhance analyses of the poor, dividing the "mass" of poor people into four substrata, starting from the completely destitute poor who are starving and ending with the poor who are straddling the poverty line. This elaborate dissection is unique in the ancient literature and unique to the Roman world, and it confirms the opinion of researchers who felt that there was a need for better (i.e., more precise) stratification, but who could not substantiate their feelings by recourse to the relevant sources. It is also helpful to better

---

139   De Ligt, "Peasantry," 24–56, translating the finds of Tchalenko, *Syrian Villages*, 358.
140   See Jongkind, "Corinth and Class," 139; and Allen, "Prosperous Romans."
141   See Wallace-Hadrill, *Houses and Society*, 67, 90, 99. See also Wallace-Hadrill, "Roman Atrium."
142   Richardson, "Typology of Houses," 55–61.
143   The inscription was cited by Garnsey, *Famine*, 263–264.

understand the lower echelons of ancient society by providing a scale with which to evaluate levels of poverty that is based on contemporaneous sources rather than on modern conceptualizations of poverty that are retrojected onto the past. In our case, a deeper understanding of poverty in Roman Palestine can assist scholars in researching a whole host of socioeconomic issues in the Roman Empire as a whole.

11 Rabbinic Attitudes toward the Poor after the Destruction of the Temple

The information presented above shows how the rabbis analyzed various levels of poverty in their time. Research into the rabbinic sources after the destruction of the Temple also shows a noted change in attitude toward the poor in a number of areas, and we will explore this issue below.

11.1 *Interest in the Poor and Poverty*

One important difference is the proportion of discussion of the poor and poverty. After the destruction, this is a major issue that is discussed on all levels of *halakha* (rabbinic law). The rabbis dealt extensively with the legal and moral aspects of poverty, showing that they were well aware of the poor in society, and they addressed their special status accordingly.[144]

In rabbinic literature, "poor" and "rich" are the most common sociological terms. The statistics relating to the use of the term "poor" in rabbinic literature are rather impressive. It is used 225 times in the Mishnah, 250 times in the Tosefta, 22 times in Mekhilta de-Rabbi Yishmael, 13 times in Mekhilta de-Rabbi Shimeon bar Yohai, 78 times in Sifra (Leviticus), 53 times in Sifre on Numbers and Sifre on Deuteronomy, and 6 times in Sifre Zuta on Numbers. Poverty is treated by the sages in numerous other contexts as well where the specific terms were not used. These contexts therefore do not appear in these statistics.

The rabbis, following the biblical decree, warned against giving the rich preference in legal jurisprudence.[145] At the same time, there was also a prohibition against preferring the poor.[146] However the rabbis were aware that it took courage to rule in favor of the poor against the rich and powerful even

---

144 Regarding methodological aspects of studying ideological concepts in rabbinic literature, see Gray, "Redemptive Almsgiving."
145 Sifra Kedoshim 2:4 (Weiss ed., 87c).
146 Mekhilta de-Rabbi Yishmael, *Mishpatim*, Kaspa 20 (Horowitz ed. 326); Mekhilta de-Rabbi Shimeon bar Yohai 23:3; Sifra Kedoshim 2:4 (Weiss ed., 87c).

when the poor man was in the right.¹⁴⁷ The intricate details of poverty described in the legal and moral context show that the rabbis were familiar with their difficulties.¹⁴⁸ There is a midrash that describes various "types" of poor according to the different names found in the Bible. They say:

> Seven names he is called: *ani, evyon, misken, dal, makh, rash, and dakh. Ani* as it means, *evyon* that he sees food and cannot eat, sees drinks and cannot drink, desires everything. *Misken* who is despised by all, *dal* who has little property, *dakh* is depressed, *rash* loses money and *makh* is like the bottom step for all.¹⁴⁹

It seems that the *evyon* is more destitute than the *ani* and the *dal*.¹⁵⁰ The rabbis interpret the other terms to reflect the social and psychological aspects of poverty such as humiliation, degradation by the wealthy, low esteem on the social scale, and lack of assets. This is the only source in which the rabbis relate to the various biblical terms for poor. The rabbis chose to use only the term *ani* and not to use the other terms unless they are interpreting a specific Bible verse that used that term.¹⁵¹

Indeed, the rabbinic amendments aimed to help the poor created a need to define who would be considered poor. One definition is found in the Sifre on Deuteronomy, stating that a poor man is someone who is in need of something; the inference here is that, if he has everything he needs, he is not poor.¹⁵²

---

147 Mekhilta de-Rabbi Shimeon bar Yohai 18:23; *T. Sanhedrin* 1:8.
148 For example, see *M. Shabbat* 1:1; *M. Eruvin* 4:9; *M. Ketubbot* 6:6; *M. Gittin* 3:7; *M. Arakhin* 4:1–2; *M. Kelim* 16:7; and *M. Mikva'ot* 10:3. The sources show that the poor had a unique material culture as well. This is an issue that merits further research.
149 See Midrash Tannaim, Devarim 15:7 (Hoffman ed., 81). This source is not very reliable when it comes to reflecting early rabbinic thought, but it has the definition of the words that, in the Bible, represent the poor. It is found with some minor changes also in Avot de-Rabbi Natan, version 2 (Schechter ed., 122). This last source is late with a nucleus that is tannaitic. See also Leviticus Rabbah 34:6 (Margaliyot ed., 782 and esp. n. 5).
150 See also Mekhilta de-Rabbi Yishmael, Mishpatim, Kaspa (Horowitz ed., 326), comparing *ani, dal,* and *evyon*.
151 Statistically, the word "*dal*" appears in the contemporary literature only 27 times: 3 in the Mishnah, 4 in the Tosefta, 3 in Mekhilta de-Rabbi Yishmael, 3 in Mekhilta de-Rabbi Shimeon bar Yohai, 8 in the Sifra, 2 in the Sifre Deuteronomy and 4 in Midrash Tannaim, Devarim. The word "*evyon*" is mentioned 45 times: 2 times in the Mishnah, 1 in the Tosefta, 7 in Mekhilta de-Rabbi Yishmael, 7 in Mekhilta de-Rabbi Shimeon bar Yohai, 3 in the Sifra, and 25 in Sifre Deuteronomy. In most of the uses, it is a quote from the Bible. See Bar-Asher, *Studies*, 1:304–305.
152 Sifre Deuteronomy 110 (Finkelstein ed., 171).

The Mishnah, mentioned above, describes five levels of "poor," and for each level there is a different form of communal assistance.[153]

The rabbis made special rules in order to give the poor a feeling of being part of society. They made rules concerning the bed on which the dead body of a poor person was carried so that it should be affordable to the poor and not be embarrassing to them. Even the vessels containing food for the mourners were relegated to modesty so that all could participate.[154] In addition, the rabbis ruled that if a poor person gave charity to the communal collection, then his charity would be accepted, but they did not obligate him to contribute.[155] It is in this light that one should understand the uncompromising statement in *Pesahim* that a poor man must have four cups of wine on the night of the Passover meal. The destitute are also part of the Jews who were redeemed on the first night of Passover.[156]

When the rabbis wish to show a case of betrothal that is annulled because it was created on a false premise, they use the example of someone who becomes betrothed to a woman on the condition that he is poor and it turns out that he is rich or vice versa. The majority opinion is that she is not betrothed. Rabbi Simeon states that if he misled her to think he was poor and was really rich, she is betrothed because she prefers rich to poor.[157]

There is a minority opinion attributed to Rabbi Akiva (c. 90–135 CE) and his disciple Rabbi Simeon (mid-second-century CE) that champions the position of the poor in society and says: "All Jews are princes" (כל ישראל בני מלכים). Although the majority disagreed with the halakhic ramifications of this opinion, it was nevertheless was a voice that existed in rabbinic Judaism.[158]

The rabbis warn against interfering with the process of claiming the tithes for the poor from the field, prohibiting the owner of the field from excluding some poor from collecting it or even helping some poor obtain more of the tithe than others. They consider this theft from the poor.[159]

The above sources show that the rabbis dealt extensively with the poor and poverty and related to the unique circumstances of the poor versus the rich in many different areas and contexts. They showed knowledge of the way society relates to the poor and of the difficulties and needs of the poor.

---

153 This system and stratification of the poor is described by Rosenfeld and Perlmutter, "The Poor," 282–294.
154 *T. Niddah* 9:16–17.
155 *T. Pe'ah* 4:10.
156 *M. Pesahim* 10:1.
157 *M. Kiddushin* 2:2.
158 *M. Shabbat* 14:4.
159 *M. Pe'ah* 4:9; *T. Pe'ah* 1:6; *Sifra Kedoshim* 1:1 (Weiss ed., 85b).

11.2   *Encouraging Charity for the Poor*

The rabbis preached for giving generously to the poor. They also took action to provide more for them. First and foremost, they state that whoever says "yours is yours and mine is yours, is a Hassid."[160]

This praise applies to those who do not take presents but give charity. The following source shows that the rabbis invested thought in analyzing the nature of charity givers:

> Four measures in givers of charity: He, who says I will give and others will not, has a bad eye toward others. He who says others should give and not I has a bad eye to his. I should give and others as well—a Hassid (pious). I will not give and others should not give—evil.[161]

In all generations and societies, it is a challenge to convince those who have to share with the have-nots. The rabbis were aware of this and used creative persuasion to convince the rich to give to the poor beyond stating the command of the Torah to do so. An example of the way the rabbis preached that people should not refuse to give charity is found in the Midrash known as the Mekhilta de-Rabbi Yishmael (third century CE):

> A poor man who asked the homeowner for alms and he gave him God enlightens both of them. But if he asked for alms and the homeowner refused to give him, God created them all. He who was rich will be made poor. He who was poor will be made rich.[162]

The message is that the rich man is temporarily rich. If he does not give charity, he will be punished and made poor.

Another method for encouraging the giving of charity was to tell stories about the charity of popular personalities from the glorious Jewish past. The rabbis told a story about the famous convert to Judaism King Monobases, who used his money to support the poor in a drought year. His relatives scolded him for giving away the family's wealth. He responded that he merely transferred the wealth from this temporary world to the permanent "world to come."[163] This story coincides with Josephus's story about Helena (Helena the Queen, who was the wife of King Monobases the First), who had recently immigrated

---

160   *M. Avot* 5:14.
161   Ibid., 5:13.
162   Mekhilta de-Rabbi Yishmael, Yitro, Amalek (Horowitz ed., 201–202).
163   *T. Pe'ah* 4:18 (Lieberman ed., 60).

to Jerusalem from the Kingdom of Adiabene and gave out much wheat to the poor in Palestine during the drought year of 49 CE.[164] The story about Monobases presents the idea of supporting the poor as a Jewish idea unknown to the king's countrymen. King Monobases was a perfect example cited by the author of the tosefta to convince the people of the importance of charity.

The above story is followed by a dramatic statement in favor of charity and benevolence (*gemilut hasadim*). The Tosefta states that the latter concept "weighs as much as all commandments in the Torah."[165] Rabbi Joshua ben Korha (c. 170 CE) completes the above idea by presenting the other side of the above statement: "He who hides his eyes from charity it is as if he is worshiping idols."[166] Two generations later, Rabbi Elazar son of Rabbi Yossi (c. 200 CE) continues this thought, stating that charity and benevolence cause "great peace" and are excellent attorneys representing the Jews to their "father in heaven."[167] The editor of the Tosefta, which is generally a legal work, did something extraordinary in rabbinic legal literature by citing a story and three statements to enhance the giving of charity in Jewish society. A similar statement is found in the Sifra and it was spoken by Rabbi Avardimos son of Rabbi Yossi (c. 200 CE), who says that one who separates the tithes for the poor from his field's produce is similar to the one who offers sacrifices in the Temple, and that the one who does not separate the tithes is similar to someone who is living during the existence of the Temple but does not offer sacrifices.[168]

Rabbinic literature after the destruction of the Second Temple describes the functioning of a community organization that presumably supplied consistent support to the poor and mentions three different mechanisms that it employed to do so: the *tamhui*, the *kupa*, and the clothing fund. It also describes the responsibilities of the *gabbaim* and *parnasim* who collected and distributed the charity collected from the entire community. These officials

---

164   Regarding the Kingdom of Adiabene and its contacts with Jews, see Josephus, *Ant.* 20:17–96; *War* 5:250–251. At *War* 2:520, he mentions a relative of this family who fought alongside the rebels in the Great Revolt against the Romans. See Lieberman, *Tosefta Kifshuta*, Zeraim, part 1, 190–191; and Kalmin, "Royal Family," 61–77.
165   *T. Pe'ah* 4:19 (Lieberman ed., 60). Actually, the source then proceeds to show how benevolence is even more comprehensive than charity. There are few commandments that have this status. They are circumcision (*T. Nedarim* 2:6), living in the Land of Israel (*T. Avodah Zarah* 4:3), and prohibition of idol worship (Mekhilta de-Rabbi Yishmael, Bo, Pisha [Horowitz ed., 5]), *tzitzit* (Sifre Zuta, Numbers 15:40 [Horowitz ed., 289]), and using a different expression studying Torah (*M. Pe'ah* 1:1).
166   Ibid., 4:20 (Lieberman ed., 61).
167   Ibid., 4:21 (Lieberman ed., 61).
168   See Sifra Emor, parsha 10, chapter 12 (Weiss ed., 95c).

describe themselves as being involved in the policymaking for the collection and distribution of these funds.

The Mishnah reports a rabbinic amendment that was meant to use religious legislation to enable the wealthy to give produce to the poor that was not fit for themselves without separation of tithes. It states: "You may feed the poor *demai*."[169] *Demai* is fruit that was raised and sold by people that the rabbis suspected of not separating all the tithes from the produce of their fields. They decreed that this fruit should not be eaten prior to separating minimal tithes from it. According to rabbinic literature, it was an ancient stringency dating to the early Hasmonean period or even earlier.[170] Despite their decree, they allowed feeding the poor this produce without separating the tithes in order to provide more to the poor and to give an incentive to farmers to feed the poor.[171]

The Mishnah continues with the following statement: "Rabban Gamaliel fed his workers *demai*."[172] This statement is quoted as an example for the rule that one can feed the poor *demai*. The important sage and leader Rabban Gamaliel (c. 85–115 CE) acted according to this rule and fed *demai* to his workers who were poor.[173]

There is also a change of direction when it comes to the rabbis' preferences in allocating charity to the poor. One halakhic Midrash contains a decree with regard to a hierarchy for providing financial assistance: relatives are first, then the poor of the city of the poor person, and then come the poor from outside the city.[174] The rabbis obligate the individual to first help those who are closest to them and then afterward help the rest of the poor. Similarly, the sources show that the local poor were supported by the community before the community extended relief to poor from other locations.[175] This hierarchy indicates that the consideration of the former status of the poor—*bnei tovim*—which had played an important part in the consideration of granting assistance prior to the destruction of the Temple, is not the criterion for extending aid to the poor. The new criterion is that family relationship and geographical proximity determine which poor persons should be supported first.

---

169   M. Demai 3:1.
170   See *M. Ma'aser Sheni* 5:15; and *M. Sotah* 9:10. The entire tractate *Demai* is devoted to this issue.
171   See also Sifra, Behar, parsha 1, chapter 1 (Weiss ed., 107b), which says that the sage Rabbi Judah maintains that there is a leniency for the poor concerning eating fruit of the Sabbatical year.
172   *M. Demai* 3:1.
173   See Goodblatt, *Monarchic Principle*, 176–275, esp. 256–257.
174   Mekhilta de-Rabbi Yishmael, Mishpatim, Kaspa 19 (Horowitz ed., 315).
175   Ibid.

Nevertheless, the financial status of a formerly wealthy person who lost his fortune was still a factor in determining how much assistance was given:

> If he was used to use silk clothing they give him silk clothing, if he had a *me'ah* they give him a *me'ah*; a dough they give him a dough, a bread they give him a bread; to put the food in his mouth, they put food in his mouth ... even a slave even a horse ... a wife.[176]

The rabbis continued the policy that a poor man should be given enough charity so he could maintain the lifestyle that he was used to. This approach corresponds well with the words of Rabbi Akiva: "Even the poor of Israel, we see them as rich people who lost their fortune as they are the sons of Abraham, Isaac and Jacob."[177] Rabbi Akiva awarded a poor woman compensation for embarrassment just like he would a rich one. The majority opinion argued with this position. However, the ideology that the Jewish people are essentially all *bnei tovim* seems to be accepted by all, though they still differentiated between status levels regarding embarrassment. Charity and financial help are extended to all poor regardless of their previous history.

11.3 Assuming Community Responsibility for the Poor

When rabbinic literature after the destruction of the Second Temple discusses the issue of poverty and charity, it provides evidence for the existence of a more comprehensive sense of communal responsibility and organization for the relief of the poor. This indicates a change in the rabbinic attitude toward the poor. The poor person is one of us, an individual who observes the covenant and therefore needs to be helped and protected by social policy. They do not refer to him as lazy, and do not insert into the calculations for supporting him that he is righteous or a sinner. Poverty is now viewed as a social problem that can affect ordinary people who do their best to support themselves but do not succeed. Therefore, the problem needs now to be dealt with on a general level as well as on an individual level.[178]

An important source indicates the local organization of support for the poor: the *tamhui* and the *kupa*, which are both described earlier in this chapter. The Tosefta also alludes to a clothing provision given by the community for the

---

176   *T. Pe'ah* 4:10 (Lieberman ed., 58).
177   *M. Bava Kamma* 8:6. Rabbi Akiva was active c. 90–135 CE.
178   Below, it will be shown that the rabbis developed a new theology concerning the reason for poverty.

local poor. A newcomer to the community who lived there for one month was entitled to take from the *kupa*, but only after six months of residence could he receive clothing from the community fund. In addition, if the community knew of a wandering poor person and wanted to help him, they would give him clothing as well.[179] It seems that money for this fund was collected separately, but the sources do not tell us where the funding for clothing for the poor came from.[180] There is also a mention of burial expenses covered by community funds (*zedakah*).[181]

Even though the community started to assume responsibility for the poor, it did not completely replace individual giving. Some poor preferred to go door to door as it states in the Tosefta concerning the communal charity system: "If he collects from door to door, we do not care for him at all."[182]

The care for the poor was advocated by the rabbis, but according to one description in rabbinic sources, it was lay leadership that actually gathered and distributed the funds. The *gabbaim* collected the alms for the poor and distributed them. There is also mention of *parnasim* who took care of general community needs and also the care of the poor. It is possible that large communities had both *gabbaim* and *parnasim* while small communities had only one of them who organized the charitable activities in addition to performing other communal duties.[183] Historically, it is unclear whether the rabbis initiated the charity funds or whether they regulated a grassroots movement that started with the lay leadership or even the people themselves. It is also possible that the rabbis are describing a utopian community, and that the system was not as efficient and organized at it seems from the literary sources.

Rabbinic literature from after the destruction of the Temple describes community operations that were meant to provide help to the poor. The poor were given supplies by the community according to their needs: a daily food provision from the *tamhui*, a weekly allowance from the *kupa*, help with clothing, and assistance with burial costs. There is no evidence of the existence of a similar system prior to 70 CE.[184]

---

179   *T. Pe'ah* 4:8 (Lieberman ed., 57).
180   Ibid., 4:9 (Lieberman ed., 57–58).
181   *T. Ketubbot* 9:3 (Lieberman ed., 87).
182   *T. Pe'ah* 4:8 (Lieberman ed., 57).
183   Concerning *parnasim*, see esp. *T. Meggilah* 2:15. *Gabbaim* managing charitable donations are mentioned in *M. Demai* 3:1. See Fraade, "Local Leadership" and "Language."
184   On burial practices of the poor in the second temple period see Magness, *Stone and Dung*, 155–164.

11.4   Recommended Strategy to Avoid Poverty

An important result of recognizing poverty as a community problem is the effort that the rabbis made to suggest ways to prevent poverty.[185] The rabbis say that parents are obligated to teach their children a profession (*omanut*) in order to ensure that they can earn a living. This obligation is mentioned alongside the obligation to teach a son Torah and to help him marry.[186] Rabban Gamaliel (c. 85–115 CE) compares a person who has mastered a vocation to a vineyard surrounded by a fence that is protected from damage. Rabbi Yossi (two generations later), adds that a man with a profession is similar to a woman who has a husband and who is therefore protected both physically and morally.[187]

The rabbis also suggest a specific kind of financial conduct to help avoid poverty. The Tosefta states that one should not sell the field that he has inherited unless he becomes poor. Similarly, it discourages selling oneself into slavery or selling one's daughter in order to have cash or to buy an animal, unless one lacks basic necessities because one is poor.[188] They believed that land and human manpower was a commodity that should be safeguarded in order to provide constant income. Selling them for cash to spend is an economically irresponsible act and could lead to poverty down the line.

Sifra, a work of halakhic exegesis, edited in the third century, provides further advice:

> A person should not sell his property unless he became poor; and he should not sell it all. Rabbi Elazar son of Azariah says: "If someone is not allowed to donate all his property to the Temple, certainly one should not sell all he owns."[189]

Sifra states that even if one has to sell his property he should sell it gradually, leaving as much as possible for future income. Rabbi Elazar son of Azariah (c. 90–120 CE) learns this principle from the fact that one is warned not to

---

185   The Roman writers also saw poverty as something to be avoided. See Morgan, *Morality*, 48.
186   *M. Kiddushin* 4:14 is a recommendation. *M. Kiddushin* 1:7 mentions it among the obligations of a father toward his son. This is specified in *T. Kiddushin* 1:11 (Lieberman ed., 279–280). See Albeck, *Mishnah, Kiddushin* 1:7 (Vol. 3, 315). In Modern Hebrew, *omanut* means "art." In Rabbinic Hebrew, it means "trade" or "profession."
187   *T. Kiddushin* 1:9. All the parables are attributed to Rabban Gamaliel of Yavneh (c. 85–115 CE). The sages that elaborated on the topic were active after the Bar Kokhba Revolt (132–135/6 CE).
188   *T. Arakhin* 5:6–8.
189   Sifra, Behar, parsha 3, chapter 5 (Weiss ed., 108b).

donate all his property to the Temple because that will leave him poor and dependent on the community for sustenance.

The Rabbis also utilized the desire of the people for wealth in order to further their religious values. Rabbi Akiva (c. 90–135 CE) said:

> [Giving] tithes is a road to wealth.[190]

And:

> He who needs to take (charity) and does not take does not leave the world before he supports others.[191]

Rabbi Yonatan, a generation later, said:

> He who observes the Torah in poverty will observe the Torah wealthy.[192]

In addition, they felt a need to admit that religion alone is not enough to provide the necessities:

> If there is no flour, there is no Torah; if there is no Torah, there is no flour.[193]

In short, the rabbis devoted much thought to the issue of poverty and formulated certain economic behavior that was expected to prevent poverty. They urged people to provide their children with a vocation so they can make a living. And they admitted that one cannot learn Torah when one does not have a way to make a living, while at the same time they promoted religious observance as a way to become wealthy.

11.5 Rabbinic Theological Approach to Poverty

There are a number of rabbinic sources that portray poverty as a result of immoral conduct or religious offence. The Mishnah mentions that the person dealing with the money donated to the Temple had to be very careful not to be suspected of stealing the money, because he may become poor and people will say that it was because of the theft from the Temple. Alternatively, he may

---

190 *M. Avot* 3:17. *M. Avot* 3:20 describes vividly the process of borrowing money and the difficulty of paying it back.
191 *M. Pe'ah* 8:9. This mishnah advocates good character as a merit for becoming rich.
192 *M. Avot* 4:11.
193 *M. Avot* 3:21. The saying is attributed to Rabbi Elazar son of Azariah (c. 90–120 CE).

become rich and people will suspect that the money came from stealing from the Temple.[194] This shows that people would connect a loss of money to an act of embezzlement from the Temple, but at the same time could conceive that someone could get rich by stealing from the Temple and would not be punished immediately.

The following statements point to fault in religious behavior as an explanation for poverty:

> He who neglects the Torah when he is wealthy will neglect the Torah when he is poor.[195]
>
> He who does not need to take charity and does [take] does not leave the world before he [actually] needs charity.[196]

The Mishnah in *Kiddushin* states that poverty is not a result of the vocation that is chosen by a person; rather, it is a result of his merit (or lack of it). It recommends that the person should ask for wealth from "he who owns all wealth"—that is, he should pray to God.[197] Despite their theological approach, the sources do not seem to state the logical opposite: if someone is poor that means he is evil and should not be helped. To the contrary, as shown above, the rabbis advocate the financial support and social encouragement of the poor.

It is possible that the rabbis also had other explanations for poverty. There is a mishnah that seems to state that there is a hereditary component to wealth and poverty. It says: "A father bestows on his son beauty, strength, wealth."[198] A midrash tells about Rabbi Yohanan son of Zakkai (active before and after the destruction of the Temple), who encountered the daughter of Nakdimon son of Gurion, one of the wealthiest people in Jerusalem (before 70 CE). She was collecting kernels of grain from the stools of a donkey belonging to a nomad. He attributes her state to the fact that the Jewish people did not want to worship God properly, and so instead they suffered. This midrash is quoted in a number of places and seems to be formative for the philosophy of the Jewish people after the destruction.[199] Reading between the lines of this story shows

---

194 *M. Shekalim* 3:2. This source is attributed to the period of the Temple. The punishment is monetary just as the sin was monetary. However, sources that we will mention below speak of poverty as a punishment for unspecified sins.
195 *M. Avot* 4:11.
196 *M. Pe'ah* 8:9.
197 *M. Kiddushin* 4:14.
198 *M. Eduyot* 2:9.
199 Mekhilta de-Rabbi Yishmael, Yitro, Bahodesh 1 (Horowitz ed., 203); Sifre Deuteronomy, 305 (Finkelstein ed., 325). A short account is already present in *T. Ketubbot* 5:10.

that poverty is no longer seen by the rabbis as the problem of the individual; rather, it is the result of foreign rule, which was a means of punishing the Jewish people for their sins. This insight can help explain the compassion that the rabbis now had toward the poor and destitute—compassion that we do not find so extensively prior to the destruction. Since poverty is a byproduct of foreign domain, being poor does not afflict only the unworthy. The poor are suffering for the sins of the nation.

This approach corresponds with a midrash to the above passage in the Torah that states: "There will always be poor."[200] On the other hand, the Torah seems to contradict itself, saying that there will not be any poor people when God blesses you.[201] The answer is that if the Jewish people follow the way of God there will be no poor, and if they do not follow the way of God there will be poor.[202] It is also the spirit of the words of Rabbi Yishmael: "The girls of Israel are pretty, but poverty makes them ugly."[203]

Between the lines of the rabbinic opinions it is possible to see what the people believed regarding the issue. The Mishnah, at the end of the tractate *Kiddushin*, discusses appropriate professions for a Jew. In the conclusion of the discussion,

> Rabbi Meir said that a person should teach his son an "easy and clean" profession and he should pray to "the owner of wealth and property" because there is no profession that does not have wealthy and poor. Poverty does not come from the profession, and wealth does not come from the profession; rather, it is all according to his merit.[204]

According to Rabbi Meir, a person's wealth or lack of it is a derivative of his spiritual accomplishments. If he deserves to be rich, he will be rich and if not, he will not.[205] However, it indicates that the people attributed wealth and lack of it to profession, talent, and initiative. This caused people to choose professions

---

200 Deut. 15:11.
201 Deut. 15:4.
202 Sifre Deuteronomy, piska 118 (Finkelstein ed., 177).
203 M. Nedarim 9:10; T. Nedarim 5:6.
204 M. Kiddushin 4:14.
205 M. Shekalim 3:2 mentions that if the official who managed the Temple's money would become poor, people might see this as a punishment for embezzling from the Temple. Therefore, precautions were made so there would be no reason for suspicion. This seems to indicate as well that people thought there was a connection between sin and poverty. However, it cannot be determined whether this attitude reflects a position that people maintained during the period in which the Temple stood, or whether it reflects the way people thought when this specific mishnah was compiled.

that the rabbis felt could damage their religious commitment. They therefore wished to detach the connection between choice of vocation and wealth or poverty. On the other hand, the rabbis (as cited above) advocated teaching children a vocation because they connected mastering a profession with the possibility of obtaining sustenance honestly.

11.6   *Summary*

There are a number of voices in rabbinic circles speaking about the reason for poverty. On the one hand, they advocated attaining a profession, but at the same time they maintain that the economic status that will be achieved by a person will not strictly derive from his profession, but from other factors like merit and prayer. There are voices that hold the poor responsible for their plight and others that see them as victims of the situation of the people or of hereditary restrictions. Nevertheless, the rabbis realized that poverty is a social problem and that it required attention from the leadership of the community.

It seems that after the destruction of the Second Temple the rabbis assumed a more compassionate attitude toward the poor than they had prior to the destruction. Before the destruction, they seemed to be suspicious of the poor and have a positive attitude primarily toward the formerly rich. After the destruction, however, they see the poor as an integral part of Jewish society who must be cared for by an organized system in the Jewish communities. They advocate giving charity to the poor and treating the poor as human beings. They relate to the poor in all halakhic rulings in which a lack of assets could cause difficulty in fulfilling religious obligations.

CHAPTER 3

The Laborer (*Po'el*): On Both Sides of the Poverty Line

The word "*po'el*" (or "*po'alim*" in plural) in the Mishnah is an expression, or term of art, that refers to an unskilled laborer. From the way it is used in rabbinic literature, it can be seen that the rabbis saw the *po'alim* as belonging to a distinct social entity with common characteristics for which they provided specific guidance and legislation. For the sake of simplicity, we will refer to them here simply as laborers. This group of people worked for a living, in contrast to the "poor," who primarily begged or enjoyed social charity. On the other hand, they did not own income-producing property such as a field or a factory, and depended for their livelihood on being employed by others.[1] The vast majority of laborers were employed in Palestine in two sectors. Most worked in agriculture, while others worked for nonagricultural enterprises, the largest of which was construction. Though the sources do not state as much, it is highly likely that this sector as well had a graduated level of income depending on various factors such as health, available employment, expertise, and family size. Nevertheless, it seems that they were on the lower level of the middling groups or even within the ranks of the poor.

The category of laborer has its own chapter, though there were many times when the laborer could have simultaneously met the criteria for being part of the poor; he would have been entitled to social help or to tithes from the fields. This is because the sources have different definitions for him, sometimes in the same sentence. The laborer was someone who worked while the poor lived from charity, though this definition does not fit every pertinent individual. There were probably poor who collected charity but who sometimes worked, and laborers who collected charity to supplement their income when they had no work.

---

1   This aspect they shared with some craftsmen. It will be further discussed below in Chapter 4, which is devoted to them.

1 The Use of the Word *Po'el* from the Bible to Second Temple Literature

The word "*po'el*" is used in the Bible to denote one who *does* certain actions; the verb *pa'al* means "to do." For example, *po'alei aven* relates to people who regularly do evil, whereas *po'alei tzedek* refers to people who do good.[2] The relevant passages in the Bible discuss men who do good deeds and/or evil deeds, but they do not offer us a clear definition of the persons' status.

In the Bible, a wage-earning worker is called "*sakhir*."[3] The work or produce of the wage earner was called "*pe'ulat sakhir*"—and the activity or produce of the worker was also a reference to his salary.[4] In Second Temple literature and the Dead Sea Scrolls, the word for laborer is still "*sakhir*" and the word for his salary is "*pe'ulah*."[5] It seems that the first time the word "*po'el*" itself is used to refer to a laborer is in the first century CE.[6]

2 The Laborer in Josephus and the New Testament

Though we do not have the original Hebrew, it is possible to see from the context that day laborers are described in the writings of Josephus and the NT and

---

[2] For evildoers, see Isa. 31:2; Hos. 6:8; Mik. 2:1; Prov. 10:29; 21:15; and Ps. 5:6; 6:9; 59:3. For those who did good deeds, see Ps. 15:2. There are other similar uses such as *rav pa'alim*: 2 Sam. 23:20.

[3] On the historical background of the workers in the Ancient Near East and the Bible, see, for example, Powell, *Labor*, esp. 1–41, and the index, s.v. labor–work crew; and Radner, "Hired Labor," 185–226.

[4] For sources that refer to the products of the worker, see Jer. 31:16; Prov. 10:16, 11:18; and Ps. 28:5, 17:4, 109:20. There is an example where it refers to salary in Lev. 19:13: "Do not hold back the wages of a hired worker overnight" (NIV). See also Lev. 25:53 regarding someone hired to work for a year. Deut. 24:14 talks about a laborer who is poor or destitute. Job 7:2 reflects the dependence of the laborer on his wages. See also Hatch and Redpath, *Concordance*, 930, a.c. *sakhir*; C. VanDam, "skr, sakir," 3:1241–1246 (VanGemeren, *Dictionary*); Koehler and Baumgartner, *Lexicon OT*, 3:1327–1328 (*skr*) day laborer, hired laborer, hireling; and Ben Iehuda, *Dictionary*, 16:7564.

[5] Ben Iehuda, *Dictionary*, 10:4850–4851; Koehler and Baumgartner, *Lexicon OT*, 3, 950/1, labourer; E. Carpenter, "p'l," 3:646–649 (VanGemeren, *Dictionary*); Hatch and Redpath, *Concordance*, 541c (*ergon*); G. Bertram, "ergon," *TDNT*, 2:635–655, "*cunergon*," 7:871–876.

[6] Ayali, *Workers*, 27, n. 1, posits that the term is used in Sir. 37:11 (Segal ed., 321). See also Skehan and Di Lella, *Ben Sira*, 425 (they translate the term to "an indifferent worker"), 429. However, in Ben Sira, Academy of the Hebrew Language Edition, 37 (text), 256b (index), it was not understood as a professional term, but as a verb. This can also be seen from comparison with page 327 in the above definition indicates a different understanding of the passage. See also Hatch and Redpath, *Concordance*, 541c–544b, and index, 32; Kloppenborg, "Tenancy," esp. 31–38.

that it is likely that in the original Hebrew text (of the NT, if there was one) the term *"po'el"* was used. When describing the erection of the First Temple, Josephus states that King Solomon hired 30,000 workers: ἐργάτας τρισμυρίους (*Ant.* 8:58). He uses the same term when he writes that Hyrcanus son of Joseph (son of Tuvia) gave out meat to the workers: he uses the term "τοῖς ἐργάταις" (*Ant.* 12:194). This word seems to describe groups of unskilled laborers hired for physical work.

In *Jewish Antiquities* (*Ant.*) 15:390, when describing the rebuilding of the Temple by King Herod, Josephus mentions that Herod chose 10,000 experienced workers (ἐργάτας δὲ μυρίους), "training some to be builders and others as craftsmen." This passage shows that Herod first hired general manual workers and then taught them a specialty related to the construction of the Temple. It is unclear how he would refer to them after they would have completed their training.[7] Indeed, later on (*Ant.* 20:220), when discussing workers at the Temple, Josephus uses two terms: τεχνιτῶν for the professionals and ἐργάσαιτο for what they created. Here, the word refers to the actions of the professionals and not to those of the manual laborers.[8]

In *Jewish War* (*War*), Josephus refers to the uprising of the Jews against the Romans. He mentions that the rebel leader Simeon murdered workers, ἐργατῶν, who were on their way to work (*War* 4:557). When discussing the laborers at work on the Dead Sea, he says: "Προσελαύνοντες δὲ οἱ τῆς λίμνης ἐργάται" (*War* 4:480). It is interesting that all mentions of laborers in Josephus link them with nonagricultural pursuits. Perhaps it is because Josephus was active primarily in Jerusalem and later in Rome and was aware of the workmen in the city more than those in the countryside.

The laborer appears more clearly in the NT.[9] He appears a number of times in Matthew, a few parallel times in Luke, and a few times in Acts.[10] In all of these sources, there is a description of events that took place in Palestine. In

---

7 Van Henten, *Judean Antiquities*, 15:296 and nn. 2772–2775.

8 Compare Rengstorf, *Concordance Josephus*, 2:199b–c, s.v. ἐργάτης.

9 Regarding the term *"po'el"* in the NT, see Danker, *Dictionary*, 390, s.v. ἐργάτης. This Greek word refers to a laborer according to the verb "to do." There is another term that relates to actions in general, s.v. ἔργον, on pages 391–392. That term refers to actions, actions of a God or man. It has various uses.

10 The term does not appear in Mark, which was compiled between 60 and 80 CE. Perhaps Mark reflects an earlier tradition that does not contain the term. Matthew and Luke were compiled later, around 80 to 90 CE, and possibly the term was used more often at that time. Regarding the background editing of the parables of Jesus, see Ewherido, *Matthew*, esp. 197–253; Basser and Cohen, *Matthew*, 281–298, 512–520; and Vine, *Matthew Audience*, 33–78.

Matthew 20:1–16, there is one source that stands out as a vivid description of employer–laborer relations in this period:

> I ... householder (οἰκοδεσπότῃ), who set out early in the morning to hire (μισθώσασθαι) workers (ἐργάτας) for his vineyard; 2. And when he had agreed with the workers (τῶν ἐργατῶν) for the one *denarius* a day, he sent them into his vineyard. 3. Going out about nine o'clock, he saw other men standing idle in the marketplace (Gr. *agora*) and said to them, 4. "You go into my vineyard, too, and I will give you whatever is right," and so they went. 5. Going out again at midday, and at three o'clock, he did the same. 6. At about five o'clock, he went out and found others standing. He said to them, "Why do you stand here all day idle?" 7. They answered him, "Because no one has hired us." "You too go into the vineyard," he said. 8. When evening came, the owner (ὁ κύριος) of the vineyard said to his steward (τῷ ἐπιτρόπῳ), "Call the workers (τοὺς ἐργάτας) and give them their wages, beginning with the last, and so up to the first." 9. When those who were hired at five o'clock came, they each received a *denarius*. 10. When the first came, they supposed that they would receive more, but they each received a *denarius*. 11. On receiving it they grumbled to the owner (τοῦ οἰκοδεσπότου), 12. "The last only worked an hour, but you have made them our equal, and we have borne the burden and heat of the day." 13. But he answered one of them, "My friend, I am not doing you an injustice. Did you not agree with me for a *denarius*? 14. Take what is yours and go. I choose to give to the last what I also give to you. 15. Am I not allowed to do what I wish with my own property? Or is your eye evil, because I am good?" 16. So the last shall be first and the first last.[11]

This long parable is the earliest and the most complete source that describes day laborers based on the background of Roman Palestine in the first centuries CE. In this parable, there are a number of details that seem to depict the real situation of the laborer:

a) The laborer waited for the employer to seek him out at a location that was known to employers and workers. Workers who were not hired waited to be hired in the course of the day for a partial workday.
b) Laborers were hired for a day at a time. The typical workday began with dawn and ended at dusk.

---

11   From Albright and Mann, *Matthew*, 236. For a comparison, see James 5:4, where it talks of laborers who harvested the fields but have been cheated out of their wages. God will punish those employers. See Johnson, *James*, 291, and commentary on 301–303, 308–309.

c) The relationship between the laborer and employer lasted for the day only. At the end of the day, the worker was paid and he may or may not be rehired the next day. This agreement prevailed whether the job was finished or not.
d) The owner was not always present at the workplace. Sometimes, he sent an overseer to hire the workers.
e) The nature of the task was not a factor. The laborers were available for many different jobs. This differentiated them from the *uman*, who was an expert in a specific area.
f) The pay for a day's work was 1 *denar*. It is implied in the discussion in the parable that when the laborer was hired for less than a day the pay would be lower.[12]

In the aforementioned case, it seems that there were plenty of workers and that the employer had only to choose who to hire. There is another story in Matthew 9:37–38, where there is a shortage of workers, which comes to symbolize the shortage of people devoted to the service of God:

> There is an abundant harvest, but there are few workers (ἐργάται); therefore, ask the chief harvester to send workers (ἐργάτας) into his Harvest.[13]

The setting here is agricultural. There is such a shortage of workers that there is a need to pray that workers will come to harvest the field. In another context, Matthew (10:10) says: "The worker (ὁ ἐργάτης) deserves his keep." This seems to be a case where the pay of the worker is in question. In comparison, the man of God also deserves to have his basic livelihood supplied by the public, which benefits from his (i.e., God's) emissary.[14]

3 The Laborer in Rabbinic Sources

3.1 *The Laborer and His Working Conditions*

Tannaitic sources that were compiled a few generations after Josephus and the NT continue to expound on the day laborer, and they supply many additional

---

12 In the parable, the employer paid all the workers equally even though some worked less than others. Those that worked the whole day complained. The employer said he can do what he chooses with his money.
13 This is also mentioned in Luke 10:2 and James 5:4.
14 See also in Luke 10:7; 1; Tim. 5:18. This comparison of the apostles to workers is found also in Phil. 3:2, where the author is criticizing certain religious preachers by blaming them for evil behavior. See Reumann, *Philippians*, 461–463.

details. The term "*po'el*" appears 41 times in the Mishnah, 77 in the Tosefta, and 35 in halakhic Midrash, which totals to 153 times in Tannaitic literature. This is a significant amount. In most cases, the term appears in plural. This may indicate that the workers tended to be seen as groups more than as individuals. The following source shows that there was a social distinction between the laborer and the poor man:

> A sheaf which workers forgot but which the householder did not forget ... [or if] poor people stood in front [of a sheaf] or covered it with straw.[15]

In the above source, the "worker," "poor," and "homeowner" are mentioned side by side. Indeed, there are sources that indicate that the workers were considered "poor."[16] However, the difference is that in rabbinic literature when the worker is trying to make a living from work he is called a "worker." When one is collecting alms or tithes, he is defined as a "poor man." A *po'el* who could not find work could decide to collect alms, and his status would therefore change. The difference between the poor man and the *po'el* can also be seen in their daily income. As will be seen below, the daily salary of the *po'el* was one *denar*, while the community would give the poor man a loaf of bread worth a *pundion*, which was one-twelfth of a *denar*.[17]

In addition, we find the term "*po'el*" used alongside the "poor" in the Tosefta *Bava Kama*: "A worker and a poor man who climbed a tree and broke off the branch."[18] Similarly, the poor man climbs the tree to collect tithes, and the worker climbs to pick the fruit for the owner or to trim the branches. Here, the workers work in the field and the poor collect the tithes, a situation that shows a difference between them. Indeed, the salary of a *po'el* is considered a low one in comparison. The Mishnah states (*Bava Metzia* 5:4):

> They do not set up a storekeeper for half the profit ... unless one pays him a wage as a worker.[19]

---

15   *M. Pe'ah* 5:6–7, the translation is based on Neusner ed., 25. For additional sources that mention the poor and the worker side by side, see *T. Bava Kama* 10:29 (Lieberman ed., 56); Sifre Devarim, piska 282; and Midrash Tannaim 24:19.
16   *M. Pe'ah* 5:5–6 prohibits allowing the worker to bring his son to collect the poor tithes from the field.
17   Regarding the salary of the worker, see above for the testimony from the NT and below for the testimony of rabbinic sources. See also Katsari, *Monetary System*, 206. Regarding the value of public alms for the poor, see above in Chapter 1.
18   *T. Bava Kama* 10:29 (Lieberman ed., 56); the translation is based on Neusner ed., 4:67.
19   The translation is based on Neusner ed., 4:541.

THE LABORER (PO'EL)

This source discusses a case in which a silent partner invests in the inventory of a store and has a storekeeper operate the store. The income is divided between them. In this economic arrangement, the rabbis consider the storekeeper to be the owner of half the merchandise and the partner to be the owner of the other half. The storekeeper owes money for his half and will pay it from the income of the store. In addition, he gives the investor half the profit on the principal, which is in effect paying interest, since he is doing all the work in the store. Therefore, in addition to dividing the profit, the owner must pay him "like a *po'el*." This means that the payment of a *po'el* was considered a basic wage, differing from the payment of the expert or craftsman, who is termed "*uman*," who makes more for his efforts (for more about the craftsman, see Chapter 4). The Tosefta establishes that the salary that the storekeeper must receive is that of an "idle worker."[20] This is even lower because it takes into account that the *po'el* does hard manual labor while the storekeeper has an easy job. According to this source, it is possible that a hired storekeeper who is not a partner would receive a lower salary than the *po'el* because the work is light and does not require specific knowhow.

Similarly, the Mishnah in *Bekhorot* prohibits taking money to judge, testify, or purify. However, it allows one to take money "like a *po'el*." This shows that the salary of a *po'el* was not high.

As stated above, the historical background for the creation of the Hebrew term "*po'el*" seems to be the progressive deterioration of the economic situation of the Jews of Palestine under Roman rule, especially in the wake of the destruction of the Second Temple.[21] The loss of land forced many peasants to become sharecroppers on land they used to own, or, worse, to become day laborers without permanent employment.[22] This created a large group of people that would be day laborers, and it was necessary to have a term that would describe them. It also differentiates them from another group of workers—the craftsmen who were professionals that earned a higher daily wage than the *po'alim* and sometimes had a business that they operated from their homes or workshops.[23]

---

20 T. *Bava Metzia* 4:11 (Lieberman ed., 83).
21 See Alon, *History*, 93ff. See also Ayali, *Workers*, 29–30.
22 On the importance of ownership of real estate in the ancient world, see Aristotle, *Politics* 1:1256A, 19–21, 29–40; Watson, *Roman Law*, 139–141; Osborne, "Roman Poverty," 4–5; and Kehoe, *Law Rural Economy*, 5–9.
23 See Epstein, *Introduction Mishnah*, 444a, for the philological distinction between *po'el* and *uman*. See also below in the chapter devoted to the craftsman. Indeed, there is often confusion between the *po'el* and *uman*. The Mishnah or Tosefta can start discussing one

Po'alim were employed for various projects. They were hired to plow,[24] to plant,[25] to weed,[26] to harvest,[27] to collect vegetables,[28] to hoe around trees or plants,[29] and to bundle onions.[30] Laborers were hired to transport objects from place to place.[31] There were cases where the owner had an overseer who hired the workers.[32] The payment could also be given out by an overseer or messenger.[33] Though the sources do not define the status of the representative, it is likely that they refer to a manager or overseer that hires workers and supervises their work. This was found in other parts of the Roman Empire, especially on royal estates and those of the very wealthy absentee owners who had a manager that administered their entire holding. In other cases, the manager was responsible for one branch or asset.[34] Women also hired workers.[35] It was prohibited to hire workers on the Sabbath to work after the Sabbath.[36]

The classic situation for hiring *poa'lim* was when the owner came to the workers and hired them for the day:

> R. Yohanan b. Matya said to his son, "Go, hire workers for us." He went and made an agreement with them.[37]

---

and bring an example of the other. It is because the terms were not completely defined and it is likely that some people did not know the difference between them.

24 *T. Bava Metzia* 7:1 (Lieberman ed., 97); 7:5 (Lieberman ed., 98).
25 *T. Shviit* 4:13 (Lieberman ed., 182). The source does not state explicitly what the workers were hired to do, but the most logical interpretation is that the workers planted the barley, found the greens, and took them as abandoned property.
26 *T. Maasrot* 2:15 (Lieberman ed., 235); *T. Bava Kama* 7:5 (Lieberman ed., 98).
27 *M. Kilayim* 7:6. It seems from there that there were cases in which workers were hired to harvest, but sometimes the owner harvested himself. *T. Pe'ah* 2:3 (Lieberman ed., 46); *T. Bava Metzia* 7:1. Harvesting onions: *T. Maasrot* 2:16 (Lieberman ed., 235). Picking fruit: *T. Maasrot* 2:14 (Lieberman ed., 234–235).
28 *M. Maasrot* 5:5.
29 *T. Maasrot* 2:13 (Lieberman ed., 234); *T. Bava Metzia* 7:5 (Lieberman ed., 98).
30 Ibid., 2:16 (Lieberman ed., 235).
31 *M. Avodah Zarah* 5:1; *T. Bava Metzia* 7:4. In the latter source, it seems to involve purchasing as well.
32 *M. Shabbat* 23:3; *T. Ketubbot* 9:3 (Lieberman ed., 88), regarding the household member who hires and fires workers; Matthew 20:1ff.
33 *T. Shevuot* 7:5, where the storekeeper is asked to pay the workers in kind; *T. Ketubbot* 9:5.
34 Aubert, "Production," 99–110.
35 *M. Kiddushin* 3:6.
36 *M. Shabbat* 23:3.
37 *M. Bava Metzia* 7:1 (Neusner ed., 4:546). This is also seen in *M. Nedarim* 4:7, where the owner goes "to the workers."

THE LABORER (PO'EL)   75

However, there were also cases in which laborers were hired for other periods of time, for another source states:

> He who hires a worker to watch his cow for him, [or] to watch his child for him, does not pay him a salary for the Sabbath. Therefore [the watchman] does not bear responsibility [to make up any loss which takes place] on the Sabbath. But if he was hired by the week, by the month, by the year, or by the septennate, he does pay him a salary covering the Sabbath. Therefore, [the watchman] does bear responsibility to [make up any loss] on the Sabbath. [The watchman] may not say to him, "Pay me my salary for the Sabbath." But he says to him, "Pay me my salary for a ten-day period."[38]

In the context of the prohibition against being paid money for working on the Sabbath, the source deals with long- and short-term employment that differ from the daily employment mentioned above. The jobs mentioned involve actions of guarding that are permissible on the Sabbath, but receiving payment for work on the Sabbath is problematic. When the pay is global for all the days of work and the Sabbath is included, it is permissible. This indicates that there was also longer-term employment for more than one day in the labor market of the time, though the discussion may relate specifically to nonproduction employment.

Regarding payment for work, it seems that there was often a set daily wage that was determined by "the practice of the city (*minhag hamedinah*)."[39] The Tosefta establishes the right of the city leadership to determine the salary of the laborers.[40] There is no source in Tannaitic literature to support the idea that the *po'el* negotiated the salary with his employer; there is only evidence

---

38   *T. Bava Metzia* 8:1 (Neusner ed., 4:116). See the parallel in *T. Shviit* 5:21 (Neusner ed., 230, Lieberman ed., 189) with little change. See also Sifra, Behukotai, parsha 1, chapter 2, 5: "The worker who did work for him over a long period of time" (Neusner ed., Sifra, part 3, 248); the source distinguishes between the long-term worker who was paid much money and the short-term workers who earned less.
39   *M. Bava Metzia* 7:1.
40   *T. Bava Metzia* 11:23 (Lieberman ed., 26). See Lieberman, *Tosefta Kifshuta*, 9:321. He posits that it is a maximum and minimum leaving room for negotiation between the worker and owner.

for the negotiating of certain benefits or conditions.[41] It seems that there were some jobs that had a set fee that was the norm.[42]

When the work was urgent and needed to be done at a time that people did not like working, such as the days between the holidays (*hol hamoed*), it was sometimes necessary to pay the workers extra. In other cases, the rabbis demanded that one hire a number of workers to harvest a field quickly rather than doing it himself, so that it would not seem like the Jew is maintaining wheat in a vineyard and thus transgressing the prohibition against mixing different species of seeds in the tractate *Kilayim* (lit. "cross-breeding").[43]

There are cases mentioned in which a Jew hired non-Jews as workers or non-Jews hired Jews as workers.[44] There is a prohibition against hiring non-Jewish workers to harvest wheat because they do not know that they have to leave the poor the individual stalks that fall on the ground.[45] In some cases, the worker separates the tithes for the priest on behalf of the owner.[46]

The expectations from the worker were high. The rabbis required that he put into his work every ounce of energy that he had. This rule stands in contrast to the rule stipulating that the Jewish slave was to be treated gently.[47] Indeed, the Mishnah in *Avot* shows the common situation in which the "workers are lazy" and the "owner is demanding."[48] It should be noted that the source also says "and the pay is great." That is clearly only relevant to the way the author wants to present the pay that God pays his devotees, and it shows that when the pay

---

41   *M. Bava Metzia* 7:6. There he negotiates receiving more money on the condition he will not exercise his right to eat from the produce while he works. *M. Bava Metzia* 6:1 mentions a case in which they "mislead each other." *BT Bava Metzia* 76a establishes that the case was that there was misinformation regarding the fee that had been agreed. However, Albeck, *Mishnah, Bava Metzia*, 94, explains that the misleading was concerning what the fixed rate was and that he would follow the assumption that in most cases the fee was not negotiated.

42   *M. Bava Metzia* 5:4. This also can be seen in *M. Bava Metzia* 7:1, which mentions the "practice of the country" being the supplying of workers with food and beverage.

43   *M. Kilayim* 7:6.

44   *T. Halah* 1:3 (Lieberman ed., 275). In this case, the source discusses whether the tithe from the dough must be separated or not. There is a similar discussion in *T. Pesahim* 2:3–4 regarding *hametz* (leavened bread, prohibited on the Passover festival). It may have belonged to a non-Jew who worked at the site.

45   *T. Pe'ah* 3:1.

46   *T. Terumot* 1:7–8 (Lieberman ed., 108–109).

47   Sifra Behar 6:6 (Weiss ed., 110a). See also Varro, *De re rust.* 1.17.3. He recommends doing hard or unhealthy tasks with hired workers not slaves, though his reason was probably not to damage the slaves that were part of the property of the master.

48   *Avot* 2:15. The statement is attributed to Rabbi Tarfon, who was active in the beginning of the second century CE.

is more than usual the workers are motivated to work harder and the employer can demand more from them. The Tosefta states:

> A worker has no right to do his own work by night and to hire himself out by day, to plow with his cow by night and to hire it out in the morning (*shaharit*). Nor may he deprive himself of food and starve himself in order to give his food to his children. On account of the robbery of his labor which belongs to the householder [who hires him].[49]

The source implies that there were laborers that would do the above actions in order to earn more and improve their economic situation. The employers certainly were unhappy with this practice, and in this case the rabbis sided with them. The rabbis were so keen that the laborer work the hours for which he was hired that they legislated leniencies for workers regarding religious obligations so they would not have to take away much time from the employer. The Tosefta states:

> The workers may recite [the *shema'*] while in a treetop, and recite the prayer while atop an olive tree or atop a fig tree ... But a householder (the owner) must always climb down an [then] recite the prayer [since the height will distract him].[50]

Similarly, laborers were allowed to use a shortened version of the blessing after food (*birkat hamazon*). If the owner is eating with them or they are receiving their food as their salary, they should say all the benedictions.[51]

The person who hires the workers is usually referred to as the "homeowner."[52] This concept is discussed below. Here, it is important to point out that the term was likely used to denote more than just a homeowner. It likely refers to an entire economic entity that could include a field or fields and other installations. The employer usually belonged to a higher stratum of society than the employee, though it is possible that the employee would be a field owner who would rent out his work during periods in which his land did not require labor. Employers that were wealthier than the average homeowner would have a bailiff or an overseer who would hire the workers and pay them. The former would not do the hiring and paying themselves.

---

49 *T. Bava Metzia* 8:2 (Neusner ed., 4:116; Lieberman ed., 103).
50 *T. Berakhot* 2:8 (Neusner ed., 1:7). Compare *M. Berakhot* 2:4.
51 *M. Berakhot* 5:24 (Lieberman ed., 29). They say only two benedictions rather than four.
52 *M. Berakhot*; *T. Pe'ah* 2:7 (Lieberman ed., 46–47); and *T. Demai* 8:6 (Lieberman ed., 102).

The sources mention that on top of their salary the workers would be entitled to certain benefits as well. The rabbis interpreted a passage in the Torah as allowing workers to eat from the fruit they are working with if their work involves the harvesting or collection of that produce.[53] There is much discussion about the boundaries of this benefit.[54] The worker may eat from agricultural produce only, and only when it is harvest time. Once it was harvested and collected, it could not be eaten without the consent of the employer.[55] A worker may eat only from the type of fruit he is working with. If he is working with figs, he cannot eat grapes.[56] The Mishnah mentions cases in which the worker and employer agree to allow the worker's son or family to eat from the fruit with which he is working. This can be in addition to his salary or instead be a part of the salary or all of it.[57] It seems that a benefit consisting of food during or after work was common, as we find such a benefit being referred to in numerous contexts.[58] The cases in which the worker is willing to lose money in order to feed his family from the fruit he is working with seem to be cases in which there is an abundance of workers and the worker is desperate to keep his job. He is therefore willing to accept some of his pay in kind rather than in cash.

In addition, it seems that in other jobs that did not provide this benefit, such as plowing, planting, or weeding, there were occasions on which the workers would be provided with food. Rabban Simon son of Gamaliel stated that this is done "according to local practice."[59] It is also found that Rabban Gamaliel fed his workers *demai* (lit. "dubious" produce), which shows that he too gave food to his workers.[60] There is mention of breaks in work for the sake of eating.[61]

---

53   *M. Bava Metzia* 7:2–5, based on Deut. 23:25–26. Compare *T. Maasrot* 2:13–16 (Lieberman ed., 234–235).

54   *M. Maasrot* 2:7 determines that when the laborer is granted the right to eat by law, he does not have to separate tithes for the priest and Levite from the produce. If the right to eat is given to him by his employer he must separate tithes.

55   *M. Bava Metzia* 7:2.

56   Compare *M. Maasrot* 2:8: when working with one kind of fig, he may not eat from another.

57   *M. Maasrot* 7:7. Whenever it is not the worker himself who is eating the Mishnah states that he must separate tithes. This is regardless of whether the food is at the expense of his salary or in addition to his salary.

58   In addition to those mentioned above, see *M. Maasrot* 3:1–3.

59   *M. Bava Metzia* 7:1. The majority opinion agrees with the principle that food for the workers depends on the local practice. It, however, posits that when the employer promised verbally to feed the workers he was obligating himself to providing them with extra food. See also *M. Bava Metzia* 7:4, 5, and 7.

60   *M. Demai* 3:1. This was because the rule was that one could feed the poor *demai*. Rabban Gamaliel's workers were poor and therefore he fed them *demai*. See also *M. Terumot* 6:3 and *T. Terumot* 3:15 (Lieberman ed., 76) that mentions feeding workers.

61   *T. Demai* 5:7 (Lieberman ed., 88); *T. Maasrot* 2:13 (Lieberman ed., 234).

THE LABORER (PO'EL)

There are cases in which the employer gives his workers money and tells them to buy food with it.[62]

The sources relate occurrences in which there is a religious discrepancy between the employer, who does not separate tithes from his produce, and the worker, who does. The Mishnah advises the worker on how to conduct himself.[63]

The rabbis decreed that a day laborer should be paid on the following night, and that a night worker may be paid on the following day.[64] An exception to the rule is someone who was hired for a longer period starting at a week: if he finishes his work during the day, he should be paid that day, and if he finishes his work at night, the employer has until the end of the following day to pay him.[65]

The worker also had rights. The Mishnah states that if someone hired a laborer to do a certain job, then he could not force him to do a different job. If he hired him to plow a certain field, then he cannot force him to plow another field.[66] Typically, the workday started in the morning and ended in the evening, as the Mishnah says: "A man comes from the field in the evening."[67] The Mishnah states that the employer cannot force his workers to come early or to leave late.[68]

In order to encourage employers to pay their employees on time and not to postpone payment, the sages stated that if an employer does not pay on time he transgresses the positive commandment that one must pay "on the day" and also the negative commandment not to wait to pay until the following morning. The rabbis expand on this decree to include not only the payment for labor but also for the rental of animals or equipment.[69]

---

62   Ibid., 5:14 (Lieberman ed., 89).
63   *M. Demai* 7:3. This too is a case in which the employer took it upon himself to feed the worker as a benefit. See also *T. Demai* 8:6 (Lieberman ed., 102).
64   This is based on a passage from the Torah (Lev. 19:13).
65   *M. Bava Metzia* 9:11. On the distinction of the long-term worker, see also *T. Shviit* 5:21, which says that, in contrast to the day laborer, the long-term laborer may be fed produce from the seventh year. There, the long-term worker is called a "*sakhir*" possibly to separate him from the day laborer.
66   *T. Bava Metzia* 7:506, 508 (Lieberman ed., 99–100).
67   *M. Berakhot* 4:2. See also *T. Arakhin* 4:1 and *T. Avodah Zarah* 7:10. Sifra, parsha 1.1 seems to indicate that the laborers leave for work at sunrise. It is clear from the Mishnah that different locations had different practices.
68   *M. Bava Metzia* 7:1. See Epstein, *Introduction Mishnah*, 1, 354, 376.
69   Ibid., 9:12.

There are also leniencies for the employer. If the worker does not ask for his pay, the employer does not transgress the rule on prompt payment.[70] Similarly, if he refers the worker to receive his money from a banker or a storekeeper, he is fulfilling his obligation.[71] On the other hand, the employer may not offer the worker the option of taking some of the material he worked with instead of money.[72]

When the worker claims that he was not paid and the employer claims that he was paid, it is stated that the worker can get his pay as long as the claim was made during the payment period, in which case the workers are allowed to "swear and collect."[73] If the claim was made late and the employer claims that he paid on time, the employer swears and does not have to pay.[74]

There were cases in which there were disagreements and claims of fraud between the employer and the employees. Sometimes the workers were hired and they did not come or stopped working in the middle of the day.[75] When the work was not done due to uncontrolled circumstances, the worker had the upper hand. If the worker got sick or had to mourn, the employer had to pay him for the part of the job that he had already carried out.[76] Similarly, if the worker went to do the work but it turned out to be unnecessary, the owner had to pay him in full or like an idle worker, depending on the specific case.[77] This source needs a closer look, because it provides some interesting details about the nature of the work of the laborer. It also shows that the worker is hired only for the job that was presented to him. He is not a general worker and can refuse to do a harder job for part of the day. On the other hand, the employer may switch him from a hard job to an easier job. He cannot have him do the same kind of work in someone else's field. If he notified the worker in advance that he may change the job midway through and/or have him work another's

---

70 Ibid., 9:12.
71 Albeck, *Mishnah*, 103, explains that the storekeeper is to give him merchandise for his pay. That would mean that the employer can force the worker to receive pay in kind rather than cash. However, it is possible to say the storekeeper was asked to give the worker an option of merchandise or cash.
72 M. Bava Metzia 10:5.
73 See also *M. Shevuot* 7:1. Albeck, *Mishnah*, 265, explains based on the JT that the employer is busy with his various enterprises and therefore may forget to pay and mistakenly think that he paid.
74 M. Bava Metzia 9:12.
75 M. Moed Katan 2:1–2. T. Bava Metzia 7:1 (Lieberman ed., 98) states that if they decided to refrain from finishing the job, they did not lose their entire pay for the day, and if the owner stopped the work in the middle, he must pay them like "an idle worker."
76 T. Bava Metzia 7:3 (Lieberman ed., 98–99).
77 See the above source in addition to T. Bava Metzia 7:4 (Lieberman ed., 99).

field, he would be able to do as much. The Tosefta in *Bava Metzia* also teaches us about what workers would do if the job was not completed:

> Under what circumstances? In a case in which they did not begin [the work]. But if they had actually begun the work, lo, they make an estimate for him [how much of the work actually had been done]. How so? [If] one undertook for the householder to cut down his standing grain for two *sela*, [and] had cut down half of it and left half of it, [or if he undertook] to weave a cloak for two *sela* and [had woven] half of it and had left half of it—lo, these make an estimate for him. How so? If what he had made was worth six *denar*, they hand over to him a *sela* [four *denar*] or he completes his work. And if it was worth a *sela* they hand over to him a *sela*. R. Dosa says: "They make an estimate of the value of what is going to be made. If that which was going to be made was worth five *denar* they give him a *shekel* or he finishes the work. And if it was worth a *shekel* they give him a *shekel*."[78]

The source proceeds to describe various situations in which the workers mislead the employer, such as when they change their mind before they started working or during the workday. In the latter case, they receive part of their pay. The source also distinguishes between a situation in which a delay in the work will cause a loss for the employer and cases in which it will not cause a loss for the employer.

It can also be seen in this source that sometimes the workers were hired to complete a certain task rather than to work for the day. What if they were hired to harvest a field of wheat for two *sela* and they did only half the field? Here, there is a disagreement between Rabbi Dosa and the majority opinion. Rabbi Dosa safeguards the right of the employer to have the job finished at the expense of the pay for the workers for what they did. The majority opinion says that the workers receive one *sela*, which was half the salary for the harvesting of the field, which was two *sela*.

There is a need to see the nature of the employment agreement under discussion. Two *sela* for harvesting the field is eight *denar*. The daily pay for a laborer was a *denar*. If the field could be harvested in one day, then it would be a very generous payment. It is more likely that the job was to take several days.[79] This can also be seen in the story of Ruth, where the relevant passage

---

78   *T. Bava Metzia* 7:1 (following Neusner ed., 4:110 and Lieberman ed., 98).
79   This is probably the way to understand *T. Shevuot* 6:1, in which the employer says "I owe you one *sela*" and the worker says "you owe me two *sela*." It is not talking about a one-day job but rather a job that was to be paid for on completion.

tells us that she collected the poor man's tithes in Boaz's field "all the days of harvesting the wheat and the barley," indicating that the harvest was more than one day.[80] The actual daily pay was probably lower than a *denar* because the worker was ensured employment for a number of days without the need to seek out a new job every day. The Sifra mentions a situation in which a king hired workers and one of them worked for the king for many days. The king told him to let him finish the small account that he had with the other workers and then he would get to his large account.[81] The reason for the higher pay for the worker who worked more seems to be merely that he worked more "days." This indicates that it was a job that was billed by the day.

The Tosefta in *Shviit* tells us that there were workers who were hired by the public through the leaders of the community. There were towns that hired workers to collect the fruit off the trees in the Sabbatical year and to distribute them to the people. The workers would process the fruit until it could be stored. It is unclear whether the same workers did the distribution or whether the court itself did it.[82]

4 The Laborer's Economic Situation

There are a number of sources spanning various periods that indicate that the daily wage for the laborer was one *denar* per day. As noted above, in Matthew the homeowner hires workers for a *denar* a day. However, the source also mentions workers who worked less than a day and expected to earn less.[83] There is a mishnah that points to that wage as well.[84] The Tosefta, however, is more explicit:

---

80 Ruth 2:23. See also the previous passages in which she happens to collect in Boaz's field and Boaz tells her to come to his field every day. Of course, the time for harvesting a field would depend on its size. It is also possible that Boaz, who was a wealthy man, had a number of fields.
81 Sifra, Behukotai, parsha 1:2:1.
82 *T. Shviit* 8:1 (Lieberman ed., 200).
83 Matt. 20:1–7. Curchin, "Labour," 179, posits that the sum must be realistic because the parable was meant to influence the people that listened to it. See also Tobit 5:15. In this ancient source from the third century BCE, the pay for the worker is a *drachma* a day, which is equivalent to a *denar*. However, it must be noted that in that case the employment was long term and there were familial ties involved.
84 *M. Bava Metzia* 7:4 mentions that a worker may eat from the fruit even the sum of a *denar*. Rabbi Elazar son of Hisma says that a worker should not work more than his pay and more than the rabbis allow. It is possible to derive from this that the pay equaled a *denar*.

THE LABORER (PO'EL)

> He who says to a worker, "Here's this *maneh*, and let it be in your hand, so you'll work with me at the harvest time at the rate of a *denar* a day," while the work is worth a *sela* a day, it is prohibited. "[Charge] against it at the rate of a *denar* a day," while the work is worth a *sela* a day—it is permitted.[85]

The Tosefta shows that the daily salary for a worker at harvest time was a *sela* a day, which was four *denar*. This is probably because at harvest time there was great demand for workers and a limited amount available. In this case, the money was paid in advance for a relatively long period of employment and the employer wished to pay the standard one *denar* even during high season, which is when the pay was usually higher.[86]

A source from the Roman world seems to mention a lower wage found in other parts of the Empire primarily in transport.[87] Scheidel measured the pay of the Roman laborer in kind. He states that the pay was four to five liters of wheat for a day's work. In contrast, the Mishnah states that one *sela* equaled four *denar* and could purchase four *se'ah* of wheat.[88] This means that one *denar* could purchase one *se'ah* of wheat. Each *se'ah* was six *kav*, and each *kav* was 1.8 liters, making the *se'ah* approximately ten liters. The above-mentioned pay of the laborer in Rome was therefore half a *denar* or less.

If indeed the pay in Roman Palestine was one *denar* a day, then the laborer could accumulate in that way 300 *denar* a year (without the Sabbath and holidays), assuming that he and his family are healthy throughout the year. Ayali deducts rain days as well and reaches in her study 275 days of work.[89] The price of a loaf of bread from the baker was one *pundion*, which was one-twelfth of a *denar* (one *denar* was six *isar*, one *isar* was two *pundion*).[90] Assuming that the laborer was feeding a family of five, he would need three loaves of bread a day; each loaf would equal two adult meals; and children would eat half of

---

85 *T. Bava Metzia* 6:15 (Neusner ed., 4:108). See also Sifre Devarim, piska 307, which mentions a *denar* and perhaps a bit more. A general statement is found in the Mekhilta de-Rabbi Yishmael, Beshalah, Massekhet Shira 8: "A coin he gives him." Similarly, it is found in Mekhilta de-Rashbi Shimeon bar Yohai 15:11.
86 Since a *maneh* is 100 *zuz*, which is 25 *denar*, the worker was hired for 25 days, which is probably really a month because no work was done on the Sabbath.
87 Cato, *De Agr.*, 22.3. Curchin, "Labour," 179, assumes that the pay was even lower in the villages. However, he concludes that in agriculture the pay was higher than in transport (180–181).
88 *M. Pe'ah* 8:7. See Albeck, *Mishnah, Zeraim*, 65.
89 Ayali, *Workers*, 55.
90 *M. Pe'ah* 8:7. See also *M. Bava Metzia* 4:5, Albeck, *Nezikin*, 80. "A loaf for a *pundion*" is also mentioned in *T. Shviit* 6:21 (Lieberman ed., 192–193).

that amount.[91] If the wife of the laborer could take the wheat herself to the mill and bake the bread herself, they could save additional money. Alternatively, they could eat the wheat as cereal by chopping it in half, into thirds, or into quarters.[92] It is likely that the family would need to add to the bread also *kitnit*—legumes for protein as described in the Mishnah (*Bava Metzia* 7:1) as the typical laborer's meal; the expense, then, could reach four to five *pundion* a day for food. This means that there would be money to save, enabling the worker to accumulate a sum of 200 *zuz*, which would place him in the middle class. Of course, this calculation depends on the worker accumulating enough workdays.[93]

Ayali calculates it slightly differently. With one day's payment, the worker could buy a *se'ah* of wheat (approx. ten liters), and prepare from it 18 small loaves of what was considered the bread of the poor (this follows Rabbi Simeon's opinion that there would be three loaves per *kav*). This would supply the bread needs of the family for the week, since each loaf provided two adult meals and four child portions.[94]

In addition, he assumes that the poor man needed other food items that were supplied, according to the sources, to the poor as part of the "poor tithe." They included a half a log of wine, though Rabbi Akiva said a quarter, and a quarter of a log of oil, though Rabbi Akiva said an eighth.[95] He assumes that these extra food requirements would cost another *denar* a week like the bread. To this must be added the expenses for clothing and other important items. The following table was compiled by Heichelheim in order to calculate the various basic needs of a man.[96]

---

91 According to *M. Eruvin* 8:2; Albeck, *Mishnah, Moed*, 115, says the loaf of bread that was two meals equaled 12 eggs. It should be noted that Rabbi Simeon mentioned in that mishnah has a smaller bread of which two-thirds equals two meals or five eggs and a third. This could be the bread of the poor or, the opposite, the bread of the rich man, who ate many other things with the bread. Both opinions are cited in *M. Keilim* 17:11. The first opinion is attributed there to Rabbi Yohanan son of Broqa.

92 *T. Moed Katan* 4:13. There, it is called *"hilka," "tigris,"* and *"tisni."* BT Moed Katan 13b explains that one of them refers to kernels of wheat split into two, the other refers to kernels of wheat split into three, and *tisni* refers to kernels of wheat split into four.

93 Researchers of the Roman world came to a similar estimation of the income of the average laborer. See below.

94 However, it could be that a poor man's bread was even cheaper. It was called *"pat kivar"* because he would mix into the flour also bran that was cheaper. See *M. Makhshirin* 8:2; and Albeck, *Mishnah, Taharot*, 420. See also Sifra Behar, parsha 1, chapter 7 (Weiss ed., 109, 2–3).

95 *M. Pe'ah* 8:5.

96 Heichelheim, "Roman Syria," 180.

THE LABORER (PO'EL)

	Bread	Food	Clothing	Misc.	Total (*denar*)
Approximate annual amount	96	96	50	33	275
Amount per day	0.275	0.275	0.140	0.095	0.785

The above calculation assumes a cost of 50 *zuz* for the year for a family of five. The price given in the Mishnah for a *haluk*, a kind of undergarment, was between 12 and 25 *denar*, and the *tallit*, which served as the overgarment, was an additional 25 *denar*.[97] The assumption is that the laborer would buy clothing every two years for his wife and himself, and from the old clothes sow together clothing for the children.[98] According to this calculation, the laborer would at best make ends meet if he worked every available day, he and his family were healthy, and there was no famine to raise the price of food.

However, there are a number of things that can change this calculation in the favor of the laborer:

1. Ayali himself reasons that the laborer usually ate at least one meal on the job.[99]
2. During the harvest season and fruit-picking season that spanned most of the summer and some of the winter, the laborer would be able to eat from the produce that he harvested according to the Torah decree mentioned above.[100] In addition, if indeed in the high seasons such as the harvest the wages were doubled (or raised even higher), it would make a difference.
3. *T. Shviit* states that it is permitted to give a Samaritan fruit that is from the Sabbatical year "up to 4 *isar*" (*isar* = *as* = 1/24 *denar*; 4 *isar* = 1/8 *denar*). Lieberman explains that this equals four meals: two for him and two for his wife. This should lead to the conclusion that the money needed for

---

[97] The price of the *haluk* is based on *M. Meilah* 6:4. The price of the *haluk* and *tallit* is based on *T. Bava Metzia* 3:14 (Lieberman ed., 76).
[98] Ayali, *Workers*, 56.
[99] As stated in *M. Bava Metzia* 7:1, in places that the laborer was given food he could expect "bread and legumes." The above source also mentions that some employers would provide "sweets" for the workers.
[100] See, for example, *T. Bava Metzia* 8:3 (Lieberman ed., 102). The worker is allowed to dip his bread into vinegar in order that he should eat many grapes, and the farmer may feed him wine so he does not eat many grapes.

extra food required by the poor is only four *isar* a day, much less than the expense of bread, which goes against Heichelheim's calculation.[101]

4. The *haluk* mentioned in the Mishnah costs 12 to 25 *denar*. This cost probably related to the middle class. There were undergarments that were as cheap as one *denar* in value.[102]

5. It is likely that the laborers wore only a haluk and not a *tallit*.

Although it seems that the usual pay for workers in Roman Palestine was in cash, the sources mention cases in which there was pay in kind. The Mishnah mentions payment in kind (part of the harvest) to workers who harvested the field.[103] The following passage from the Tosefta shows that the norm was to pay in cash, not in kind:

> [If the employer] gave him a draft on a storekeeper or moneychanger [M. Bava Metzia 9:12], they are subject to transgressing on his account [the rule against keeping back wages, if they do not pay up]. But he does not transgress [the biblical requirement]. And if he stipulated with him at the outset in this regard [in that the wages would be deposited as specified], then even they are not subject to transgressing [the biblical law] on his account. And if he told someone to pay him, this one and that one are not liable to transgressing the law on his account.[104]

In Tosefta *Berakhot*, there is mention of laborers who "work for their food." The rule there is that, even though regular laborers may say a shortened benediction after their meal so they may quickly get back to work, when their pay is their meal they must say the entire benediction.[105] Ayali explains that this must have been in a period of unemployment when wages were down or in a

---

101 *T. Shviit* 6:20 (Lieberman ed., 192). Lieberman comments that the sum of four *isar* squares with *M. Pe'ah* 8:1.

102 *M. Meilah* 4:6; Sperber, *Money and Prices*, 103–106. In the inflation period of the Roman Empire in the middle of the fourth century CE, the prices were very high but there were still three levels of prices for garments. A superb *haluk* from Beit Shean would cost 11,000 *denar*. A simple one would cost 2,500 *denar*, and one for a slave or poor man would cost only 1,000 *denar*. See Jones, *Economy*, 353, 355.

103 *M. Pe'ah* 5:5. Of course, this type of agreement was practical only in harvesting and not in other agricultural work that did not yield produce that could be used as immediate pay.

104 *T. Bava Metzia* 10:5 (Neusner ed., 4:135). See, similarly, *T. Bava Metzia* 7:4 (Neusner ed., 4:98–99). Here, one must accept the opinion of Ayali, *Laborer*. He posits that pay in kind was not the norm and therefore could not be offered to the worker. Krauss, *Lehnwörter*, 2:105, wanted to deduce the opposite—that it was the norm to pay the worker in kind.

105 *T. Berakhot* 5:25 (Lieberman ed., 29).

time of famine when the food would be worth the daily pay.[106] On the other hand, in times when the owner needed the work done quickly he would have to pay more or, as the Mishnah states, "until a third."

The agreement between the worker and employer involved only the pay and benefits for the worker himself. If he wanted his son to eat from the produce, then he was required to have it deducted from his pay.[107]

5   Summary

The term *"po'alim"* relating to a distinct social category of laborers who were paid for their general work and not for a particular skillset is first found in Jewish literature of Roman Palestine in the second half of the first century CE in Josephus, and shortly after it is found in the NT. In the second and third centuries, this group receives a lot of attention from rabbinic sources. Such laborers existed prior to this time as well, but were not specifically identified as a distinct group. This indicates that the phenomenon of the day laborer who went every day to wait to be employed, as described in detail by the NT and rabbinic sources, gained a great deal of significance in the period here under discussion or somewhat earlier. The historical background for the proliferation of the day laborer in this period is connected to Empire-wide processes of urbanization that brought many laborers from villages to look for work in the cities, as well as to the unique circumstances of Jewish society in Roman Palestine: many people lost a lot of land because of the revolts and wars and there was a need for hired labor during the labor-intensive periods of agriculture—especially in the absence of extended family members.[108]

Day laborers were found in agricultural as well as nonagricultural occupations. On the one hand, in contrast to the poor, they worked for a living and did

---

106   Ayali, *Laborer*, 44.
107   As it is stated in *T. Bava Metzia* 8:2 that the laborer may not deprive himself and feed his family because that is at the expense of the employer. This of course also involves the private food of the laborer: he must eat his portion of food so he will be strong for his work. In *M. Maasrot* 2:7, the worker suggests that his son eat from the produce at the expense of his salary. It could be that the entire salary would be lost; it is more likely, though, that an amount was to be deducted.
108   This issue of the breakdown of the extended family when nuclear families had to live by themselves and attain their livelihood was discussed in previous chapters. This phenomenon contributed to the proliferation of day laborers during labor-intensive periods, when demand for their work was high, and to the supply of laborers who lost their land and had to work for other people.

not collect tithes or go begging. On the other hand, their employment was unstable, their pay was low, and they lived on the edge of sustenance. The laborers were independent and could choose whether to work for a certain wage or not, but they probably could not afford to miss a day without having to deprive themselves or their family of various necessities. They were also similar to the poor, in that most of them did not own land or any income-providing assets; they may not have owned the home they lived in. Their livelihood therefore depended on employment they gained from the *ba'al habayit* ("homeowner") that owned their own land and used hired labor. This was a group that was broad, including middle-class smallholders as well as wealthy landowners that used bailiffs and foremen to hire and supervise laborers.

The laborer was usually hired for a day at a time. Sometimes, he was hired for a season for harvesting or planting, and at other times he was hired for a few hours or to complete a specific job. Employment conditions varied according to the time of year and according to location. The average pay was one *denar* for a day's work. However, there are other arrangements mentioned in the sources. It also made a difference if the employer provided food during the day's work or not. There were also extreme situations in which the worker agreed to work for food.

Most employment agreements were oral, and there were sometimes misunderstandings, instances of fraud, and occasions on which people changed their minds. The workday lasted the entire day from sunup to sundown. Biblical law allowed the worker to eat from the fruit that he harvested. This too sometimes caused disagreements between the worker and the employer. The Mishnah and the Tosefta devote a lot of space to the discussion of these issues, giving us a detailed picture regarding a group in society that Roman historians said they knew existed but about which they said they knew little.

From the laborer who lived close to sustenance, our discussion will move to the craftsman, who was in better financial shape and who varied in his economic situation from living in poverty to living as part of the middle class.

6   Laborers in the Roman World

On the one hand, research on the Roman world tends to place workers of all kinds into one category.[109] On the other hand, there seems to be a con-

---

[109]   Park and Maxey, *Two Studies*, esp. 67–86; Brunt, "Labour," 701–716; Joshel, *Work Identity*, esp. 69–91; Kolendo, "Peasants," 199–213. Giardini's "The Romans" differentiates agricultural workers called "peasants" from "craftsmen," who are discussed in a separate chapter.

sensus that in the Roman world the economy was by large a result of market forces and of the law of supply and demand. The same was true in terms of labor. Workers were hired in many different ways and under many different conditions. Nevertheless, there were more work options in the cities than in rural areas.[110]

One of the reasons for the scant information concerning laborers is that most literary sources and archeological findings represent the viewpoint of the minority upper classes of society. Therefore, any venture to go beyond that milieu is so daunting that the small differences that one may find in the sources seem to be relatively insignificant. Another reason is that "extremely little is known of the working population in general but more of the slaves than of any other section of it. Since slaves were property they were of constant concern to the jurists who provide our most valuable information."[111] Since there was little litigation concerning free laborers, there are few documents available that refer to them. All the above makes it difficult to find information about the unskilled free laborer. However, despite the above-mentioned limitations, one can piece together hints found in various places in an effort to try to learn something about him.

Most laborers in the Roman world worked in the fields, performing agricultural tasks.[112] The ancient first-century BCE Roman writer Varro said: "All agriculture is carried out by human beings, either by slaves, or by free persons, or a mixture of both" (*De re rust.* 1.17). Brunt points out, however, that, while in the rest of the Empire there was much slave labor, in Egypt and Palestine most labor was carried out by free men.[113] In the rest of the Roman world, the craftsman or peasant could purchase slaves, who would comprise a labor force needing only to be fed and minimally clothed. Brunt adds that "very probably slave competition held down the remuneration that the free poor could expect for their labor especially in agriculture and mining."[114] Interestingly, the orator and statesman Cicero wrote that a casual laborer hired for the day would

---

For Latin terms for laborers, see Glare, *Oxford Latin Dictionary,* 990 a–c, 991a (*labor*), 1251 a–c (*opera, operarius*); 1261a–c (*opus*); De-Vaan, *Dictionary Latin,* 320 (*labor*), 386 (*moles*), 432 (*opus, operarius*). This can be seen from the inscription on the tomb of the Mactar Reaper, who mentions that in the beginning of his career he was a laborer hired to harvest wheat. The epitaph is dated to 260–270 CE. For the source of the epitaph, see Dessau, *ILS,* II, 781–782, no. 7457.

110 Temin, "Labor Market," 513–538; Allen, "Prosperous Romans," 327–345; Scheidel, "Real Wages," 425–462; Lis and Soly, *Worthy Efforts,* 54–98.
111 See Brunt, "Labour," 708.
112 See Ibid., 701.
113 See Ibid., 703. Serfdom also did not exist in Palestine and Egypt (ibid., 704).
114 See Ibid., 708.

earn three *sestertii*.¹¹⁵ This is three-quarters of a *denar*, which is 75 percent of the estimated income of a day laborer in Palestine, where there was no slave labor to compete with. Brunt points out that while slaves cultivated the land all year round, harvest, plowing, and planting required large numbers of unskilled workers and so free laborers would be hired even in Italy.¹¹⁶ Garnsey adds that some of these workers would have been smallholders that used the extra income to supplement the meager returns of their smallholdings.¹¹⁷ Another area in which work was seasonal was the erection of large monumental buildings. Workers would be hired for the job and let go when it ended; there was no need to employ slaves. Maritime trade operated only in the summer, not in the winter, and therefore dock workers would be free men and not slaves.¹¹⁸

Brunt points out that the reason the Roman jurors rarely mention salary earners is because most labor was hired on a daily basis. If the employer was unhappy with the work, he would dismiss the worker early and not pay him. The worker rarely had the ability to sue the employer for his wages. The author of the Epistle of James (5:4) voices the complaints of laborers whose wages were held back fraudulently. Perhaps the reason why he voices these concerns is because in the Torah it was considered a religious transgression to not pay workers for their labor.

There is little account of the lives and careers of laborers. As described above, a laborer that did not own land of his own would live on the border of subsistence and would depend on all other factors of his life being positive.¹¹⁹ There is very little evidence of laborers who managed to accumulate enough wealth to leave an epitaph that told their story as some artisans elsewhere in the Roman world were able to do. There is the story of the "Mactar Reaper" from North Africa (260–270 CE), which seems to be an exception. He left a lengthy epitaph that describes how he rose from being a day laborer during the harvest to being a foreman of workers. It goes on to say that he was later able to purchase land and build a villa.¹²⁰

---

115 Cicero, *Q. Rosc.*, 28. Kay, *Economic Revolution*, 287, assumes that the laborer could find work for 250 days a year.
116 Paterson, "Production," 181–207.
117 Garnsey, "Introduction."
118 See Brunt, *Italian Manpower*.
119 Curchin, "Labour," 177–187, describes the situation of the laborer in Roman Spain.
120 Cited by Lis and Soly, *Worthy Efforts*, 86–87 and n.97.

CHAPTER 4

Craftsmen and Artisans: the Low Middle Class

> Who will personally invite a foreigner; unless he is a craftsman, a diviner, a healer, a carpenter.… These are the ones among men who are sought on the broad earth.[1]

∴

> Whoever has a trade, to what is he compared? To a vineyard surrounded by a fence, to a furrow surrounded by a border.[2]

∴

Contemporary studies have probed the social situation of the craftsmen as portrayed in archeological and epigraphic findings and literary texts from the Roman world. The evidence demonstrates that this group of people engaged in professional, nonagricultural production and had skills that differentiated themselves from other members of the lower class.[3] It was posited that those belonging to this group shared a certain amount of prestige and a certain identity, and were less destitute than those who lacked land or a store and did not master a craft.[4]

---

1 Homer, *Odyssey* 17.382–386.
2 *T. Kiddushin* 1:8.
3 On the social location of the craftsman, see Frank, *Economic History*, 324–325; and Costin, "Craft and Social," 1–13.
4 See Meeks, *Social Paul*, 53–58; Aubert, "Workshop Managers"; Harris, "Workshop," 69–77; Scheidel, "Human Mobility," 1–5; Friesen, "Poverty Pauline," 323–326; Mayer, *Middle Classes*, 66–74,104–105, 114–120; Rosenfeld and Perlmutter, "Craftsmen"; and Wilson and Flohr, "Introduction," esp. 3–8. Hawkins, *Artisans*, 23–65, 268–272, posits that the Roman artisan had an unstable income and was dependent on loans. This evidence is not found in rabbinic literature possibly because said literature reflects a more rural setting, describing villages and small towns rather than large cities. On salaries of craftsmen see: Frank, Economic History 335–336 that quotes Diocletian's edict that gives an unskilled laborer half the salary of the lowest expert.

The vast majority of the population in the ancient world made its livelihood from farming the land.[5] Ten people tilling the ground were necessary to produce enough food for one person to live away from the land.[6] Lenski, in his analysis of ancient society, identifies the artisan as a "dispossessed farmer" and establishes his place in society below that of the farmer and close to the bottom of the societal ladder.[7] He estimates that craftsmen made up only 3 to 7 percent of society.[8] Initially, this was most likely true, and this is one of the reasons why the artisan in Greco-Roman and Persian society was considered to have a lower status than the farmer.[9] However, there is evidence that indicates

---

5   Hopkins, "Economic Growth," 35–39; Garnsey and Saller, *Economy and Society*, 43; Bang, "Trade and Economy," 25; De Ligt, *Markets*, 149–154. De Ligt says that the ancient world was a "peasant world which represented 80 to 90% of the population," and s.v. population, growth; De Ligt, *Peasants*, 13–30, 230–233; and Bowman and Wilson, "Roman Agriculture." Regarding Roman Palestine, Josephus, *Contra Apion* 1:12; Safrai, *Economy*, 352; Oppenheimer, *Between Rome and Babylon*, 197–242; Balch, "Rich and Poor," 214–218; and Oakman, "Jesus Peasant," 125–137 state that the same picture emerges from the NT. Regarding the second and third centuries, see Sperber, *Land*, 178. See also Horden and Purcell, *The Corrupting Sea*. Horden and Purcell show in this work that there were common economic conditions in all the lands that bordered the Mediterranean Sea.

6   White, "Technology Expansion." White was quoted by Fiensy, "Leaders," 5, n. 6. However, he mentions researchers that maintain that only 70–75 percent of the population in ancient Italy were peasants, meaning that fewer peasants were necessary to support the urban population. Nevertheless, it seems that it is impossible to compare Italy to the Roman provinces because much of the agricultural produce was imported to Rome in the form of tax from the provinces.

7   Lenski, *Power and Privilege*, 278–279. Harris, "Workshop," 80–81, claims that little investment was required in order to set up a workshop but that the income was low. However, this is in comparison to agricultural estates. The craftsman was in a good financial position in comparison with the city poor and the unskilled farm workers. Frank, *Economic History*, 324–331, concludes that many of the professionals in rich Roman households and estates were slaves and that independent craftsmen served the middling groups or existed in the smaller towns and the provinces, where slave labor was not as common.

8   See Lenski, *Power and Privilege*, 279; and Fiensy, "Leaders," 6.

9   Herodotus 2.167, based on Egyptian attitudes; Aristotle compares them to slaves in *Pol.* 1.5.10. and considers them inferior to farmers in ibid., 6.2.7, 7.8.2. On the other hand, he concedes that crafts are necessary for society. See *Pol.* 4.3.11–12, and Plato, *Rep.* 2.396b–371e. Xenophon has Socrates denigrate artisans (*Oec.* 4.1–4), and later Greek authors such as Dio Chrysostom maintain a similar attitude (see *Or.* 7.110). Some Roman authors, such as Lucian of Samosata (*Fug.* 12–13), Celsus (Origen, *C. Cels.* 6.36), and Cicero (*Off.* 1.42 and *Brut.* 73) share this view. However, Cicero and Livy admit that artisans are useful to the city (Cicero, *Rep.* 2.22, and Livy, *AUC* 20.2.25); see Harries, *Cicero*, 185–203 and esp. index, s.v. citizenship, *societas*. As will be shown below, this attitude was not shared by Palestinian-Jewish thinkers, or by Roman craftsmen who described their profession on their epitaphs. See Mayer, *Middle Classes*, 100–133; and Saldarini, *Pharisees and Sadducees*, 139.

that this relative positioning changed with the economic development of the Roman Empire.[10]

Epigraphic findings show that in the first centuries CE a substantial number of craftsmen acquired enough wealth to mention their profession on their gravestones and to establish *collegia* in Rome.[11] A similar picture emerges from inscriptions found in Asia Minor in the first centuries CE. Epitaphs found show the variety of professions held by craftsmen as well as their professional pride. They were organized into *collegia*, and some of them had funds to pay membership fees as well. Some *collegia* were wealthy enough to construct decorated graves for their members.[12] Some researchers see the development of the crafts and the appearance of artisans as one of the first signs of progress toward a more complex society involving economic development and technological innovation (along with the development of commerce).[13]

Research on Jewish society in Roman Palestine in the first centuries CE shows that there was gradual development of groups of craftsmen who advanced beyond the level of "dispossessed farmers achieving a modest level of financial security."[14] Some of these professionals also achieved social status

---

10   There are other reasons mentioned for the lack of status of the craftsmen. Socrates and Dio Chrysostom mention the disfiguring of their bodies from the repetition of tasks and, on the other hand, their soft bodies from their sedentary lifestyle (Socrates in Xenophon, *Oec.* 4.1–4 and Dio Chrysotom, *Or.* 7.110). Another criticism was that a craftsman was not an adequate defender of the city (Socrates in Xenophon, ibid.). See also Hock, *Social Paul*, 20–27, 31–37, about the time it took for the artisan to produce and how manual labor resembled slave labor in the eyes of society. However, it is likely that the attitude to craftsmen improved when technology improved, enabling them to improve their economic standing, as well as their diet and health.

11   On epitaphs of craftsmen, see Vitruvius, *De arch.* 6, pref. 5; Frank, *Economic History*, 331–332; Stuart Jones, *Sculptures*, 76–77; CIL VI 1975; Zimmer, *Occupations*, 197–198. On Roman *collegia*, see Frank, *Economic History*, 328–329; Jongman, *Pompeii Society*, 168–170; Cotter, "The Collegia"; Arnaoutoglou, "Collegia Asia Minor"; Poblome, "Production," 493; Sodini, "Archaeology," 43–44; Liu, *Collegia*, 162–212; Gibbs, "Collegia"; Salvaterra and Cristofori, "Italian Scholarship"; and Hawkins, *Artisans*, 101–129. Other portraits of Roman craftsmen can be found in Lippold, *Vatican Sculptures*, 317, no. 52; Zimmer, *Occupations*, 36, 157–158, no. 80; D'Ambra, "Smith's Tomb," 94–95, fig. 58; Varner, "Replications," 290–292; and Stewart, *Roman Art*, 27.

12   See Van Nijf, *Associations*, 191–206, and index, s.v. associations, occupations (full list); Kloppenborg and Ascough, *Associations*, esp. 2–15; and Ascough, Harland, and Kloppenborg, *Associations*, esp. 1–11.

13   See Schortman and Urban, "Craft Economy"; and Scheidel, "Economic Growth." On the definition of Roman craftsmanship, see recently Hawkins, *Artisans*, 3–5; Brun, "French Approach"; and Ruffing, "Specialization."

14   There is not sufficient evidence to estimate how many such craftsmen existed. Regarding the financial situation of craftsmen in general, see Mossé, *Ancient Work*, 79; Burford,

that exceeded their economic gains because they provided society with a service or product that was needed and respected. This drew the attention of the spiritual leadership, who mention crafts in legal and religious contexts.[15] However, the surviving archeological findings are not as elaborate in Roman Palestine as they are in other parts of the Empire, and epitaphs found in Palestine do not usually contain the profession of the deceased. It is possible that there were epitaphs of this nature that were lost due to the wars and due to the conquering armies that passed through the region.[16] It is also likely that the economic situation of Roman Palestine was not as developed as that of other parts of the Empire. Perhaps religious and cultural considerations prevented the creation of postmortem records of the professions. Nevertheless, literary sources indicate a gradual increase in the appreciation of craftsmen and their professional skills in rabbinic circles. We are unable to discern whether this reflects the attitudes of the general Jewish population or only of the rabbinical circles; however, it is definitely a change when compared to attitudes that were prevalent in earlier rabbinic circles.

Our discussion here begins with a more detailed survey of the research that has accumulated concerning the artisan and craftsman in the Roman Empire. We will also present a survey of the research on Roman Palestine, which we will follow up with a survey of the relevant Jewish literature.[17]

It can be difficult to characterize the ancient craftsman or artisan, since individual workmen often did various crafts, and sometimes farmers supplemented their income by providing technical services to their neighbors. Zacaggini defines craftsmen as "specialists who perform activities other than those strictly connected with primary production or those activities based upon rudimentary knowhow."[18] Harris notes that in classical Greece there was a variety of professions—he estimates 170 professions—but there was little vertical specialization.[19] In other words, craftsmen did all the work needed to

---

Craftsmen, 141; and Ulrich, "Artisans." They also conclude that the craftsmen were able to earn enough money to live simply.

15 On criteria for social stratification, see Friesen, "Poverty Pauline," 323–331, Scheidel, "Stratification," 43–54; and Longenecker, "Economic Middle," 262–272.

16 This can explain why there are few epitaphs in Roman Palestine depicting the trades of the deceased. Also, the Jewish religion put emphasis on the deceased's religious devotion so that he would merit enjoying the "world to come."

17 For previous research on the artisan in Jewish society, see Ayali, *Workers*; and Aberbach, *Work and Crafts*. See also Safrai, *Economy*, 353–354, 370. Safrai states that the municipal officials encouraged the artisans with subsidies and could therefore control when they traveled, as is evident in *T. Bava Metzia* 11:30.

18 Zaccagnini, "Mobility," 246.

19 Harris, "Workshop," 67–70.

produce a single product, and society at that time lacked a coordinated division of labor. The terminology that distinguishes the professional craftsman from the person who occasionally performed certain tasks developed in this period first in literature and, in the third century CE, in spoken language as well. There is a record of a variety of professions, both in Jewish and non-Jewish sources, indicating the development of a large variety of crafts that preceded the emergence of commerce and industry.

1   Crafts in the Roman Empire

The economic development of the eastern parts of the Roman Empire in the first century CE increased urbanization and encouraged trade. The result was the development in production and technology that increased the wealth of the middling groups and enlarged their population, further creating a market for additional manufactured products. Thus, the status and skills of the craftsmen developed, while some of them, especially those who resided in cities, enjoyed a certain level of economic prosperity. This is seen in the proliferation of the *collegia* (workers' associations) in this period that organized members of the various professions. The *collegia* built clubhouses (*scholae*), sanctuaries, tombs, and monuments honoring the names of the professional associations.[20] There are records of 40 *collegia*, which organized the Roman artisans and assisted them with anything from celebrations to funerals. (There were probably many more *collegia*, and 40 is likely a mere fraction of the total.) The organization of workers indicated economic ability and the development of the social world of craftsmen.[21] Ruffing found 160 terms for crafts from the city of Rome alone and 225 designations for occupations in the western part of the Empire.[22]

Archeological findings show that Roman marketplaces included workshops for individual artisans. There were streets in Roman marketplaces that were named after the type of craftsmen who worked there. For example, there was

---

20   On the *scholae* of the guilds, see Mayer, *Middle Classes*, 85–99, who describes in detail *scholae* that were found in various sites, the cost involved in erecting them, and the income they would bring the guilds. On the guilds in general and the fabric industry in particular, see Liu, *Collegia*.
21   On the *collegia*, see, for example, Jongman, *Pompeii Society*, 168–170; Van Nijf, *Associations*; Arnaoutoglou, "Collegia Asia Minor"; Poblome, "Production," 493; Sodini, "Archaeology," 43–44; Liu, *Collegia*, 162–212; Gibbs, "Collegia"; Kloppenborg and Ascough, *Associations*; Ascough, Harland, and Kloppenborg, *Associations*.
22   Ruffing, "Specialization," 113.

Glass Street and Harness-Maker's Street.[23] These streets were lined with shops where the artisan-merchants worked and lived. This phenomenon developed from the third century BCE in Greece, intensifying at a later period in the Roman Empire.[24] The sheer number of workshops and associated businesses shows that there were economic opportunities for artisans and traders who shared the same market situation. In Weberian terms, "they depended on their skill and their sales and not on working their own land or that of others."[25]

Names of professions have been found on tombs of artisans, indicating that they saw their profession as being important. In some cases, their family would hire artists to depict the professions in pictures on the epitaphs. Loane cites images from "miniature factory scenes":

> The central figure carrying the roll is evidently the owner of the establishment; to his left one man works with a bow and drill, another with a saw and still another with an ax. To the right a craftsman is splitting the wood with a chisel and hammer, while a second is carefully cutting out a carved leg and a third is finishing off a bit of metal decoration.[26]

The self-image of Roman artisan funerary inscriptions, where the family of the deceased or his *collegia* mention his craft, indicate that the artisans themselves considered their craft to be a positive aspect worth advertising, even posthumously. In addition, Stewart points out that we find a significant number of Roman craftsmen who bore names of famous Greek artists, such as the goldsmith Zeuxis (*CIL* VI 3927) or the sculptor Myro (*CIL* VI 29796).[27] The development of the craftsman in Rome is exemplified by Vitruvius, who lived in the late first century BCE. He wrote a book about architecture, in which he describes the architect as someone who must know literature, drawing, geometry, history, philosophy, music, medicine, law, and astronomy. He describes himself as not working for a wage but as doing a "favor."[28] Another example is Titus Statilius Aper, who was a surveyor or builder. The funerary inscription created by his family in his memory documents his profession.[29]

---

23 On the Roman glass industry, see Frank, *Economic History*, 225.
24 Loane, *Industry*, 90–97.
25 Mayer, *Middle Classes*, 19.
26 Loane, *Industry*, 98.
27 See Stewart, *Roman Art*, 22. See also *CIL* VI 857: "Phidias and Ammonios, both sons of Phidias, made [this]"; and Arnaoutoglou, "Craftsman Associations."
28 See Vitruvius, *De arch.* 1.1.3, and 6, pref. 5. On a relief of a Roman architect, see Cohon, "Tools," 94–100.
29 See Zimmer, *Occupations*, 197–198; Stuart Jones, *Sculptures*, 76–77; and *CIL* VI 1975.

On the other hand, a portrait from a second-century altar depicting a sculptor at work shows that the sculptor is far from being high-class. He is bearded and wears a working-class short tunic, and his scrawny feet are bare. The woman who seems to have ordered his services is dressed in a respectably long tunic that falls modestly to the ground, with a mantle draped around her hip and over her shoulder. She has an elaborate coiffure, a fashionable style in this period, and seems to be holding a bag of money, both depictions being indicative of high society. It is unclear from the image whether it is primarily depicting the sculptor or the woman. However, the social gap between the two figures indicates that most artisans were far from being members of the upper classes, even if they were artists and even if they worked for the upper classes.[30]

Recent research, based on archeological finds in Asia Minor, further clarifies the status of craftsmen. Öğüş analyzes hundreds of *sarcophagi* found in excavations in Asia Minor and concludes that many of them belonged to "an archaeologically demonstrable group of individuals who had middling fortunes, modest professions, and names that set them apart from the aristocrats within the context of the Roman Empire."[31] He demonstrates that this phenomenon was characteristic of the first centuries CE and had not been seen previously. In his opinion, the Severan dynasty developed Roman economics and urbanization to the point that craftsmen could achieve sufficient wealth and sufficient status for building monuments and purchasing *sarcophagi* for their burial. These findings correspond with the time frame that scholars have established for the development of the crafts in Roman Palestine.[32]

There is little research regarding the substratification of craftsmen as a group. Generally speaking, Beechey finds that poverty existed in Roman society primarily in cases of individuals who lacked a profession or a vocation.[33] Stewart posits that the social status of the artisan was positively correlated with the level of the required theoretical expertise. Design and measurement were considered cognitive skills. The harder the manual labor involved, the lower the status of the artisan. Kehoe points out that there was economic expansion in the provinces of the Roman Empire during the first centuries CE,

---

30   Lippold, *Vatican Sculptures*, 317, no. 52; Zimmer, *Occupations*, 36, 157–158, no. 80; D'Ambra, "Smith's Tomb," 94–95, fig. 58; Varner, "Replications," 290–292; Stewart, *Roman Art*, 27; Ulrich, "Artisans."
31   Öğüş, "Sarcophagi," 119.
32   Ibid., 113–120.
33   Beechey, "Rethinking Work." On this issue, see, for example, De Ligt, *Markets*, 205–211, and index, s.v. cities, craftsman, villages, *Peasants*, esp. index, s.v. towns, urbanization; and Holleran, *Shopping*, esp. index, s.v. craftsman.

and this advancement would have assisted artisans and merchants more than it would have helped farmers.[34]

2   The Craftsman in Archeological Finds in Roman Palestine

There is evidence of products made and consumed in this period that required expert manufacturing in workshops, which indicates that, to a certain degree, they were mass-produced. Pottery was manufactured and marketed all over Palestine similarly to the way it was marketed all around the Roman world.[35] In Scythopolis (Beit Shean), flax workshops manufactured clothing for the Roman army as well as for the rest of the Empire.[36]

Rabbinic sources from the early Roman period describe manufacturing on a small scale, which corresponds with the archeological evidence of garments uncovered in the Judean Desert as well as in the Galilee, which were manufactured locally from linen or wool. This economic activity involved many professional skills such as spinning, weaving, sewing, and dyeing.

Meyers, who conducted several archeological digs in Meiron, noted that area M1 on the site had buildings divided into many rooms that were interconnected, which meant that there was little privacy. There is disagreement among researchers about whether each room housed a family, or whether each family owned a number of rooms. Meyers mentions that the buildings were constructed with good materials, had decorated doorposts and lintels, a ritual bath (*mikveh*), and stores and workshops with equipment underneath them. These features indicate that the structure belonged to a group of craftsmen who were financially secure and were able to attain comfortable living and working conditions.

Evidence of the manufacture of pottery was discovered in a number of sites in the Galilee in recent years. Adan-Bayewitz describes a manufacturing center in Kfar Hanania that produced cooking pots, bowls, and jugs. He also excavated Shikhin, where storage jars were produced.[37] Similar items were produced at Yavor.[38] Findings from Yodefat included a "potter's quarter."[39] It is clear that

---

34 Kehoe, *Law Rural Economy*, esp. 1–52. See also Kehoe, "State and Production," 33–54.
35 On the distribution of pottery in the Roman Empire, see Frank, *Economic History*, 220–227. Iacono, "Pottery Trade"; and Poblome, Malfitana, and Lund, "Pottery, Roman Empire."
36 See Rosenfeld, "Linen."
37 Adan-Bayewitz, *Pottery Galilee*, 23–41, 78–80.
38 See Safrai, *Economy*, 204, fig. 46, Giv'at Yavor (1674.2558); and Crossan, "Relationship," esp. 153–154.
39 See Adan-Bayewitz and Aviam, "Iotapata"; and Edwards, "Jotapata."

there was local manufacture of oil lamps as well.[40] The excavators identified a "Jerusalem type" and a "northern type."[41] These factories were not described in rabbinic sources, but they do mention various kinds of pottery.

Another product was the stone vessel. Literary evidence for the usage of stone vessels is found in the NT in the episode of the miracle of changing water to wine at Kfar Qana (John 2:6).[42] The archeological find of a Galilean stone vessel workshop northeast of Nazareth proves that at least some of the stone vessels were produced in the Galilee, though most were produced in Judea prior to the Bar Kokhba Revolt. Evidence for the continued use of stone vessels after the destruction of the Temple and into the second century CE was recently discovered at a new excavation at Arbel.[43] There is also evidence for the manufacture of glass and wood products, as well as for the production of Balsam oil, which indeed required specialist knowledge.[44]

Another artisanal trade that has left archeological evidence is the baker of bread. Excavations have revealed seals of bread-bakers in Palestine from the first to the fourth century CE. This shows that they took pride in their profession.[45] It corresponds to the literary descriptions of the central bakery—*nachtom*—in the town and city economy.[46]

3 The Literary Sources

To show the development of the crafts and the status of craftsmen, it is necessary to survey the description of craftsmen in various stages of the development of Jewish-Palestinian literature. The survey will start from the OT, proceed through Second Temple literature and the NT, and finish with the rabbinic sources. Generally speaking, the relevant comparative literature portrays only part of the development seen in the archeological record. This

---

40 Frank posits that all manufacture of oil lamps was local and that the molds copied the designs of maufactures because there was no copyright law. In contrast to pottery, there was no expertise involved in working the clay for cheap lamp molds. See Frank, *Economic History*, 222–223.
41 See Sussman, *Jewish Oil Lamps* and *Roman Period Oil Lamps*.
42 See Edwards, "Khirbet Qana," 101–132; and Edwards and Eshel, "Language and Writing."
43 See Aviam, *Galilee Second Temple*, 18–19, and n. 8.
44 Leibner, "Arts," is a summary of the archeological findings on the artists and their professions in Palestine. See also Sperber, *Material Culture*; Gorin-Rosen, "Glass," "Ancient Glass"; Harris, "Wood"; and Foy, "Glass."
45 There are many findings concerning bakers and bakeries from the Roman Empire. See recently Monteix, "Pompeian Bakeries."
46 See Amit, "Bread Stamps," 159–174; and Broshi, *Bread, Wine, Scrolls*, 111–112.

disparity can be attributed to the fact that the relevant literature is primarily legal and was not intended to be a historical narrative. On the other hand, both literary and archeological sources from Roman Palestine portray the development of crafts and manufacturing centers both in rural areas and in urban locations. This finding should raise questions concerning the prevailing assumption among scholars that there was little manufacturing in rural centers in the Roman world.[47] Recently, it was suggested that the rural regions of the Mediterranean basin were more connected to manufacturing and commerce than had been previously thought.[48]

4   The Craftsman in the Old Testament

Craftsmen are featured in Exodus in the episodes concerning the construction of the Tabernacle (*mishkan*) when the Jews were wandering in the desert.[49] Later, large numbers of craftsmen and artisans were involved in the building and maintenance of the Temple built by King Solomon in Jerusalem (the First Temple).[50] The primary term used in the OT for the description of the professional craftsman is "*hārāš*."[51]

The prevalent term for production and manufacturing is "*melakha.*" However, that term is used for occasional expert work as well as for professional craftsmanship. Jonah the prophet was asked "what is your *melakha*?" meaning "what is your profession or trade?"[52] The distinction between permanent vocation and occasional endeavor is blurred.

In addition, we find the phrase "*hoshev mahashavot laasot*" used to describe the skill involved in planning and executing the work of the craftsman.[53] Craftsmen are mentioned in ancient sources primarily in the context of royal or religious construction projects. It seems that the average person had little

---

47 Mayer, *Middle Classes*, 16–21. On urban middle-class culture, see also ibid., 61–100.
48 See Witcher, "Agrarian," 342.
49 Exod. 28:2–4, 31:1–6.
50 Concerning the Temple, see 1 Kgs 6:1–38, 7:14–51. Regarding maintenance and upkeep of the Temple; see 1 Kgs 2:1–18. It is logical that large numbers of craftsmen were involved in building Solomon's palace, though one central one is mentioned. See 1 Kgs 7:1–14.
51 Gen. 4:22; 1 Kgs 7:14; Jer. 17:1. On the craftsman in the OT and the crafts mentioned, see Aberbach, *Work and Crafts*, 7–19. On the terminology for the craftsman in the OT, see Cornelius, "haras"; and Gluska, *Hebrew and Aramaic*, 264–265.
52 Jonah 1:8.
53 See Exod 21:3 and 35:32–22. In the OT, they are called "those who do *melacha*," while *ba'al melacha* refers to the individual ordering the product or the work. See Ayali, *Workers*, 5; and Cornelius, "hoseb."

use for the professional. The average farmer was adept at most of the crafts that he needed for himself and his household, albeit using a low level of technology.

The term *"uman,"* which is used commonly in rabbinic literature to describe professional craftsmen, is mentioned once in the OT in the context of artistic creativity: *maase uman* refers either to something created by an artist or to something that was a work of art, but it does not indicate a permanent profession.[54] The distinction between an artist who created art and an artisan who manufactured useful products was unclear.[55] The term *"uman"* originated in eastern Aramaic and was rarely used in Palestine. Therefore, it seems that it was not well known in Palestine at this stage.[56]

The OT also uses terms that characterize the professions of specific artisans: the *yotzer* made pottery, the *tzoref* made jewelry, and the *hārāš* worked with metal, stone, and wood.[57] In the clothing industry, the weaver is mentioned, but the tailor (*hayat*) is missing. The term for the tailor was imported from Aramaic during the rabbinic period.[58] The shoemaker (*sandlar*) is also missing from biblical literature, and the Hebrew rabbinic term emanated from the Latin *sandalarius*.[59] This shows that certain crafts were recognized in language as deserving a specific term to define them, while others were not.

5   The Craftsmen in Non-Biblical Second Temple Literature

In Ben Sira, there are many descriptions of artisans, which mention the hard work involved as well as the difficulty of studying and being wise when one is engaged in intensive physical labor.[60] The author compares this form of

---

54   Song of Songs 7:2. The LXX (Septuagint) translates the word *"uman"* in this passage as "τεχνή." This word can assume two meanings. Pope, *Song of Songs*, 593, translates the term as "artist," while Longman, *OT Commentary*, 194, translates it as "artisan." Keel, *Song of Songs*, 234 (see also Hope, *Song of Songs*), mentions both possibilities. However, in the rest of the OT the term *"uman"* for artisan is not found. Longman's translation is therefore based on the later usage of the term in the Mishnah. The proper translation should therefore be "artist." See also Cornelius, "umman."
55   See Stewart, *Roman Art*, 19–21.
56   Gluska, *Hebrew and Aramaic*, 264–265.
57   *Yotzer* means "potter." See Isa. 45:9. *Tzoref* for precious metals: Isa. 40:19. *Hārāš* refers to various materials: for metal, see Gen. 4:22, 1 Kgs 7:14, Isa. 44:12; for stone, see Exod. 28:11, 35:35; and for wood, see Isa. 40:20, 41:7, 44:13.
58   Weavers: 2 Kgs 23:7; Isa. 19:9. Tailors: Even-Shoshan, *Dictionary*, 629.
59   See Even-Shoshan, *Dictionary*, 2212.
60   Ben Sira, Segal edition (Segal, *Ben Sira*), 38, 25–34, 252–254; Sauer, *Jesus Sirach*, 598–599; Skehan and Di Lella, *Ben Sira*, 445–446. See Finkelstein, *Pharisees*, 219–222, who claims that these passages show that the sages at that time belonged to the social elite and

employment to that of a scribe and finds that it is better to be a scribe because there is more time to study. He describes craftsmen routinely working outside in the context of large public construction projects as in biblical times. On the other hand, his terminology is identical to that of the Bible. He uses the biblical terms "*hārāš*" and "*hoshev*," and not the terms developed in later literature. It is hard to determine his exact terminology because the manuscripts for the relevant chapter are sometimes missing and, where they are available, they are often contradictory.[61]

The term "*uman*" is also absent in Qumranic literature, which also uses biblical terminology to describe the crafts.[62] A look at contemporaneous Jewish-Greek literature, translations, and commentaries on the OT should shed light on the ancient use of the terms for craftsmen during the first few centuries CE. In this literature, the distinction between the professional and nonprofessional worker and between different kinds and levels of craftsmen is clearer than it is in the biblical terminology that preceded it. The LXX (Septuagint), Philo, and Josephus all describe unskilled labor with the term "ἔργον" and hired day laborers with the term "μίστος." There are differences between early and late Jewish-Greek literature regarding the terms used to describe professional craftsmen. The LXX translates the passages relating to craftsmen building the Tabernacle as "τέχνης."[63] The head builders of the Tabernacle were called "ἀρχιτεκτονεῖν."[64] In translation of 1 Kings, the LXX uses the term "τέκτων."[65]

Philo, the Jewish philosopher of Alexandria, has a similar term, ἀρχιτέκτων, which he uses to refer to professional craftsmen, though he often uses this term in reference to the Creator. He describes the Jewish community in Egypt

---

looked down on the artisans. Segal argues with him and claims that Ben Sira is not criticizing the professions themselves only the inability of those involved in skilled labor to rise in the study of Torah and to serve as sages and judges.

61 See Skehan and Di Lella, *Ben Sira*, 450–452. The word "*umanut*" seems to refer to expertise, though it is doubtful. Nevertheless, it refers not to the professional but to the precise workmanship of a professional. It is also clear that the Greek versions cannot be used to determine the meaning of term because it is impossible to know what the original term was based on the Greek translation. See also Cornelius, "hoseb" and "haras."

62 See *The War of the Sons of Light against the Sons of Darkness* (aka the *War Scroll* or the *War Rule*) 5:5, 6, 9, 10, 11. Scholarly editions are Yadin, *The War*, 280, 282; and Schiffman and VanderKam, *Dead Sea Scrolls*, 63–67, 231, 264, 606–610, 773–779; for recent commentary, see Schultz, *Conquering*, 240–255.

63 See Exod. 28:11 regarding the stone carver and 30:25 regarding the perfume-maker for the Tabernacle.

64 Exod. 31:4, 35:32, 37:21, 38:23. See also Hatch and Redpath, *Concordance Septuagint*, 166.

65 1 Kgs 13:19 is one example. See Hatch and Redpath, *Concordance Septuagint*, 1342, and the sources cited there. They translate the term to the biblical *hārāš*.

as being involved in professional labor in order to present its members as a positive element in society. His terminology is identical to that of the LXX.[66]

Josephus follows the LXX when describing the work of Bezalel and Eliav, the architects and supervisors of the building of the Tabernacle, whom he calls "ἀρχιτέκτονας" when referring to their expertise. However, when referring to their position of leadership, he refers to them as "ἄριστοι τῶν δημιουργῶν," the leaders (lit. "the best") of the craftsmen.[67] He also uses the word "δημιουργός" to describe the skilled workers who constructed the Tabernacle, which is translated literally as "master of craft." This term does not have this connotation in the LXX.[68] Josephus also uses the terms "τέκτων" and "τέχνη" to describe the builders of the Tabernacle.[69] The relevant dictionaries do not provide clear definitions for the different terms. Nevertheless, an examination of the examples shows that Josephus seems to use τέκτων for the actual worker and δημιουργός for the professional craftsman, especially with regard to construction.[70] He never uses the word "βάναυσος" ("handicraft," "artisan") or its variations.[71] He describes how Herod trained priests to be stoneworkers and carpenters in order to rebuild the Temple.[72] He also praises the skills of the craftsmen that built the Temple (*Ant.* 3:200, 8:76), made the sacred vessels (*Ant.* 12:59–12:84), and built the towers protecting Jerusalem (*War* 5:175). This indicates that the large-scale construction project demanded many craftsmen who were not readily available. The same source talks about Herod recruiting 10,000 experienced workers.[73]

There seems to be a development and diversification of terms pertaining to craftsmen in Josephus as compared to previous Jewish-Greek literature.

---

66 Philo, Creator: *Opif.* 17, 20, 24; *Mut.* 30; *Som.* 2:8. Bezalel: *Leg.* 3:95; *Som.* 1:206.
67 Josephus, *Ant.* 3:104, 200. See also 3:10, 56, and 199. See other sources in Rengstorf, *Concordance Josephus*, 2:436.
68 Josephus, *Ant.* 3:106, 289. See other uses in Rengstorf, *Concordance Josephus*, 1:199–200, 436. Regarding the LXX, see Hatch and Redpath, *Concordance Septuagint*, 295–296.
69 For the former, see 3:204 concerning the generous payment that Moses gave the craftsmen. This payment is not mentioned in the Bible, but Josephus added it, and it seems to have been the practice in his time. For τέχνης, the example regarding the construction of the Tabernacle is to be found in *Ant.* 3:197. He, however, uses this term often in other contexts; see Rengstorf, *Concordance Josephus*, 4:182; τέκτων, 4:171.
70 See Josephus, *Ant.* 3:200–204.
71 Liddell and Scott, *Greek Lexicon*, 305.
72 Josephus, *Ant.* 15:390.
73 All this indicates a labor market in Roman Palestine, which is contrary to Finley's assumption that there was no such thing in the Roman Empire. See Temin, "Labor Market," 513–538, who argues with Finley.

Josephus has different terms for skilled and unskilled laborers. He distinguishes between technicians who just do the labor and architects who use planning and design for their professions. He also has terms for experts and directors. This seems to indicate an advancement of sorts in crafts toward the end of the Second Temple period. Fine shows that this terminology existed also in Roman literature at that time and that it indicates the development of crafts in the Roman Empire, the existence of a large variety of professions, and the recognition at this time of various levels of expertise.[74]

Together with these developments, the successful craftsmen became established economically, created *collegia* for mutual support, and were noticed more by society. It is possible that this development was introduced to Roman Palestine as a result of the abundance of craftsmen that King Herod used during his reign for his various monumental building projects, including their décor, furnishings, and supplies. This, of course, included the renovation of the Temple, a project that employed many craftsmen, as described by Josephus.

6 The Craftsmen in the New Testament

Researchers of the NT are generally interested in the status of the craftsman because tradition maintains that Joseph, husband of Mary, was a carpenter, that is, a craftsman.[75] According to Mark, Jesus himself was a carpenter.[76] However, in the Synoptic Gospels there is no mention of the term "*uman*," even though there are descriptions of various craftsmen. Jesus's closest disciples came from the nonagricultural sector.

Two brothers, Simon (Peter) and Andrew were fishermen, as well as Simon's partners James and John, sons of Zebedee.[77] The NT mentions a laundryman,

---

[74] Fine, *Art and Judaism*, 21–36, shows that a similar terminology was used at the same time in Roman documents.

[75] Matt. 13:54–56. See Weber, *Economy and Society*, Vol. 1, 481. Oakman, "Agrarian Palestine," 62–64, emphasizes that he was a rural artisan not an urban one and therefore came from the lower classes and not the middle class. For a summary of opinions concerning Jesus's lineage, see Hanson and Oakman, *Palestine Jesus*, 57–61, with additional references there. Saldarini, *Pharisees and Sadducees*, 151, explains the rejection of Jesus in Nazareth as a result of his low social status being a carpenter. However, Fiensy, "Leaders," argues that Jesus had connections with the local elite through his vocation as a carpenter.

[76] Mark 6:3. Fiensy, "Leaders," argues that Jesus was indeed a carpenter and that he learned the vocation from Joseph.

[77] Matt. 4:18; Luke 5:1–7, 10; John 21:3.

doctor, scribe, clerk, saleswoman, and silversmiths.[78] This could indicate that the pursuit of a nonagricultural profession enabled mobility and released the individual from attachment to the land or to a permanent employer, thus allowing for religious contemplation.[79] On the other hand, all of Jesus's parables are taken from agricultural situations. The reason behind this is that he came from a background where he was a village artisan supplying local farmers.[80]

Paul says that he worked as an artisan in the tent industry during his missionary travels.[81] Hock concludes that Paul was a member of the lower classes.[82] However, Acts mentions two disciples of Paul, Aquilas and Prisca, who manufactured tents and hosted the communal dinners of the local Christian community at their house. This indicates that their economic situation was better than that of other followers; they were able to host the event.[83] It is possible that they owned a workshop and that Paul was a worker who moved from place to place, which could explain the economic disparity between them.[84]

In Acts (19:24–25), there is a case of a craftsman who employs workers, which shows that there were laborers in other industries as well:

> A silversmith named Demetrius, who made silver miniature shrines of Artemis and created no little business for his craftsmen called a meeting of them and other workers (ἐργάτας) in related crafts.[85]

---

78   Laundryman: Mark 9:3. Doctor: Matthew 9:12; Mark 2: 17; Luke 5:31. Scribe: Mark 12:32; Acts 19:35. Clerk: Matthew 20:8; Acts 20:28; 1 Tim. 3:2. Salesman: Acts 16:14. Silversmith: Acts 19:23–25.

79   See Fiensy, "Leaders," 21.

80   On the difference between urban and rural culture in antiquity, see De Ste Croix, *Class Struggle*, 10. Fiensy, "Leaders," 24–26, claims that Jesus had contact with the urban elite. It is a possibility with no solid proof. Clearly, his upbringing was in an agricultural setting.

81   1 Thess. 2:9; 1 Cor. 9:6, 18:3.

82   Hock, *Social Paul*, 20–27, 31–37.

83   Acts 18:2–3, specifically they were tentmakers. See Horrell, "Meetings," 367 and n. 82.

84   On the other hand, Luke-Acts turns Paul into a highly educated, well-connected, and active Pharisee who was a Roman citizen (25:11) and who studies with a sage named Gamaliel (22:3). He had enough contact with the High Priest to ask for letters of introduction to the Jewish community in Damascus (9:1–2, 22:4–5, 26:12). On this discrepancy, see Saldarini, *Pharisees and Sadducees*, 134–143.

85   Fitzmyer, *The Acts of the Apostles*, 654. Fitzmyer (657–658) explains that Demetrius was involved in the manufacture of materials for the temple of Artemis in Ephesus, where this event took place.

The above example depicts an entrepreneur who seems to have created an industry in which he creates religious articles in vast quantities and who hires craftsmen to execute the work.

The terminology in the NT describing the artisan and craftsman is similar to that of the OT and Ben Sira, while the terminology for the craftsman in the Greek versions [of the NT] is more like that of the LXX, using the term "τέχνη" and not the more complex terms found in Josephus and Philo.[86]

7 The Craftsmen in Rabbinic Literature

Rabbinic literature contains numerous words that define various crafts and vocations. These terms were gathered separately by Ayali and by Aberbach, who counted more than 200 professions in rabbinic literature.[87] This indicates the existence of specialization and a diversity of craftsmen, facts that were not evident in previous sources. These professions can be subdivided into various categories according to level of expertise and social standing; however, an analysis of the terms for the various crafts is beyond the scope of this study. We will use the word "*uman*," which is a common rabbinic term describing craftsmen in general, as a case study to analyze the phenomenon of the development of the crafts in the first centuries CE.

In Tannaitic literature, the biblical *hārāš* was replaced by *uman*, which refers to professional artisans of all kinds.[88] This term originates from the Assyrian *ummânu* and Aramaic *umman*. It has a wider definition than *hārāš*, since it includes all expert workers, not only metalsmiths. Gluska posits that the intellectuals imported the term "*uman*" from Aramaic and that it gradually spread from literary to popular use. The reason for this transfer was the need to differentiate between professionals and laymen who do the same work.[89] Hebrew was importing words from Aramaic at the time because Hebrew often seemed constricting to its speakers and so words were borrowed from its sister language. In some Jewish circles, Aramaic took over from Hebrew as the popular language.[90]

---

86 See Acts 18:2–3 in the Greek version.
87 See Ayali, *Laborer, Workers*; and Aberbach, *Work and Crafts*.
88 In Tannaitic literature, the biblical term "*hārāš*" is used as a word pertaining to a carpenter and not to all craftsmen. See *M. Ohaloth* 13:3.
89 Gluska, *Hebrew and Aramaic*, 264–265.
90 Naveh, "Hebrew versus Aramaic 1," "Hebrew versus Aramaic 2"; Segal, "Mišnaic Hebrew" summarizes the research on the relationship between Mishnaic Hebrew and Aramaic. See also Breuer, "Aramaic"; and Bar-Asher, "Mishnaic Hebrew." On the tension between

Epstein states that the artisan can be compared to the German *meister* while the *po'el* (day laborer) refers to the *arbeiter*.[91] The difference is that the work of the *uman* involves not only physical effort but also technical ability, while the work of the *po'el* only consists of the former. This distinction corresponds to the social scientific differentiation between skilled and unskilled labor.[92] In rabbinic literature, these terms are used quite frequently, in contrast to the rare mention of these terms in early Second Temple literature.

Analysis of the various uses of *uman* shows that the word usually indicates a self-employed artisan who does his work in his home or shop, such as the *tsaba*, dyer of garments, and the *qadar*, the potter.[93]

A further development in Tannaitic literature is the term "*umanut*."[94] It appears a few times in Tannaitic Midrash and more often in the Mishnah. A few examples can be used to illustrate its usage. The sages requested that a father teach his son *umanut*.[95] Examples for *umanut* can be found in the last mishnah in tractate *Kiddushin*, which defines it as a profession that is studied and acquired. It also mentions that animals, as opposed to humans, live well without studying a profession.[96] The following source deals with the *uman*, the craftsman:

> These are the tools that the artisan is not permitted to sell during the Sabbatical year: a plough and all its accessories, a yoke, a pitchfork, and a mattock. But he may sell: a hand sickle, a reaping sickle, and a wagon and all its accessories.[97]

---

the uses of the two languages already in the second century BCE, see Tigchelaar, "Aramaic Texts."

[91] See Epstein, *Introduction Mishnah*, 444, that *uman* refers primarily to nonagricultural workers. On the difference between agricultural and nonagricultural workers, see Freu, "Labour Status," 163–164.

[92] On skilled labor as a factor of stratification, see Giddens, *Sociology*, 218, 226; Temin, "Labor Market," 514–516; Freu, "Labour Status," 161–179; and Erdkamp, "Economic Growth," esp. 10–13.

[93] The *uman* is mentioned in Tannaitic literature 170 times. For example, see *M. Shviit* 5:6, *M. Pesahim* 4:7, *M. Betzah* 1:10, and *M. Moed Katan* 1:8. The *tsaba* is mentioned in *M. Bava Kama* 9:4.

[94] *Umanut* also appears a number of times. See, for example, *M. Kiddushin* 4:14, *M. Sanhedrin* 3:3, and *T. Bava Metzia* 2:13.

[95] *T. Kiddushin* 1:11 (Lieberman ed., 279).

[96] *M. Kiddushin* 4:4; *T. Kiddushin* 5:13.

[97] *M. Shviit* 5:6.

In this case, the *uman* is a blacksmith who makes metal utensils. He manufactures a large selection of essential utensils for the farmer. He is instructed not to sell them to farmers during the seventh, Sabbatical, year, because he would be assisting them in violating the religious edict prohibiting farming during that year. This source shows that people referred to as "*umanim*" were involved in the manufacture and sale of utensils, which is a large enterprise in all economies.[98]

Speaking of *umanim*, the plural of *uman*, we find the following use in the Mishnah: "If one hired *umanim* and they tricked each other."[99] This source deals with a number of craftsmen and describes multiple craftsmen working for the same employer at the same time. The following chapter in that tractate discusses hiring *po'alim* who are day laborers, the lowest level of the working class.[100] The two sources discussed define two kinds of skilled workers that existed in that period: workers who were also entrepreneurs, working in their house or workshop, and the professional who worked with a team on a construction site or in other similar situation, whose incomes were lower than that of the independent artisan, though higher than that of the *po'el*, who was an unskilled worker.[101] This exposes a hierarchy within the working class that is dependent on expertise, the nature of the profession, and the ability to set up an independent workshop.[102]

Rabbinic legal sources use the term "*maase uman*," expert work that defines the skillset of the craftsman in comparison to the novice. This distinction has legal ramifications regarding the laws of observing the days of *hol hamoed* (the middle days of the festivals of Passover and Sukkoth). On the holiday, an unskilled person may sew in the usual way, but an expert must sew with irregular stitches.[103] The novice is permitted to make a parapet for a roof or a porch in an unskilled manner, but not in the manner of a skilled craftsman.[104]

---

98 This person is hardly an "impoverished peasant" and is likely to be financially comfortable.
99 *M. Bava Metzia* 6:1.
100 Ibid., 7:1.
101 See also *M. Shekalim* 4:5 about the payment to the *umanim* in the Temple.
102 On the situation of skilled labor in the Roman world, see Erdkamp, "Growth Economy," esp. 15–18; Scheidel, "Real Wages," 425–462; Temin, *Roman Market Economy*, 118–119; and Freu, "Labor Status," 161–162.
103 *M. Moed Katan* 1:8.
104 Ibid., 1:10.

8 Further Development of Terminology of Craftsmen

8.1 Ba'alei Umanuyot

The following source deals with a group of craftsmen, each with a private workshop. Therefore, a double plural term is used to describe them: *ba'alei umanuyot*. This phrase seems to indicate a recognized social group of craftsmen that shared a common street in which they had workshops. Someone who wanted to seek out a craftsman would go to that part of Jerusalem. This term is used in the context of people entering the city of Jerusalem, bearing the offering of the first fruits to the Temple:

> And all the craftsmen (*ba'alei umanuyot*) of Jerusalem, stand before them and greet them [saying]: "Brothers, men of such and such a place, you have come in peace."[105]

This mishnah indicates that in Jerusalem, prior to the destruction of the Temple, the main street was lined with storefronts in which many craftsmen worked. When the bearers of the first fruits would pass, the artisans would stop working and greet the pilgrims. Safrai shows that these shops were separate from the dwelling places of the artisans and that the occupancy of a shop therefore meant that one had a business facility in addition to a home.[106] The main street of the city or its main square was a strategic location in which the best and wealthiest craftsmen would work.

8.2 Beit Ha'uman: *the Workshop of the Craftsman*

The expression "*beit ha'uman*" refers to a craftsman who has a place to ply his trade, either a house or a workshop. For the most part, he would take his work home and, using the tools and/or machines in his possession, he would manufacture or mend the relevant objects. This indicates a certain level of economic success because the artisan is not merely selling his labor and skill, but he has an investment as well. One example is as follows:

> They do not bring utensils (clothing) from the workshop [*beit ha'uman*] of a craftsman [during the festival].[107]

---

[105] M. *Bikkurim* 3:3.
[106] Safrai, *Economy*, 214–219, 230–231, 352–354.
[107] M. *Moed Katan* 2:4.

This source illustrates that some artisans had a specific location where they practiced their trade. Even if they resided at the same location, it became known to people as the "house of the craftsman" and became his place of manufacture and sale.[108]

The *beit ha'uman* would be a parallel term to the *tabernae* of the Roman Empire described by archeologists. *Tabernae* were shops that lined the streets in the center of Roman towns in the period of the Empire. Recent research shows that the *tabernae* served artisans and craftsmen as well as vendors and merchants. *Tabernae*, though modest in size, proved to be bases for the large-scale manufacture and sale of tools, religious articles, and household utensils. Some *tabernae* had decorated walls and graffiti documenting the amounts sold and the volume of transactions carried out, which indicated that they had substantial inventory and took in a significant amount of income.[109]

8.3   *The Expert:* Tsaba Uman, Rofeh Uman

Further evidence of increased professionalism can be found in the differentiation in the sources between a "regular" professional and one who is known to be an expert. There are a number of places where the sources refer to a "professional doctor" or a "professional butcher," who worked with permission from the court.[110] Regarding the butcher, in the recent excavations at Sepphoris an area was identified as a slaughterhouse and included an inscription. This large area indicates the former presence of an organization of butchers in Sepphoris in the period of the Mishnah.[111]

Medicine was a profession. However, the use of a special term for an "expert" doctor already creates a hierarchy of professionals according to their expertise. This also indicates that a more complex society of professionals developed during the period under discussion. Illustrating this hierarchy among doctors is the following passage:

> They brought buckets of bones from Kefar Tabya, and they left them in the open air at the synagogue in Lydda. Theodoros the physician came in, with all the physicians with him. They said: "There is not present a backbone from a single corpse nor a skull from a single corpse." They said:

---

108   On the ancient workshop, see Harris, "Workshop," 67–99. For research on the employment terms related to the ancient workshop, see Silver, "Hired Workers," 259.
109   See Mayer, *Middle Classes*, 66–85. See the archeological sources quoted there.
110   *T. Bava Kama* 6:6.
111   See Grantham, "The Butchers of Sepphoris."

"Since some present declare unclean and some present declare clean, let us arise for a vote." They began from Akiva, and he declared [them] clean. They said to him: "Since you, who [in the past] declared unclean, have declared clean, let them be clean."[112]

The sages brought doctors to the courtyard of the synagogue in Lydda for a consultation concerning the anatomy of the human body in order to determine the status of boxes of bones that were brought to them. The doctors expressed their opinion, and accordingly the rabbis ruled on the religious issue. This occurrence is attributed by the source to Rabbi Akiva as the youngest scholar present and therefore the first to express his opinion. Rabbi Akiva was a young disciple of the sages of Yavneh in its first generation—the end of the first century CE. The doctor had a Hellenized name, Theodoros, and entered into the synagogue with "the doctors." It is clear that Theodoros is not only an expert doctor, but is also the leader of a group of doctors who work under him. Theodoros may have been the senior city doctor. This position has been shown to have existed in some Roman cities in that period. These doctors were called "*archiatri*" (sg. "*archiatros*") and enjoyed much prestige.[113]

The doctors that accompanied him may have been civic doctors that were appointed by the local civic administration and who in other Roman cities were paid well by the local authorities. They did not receive pay from their patients though they were allowed to receive presents for their service. These doctors were exempt from paying taxes and from compulsory military service.[114] It is likely that such doctors were employed in the city of Lod as well as in other Roman cities. Theodoros was the chief doctor and in charge of the other city doctors.[115]

---

112   *T. Ohaloth* 4:2 (Neusner ed., 5:87–88).
113   Nutton, "Archiatri," esp. 194; Van Nijf, *Associations*, 149–183, index, s.v. occupations; Israelowich, *Patients and Healers* 47, n. 240, 124–134.
114   See Scarborough, *Roman Medicine*, 110–112; Nutton, "Archiatri," *Ancient Medicine* 10, 255–256, 301, 403, n. 61, 409, nn. 70–71.
115   There was much demand for the position of civic doctor because of the good employment conditions, but it was a burden on the population of the city that was taxed to pay for it. Therefore, around 160 CE Caesar Antoninus Pius limited their number to ten in the big metropolises, seven in large cities, and five in small cities; see Jackson, *Doctors*, 57. It is possible, therefore, that there were five civic doctors in Lod as in other small cities of the Empire.

9 Historical Background

The craftsman in the pre-Roman world was a specialist who was involved in royal and religious construction projects or who worked for the rich in large cities. The common person had little interaction with craftsmen. A peasant would generally purchase his farming tools from a professional, but would fix them himself or with the help of a neighbor. He would manufacture his own clothing and attach straps to his own sandals.[116] Over time, society gradually became more complex and included more services and crafts for the average person. During the Roman Empire, the contact between the expert and the individual rose to a new level, especially in the area of personal service.[117] Urbanization and semi-urbanization of large villages positively affected growth in the crafts market because the town or city would have numerous professionals who were not found in the rural areas. This was true of personal services, such as those offered by doctors and barbers, and also of professional services like those offered by builders and architects.[118] This resulted in the variations of the term *"uman"* that were used to describe these professionals.

It is evident in the sources that it was necessary to have a term that characterized professionals in general, since this segment of society shared a similar position in rabbinic law and were equally important parts of the social fabric of society. The term *"uman"* is used in rabbinic literature to refer to the blacksmith who manufactured agricultural equipment;[119] the shoemaker;[120]

---

116 See *M. Bava Kama* 10:9, which says that women would manufacture wool clothing. The theory of peasant society was developed by Chayanov, *Peasant Economy*; and Dalton, *Tribal and Peasant*. Other researchers described the ancient economy in a similar way. See Hopkins, "Taxes," 104; Shanin, *Peasants*, 2–9; and Moreland, "Galilean Response," 38. For recent discussion of peasant theory, see Erdkamp, *Grain Market*, 56–61, 79–120; Bang, "Trade and Economy," 3–33, "Grain Market," 228–230; Silver, "Roman Bazaar"; Killebrew, "Village"; and Butcher, *Roman Syria*, 180–218. The researchers showed that, in a rural economy, fishermen and hunters could share the behavior of self-provision that characterizes peasant society.

117 See the list of professionals in *M. Shabbat* 1:2–3; all of them are connected to personal service: the barber, the tailor, and the scribe. It also mentions the bathhouse.

118 On the urbanization of Roman Palestine, see Jones, "Urbanization," *Cities Eastern*, 269–280; Yeivin, "Towns"; Horrell, "Meetings," 358–359; Zangenberg and Van den Zande, "Urbanization." On the connection between urbanization and nonagricultural pursuits, see Safrai, *Economy*, 370.

119 *M. Shviit*, 5:7.

120 *M. Betzah* 1:10; *T. Betzah* 1:23 (Lieberman ed., 285).

textile production;[121] construction work;[122] lock and key production;[123] oven manufacture;[124] table utensils such as pots, plates, forks, and knives;[125] woodworkers and carpenters;[126] bankers;[127] food preservation experts;[128] manufacturers of mats and tents;[129] leather tanners;[130] barbers; sailors; shepherds; and shopkeepers.[131] Furthermore, there were more complex craft operations that required a number of artisans with different skills. This spurred the need for the word *"umanim,"* a plural form that could relate simultaneously to a wide variety of artisans.

This increase in the amount of experts and areas of expertise created a hierarchy in the levels of expertise, as shown above. As a result, it created a stratum of experts that were on a higher economic level than the rest of the artisans, though not as high as those who supplied services to kings and temples.[132] The increased awareness of the opportunities involved in vocational pursuits can also be seen from the rabbinic recommendation to train children to be craftsmen, which we will describe below.

10 Rabbinic Endorsement of Craftsmanship

Another indication of the status of the artisan in Jewish society in the period of the Mishnah is the recommendation by the rabbis that a person teach his son *umanut*, a craft. Some sages saw this obligation as a legal requirement.[133] Most people in the world, as well as in Jewish society in the time of the Tannaim, were farmers. The art of farming passed naturally from father to son. Nevertheless, we find statements attributed to Tannaim, who lived in the

---

121 *M. Pesahim* 4, 6–7, *M. Moed Katan* 2:4; see Albeck, *Mishnah* (Vol. 2, 379), explaining *M. Bava Metzia* 2:2, *T. Sabbath* 1:8 (Lieberman ed., 2), and *T. Kiddushin* 5:14 (Lieberman ed., 297).
122 *M. Moed Katan* 1:8; *T. Kelim*; *T. Bava Batra* 2:2.
123 *M. Bava Metzia* 8:7.
124 *M. Kelim* 5:4, 8:9.
125 *T. Mikva'ot* 6:15–16.
126 *T. Kelim* 1:12.
127 *T. Sabbath* 1:5 (Lieberman ed., 2), according to the words of Rabbi Judah.
128 *T. Betzah* 4:11.
129 *T. Kelim, Bava Metzia* 1:14.
130 *T. Bava Metzia* 11:16.
131 *M. Kiddushin* 4:14.
132 On craftsmen in the context of temples and palaces, see Zaccagnini, "Mobility."
133 *T. Kiddushin* 1:8 (Lieberman ed., 279).

period following the destruction of the Temple, in favor of acquiring a trade or a profession, indicating that agricultural proficiency alone was insufficient to guarantee economic survival. This is reflected in the statement, found in the Tosefta, attributed to Rabban Gamaliel the Second of Yavneh:

> Whoever has a trade, to what is he compared? To a vineyard surrounded by a fence, to a furrow surrounded by a border. And whoever does not have a trade to what is he compared? To a vineyard not surrounded by a fence, to a furrow not surrounded by a border.[134]

In the generation following the Bar Kokhba Revolt, circa 150 CE, the need for a profession became more of an imperative. The following statement is attributed to Rabbi Judah son of Ilai, one of the leading sages after the Revolt:

> One must teach his son *umanut* (a craft). Rabbi Judah says: "He, who does not teach his son a craft, is teaching him thievery."[135]

Similarly, in the last mishnah in the tractate *Kiddushin*, there is an extensive discussion between Tannaim of that very period as to what kind of trade or profession is desirable. Rabbi Meir recommends teaching the child a craft that is "easy and clean."[136] The same Rabbi Meir is quoted in the Tannaitic Midrash praising the involvement in *melacha*, that is, some form of productive work.[137]

The historical background for the emphasis on work and craftsmanship in this period of history is that the failed Bar Kokhba Revolt resulted in a loss of land for many Jewish farmers, primarily in Judea.[138] Apparently, the sages who lived after the Revolt saw the crafts as appropriate occupations for those who could no longer derive their livelihood from farming. Some of those who

---

134   Ibid., 1:9.
135   Ibid., 1:8.
136   M. Kiddushin 4:14. See the parallel in T. Kiddushin 5:15 (Lieberman ed., 297–298). There, the sage speaking is Rabbi Judah the Prince one generation later.
137   Mekhilta de-Rabbi Yishmael (Horowitz ed., 291–292). Compare praise of work in Mekhilta de-Rabbi Shimon Bar Yohai (Epstein-Melamed ed., 149). There, statements in favor of work are attributed to Rabbi Elazar son of Azariah, Rabbi Yossi the Galilean, Rabbi Akiva, all from the Yavneh generation, and Rabbi Simon son of Yohai from the following generation, which was the generation of Rabbi Meir and Rabbi Judah.
138   See Mor, "Bar Kokhba Revolt"; Eshel, "Bar Kochba"; Safrai, *The Economy*, 324–325; and Sperber, *Land*, 160–176.

lost their land turned to robbery. Others looked to other professions, or left for Babylon or other places where Jews could buy and cultivate land freely.[139]

11   Summary

The Hebrew words *"uman"* and *"umanim"* were borrowed from Aramaic, which had adopted them from Akkadian. They were incorporated into the Hebrew language sometime before the Tannaitic period. The reason seems to have been the need to describe a significant segment of society employed in crafts and trades that had a common status in society and religious law. This sector grew during this period because urbanization brought the individual into closer contact with craftsmen engaged in construction or manufacturing as well as professionals who provided personal services, such as tailors, shoemakers, and barbers. This conclusion is bolstered by legal literature that emphasized the need for the study of a profession, especially in the generations after the destruction of the Temple and even more so following the Bar Kokhba Revolt. This is the reason why most of the rabbinic statements on learning a vocation come from this period. Archeological evidence from sites in Roman Palestine points to the manufacture of various products in Roman Palestine during this period. In addition, various crafts are mentioned in inscriptions. The emergence of craftsmen as a distinct group of people in Roman Palestine mirrors the situation in the rest of the Roman Empire, where artisans were organized into *collegia* and were proud enough of their profession that they or their relatives inscribed their profession on their tombstones. This development indicates the emergence of a new social stratum that was higher than the *po'el*, the unskilled worker. Those who were successful were close in status to the "homeowner," who was part of a distinct middling class in that society.[140] This newly emerging stratum, in turn, was subdivided into levels of expertise by ownership of a venue and machinery and by the receiving of income.[141] Some members of this stratum were economically and socially comfortable, which motivated the religious Jewish leadership to recommend that their fellow Jews pursue vocational training.

---

139   Lenski, *Power and Privilege*, 278–279, posited that all artisans of the ancient world were in effect peasants who lost their land. However, Ulrich, "Artisans," posits that the artisans worked in both agriculture and their specific trade.
140   The homeowner will be discussed in the following chapter. See also Rosenfeld and Perlmutter, "Landowners."
141   Knapp, *Invisible*, 5–7, 97–124, posited that urban craftsmen were better off than villagers.

CHAPTER 5

The Independent Farmer (*Ba'al Habayit*)

An important phenomenon in Jewish society in Roman Palestine in the first, second, and third centuries CE was the proliferation of the independent peasant-landowner, indicating that there was a considerable group of people who were well-off compared to the poor but who were at the same time not wealthy. The Hebrew expression "*ba'al habayit*" (landowner, lit. "master of the house") was used frequently in contemporaneous literature, a term that, it turns out, requires further cross-cultural, legal, historical, archeological, and sociological research.[1] The frequency with which this term appears indicates that the *ba'al habayit* was considered by the rabbis to be the backbone of Jewish society in the Mishnaic period (100–250 CE), and that it was a broad term that covered various economic situations, most of which were occupied by people belonging to the middling groups in society.[2] Defining the precise social and economic parameters of this Roman-Palestinian segment of society will assist us in expanding our understanding of the place of the peasant-landowner elsewhere in the Roman Empire as well.[3] This, in turn, will contribute to the understanding of middling groups in Roman society and the situation of the small landowner.[4]

The original biblical expression "*ba'al habayit*" simply meant "homeowner." This pair of words underwent a transformation that reflected historical and socioeconomic processes that caused the expansion of its meaning to encompass "landowner" by the second half of the first century CE. This group consisted of people at different economic levels and included the large estate owner, who was a member of the elite, as well as the small landowner, who was neither rich nor poor. In turn, this group of small landowners was subdivided into numerous economic and social subgroups. As will be shown below,

---

1 According to a search conducted with the help of the Responsa Project, Bar-Ilan University, there are more than 300 uses of the expression "*ba'al habayit*" in Tannaitic literature (i.e., Mishnah, Tosefta, and halakhic Midrash).
2 The private landowner, large or small, held most of the land in Palestine even after the first revolt. See Safrai, "Agrarian Structure," 107–109. For numerous examples of farmers who were landowners in Roman Palestine, see Dar, *Landscape and Pattern*, 21–87.
3 On freeholders in the Roman Empire and primarily the eastern provinces, see Garnsey, "Peasants," 96–97.
4 Regarding similarities and differences between various parts of the Roman Empire in social aspects, see Bagnall and Frier, *Demography*, 171–173.

the Hebrew term developed in parallel to similar Greek and Latin terms; this was especially true with respect to legal terminology. This chapter will demonstrate how rabbinic legal literature inadvertently provides a vivid picture of the daily life and daily economic activity of the *ba'al habayit*; it will conclude with the historical background that will explain the reason for the expansion in the semantic range of the term to refer to middling groups in society in general and to peasant landowners in particular.

To understand the economic status of the small landowner, it is useful to compare him to the *aris* (the sharecropper) and the *hokher* (the renter). The small landowner worked his own land and pocketed all the profits after tax and expenses. The sharecropper and renter worked someone else's land, putting in the same amount of work as the landowner but receiving only part of the profit. It was probably still more profitable to be a landowner, however small the land under ownership, than a sharecropper.[5]

1 The Term "*Ba'al Habayit*" ("Homeowner") from Biblical Times until the First Century CE

The term "*ba'al habayit*" is mentioned only three times in the OT, and it consistently has the same meaning: an individual who owns a dwelling.[6] Similarly, in Second Temple Hebrew, there is no change in the meaning of the term. In the Septuagint, the translation of the biblical *ba'al habayit* is simply κύριος, "master of the house," which relates only to the ownership of a house.[7] The Apocryphal literature does not mention the term.[8] Indeed, we also find individual uses of this term in classical literature from the fourth century BCE in reference to astrological concepts.[9] Even Josephus, writing at the end of the first century CE, does not mention an equivalent term for *ba'al habayit*. He does, however, use the Greek term "οἰκοδεσπότης," which is the later literal Greek translation of

---

[5] See Kloppenborg, "Tenancy," 31–40; and Knapp, *Invisible*, 5–11.
[6] See Exod. 22:7; Judg. 19:22; and 1 Kgs 17:17. For a discussion of the biblical meaning of the phrase, see Clines, *Hebrew Dictionary*, 238–239; Koopmans, "Ba'al"; and Strong, *Bible Dictionary*, 3617.
[7] Septuagint, Exod. 22:7. About the οἰκοδεσπότης as homeowner, see Cox, *Household Interests*, 130–140.
[8] See Hatch and Redpath, *Concordance Septuagint*, 229c, 800b–839a, and 972a–982c. It should be noted that in one scroll from Qumran, 4Q158, there is a biblical paraphrase of the words "*ba'al habayit*" (based on Exod. 22:7), using the same meaning as in the Bible. See Allegro, *Qumran Cave 4*, 5(4Q158:10[7]).
[9] Kittel, *TDNT*, 2:49.

the Hebrew *ba'al habayit*, in a political context.[10] Josephus primarily describes political events and indirectly discusses socioeconomic conditions and developments. Therefore, we cannot expect to find a full range of contemporaneous economic vocabulary in his works. It should be noted that when the text refers to the *ba'al habayit* as a homeowner, it is also indicating that the person is a man of means, even if his means are modest. The poor man lived in a hovel not a house, and often the house was not his. Even in today's language the *ba'al habayit* is someone that is not poor. However, from this point on there was a change in the meaning of *ba'al habayit*.

2   New Testament: Home and Landowner

The equivalent of the term "*ba'al habayit*" in the corresponding Greek text is the word "οἰκοδεσπότης." Dictionaries of the NT define οἰκοδεσπότης as someone who has a family and lives in a house, a homeowner.[11] Delitzsch translates the word to *ba'al habayit*.[12] This translation follows the biblical meaning of the Hebrew term "*ba'al habayit*." Indeed, often this is the full meaning of the word.[13] However, sometimes, as will be shown, the context indicates clearly that the οἰκοδεσπότης is being used in the expanded sense of *ba'al habayit*, which is landowner, similar to the way it was used in the Mishnah. It describes a man who was not only a homeowner but also an owner of property—land and vineyards—namely, a farmer. In some cases, he also hires workers or even owns slaves. Addressing an individual as a *ba'al habayit* indicated that this individual enjoyed secure economic status; he owned land, which was a source of food, shelter, and security, and he was not merely a homeowner.[14] For example:

---

10   Josephus, *Against Apion* 2:207. See also below.
11   Kittel, *TDNT*, 2:49; Brown, *New Testament Theology*, 247–256; Danker, *Dictionary*, 220, 695.
12   Delitzsch, *Hebrew NT*, consistently translates the citations from the NT quoted in the previous note as οἰκοδεσπότης to the Hebrew *ba'al habayit*. About the economic background of the Jewish peasant before and after the destruction of the Temple, see Applebaum, "Economic Life"; and Safrai, *Economy*, 691–699. See also Sperber, *Land*, s.v. land. About the cultural background of the *ba'al habayit*, see Applebaum, "Agrarian Situation," 280, n. 22; and Saller, "Status and Patronage."
13   Such is the use of the term in Mark 14:14; Luke 12:34, 13:15, 22:11; and Matt. 10:26, 24:43. These sources talk of a homeowner, but it is also possible to read the text, according to the wider meaning, as referring to a property owner when the house is part of the property.
14   On the importance of land in the ancient economy, see Garnsey, "Introduction," 3–4; Runciman, "Capitalism Rome," 157–167; Dyson, *Community and Society*, 134–135; Watson, *Roman Law*, 139–41; and Kehoe, *Law Rural Economy*, 5–9. Joshel, *Work Identity*, 60–66,

THE INDEPENDENT FARMER (BA'AL HABAYIT)

Ἄλλην παραβολὴν ἀκούσατε. Ἄνθρωπος ἦν οἰκοδεσπότης ὅστις ἐφύτευσεν ἀμπελῶνα καὶ φραγμὸν αὐτῷ περιέθηκεν καὶ ὤρυξεν ἐν αὐτῷ ληνὸν καὶ ᾠκοδόμησεν πύργον, καὶ ἐξέδετο αὐτὸν γεωργοῖς, καὶ ἀπεδήμησεν.[15]

Listen to another parable: There was a landowner who planted a vineyard. He put a wall around it, dug a winepress in it and built a watchtower. Then he rented the vineyard to some farmers and went away on a journey.[16]

The following source will also illustrate the claim that οἰκοδεσπότης refers to a landowner, not just a homeowner. In Matthew 13:27, the slaves of the οἰκοδεσπότης tell him that they have found tares planted among the wheat.[17] The main point of this story is that the field was owned by the οἰκοδεσπότης. In the same passage, he also refers to an οἰκοδεσπότης who has "stores" that he can open and distribute—obviously grown in his field.[18] Interestingly, Matthew 20:1 describes an οἰκοδεσπότης who rises in the morning and goes out to hire workers for his vineyard. He offers each worker a wage of one *denarius* for a day's work. Here too the central issue is that this man owns a vineyard, not that he owns a house. These descriptions show that farmers hired workers to help them in the labor-intensive agricultural seasons—sowing and harvesting—and that there were some who employed slaves.

In the next chapter, we are told about an οἰκοδεσπότης who planted a vineyard and designated it for cultivation to tenant farmers whose task it was to tend to the owner's vines and to receive part of the produce. When he sends his slaves to collect the produce from the vinegrowers, they attack the slaves. Here, we are talking about a wealthy individual who has slaves to do his bidding, and who can afford to assign his vineyard to others to cultivate and harvest.[19]

164–165, shows that the aristocracy disdained any occupation that was not of an agricultural nature.

15   Matt. 21:33.
16   The English translation is based on the 1984 *Holy Bible: New International Version* (NIV).
17   The word "slaves" here could merely refer to people who are loyal to the owner of the field.
18   See also Mark 13:35.
19   Matt. 21:33–40. It is unclear from the Greek what the agreement between the landowner and the tenants was. Were the "tenants" sharecroppers that received part of the produce, or were they renters who paid rent to the owner in kind? See Albright and Mann, *Matthew*, 262; and ASBS, *Peshitta*, 30; Compare Marcus, *Mark 8–16*, 801, who also translates "tenants" and reads that the slaves of the owner asked for "some of the fruits of the vineyard." See Fitzmyer, *Luke I–X*, 1276–1277, where the text translates the term to "farmers" rather than to "sharecroppers." Knapp, *Invisible*, cites this source in order to state that the poverty line was 300 *zuz* income a year (1,200 HS).

In Luke (14:16–21), both meanings of the term are found side by side. The οἰκοδεσπότης invites his friends to be guests at his table. They give different excuses as to why they are unable to accept the invitation. One has bought a field; another has bought five pairs of oxen. The third says he has a new wife. These are the dealings of the peers of the landowner in Judea in NT times. They are involved in agricultural production and marketing.[20]

The term "οἰκοδεσπότης" did not correspond with the word "rich." The Greek language used in the NT has another term for "rich": πλούσιος. Indeed, the οἰκοδεσπότης is described in a positive light, unlike the wealthy landowner, who is despised.[21] This difference in terminology indicates that οἰκοδεσπότης is a term for members of a stratum of society who are not rich but are clearly not poor either. This is because the οἰκοδεσπότης is a member of the middle class, not a collaborator with the corrupt elites. He is secure enough economically to be independent of the upper classes, but is not one of them.[22]

3 Development of *Dominus* in Roman Legal Vocabulary

The Latin language originally used the word "*domo*" (and the word "*domus*") to represent the household and the word "*dominus*" to represent the master of the household, who was typically a Roman landowner.[23] By the second

---

20 The source does not say why the peers resisted the invitation. It is hinted at by the fact that one of them bought "five pairs of oxen" (it could also mean that he bought the yoke that pairs the oxen, which would mean that he already possessed five pairs of oxen). This man was definitely wealthy. The average farmer had at best one pair of oxen, and some farmers even had to hire a pair. This is probably a man who rented out oxen to others or bought and sold them. He did not want to come to the regular *ba'al habayit*, who sends over his only slave, for the social standing of the regular *ba'al habayit* is inferior to his own. Indeed, in passage 12, we read about "your rich friends and relatives." Luke explains that they will expect gifts when they invite you to their event. Jesus warns him about that and recommends that he instead invite the poor and destitute.

21 In the NT, the landowner is never the offender. He is usually the victim of the misconduct of others. Examples can be found in Matt. 13:27, 21:33–40, 24:43 and in Luke 12:34, 14:16–21. In Luke 20:1 and in Mark 13:35, the "landowner" is giving out rewards or punishments to his workers. The parable compares him to God. In Mark 14:14 and Luke 13:15, the οἰκοδεσπότης offers a room in his house for Jesus and his disciples to celebrate the Paschal meal. The landowner is definitely shown in a positive light.

22 The sources from the NT alone are not sufficient to reach this conclusion. This conclusion is further supported by findings from rabbinic literature, as will be seen below. Both sources in combination provide the picture described here.

23 Schulz, *Roman Law*, 334–341; Nicholas, *Law*, 107, 153–157; Rilinger, "Domus"; Saller, "Family," 352; Birks, "Dominium"; Arjava, "Paternal Power"; Cooper, "Roman Households,"

century BCE, we find it used to refer to a farmer who owned land as well. At the beginning of the Principate, during the first century CE, the meaning of the word broadened, and in legal terminology it referred to the ownership (including that of the master of the house) of property. The word "*dominium*" similarly referred to the owner of property, large or small.[24]

In the Roman world, the majority of taxes were paid from the agricultural sector and primarily from the land.[25] The expansion of the term "*dominus*" resulted from the position of the landowner as the main assessee responsible for the payment of taxes and as the representative of his estate in all legal matters. This status was a byproduct of the central place that the *dominus* held in traditional Roman society and consequently in Roman law.[26] The Roman tax system did not differentiate between the small landowner and the large plantation owner (excluding the rich who also had political connections and received exemptions from payment). Both paid the same percentage of tax on the produce from their fields. In the eyes of the tax authorities, both were *dominus* or *dominium*, the ordinary and typical landowner. The terms had to be translated to Greek for use in the eastern provinces of the Empire when the Romans took control there. Hence, the term "οἰκοδεσπότης" was created.

The source of the word "οἰκοδεσπότης" is Greek. The word "οἶκος" originally meant "house." By the third century BCE, the word "οἰκία" was in use, which related not only to the house a man lived in, but also to his source of livelihood—his field, his store, his workshop. This phenomenon was so remarkable that it was discussed by Greek philosophers.[27] The ability to conceive of the concept of "home" as including the entire estate and the income earned therefrom is one step toward conceiving of the ruler of the home as the ruler of the estate. The philosophers expanded the term "οἶκος" ("household") to include the property that supported the members of the οἶκος. In Greek, κύριος refers to the male person who was the ruler of the house.[28]

4–6; Harries, *Law and Crime*, 86–105. In late antiquity, the term evolves to include ownership of land and property (see below).

24   See Cato, *Rust.* 1.4; Glare, *Latin Dictionary*, 571, "Dominus," "Dominium"; Lewis and Short, *Latin Dictionary*, 608–609, "Dominus," "Dominium"; Schanbacher, "Dominium, Dominus"; and Rilinger, "Domus."

25   See Duncan-Jones, *Money*, 47–51; and Hopkins, *Conquerors and Slaves*, 15–19. See Garnsey, "Peasants," 96–97 about taxes paid directly by peasants being an indicator of their free status, and 152–154 on how the vast majority of taxes collected came from the agricultural sector.

26   Regarding assessment for tax purposes, see Duncan-Jones, *Structure*, 199–210.

27   See Xenophon, *Oec.* 1.5–11.

28   This is the term used by the Septuagint to translate *ba'al habayit* in Exod. 22:7. This issue was discussed in the beginning of this chapter.

Nevertheless, the NT uses a different phrase to describe a householder—οἰκοδεσπότης—and it does not use κύριος.[29] This is the first time that the term "οἰκοδεσπότης" is found meaning "master of the estate."[30] It seems that the NT was translating the Latin legal term *dominus*, which was used to describe the landowner. There was a need for this new term because the landowner was the person who had to answer to the tax authorities and the person who held the special legal status of the homeowner in Roman law and was recognized as such by the Roman government administration.[31] This term was translated to Greek for use in the eastern provinces and thus took a similar form—"homeowner"—referring to the person eligible for tax assessment and who was to be considered the legal entity in charge of the extended household.[32] Indeed, in documents found in the Judean Desert, one can see the Latin influence on the local language and on the use of Greek in legal documents.[33]

Consequently, the authors of the NT used this translated term. Alternatively, the oral (or written) tradition of the NT may have used the Hebrew term "*ba'al habayit*," the persona of the homeowner-landowner who was a key member in society under the Roman administrative machinery. Both phrases originated in the Latin *domus* or *dominus*.[34]

---

29 Lampe, *Patristic Greek Lexicon*, 939. The expanded definition of οἶκος and οἰκοδεσπότης used in NT literature is discussed also by Destro and Pesce, "Householders," 211–212. They reach a different conclusion, arguing that the household included people who were not part of the nuclear family and who participated in supporting and being supported by the homeowner. Their approach does not contradict the one suggested here. Even if the family included workers and slaves, the basic implication of the term "*ba'al habayit*" is that the master of the house had a home and a field from which to draw his livelihood.

30 Kittel, *TDNT* 2:49.

31 On the small landowner as the main taxpayer in the early Roman Empire, see Hopkins, "Rome Taxes," 195–208.

32 In the later Roman Empire, the tax system changed, but the *dominus* remained the one responsible for the payment of all taxes for his family, his slaves, his sharecroppers, and all who were part of his estate. See Grey, "Colonatus," 165–170.

33 See Lewis, Yadin, and Greenfield, *Cave of Letters*, 8, 13–21; Cotton and Yardeni, *Nahal Hever*, 135–136, 269–274; and Cotton, "Language Gaps," esp. 160. On the influence of Latin terminology in the eastern provinces, see Millar, *Near East*, 327–329, 366–375, 467–471, 545–552; Woolf, *Becoming Roman*, 4–23; and Bar-Asher, "Mishnaic Hebrew," 389–393.

34 This claim is supported by the development of the use of *ba'al bayit* and οἰκοδεσπότης at the same time. About Christianity as a translation of Jewish culture into the Greek language, see Moatti, "Translation," 116–117.

4 Ba'al Habayit in Tannaitic Sources

The expression "*ba'al habayit*" is one of the most common noun phrases in Tannaitic literature and appears, in various forms, some 366 times.[35] When one examines the different places in which *ba'al habayit* is mentioned in Tannaitic literature, one notices a phenomenon similar to the development of the term in the NT. In some places, the expression simply signifies a homeowner or family man.[36] However, most of the sources mention a *ba'al habayit* in the context of someone who owns property—a field or a number of fields. The term also indicates an employer-slaveowner, an owner of a vineyard or orchard. Since the Mishnah was edited after the NT, it can be seen how the term continued to develop and how it was used with increasing frequency to refer to a landowner rather than to a homeowner. From this point forward, we will translate the term "*ba'al habayit*" as "landowner" for the sake of simplicity.

Analysis of sources reflecting the socioeconomic and religious facets of the *ba'al habayit* as characterized in Tannaitic literature establishes the above claim and provides further information concerning this social group:

> As regards produce that grows on a trellis or [the produce of] a palm tree [either of which might be damaged if the poor attempted to collect *pe'ah*]—the landowner cuts down [the produce] and distributes it among the poor.[37]

This source deals with giving the *pe'ah*, the unharvested corners of the field mandated by the Bible, to the poor. This source says that in the case of certain kinds of fruit trees—the climbing vine and the date tree—the poor do not collect their share themselves; instead, the landowner picks the fruit and distributes it to them. In this case, the landowner is the owner of the trees and has a religious responsibility to give the tithe to the poor.[38]

Another source expands further on the meaning of the term "landowner":

---

35 This count was conducted with the help of the Bar-Ilan University Responsa Project.
36 See *M. Shabbat* 1:1: the *ba'al habayit* is presented in contrast to a "poor man." See also *M. Shabbat* 20:5; *M. Eruvin* 6:8; *M. Betzah* 3:8; and *M. Bava Kama* 3:8.
37 *M. Pe'ah* 4:1. Neusner consistently translates the term "*ba'al habayit*" as "homeowner." Here, it will be translated as "landowner."
38 See the similar use of this term in *M. Pe'ah* 4:10–11, 5:2, 7, and 6:6 regarding a forgotten sheaf that should be left for the poor. See also ibid., 7:3–4, 7–8; and *T. Ma'aser Sheni* 3:18 (Lieberman ed., 261): the sages visit a *ba'al habayit* to investigate whether he separates the tithes for the priests and Levites as required. See also *T. Ma'aserot* 2:10–11 (Lieberman ed., 234).

> Ass drivers and *ba'alei batim* who are traveling from place to place eat [non-tithed produce in their possession] and are exempt [from tithing it] until they reach the specific place [they have in mind]. Therefore, if the *ba'alei batim* designated a place for them by themselves, if they are sleeping there they must separate tithes.[39]

There are two types of landowners in this passage. One is the host, A, a landowner, who is hosting B, a fellow-landowner. B is traveling from place to place and is clearly the host's equal (hence the identical term). According to the source, the guest is exempt from giving tithes (to the priest and Levite) from his fruit, because he is still traveling and has not reached his destination. Therefore, the fruit is considered to be in transition—namely, it has not reached its final stage of preparation (*gemar melacha*), which is the last stage that obligates the separation of tithes. However, if the host gives the owner a room of his own, then it is like the guest is home and must separate tithes. This description in the source allows for a number of plausible scenarios. One is that this *ba'al habayit* grows fruit and takes it to the market to be sold. He is not wealthy enough to hire salesmen, but has enough produce to sell part of it and is growing more than he needs for subsistence.[40] The host knows the guest and gives him a place to sleep in his house for the night, or even a separate room.[41] It is also possible that he is bartering produce with the *ba'al habayit* whose guest he is.[42]

---

39 *T. Ma'aserot* 2:1 (Lieberman ed., 230).

40 There are additional sources attesting to the fact that the landowner would market his produce on his own. See *M. Demai* 5:7, where he is selling greens. A landowner gives his merchandise to donkey drivers to take to market (*T. Bava Metzia* 4:8 [Lieberman ed., 83]). In *T. Demai* 2:13 (Lieberman ed., 76), the "wholesaler" buys and sells in bulk and the salesman buys from various growers and sells to stores. It seems that the donkey riders supplied the *siton* (the "wholesaler") and the *tagar* ("intermediary salesman"). See also Rosenfeld and Menirav, *Markets and Marketing*, 88–93, 124–136; and Applebaum, "Economic Life," 687–688.

41 Compare *M. Ma'aserot* 3:2, which discusses whether the landowner would have to separate tithes when he is staying overnight if he is given a separate room from his host.

42 This interpretation is supported by the comparison of this *ba'al habayit* to donkey drivers. The donkey drivers carried merchandise from place to place. It is logical that they would stay with homeowners with whom they also did business by either buying their fruit or selling them what they needed. Thus, it is logical that the guest *ba'al habayit* would either take with him fruit grown by his host or that he would leave with him part of his produce. That would explain why the Mishnah and Tosefta chose this example rather than the example of staying in an inn, which was also widespread in this period. See Rosenfeld, "Innkeeping."

5 Landowners Representing Members of a Social Group

The Tannaitic use of the term "*ba'al habayit*" denoted social as well as economic status. According to the opinion attributed to Rabbi Meir (mid-second century CE), someone who eats at the home of an *am ha'aretz*—namely, someone who cannot be trusted to separate tithes from his produce—is not to be trusted to separate tithes from his own produce. The majority of sages disagreed with Rabbi Meir and said:

> *Ba'alei batim* never refrained from eating with one another: nonetheless, the produce in their own homes is properly tithed.[43]

This source distinguishes two kinds of *ba'al habayit*. One separates tithes from his produce and the other does not. Nevertheless, there is a strong social connection between members of these two groups. They eat at each other's houses even though this involves neglecting a religious stringency that they observe in their own households. This social interaction, eating together, overcomes religious obligation and commitment, and indicates strong social ties between the landowners. The collective partaking in meals was a well-known social activity in the Roman world as well as in the Jewish one.[44] The landowners formed a social stratum based upon their similar occupational and economic status, and this social group maintained common ties.[45]

6 The Economic Status of the *Ba'al Habayit*

The following source shows that the *ba'al habayit* belonged to an economically stable social stratum:

> Said R. Judah,[46] "At first (*barishona*)[47] they would send [word] to the *ba'alei batim* [landowners] in the provinces [before Passover of the fourth

---

[43] *T. Demai* 2:2 (Lieberman ed., 69).
[44] See Tabory, "Table" and "Paschal Meal," 62–80.
[45] This conclusion sheds new light on the Toseftan passage, discussed above, concerning landowners hosting one another. The landowner is interested in sleeping in the household of one of his peers when traveling.
[46] This saying is attributed to Rabbi Judah, whose influence was considerable around the middle of the second century CE—that is, after the Bar Kokhba Revolt (135/6 CE).
[47] The term "*barishona*" ("in the beginning") in the Mishnah and in the Tosefta can refer to early periods, or merely to a generation before. See Safrai, "Sabbatical Year."

and seventh years of the Sabbatical cycle] saying: 'Hurry to properly remove [agricultural gifts] from your produce before the time of removal arrives.'"[48]

A recognized authority would send out reminders to all the landowners to complete the removing of the tithes for the priests and Levites and the presents for the poor, a process called *"biur ma'aser"* (clearance of the *ma'aser* tithe). The authority involved wanted to remind fruit-growers to fulfill their religious responsibility. The people to whom they sent a reminder are the *ba'alei batim* (pl. of *ba'al habayit*). According to this source, landowners constituted an extensive social group involved in the supply of agricultural produce. This phrase is the only reference in the sources to a social group giving its members a name that is linked to their economic ability.[49]

Close examination of the sources concerning the landowner leads to the conclusion that the average landowner was neither rich nor poor. One source for this assumption is the vast number of times that landowners are mentioned in Tannaitic literature. This indicates that landowners had a strong presence in society and were a focus of interest in rabbinic circles. It may be that the reason is quantitative—they made up a large percentage of the Jewish population—but this point cannot be proven without additional evidence. The sources also show that the landowner was personally involved in working the land and distributing the tithes to the priests, the Levites, and the poor.[50] This differentiates him from the rich landowner who used bailiffs, superintendents, or sharecroppers to do the field work. In many sources, the landowner dealt directly with the poor regarding the division of tithes or the rights to the various leavings the poor were allowed to collect in the field during harvest time.[51] This demonstrates that the landowner was not poor. But let us look at the following source:

---

48 *M. Ma'aser Sheni* 5:8.
49 If we combine with this source a source in *T. Bava Kama* 8:14, where Rabbi Simeon Shezuri laments the destruction of his father's house (his father was one of the *ba'alei batim* in the Galilee), it is possible to conclude that in early times the term applied to wealthy landowners with large plots of land, but due to the confinement of Jewish landownership after the revolts, it was now attributed to anyone who continued to hold onto his land.
50 This explains the especially frequent use of the term *"ba'al habayit"* in the Mishnah and Tosefta of the order of *Zeraim*, which deals with religious obligations pertaining to agricultural produce and production.
51 See *M. Pe'ah* 4:1, 10–11, 5:2, 4, 7, 6:6, 7:3–4, 7, 8:4, 7; and *M. Sabbath* 1:1.

THE INDEPENDENT FARMER (BA'AL HABAYIT)

> A landowner who is traveling from one place to another, and [because he has no money] needs to collect gleanings, forgotten sheaves, *pe'ah* or the poor man's tithe; "Let him collect [what he needs] and when he returns to his home, he should repay" [the amount of produce he took as a poor person for he never actually was poor] in the words of R. Eliezer. But the sages say: "[He need repay nothing, because in fact] he was a poor person when he collected produce [designated for the poor]."[52]

A landowner who is traveling has no money to purchase food. He is allowed to go to fields in the area and to be included among the poor to whom tithes are distributed. The source assumes that a landowner has ample funds for his living expenses when he is at home, but may be in need when traveling. Hence, the source distinguishes between the poor and the landowner.[53]

Another source strengthens the distinction between the economic stability of the landowner and the fragile situation of the laborer in the field:

> Workers may recite [the *shem'a*] while in a treetop and recite the prayer while atop an olive tree or atop a fig tree ... but a landowner must always climb down and [then] recite the prayer.[54]

The laborer discussed in the sources is usually a laborer who was hired on a daily basis and paid at the end of a day's work. The above source states that he is not required to be stringent regarding the performance of his religious

---

52   M. Pe'ah 5:4. Rabbi Eliezer (son of Hyrcanus, a disciple of Rabbi Yohanan ben Zakkai and active from 70 to 110 CE) requires that the landowner repay the amount of the tithes he accepted when he returns home. The majority opinion disagrees, stating that when he was on the road he was poor and for that reason was at that time entitled to the tithes and was not therefore obligated to repay them when he returned.

53   Hamel, *Poverty*, 108–113, believes that the average farmer in this period did not manage to earn enough from his land to survive and feed himself and his family; certainly, it would be inconceivable to ask him to pay back the poor man's tithe (*pe'ah*) when he was traveling. See also Hamel, "Poverty and Charity"; and Gibson, *Social Stratification*. Others disagree and see the small landowner as economically secure. These opinions are summarized by Fiensy, *Social History*, 170–192.

54   *T. Berakhot* 2:8 (Lieberman ed., 7). There is a similar situation in *T. Berakhot* 5:24 (Lieberman ed., 29). Laborers who are working with a *ba'al habayit* recite only an abridged grace over the meal. However, if their meal is their only pay or the *ba'al habayit* is blessing for them, then they recite all the blessings. This means that the landowner is a free agent managing his own time, while the "laborers" are not. Both these sources indicate that the reference to a *ba'al habayit* does not simply mean that he owns a house, for laborers could own houses as well. It is referring to the fact that he owns the property where the labor is being done.

obligations, such as prayer during work hours. Thus he may pray at the top of a tree. However, the landowner is independent and should devote the necessary time to prayer.[55]

The Mishnah states:

> The law concerning the usurping occupant did not apply in Judah in the case of those slain in the war. From the time of those slain in the war and thenceforward, the law of the usurping occupant did apply. How? [If] one purchased a property first from the usurping occupant and then also purchased it from the landowner, his purchase is null. If he purchased it first from the landowner and then purchased it from the usurping occupant, his purchase is confirmed.[56]

The Roman authorities confiscated Jewish-owned land during and after the revolts. The above description could relate to the Great Revolt of 66 CE, in which the Temple was destroyed, or to the Bar Kokhba Revolt of 132 CE. These lands were given to the *sikrikon*, which can be translated as "usurping occupant."[57] The sources seem to indicate that this issue occupied rabbinic law throughout the period from the destruction of the Temple until the days of Rabbi Judah the Prince, redactor of the Mishnah, toward the end of the second century CE. In times of war, if a buyer purchased land from the usurper, he did not have to deal with the previous Jewish owners of the land. However, when there was no state of war, the one who bought from a usurper had to receive (or purchase) permission from the original Jewish landowner.[58] The previous owner is referred to as the landowner even after he loses his land, for he will try to regain it. Until he does so, the current owner, or another who buys it from him, is defined as the landowner. Primarily, landowners executed the buying and selling of land. The landowners were therefore a broad social class that was used to owning land and that tried to regain it when it was appropriated from them.

---

55   In light of this insight, it is possible that the reason that the term appeared so often in rabbinic literature is the fact that the sages saw the *ba'al habayit* as the typical subject for the fulfillment of religious obligations, and not that there were many of them.

56   *M. Gittin* 5:6. For analysis of the laws of *sikrikon* and their development, see Safrai, "Sikrikon"; Applebaum, "Agrarian Situation," 277–28, "Economic Life," 694–695; and Garnsey, "The Land," 700–702.

57   Research assumes it was a name referring to the benefactors of the authorities, who received the land. See sources mentioned in previous note. Albeck, *Mishnah, M. Gittin* 5:6, identifies this period as that which came after the Great Revolt of 70 CE; others identify the *sikrikon* with the period that followed the Bar Kokhba Revolt.

58   See Albeck, *Mishnah, M. Gittin* 5:6.

7 Was the Landowner, *Ba'al Habayit*, Rich?

In many sources in Tannaitic literature, the term "rich" is used to refer to anyone whose economic situation could be contrasted with that of someone for whom the term "poor" was applicable.[59] Being poor meant that one enjoyed certain financial assistance that allowed them to collect certain tithes from the fields and to atone for sins by offering a less costly sacrifice in the Temple. Consequently, the term "rich" used in the Mishnah in those cases simply refers to someone who is not poor, but it does not necessarily signify any particular level of wealth.[60]

In the following source, the description of someone as rich signifies that he is wealthy, but wealth is a relative term and has various degrees:

> "On condition that I am rich"—they do not mean that he has to be the richest of the rich, but only as rich as people in his town generally regarded as rich.[61]

The source distinguishes two types of "rich." One is a person who is rich relative to his fellow villagers and peers; the second is the "rich of the rich," who is objectively rich compared with the general population. A *ba'al habayit* may be wealthy compared to his peers and thus deserving of the description "rich" for the sake of winning the hand of the lady implied in the text quoted above, but the category of the "rich of the rich" is on a much higher scale of wealth than the landowner described in the sources.

It is difficult to assess how many landowners actually belonged to the "rich of the rich." We can compare the situation in Palestine to that of the Roman Empire as a whole. Researchers have calculated that the percentage of rich citizens in the Roman Empire was between 3 percent and 5 percent of society

---

59 The rabbinic use of the term "rich" will be explained in the following chapter.
60 Such are the following sources: *M. Shvi'it* 9:8; *M. Eruvin* 4:5; *M. Shekalim* 5:3; *M. Kiddushin* 2:2; *M. Arakhin* 4:1–2. This definition coincides with an ideological statement mentioned in the Mishnah (*Avot* 4:1), which is attributed to Ben Zoma, who was active at the beginning of the second century CE: "Who is rich?" "He who is happy with his portion." The purpose of this statement is to teach people ethics, morals, and how to achieve happiness, rather than to present a definition of the term "rich" in rabbinic literature. Chapter 5 extensively discusses the term "rich" and the social strata of the wealthy.
61 *T. Kiddushin* 3:8 (Lieberman ed., 288). The text discusses a man becoming engaged to a woman on the condition that he is rich. See Lieberman, Tosefta Kifshuta 8, 948–949.

as a whole.⁶² It is likely that this was the percentage of wealthy people living in Jewish society in Roman Palestine too. This would mean that the vast majority of landowners would not be defined as the "rich of the rich." This corresponds to the description of the life of the landowner that emerges from reading the above mishnah. In contrast with the rich, the landowner needs to work very hard for his living. He is out in the fields with his workers, and he takes his produce to the market to sell. This also indicates that most landowners did not belong to the leisured class but rather to the working class.⁶³

Indeed, we find landowners hiring workers to work in the field.⁶⁴ However, these are seasonal workers who help with plowing or harvesting. The sources tell of the landowner using "a slave" versus "slaves." The wealthy classes in the Roman Empire had immense numbers of slaves who worked their fields. The wealthy themselves were not involved in the actual work and employed overseers to do it for them. This is the "husbandman" mentioned in the NT who sends his slaves to attend to agricultural issues. The "landowner" or the *ba'al habayit* mentioned in rabbinic sources is the "smallholder" mentioned in research on the Roman Empire, and there is some disagreement as to the extent to which smallholders existed during the first centuries CE. Thus, according to rabbinic sources from Roman Palestine, the smallholders were such a considerable group in society that they had their own subculture and social relations.

8 The "House" of the "Householder" (*Ba'al Habayit*) in Archeological Findings

There is some difficulty assessing the economic status of the farmers of the first centuries CE using archeological findings, as they do not supply data concerning the yields of the fields or the possessions of the farmers. Nevertheless, there are two criteria that can be used to provide a general idea of the financial status of the farmers. One is the home: its size and the amenities it provided—that is, storage, use of a courtyard, a roof, a number of rooms, etc. The second

---

62   Some researchers assess the percentage of rich citizens at even less than 1 percent. See MacMullen, *Social Relations*, 89; Alföldy, *Social History*, 130; Rilinger, *Humiliores-Honestiores*, 302; Fiensy, *Social History*, 155–167; and Friesen, "Poverty Pauline," 340–347.
63   See *M. Pe'ah* 4:1. The landowner personally gives out the tithe from the fruit trees to the poor; and *M. Pe'ah* 5:7 about a sheaf of wheat forgotten by the landowner but found by the worker, or vice versa. In *M. Demai* 5:7, a landowner was selling "greens" in the market.
64   See *T. Berakhot* 5:24 (Lieberman ed., 29); the landowner is saying grace for his workers.

is the size of the plot of land and its quality as an indication of the financial situation of the owner.[65]

Ellis identifies three possible characteristics of a "middle-class house":

A. It lacks ornate "aristocratic" architecture, in particular a peristyle (i.e., an open courtyard within the house).
B. Its occupation of a restricted space.
C. Its poor décor, which might have included feeble imitations of aristocratic styles and trends.[66]

However, he demonstrates that members of the "upper middle class" might also have preferred to inhabit dwellings identical to aristocratic peristyle homes.

Ellis refrains from establishing criteria to differentiate between the homes of the "middling classes" and those of the "poor." Perhaps this is because his assumption is that houses of the poor would not be sturdy enough to survive the wear and tear of the time that passed since the Roman Empire.[67] Nevertheless, it is possible to point out a number of characteristics of the houses described that define them as belonging to middling-class people and not to the poor.

We can use Ellis's definition as a springboard for our search for the middling-class house in Roman Palestine. Indeed, since the *ba'al habayit* was primarily involved in agriculture, it is reasonable to search among findings from rural areas in order to locate the house of a *ba'al habayit*. Indeed, since a large percentage of townsmen in ancient times made a living from farming as well, it is hard to identify in the towns which homes belonged to the *ba'alei batim* and which homes belonged to artisans, merchants, or even the poor.

Archeological excavations and surveys bear out the above conclusions. Yeivin conducted a survey of 40 rural settlements in the Golan and Galilee of this period. Recognizing the limits of conclusions that can be drawn from a survey, the evidence reveals that the villages were full of homes that were essentially family homes. This means that the families living nearby cultivated the vast majority of fields and did not use slave labor or hired hands except for temporary help for plowing and harvesting. This means that, at worst, the inhabitants of the villages were sharecroppers and that, at best, they were the owners of the fields in which they worked. Nevertheless, division of the

---

65 On limitations on the possibility of determining the amount of space allocated to each family in complex dwellings and the way to overcome the difficulties, see Wallace-Hadrill, "Roman Luxury," 157–158.
66 See Ellis, "Middle Class Houses." Compare with the criteria offered by Wallace-Hadrill, "Roman Luxury," 156, for social stratification according to houses. See also Uytterhoeven, "Housing in Late Antiquity," 43–44.
67 Regarding homes of the poor, see Uytterhoeven, "Housing in Late Antiquity," 48–49; and Wallace-Hadrill, "Roman Luxury," 153.

amount of land available for cultivation by the number of dwelling units uncovered shows that there are about 40 *dunam* available for 60 units, giving each unit 20–30 *dunam* to work. This means that the families living in these units were far from destitute and could live above subsistence level. In these settlements as well, there is no evidence of the presence of wealthy people, as the houses are very much the same and none stand out as being much better than the others.[68]

Another rural settlement that was excavated was the village of Kefar Nachum in the eastern Galilee. This village was an agricultural settlement in which some of the inhabitants would have been fishermen. It was already known from the NT and has been the subject of much research. In intensive digs carried out in the village, a large residential area was uncovered that had been settled in the first century CE and that had developed until the peak of its expansion in the fourth century CE. Many buildings were uncovered that clearly belonged neither to the rich nor to the poor.[69]

Extensive surveys in the rural areas of Palestine were carried out by Hirschfeld, who set up criteria for recognizing types of homes in Roman Palestine.[70] One of the places he describes is the "large Jewish village of" Ein Gedi.[71] Two kinds of residential dwellings from Ein Gedi are described. The ones in the settlement were of high quality, and near the plots of land the structures were of lower quality. Researchers have argued as to their use. Safrai believes that they belonged to sharecroppers or fieldworkers or poor landowners who slept near their fields during high agricultural seasons. Here too there are various levels of farmers from the economically secure farmers who have ample sustenance, down to the peasant farmer who is struggling to

---

[68] Yeivin, *Survey Settlements*, esp. 154–183. See also Yeivin, "Towns." He surveyed many of these "towns": Einan, Korazin, Usha, and Meiron in the Galilee; Susiya in southern Judea, Nafach in the Golan; and Naaran in the Jordan Valley (see ibid., 56–61). It seems that these towns were villages that were enlarged after the Bar Kokhba Revolt (ibid., 69–71). The Jews, who had less land to cultivate, started to move from agriculture to the trades and commerce. However, they preferred staying in areas of dense Jewish population rather than emigrating to the Greek *poleis*. See also Sperber, *Land*, 102–186.

[69] See Corbo, *Cafarnao I*, 173–221, esp. 218–220; and Tsafrir, *Israel Archaeology*, 133–142.

[70] Uytterhoeven, "Housing in Late Antiquity," 58–59, says about Hirschfeld's work that it is "the best starting point for those wishing to study late antique housing in Palestine." On the value and limitations of surveys and salvage excavations, see Faust and Safrai, "Salvage Excavations."

[71] This is how Eusebius defined the village in the fourth century CE (*Onomasticon* 86).

stay above subsistence level.[72] Accordingly, the sizes of the houses varied from 40 to 240 sq. m. The Mishnah says that "every household had a main living room where the whole family slept, ate and entertained."[73]

Another important source is the work of Dar, who conducted archeological digs at a number of sites that are dated to the Roman-Byzantine period. Dar's survey of the village area of the western part of Samaria that covered a wide area showed the size of the villages from the first centuries CE, the way in which they were built, and their financial status. His research shows that the houses were built from sturdy materials, had ample space for storage and livestock, and were equipped with common courtyards that contained shared commodities such as ovens, clothes-washing basins, and sometimes even an olive or wine press or a mill. Also, he found that there was only a small difference between the most modest of the dwellings in the villages and the wealthiest, indicating a small gap between rich and poor in the villages. This social structure strongly points to a wide middle stratum.[74]

Another indication is the projected size of the plots next to the fields. Dar estimates that each family had a small plot of land that would be enough to support the family when cultivated by the family itself with outside help only for plowing and harvesting. The number of plots coincides with the number of homes, so that it seems that each family cultivated its own small plot of land. It was not the case that some families had very large estates and others had a tiny plot or no land at all. The families that owned homes and land in the villages would be the *ba'alei batim* mentioned in Tannaitic literature. Their homes were fine for a nuclear family (parents and two to three children) and did not contain signs of wealth. Therefore, according to Ellis's criteria they belonged to a middle stratum between rich and poor.[75]

Dar excavated and surveyed agricultural villages and the neighboring countryside in the Mt. Carmel region. His conclusions concerning the size of plots and houses are similar to those of his research in western Samaria. The main difference between the two areas was the mountainous nature of the Carmel,

---

72 See Hirschfeld, "En Gedi," 641–650. The abundance of "small finds" (ibid., 652–653) shows the prosperity of the village as well. See also Hirschfeld, "Property versus Poverty," 384–392.

73 Hirschfeld, "En Gedi," 645. A 40 sq. m. house would be considered large in the other villages; here, it is among the smallest. See also Cotton, "Ein Gedi."

74 On the place of wine installations, particularly with multiple presses, in determining the level of investment available for agricultural production, see Erdkamp, "Economic Growth," 8.

75 Dar, *Landscape and Pattern*, esp. 21–87, 230–254.

which required a different economic basis for the livelihood of the village inhabitants.[76] A model for Dar's excavations on Mt. Carmel is Sumaqa—the ruins of a large Jewish village that was settled between the second and seventh century.[77] In addition, Dar, Safrai, and Tepper dug in a different village/town called Um Rihan in western Samaria that was inhabited by Jews or Samaritans.[78] In both villages, the number of dwelling places matches the number of fields available suggesting that most families were working as a unit. The village homes were built close together so that there seems to have been no room for "dormitory" structures for hired labor or slaves, or for lower-class living. The structure and size of the houses were similar and indicated that in the villages there was little economic difference between the wealthy and the poor.

In different surveys carried out near the Roman road near Khirbet Mishkena (around modern-day Kibbutz Lavi) and in the Arbel Valley, a slightly different village type was uncovered. It was divided into neighborhoods according to the Roman system, which indicated Roman influence. However, considering the size of the land plots for the individual farmer and the relative standard of living of the inhabitants, it was similar to the other types of villages.[79]

The above findings point toward a logical assumption that most of the village dwellers were peasants who were working their land and paying their taxes directly to the authorities, or paying rent to an absentee landowner. Nevertheless, the remains point to middling economic living. The houses are built sturdily; there are roofs and courtyards for cattle and goods, and the living quarters are not cramped. All this confirms the image of the Jewish *ba'al habayit* as it emerges from the literary sources.

The stark division between rich and poor that is described by sources of this period is not contradicted by the archeological evidence. However, the social stratum within Jewish society for landowners is wide. This segment of society owned a portion of the most sought-after commodity of the time—land—separating it qualitatively from the poor and their plight. Within this stratum, there were those who were relatively wealthy and those who were close to living at subsistence level.

---

76 Dar, *Mount Carmel*, 15–157, esp. 168–186.
77 Dar, *Sumaqa*.
78 Dar, Safrai, and Tepper, *Um Rihan*, 8–56, 130–140.
79 Safrai, "Socio-Economic," 303–307; See also Idem, *Economy*, 288–289.

9 Historical Background

We have demonstrated above that the *ba'al habayit*, landowner, who appears in the literary sources, is represented in the houses and corresponding plots of land found in Palestinian rural settlements as shown from archeological remains. It is now necessary to understand the historical developments that produced the emergence of the wide social stratum of the *ba'al habayit* in society as part of the processes that shaped Jewish society in Palestine during the late Hellenistic and early Roman periods.

Until the Hasmonean period, Jewish society was constructed from multilayered extended families that would reside together in the towns and villages of the land. The Hasmonean Revolt of 167 BCE promoted long-term changes in Jewish society in Palestine, which included a change in living arrangements. Many Jews went from living in extended families in the countryside to living in nuclear families in towns and villages. This process was a result of the many wars fought in the region until the Great Revolt of 66–73 CE and the Bar Kokhba Revolt of 132–135/6 CE. In addition, the Roman conquest in 63 BCE caused a great deal of economic and social pressure on Jewish society; the tax burden was onerous and later became even more oppressive. The revolts, and the repercussions that ensued, led to deterioration in the living conditions of Jewish society in Palestine.[80] Families were forced to create separate units, as each nuclear family functioned separately in an effort to maximize the mobilization and utilization of labor to allow for its survival in these harsh conditions.[81]

By the first century CE, the majority of Jewish society was already arranged into nuclear units. The fortunate ones owned a plot of land and worked it, while the less fortunate worked as sharecroppers and day laborers.[82] Due to heavy taxation on farmers and their accumulation of debt, there was a shift from living in extended family structures to living in conjugal family structures. In Palestine, the fierce wars and political unrest added to the pressure and seem to have intensified and catalyzed this process.[83]

---

80 Schwartz, "Economic Life."
81 See Gabba, "History"; Schäfer, *History*, 44–161; and Rubin, "Mourning."
82 Guijarro, "Family Galilee," noted this phenomenon and attributed the change in family structure to the introduction of the market economy, which encouraged the establishment of large estates worked by hired laborers, sharecroppers, or slaves. See also Guijarro, "Family First Century," 56–61 and "Home and Family," 69, 81.
83 Bagnall, *Egypt*, 58–66, 171–173. On the evolution of these changes in the Roman Empire, see MacMullen, *Social Relations*, 24; Garnsey and Saller, *Economy and Society*, 126–147. For a general summary of this subject, see Severy, *Augustus*, 1–22.

The term "*ba'al habayit*" replaced the term "*beit av*" (lit. "house of the father"), which represented the clan, or extended family. NT literature, which was redacted in the second half of the first century CE, describes Jewish society in its nuclear family form.[84] Similarly, Tannaitic literature, which was created between 70 and 250 CE, relates primarily to the nuclear family living off the land; it is natural, therefore, that extensive attention is devoted to the *ba'al habayit*, who is the social and economic head of the household. At the same time, Roman authorities taxing the population were interested in the *ba'al habayit* because he was the party whose holdings they had to assess. He was also the representative of the nuclear family in all dealings with the authorities. The use of this unique term rather than the customary "rich" or "poor" indicates that this group was neither. It described all landowners regardless of their economic status, from the smallholder barely subsisting from his income, all the way up to the wealthy owner of large plantations administered by bailiffs and worked by slaves. This historical background explains the development of the term "*ba'al habayit*" in the first century CE, its initial use in the NT, and subsequently its extensive use in Tannaitic literature. Uncovering this group in society exposes a stratum of society that is often overlooked when describing stratification: the middling groups that are not rich or poor. In the literary sources, they are not defined explicitly as an independent economic stratum, but are rather characterized by their property and occupation: homeowner-farmer. In turn, this group was not monolithic, and among its members there were those who were wealthier than others.

10 The Small Landowner in the Roman Empire

The above findings regarding Palestine enhance our knowledge of the economic and social status of the small landowners in the Roman Empire, especially in the eastern provinces.[85] There are contemporaneous sources that establish the existence of small independent landowners in Roman society.

---

84 On the structure of the family in the Jesus Movement, see Destro and Pesce, "Householders," esp. n. 1–2. See also Shaw, "Family Late Antiquity," 3–5; Dixon, *Roman Family*, 28–30; and Harries, *Law and Crime*, 86–105. It is accepted that the structure of the Christian family was similar to that which existed in the general population in which the apostles were active.

85 On the freeholding peasant in the Roman Empire, see esp. Carandini, *Peasants*; and Garnsey, "Peasants," 91–106. He also presents evidence from Syria and Asia Minor. See Garnsey, "The Land," 691–701. Scheidel, "Stratification," 51, writes: "I find it hard to imagine

However, these sources neglect to define landowners as a unique group, thus we lack sufficient information about them. There is general agreement that Roman law is structured in such a way as to hold the owner of a field, even a small one, responsible to the administration for the payment of taxes, and to give him legal authority over his social dependents: his spouse, children, workers, slaves, and/or sharecroppers. By the fourth century CE, the majority of the land was in the hands of wealthy plantation owners, who employed slaves and bailiffs, or sharecroppers, to work the land. However, there is some controversy as to just how common this system of land tenure was in the first three centuries CE.[86] The evidence that emerges here concerning the small landowners indicates that they were a significant segment of the population, that they were a distinct social group that maintained a network of social relations, and that they even had a measure of mutual support resulting from class solidarity. On the other hand, there were economic differences between various landowners resulting from the size of their plots, their ability to employ labor, their expertise, and their fortunes.

Sources from Syria and Asia Minor indicate that the small landowner was prevalent in the landscape and constituted a significant part of the rural and urban population; thus we learn that they cooperated in order to bribe local army units. They are not presented as poor.[87]

Findings in Egypt also coincide with the above description. Rowlandson analyzed the property sizes of residents of the town of Hermopolite in the fourth century CE, and discovered that 50 percent of landowners owned portions of land that were not large enough to sustain a family (according to the criteria found in local documents), and that an additional 30 percent owned between 5 and 15 *arouras*, which would be sufficient to sustain a family if worked by the family, but which was not enough for a family to live from the rent or work of tenant farmers.[88] On the other hand, the family could work the land by itself with little or no outside help. "These lists provide a valuable corrective to the idea that small scale landowning had largely been eroded by the fourth

---

how in any reasonable scenario the number of middling property owners could be smaller than ... 20 per cent."

86 See Greene, *Archaeology*, 109.

87 Greene, *Archaeology*, 138–140; Sartre, "Syria and Arabia," 641–652; Sartre, *Middle East*, 213–216. He also comments that it may be that some of the peasants were tenants, sharecroppers, or renters.
However, it seems that there were also small landowners.

88 Rathbone, *Economic Rationalism*, xiv, estimates the *aroura* at 2,760 sq. m.

century CE."[89] Only 25 percent of city dwellers could live off their plots using hired labor. If this was true as late as the fourth century regarding city dwellers; certainly it would be more so regarding villages in the first to third centuries.[90]

Rowlandson, relying also on Bagnall's data from Karanis, concludes that in the villages probably 70 percent of landholders held enough land to live on (more than 10 *arouras*), enlarging the "middle economic stratum" significantly. This will not contradict city numbers because in the city there was the opportunity to make a living from trade and commerce with the land only supplementing the livelihood. She concludes: "The number of villagers able to live off their own holdings but with little surplus, may indeed have been the largest in numerical terms, although because of the nature of our evidence, it has left little trace in the Oxyrhynchite papyri."[91] Similar conclusions emerge from findings in North Africa. The land was divided among colonists and peasants in addition to being divided into imperial and other estates.[92]

Surveys of Roman rural settlements describe two types of settlements. One is the "villa," which was ascribed to the rich landowner, and the other, the "farm," which, it is assumed, belonged to peasant freeholders.[93] This indicates that there was a wide stratum of small freeholders and they were probably identical to the *ba'alei batim* of Roman Palestine.[94] Some of these farmers would not have had enough land to employ sharecroppers to work under them, and would have had to work the land themselves with the help of their families or with seasonal hired help.[95]

---

89 Rowlandson, *Landowners*, 122–123.
90 Ibid., 121–123. She emphasizes that the data she is using prevents the mistake of overlooking ownership of a few plots by the same family, as these are official land registers.
91 Ibid., 124.
92 Kehoe, *Economy Agriculture*, 18–20, 229, s.v. peasants, villages, *vicus, coloni*; Kehoe, *Profit Tenancy*, 18–21, 117–118, 217–221, and index, s.v. peasant agriculture, tenancy.
93 See Dyson, "Settlement Patterns"; Carandini, *Peasants*; Barker, Lloyd, and Webley, "Landscape"; Foxhall, "Dependent Tenant," claims that some of these peasants were, in effect, sharecroppers, renters, or overseers for larger landowners. However, some of the "farms" belonged to peasant freeholders. The renters and sharecroppers were also not necessarily poor and may have enjoyed secure social status. See also Saller, "Status and Patronage."
94 See Greene, *Archaeology*, 132–134, that the contrast between villas and villages indicates peasant holdings.
95 See Garnsey, "The Land," 695–701, 704.

11 Conclusion

The term *"ba'al habayit"* ("landowner") originated most probably in the second half of the first century CE as a response to the need to have a Hebrew term that represented the legal entity of the Latin *dominus*. This entity was key in the Roman system of administration, as the *dominus* was the taxpayer and a legal entity that held power over his household, his family, his property, and his workers. The biblical term *"ba'al habayit,"* relating simply to a homeowner, was expanded to accommodate this new need. The first sources that mentioned *ba'al habayit* in this new sense of the term are the Synoptic Gospels of the NT in the first century CE with οἰκοδεσπότης. Rabbinic literature compiled in the first half of the third century CE uses this term extensively. Hence, from the second century onward we find the Greek form οἰκοδεσπότης in use in the eastern provinces of the Roman Empire. A vivid picture of the *ba'al habayit* can be gleaned from the literary sources, and it is supported by archeological surveys and excavations in Palestine in contemporaneous rural communities: the vast majority of the population of these villages consisted of farmers. The *ba'al habayit*-landowner owned a plot of land from which he derived his livelihood. He was not "poor," for he owned significant property (land). On the other hand, in most cases he was not rich as he did not have enough land to employ sharecroppers or utilize slaves and had to work the land himself. His home was not marked with signs of luxury as were the homes of the rich. Sources mention other property that he may have owned: work animals, tools, and storage facilities. His actual economic status depended on the size and quality of his plot, the commodities he owned, other sources of income, natural hazards, and taxation. Within this social group, there was additional economic variation. Some owned a few fields and employed sharecroppers, while some owned slaves. Some were wealthy, and some became extremely wealthy, buying fields from others and accumulating a substantial amount of land. Others were small landowners, who owned only one small plot of land and needed to hire an ox and plow to work their fields.

The landowners shared a common social status and might support each other through acts of mutual solidarity, hospitality—overlooking religious differences—and material assistance. Thus emerges the social stratum of the οἰκοδεσπότης-*ba'al habayit*-landowner. This stratum represents a substantial group of people in Roman Palestine, who were self-sufficient and who occupied a number of economic levels from modest farmers who barely had their necessities, through the middling groups, to the rich. This research, along with the developing research of literary sources from Egypt, Syria, and Asia Minor, now enables scholars to see these landowners as a segment of society that had mutual relationships and support and a measure of class identity. This discovery could lead to an improved understanding of the social role of the independent landowners in other parts of the Roman Empire as well, though caution is required when comparing the agrarian situation from one province to the next. Indeed, there were also farmers who were closer to the economic extremes of rich and poor. However, the above sources indicate that the average independent farmer was in the middle: neither rich nor poor. He had enough to live on without collecting charity, but he had few luxuries.

CHAPTER 6

The "Rich"

In modern times, the word "rich" refers to people who possess great wealth in the form of real estate or money or both. This definition seems to be true regarding the term as it was used in Roman literature, as can be seen from the prose and poetic works of the first three centuries CE, which were penned primarily by the elite. However, it will be shown below that this definition does not hold when it comes to the discourse of the Jewish population of Roman Palestine.[1]

In the Roman world, wealth was an important social factor, dividing society into two primary strata: the upper wealthy class and the poor lower class.[2] Being wealthy in the Roman Empire meant not only possessing the ability to lead a more comfortable life, but also enjoying an elevated individual social status, one that would have drawn a following from the lower stratum of society.[3]

The Roman upper class can be divided into imperial and local aristocracies. The imperial aristocracy included the Caesar, his advisors, the senators, the equestrian order, army generals, and the senior administrators of the Empire.[4] People holding these offices usually resided in Rome; wealth outside of Rome was usually of smaller proportions. In the provinces, the wealthy enjoyed special privileges. They had easier access to Roman citizenship. They could (and did) serve on the local city council, the *curia* or *boule*, and thereby influence local politics and policy: these councilors formed a local upper stratum.[5]

---

1 On the modern definition of wealth, see Wolff, "Wealth Distribution."
2 Alföldy, *Roman Society*, 1–6. Alföldy was the first to chart Roman society as polarized between a small rich stratum and a very large poor one. He did so in his famous pyramid structure described in Chapter 1. Zanker, *Images*, 5–33, accepted this division. For a critique of this structure in terms of the wealthy stratum, see Vittinghoff, "Social Structure"; Rilinger, *Collegia*, 153–179; Winterling, *Politics*, 17–25; and Davies, "Wealth."
3 See Saller, *Patronage*, 119–143; Dyson, *Community and Society*, 90–112, 168–195, 203–225, 231–232; and Anderson, *Architecture and Society*, 288–370. On wealth and the wealthy in society, see Kerbo, *Social Stratification*, 149–201.
4 See the following works concerning the social structure of society in the Roman Empire: Joshel, *Work Identity*; Vittinghoff, "Gesellschaft"; Toner, *Rethinking Roman*, 50–51; Scheidel, "Human Mobility"; Meeks, *Social Paul*, 53–58; Friesen, "Poverty Pauline"; Verboven, "Associative Order"; and Sodini, "Archaeology," 25–26.
5 The *boule* in the Roman east was parallel to the *curia* in the west; see Jones, *Later Empire*, 1.724–725. On the *boule* in general, see Rhodes, "boule."

Their wealth and status is known from written sources and from epigraphic inscriptions left in epitaphs depicting their philanthropic achievements.[6] The provincial elite were to be found primarily in cities, but wealth could occasionally be found in villages as well.[7]

There are few accounts of Jews in this period who were as wealthy as members of the Roman upper class. Only a few individuals in the first century CE, such as those of the Herodian dynasty,[8] and Gaius Julius Alexander, Philo's brother in Alexandria, were truly wealthy in Roman imperial terms.[9] Most wealthy Jews in Roman Palestine would have been considered to be socially comparable to the provincial wealthy, who had more property than most people in their region but were far less rich than the elite of the city of Rome itself.

1 The "Rich" in the Old Testament and Second Temple Literature

In the OT, the term "rich" ("*ashir*") contrasts with the term "poor" ("*ani*").[10] It seems to refer to a wide variety of people from those who possessed moderate economic means to those who possessed an excessive amount of wealth. On the other hand, the term "*chayil*" is sometimes used to define wealth.[11] *Chayil* literally means "power," referring to the concept that a person's possessions give him power to accomplish, achieve, and attain fame and social standing. In the books of Joshua and Judges, there is little mention of wealth and riches. This is

---

6   See Sartre, *L'orient Romain*, 169–174. There was no "middle class" in ancient society similar to the middle class that existed in Europe after the Industrial Revolution. See Winterling, *Politics*, 11, esp. n. 5. However, there were groups of people that were in the economic middle between rich and poor. See Scheidel, "Stratification"; Verboven, "Associative Order"; and Longenecker, "Economic Middle."

7   On the difference between city and village in Roman architecture, see Ellis, *Roman Housing*, 73, 88–89. For the distinction between city and village in Roman Galilee and Syria, see Sartre, *Middle East*, 228–229. In Egypt, the size and construction of houses in the villages was similar to Palestine. Most of the rich of Egypt were located in the cities. See Alston, "Houses in Roman Egypt"; and Katsari, *Monetary System*, 170–174.

8   See Fiensy, *Social History*, 1–21. However, Goodman, *Ruling Class*, 109–135, points out significant differences between Judea and Rome regarding attitudes toward money and the influence of the affluent strata on society as a whole. These distinctions were mitigated after the Great Revolt (66–70 CE) and more so after the Bar Kokhba Revolt (132–135 CE). See Kokkinos, *Herodian Dynasty*, 342–362.

9   See Schürer, *History*, 3:136–137; and Kasher, *Jews in Egypt*, 86.

10 The word "rich" was always mentioned in contrast to the "poor": Gen. 30:15, Deut. 30:15. Also in Ruth 3:10, the *ashir* is merely the opposite of the *ani* (poor).

11 Deut. 8:16–17. The main use for the word "*chayil*" pertains to a contingent of soldiers as in Gen. 47:6.

commonly attributed to the system of distribution of the land in the period of settlement, which created a society that was economically homogenous.

Descriptions of the rich and riches are found, however, in the period of the kings.[12] In this period, the word "*ashir*" sometimes relates to the objectively rich; Jeremiah exclaims that the rich should not take pride in their wealth.[13] Similarly, in the wisdom literature, the term "rich" often relates to the genuinely wealthy.[14] These terms can relate to the relatively rich as well. However, there is also a variety of terms relating to the very rich: *osher* ("riches"), *osher vechavod* ("riches and honor"), and *osher u'nechasim* ("riches and property"). These terms all relate to various levels of extreme wealth.[15] In addition, the term "*hon*" refers to assets and seems to refer specifically to wealth measured in money.[16]

In the Greek version of the Bible, the Septuagint, the word "rich" appears in various forms of the word "πλούτεον," which indicates a high socioeconomic level, but the Septuagint does not contain terminology that distinguishes levels of prosperity within society. In Ben Sira, there is a stark contrast between those who have *hon*, indicating a great deal of property, and those who have nothing, the suffering poor. However, the rich are not ridiculed or considered necessarily evil. Ben Sira warns against the exploitation of the poor by the rich and against using wealth for evil deeds.[17] The rich in that period are presented as well-to-do, with plenty of money and assets as well as with the ability to accomplish great feats and the ability to govern.[18] In the Dead Sea Scrolls, the word "*hon*" is also used to indicate wealth, while the other biblical words that indicate wealth, *osher* and *nechasim*, are not used at all.[19]

---

12   Domeris, "asir."
13   Jer. 9:22. Also 2 Sam. 12:2–4; and Mic. 6:12.
14   In Ps. 49:3 and Prov. 22:2, 7, the rich person is in contrast to poor person, but it is also in contrast to one who rules over the poor. Similarly, in Prov. 10:15, 14:26, 18: 11, 28:6, 11, *ashir* relates to the truly rich. See also Eccles. 5:11, 10:6.
15   Eccles. 4:8–12, 5:12, 9:11. *Osher vechavod*: Prov. 3:18, 8:18, 22:4. *Osher u'nechasim*: Eccles. 5:18, 6:2. The two complex expressions probably relate to a higher level of riches than simply "rich."
16   This term appears 23 times in the later prophets and in the wisdom literature. In all places, it refers to portable wealth, primarily money. See also Domeris, "hon." On the rich in the wisdom literature, see Adams, *Social and Economic*, 184–192.
17   Ben Sira 10:30, 31:1–10. Ben Sira does not regard riches as evil but calls on the wealthy not to mistreat the poor or disregard their needs. The rich person enjoys life, but the poor person suffers. See Domeris, "asir"; Adams, *Social and Economic*, 192–194.
18   See Schwartz, *Jews*, 71–72 and 175–176.
19   See CD 8:5, 19:17. See Domeris, "hon"; and Adams, *Social and Economic*, 197–198.

2 The "Rich" in the New Testament

The books of the NT were redacted between the years 60 and 90 CE.[20] The most common terms for rich that are used are πλούσιος ("rich," "wealthy"), πλουτῶν ("rich person"), and πλουτέω ("to be rich"). Each one of these forms means both "plenty" and "wealth."[21] Examination of the examples leads to the tentative conclusion that the various forms refer to slightly different levels of wealth. However, there does not seem to be any kind of consistency and the terms are used interchangeably. This use of these terms is similar to how the terms are used in the Septuagint and the wisdom literature, but there are no additional words that help the reader distinguish different levels of wealth. However, another term common in the NT, οἰκοδεσπότης, relates to individuals who are homeowners, indicating that they are in a sound economic situation but are not as wealthy as the πλούσιος.[22] This reveals two types of established citizens in the NT: the homeowner and the rich person. The homeowner is usually presented in a positive light, while the rich person is portrayed in a negative light.[23] In addition, there is a distinction between the way in which wealth is described in Jesus's sayings and parables, and in the description of his encounters with the rich.

In the parables, the wealthy person is developed and presented as someone who lives a life of indulgence and does not need to work.[24] In Luke, the parables on the rich appear in one section of the book, as they are concentrated in chapters 16–18.[25] One might suggest that the rich people who Jesus meets in the first half of his journey were relatively rich but that they were not "Roman rich," as it were: they still needed to work for a living. When he

---

20 Vyhmeister, "Rich Man."
21 See Hauck and Kasch, "πλοῦτος, πλούσιος πλουτέω, πλουτίζω."
22 Luke 14:15–24. In the story there, the homeowner's friends are wealthier than him and do not want to come to his dinner, but careful analysis of their "excuses" shows that they too work for a living and do not belong to the leisure class.
23 On the homeowner, see Mark 13:35, where he is assigning tasks to workers; Mark 14:14, where he is hosting Jesus and his disciples for the Passover meal; Luke 14:16–20, where he is inviting his friends for a meal, and Luke 22:11 and Matt. 21:33, 24:43. This issue was discussed in the previous chapter. See Rosenfeld and Perlmutter, "Landowners."
24 Regarding Jesus's sayings that refer to rich people, at Mark 10:25, 18:24–25 we have the rich man who was owed 10,000 talents. The parables at Luke 12:13–21 and Luke 16:19–31 talk about the rich man who was wearing superb linen garments and experiencing pleasures every day. Encounters with the rich appear also at Mark 10:17–24, 12:41–44; and Luke 18:21–29, 21:1–4. See Derret, *Law*, 80–82.
25 On the rich in the NT, see also Adams, *Social and Economic*, 198–201. He primarily discusses Luke.

reached Jerusalem, Jesus first ran into the "leisure class" rich who conducted their lives like the rich of the Roman Empire. These rich people were primarily involved in politics and pleasure-seeking. Furthermore, every time the NT mentions the "rich" and refers to a member of the leisure class, it adds information about how wealthy this rich person was and how he looked and behaved prosperously, or it calls him "very rich." In this, the NT distinguishes between the homeowner, the rich person, and the very rich person in much the same way as the rabbis will differentiate the economic strata of Jewish society approximately 100 years later.[26]

3 The Attitude toward the Rich in the New Testament

Examination of the literary sources of the NT shows a consistent attitude toward the wealthy and toward wealth, though there are also gradual modifications in the approach to this issue in later generations. The NT does not represent the approach of rabbinic circles, as the Christians were revolutionaries who were rebelling against conservative political and religious leadership in Roman Palestine. Therefore, examination of the collective approach of the early Christian writers can help us understand a perspective on the issue of wealth that is not the rabbinic one.

The most notable incident involving wealth is mentioned in the three Synoptic Gospels, each of which tells its own subtly different version of it. In the first stage of the activity of Jesus and his disciples in the Galilee, it seems that the former is extremely critical toward wealth and consequently the wealthy. The incident (according to Mark) had to do with a rich man who has asked Jesus how he could attain the Kingdom of God. Jesus answered him, telling him that he should observe the divine commandments and went on to mention some of the Ten Commandments. The wealthy man stated that he had already been doing that.[27]

Jesus looked at him and loved him. "One thing you lack," he said. "Go, sell everything you have and give to the poor, and you will have treasure in heaven. Then come, follow me." At this, the man's face fell. He went away sad, because he had great wealth. Jesus looked around and said to his disciples: "How hard it

---

26 The prime example for this kind of rich is mentioned in Luke 16:19–31 (and the poor—Lazarus). See Bauckham, "Lazarus," 97–118. Moxnes sees the descriptions of the rich in Luke as a sign of patron-client relationships in early Christianity; see Moxnes, "Patron Client," 242; and Balch, "Rich and Poor," 214–233. There is also mention of a rich man in James interpreted in a similar way. See Vyhmeister, "Rich Man."

27 For an analysis of this part of the conversation, see Hicks, "Markan Discipleship."

is for the rich to enter the Kingdom of God!" The disciples were amazed at his words. But Jesus said again: "Children, how hard it is to enter the Kingdom of God! It is easier for a camel to go through the eye of a needle than for someone who is rich to enter the Kingdom of God."[28]

This response baffled his disciples, who asked him who could be saved, if what he said was true. He answered that only God can save. The conclusion was that Jesus's disciples, who had left all of their property behind and followed him, would receive a greater reward than others in the future.[29]

The message here is that there are rich people who aspire to be good; however, wealth is a great obstacle to religious elevation, and since the wealthy person is not willing to leave his money for his religion, he will never reach the highest level of faith in God and know the true way of living. Wealth and true faith contradict one other.[30] The strongest statement concerning wealth is definitely the sentence "It is easier for a camel to go through the eye of a needle than for someone who is rich to enter the Kingdom of God."[31]

Other incidents are less overt, but they also show a negative attitude toward wealth and the wealthy. The Parable of the Sower appears in the three Synoptic Gospels.[32] A man planted seeds. Most of them did not germinate either because they fell on the path, were eaten by birds, or fell on rocks where there was no soil, and others grew among thorns that suffocated the plants so they could not produce grain. Only the fourth group of seeds took root and produced grain. Similarly, there are four kinds of people: three kinds do not succeed and one does. The third group is the rich, who are closest to success but have deterrents: "Still others, like seed sown among thorns, hear the Word; but the worries of this life, the deceitfulness of wealth and the desires for other things come in and choke the Word, making it unfruitful."[33] There is some praise of the wealthy, in that of all people they are the closest to the truth.

---

28 Mark 10: 21. This incident is also mentioned, with minor changes in some of the details, in Matt. 19:21–24 and Luke 18:22–25. For commentary on this, see Hicks, "Markan Discipleship," 195–199. Hicks posits that Jesus relied on the prophet Malachi (5:3), who states that the wealthy mistreat their workers and therefore the only way to observe all the commandments of the Torah is to give all your property to the poor.

29 See Légasse, *Marc*, 608–625, and *Du riche*, 17–31.

30 This analysis is based on Marcus, *Mark 8–16*, 730–740. For analysis of the parallel account in Luke, see Fitzmyer, *Luke I–IX*, 1195–1201.

31 Mark 10:25. Fitzmyer, *Luke I–IX*, 1201–1206. On Jerome's commentary on this statement, see Luomanen, "Rich Man." There is also a commentary that gleans from this statement that there is tension between abundant material property and spiritual and intellectual property. See Hogeterp, "Luke Wisdom."

32 Ibid., 4:13–20. Similarly, Matt. 13:22 and Luke 8:14. See Fitzmyer, *Luke I–IX*, 710–715.

33 Ibid., 4:19. See Marcus, *Mark 1–8*, 308.

But still they fall short. They listen to the truth, but they are deceived by their wealth, which produces other desires that draw them away from it, and they have other "worries of this life."[34]

In Mark 12:41, there is a personal account of Jesus's life that has a similar message. When Jesus is in the Temple, he and his disciples see people donating to the Temple. The rich put large donations and the poor small ones. A widow puts in two pennies. Jesus states that he prefers the donation of the widow who put all she had, in contrast to others, who had a lot and were giving merely from their surplus. Here, too, the message is not against wealth per se; it is just that the wealthy do not attain the full devotion that he (Jesus) seeks.[35]

The Parable of the Rich Fool is a sharp critique of the search for wealth. Luke relates it as follows:

> Someone in the crowd said to him, "Teacher, tell my brother to divide the inheritance with me." Jesus replied, "Man, who appointed me a judge or an arbiter between you?" Then he said to them, "Watch out! Be on your guard against all kinds of greed; life does not consist in an abundance of possessions." And he told them this parable: "The ground of a certain rich man yielded an abundant harvest. He thought to himself, 'What shall I do? I have no place to store my crops.' Then he said, 'This is what I'll do. I will tear down my barns and build bigger ones, and there I will store my surplus grain.' And I'll say to myself: 'You have plenty of grain laid up for many years, take life easy: eat, drink and be merry.' But God said to him, 'You fool! This very night your life will be demanded from you. Then who will get what you have prepared for yourself?' This is how it will be with whoever stores up things for themselves but is not rich toward God."[36]

This sharp criticism is aimed at a person who spends his life in the pursuit of wealth and does not invest in his future life after death. On the other hand, it presents an extreme case of someone who thinks only about his material acquisitions and does not deal with spirituality, being benevolent, or caring for the poor. It could be that if he attends to these issues as well he would be praiseworthy despite his wealth.[37] Jesus's public speeches as they are recorded

---

34   Akin to the saying in *M. Avot* 2:8: "He who has many belongings has many worries."
35   See parallel in Luke 21:1–4. See also Légasse, *Marc*, 770–775; and Simon, "Marc 12."
36   Luke 12:13–21.
37   For an interpretation of this parable relating to wealth and desire, see Fitzmyer, *Luke I–IX*, 970–975; and Rindge, *Rich Fool*, esp. 1–7, 9–41, 217–230.

in Luke deplore the rich for not assisting the poor, but do not abhor wealth if it is used properly.[38]

The accounts quoted above seem to convey a theoretical ideology that characterizes movements in the beginning of their development as requiring fully devoted members in order to spread and take root. Jesus's followers had left their material pursuits to follow him and pursue their search for perfection and spirituality. Jesus sought to instill in them a certain pride and sense that their sacrifice was essential. However, in practical terms it will be shown that Jesus did not disconnect his movement from people that had property, including the wealthy. This seems to create a dichotomy between the theoretical abhorrence of property and wealth and the practical interaction with people and their property. On the one hand, the disciples of Jesus were required to give up private property and material aspirations, but, on the other hand, he sought to assist individuals who were sinners and outcasts, including the wealthy.

An interesting example of an interaction between Jesus and the rich comes from the story about the wealthy Joseph from Arimathea (Ramathaim in Judea),[39] who gives money to Governor Pontius Pilatus so that he would allow the former to bury Jesus after he was crucified. Joseph wraps Jesus in a sheet and buries him in a large grave.[40] This incident shows that Jesus had wealthy disciples who could use their connections in order to be received by the Roman Governor, pay money, and receive permission to bury their leader in a respectable grave. Another case is that of the tax collector:

> As he walked along, he saw Levi son of Alphaeus sitting at the tax collector's booth. "Follow me," Jesus told him, and Levi got up and followed him. While Jesus was having dinner at Levi's house, many tax collectors and sinners were eating with him and his disciples, for there were many who followed him. When the teachers of the law who were Pharisees saw him eating with the sinners and tax collectors, they asked his disciples: "Why does he eat with tax collectors and sinners?" On hearing this, Jesus

---

38   See Luke 1:53: "He has filled the hungry with good things but has sent the rich away empty." Also in Luke 6:24–25, he praises the poor that aspire for the "Kingdom of God" and the wealthy today that will be empty in the future. In Luke 14:11–14, he encourages the wealthy to invite to their table the poor and those who do not have property even though they cannot reciprocate. This is empowering the poor and acknowledging the ability of the rich to help them.
39   See Tsafrir et al., *Tabula Iudaea*, 67.
40   Mark 15:34–35; Matt. 27:57–60; Luke 23:50; John 19:38.

said to them, "It is not the healthy who need a doctor, but the sick. I have not come to call the righteous, but sinners."[41]

The tax collectors comprised a group in Jewish society; they possessed some wealth but were considered to be collaborators with the Roman authorities and therefore thieves stealing from the population. They were ostracized by the Jewish community. Jesus eats with them as well as with other "sinners." These people have property and are attached to it. Nevertheless, Jesus states that his mission is to be close to them.[42]

In Luke, there are a number of stories concerning tax collectors that are missing in Mark and Matthew. One of them is the story about the Pharisee and the tax collector who went to the Temple:

> But the tax collector stood at a distance. He would not even look up to heaven, but beat his breast and said, "God, have mercy on me, a sinner." "I tell you that this man, rather than the other, went home justified before God. For all those who exalt they will be humbled, and those who humble themselves will be exalted."[43]

The tax collector sees himself as a sinner but is praised by Jesus for not being self-righteous even though he is wealthy. In the following chapter in Luke, there is a similar story about another tax collector:

> Jesus entered Jericho and was passing through. A man was there by the name of Zacchaeus (Zakkaii); he was a chief tax collector and was wealthy. He wanted to see who Jesus was, but because he was short he could not see over the crowd. So he ran ahead and climbed a sycamore-fig tree to see him, since Jesus was coming that way. When Jesus reached the spot, he looked up and said to him, "Zacchaeus, come down immediately. I must stay at your house today." So he came down at once and welcomed him gladly. All the people saw this and began to mutter, "He has gone to be the guest of a sinner." But Zacchaeus stood up and said to the Lord,

---

41 Mark 2:14–17; Matt. 9:9–13; Luke 5:27–32. Compare also Luke 15:1–2, 7:29, 34, where a similar idea of the need to care for the sinners and tax collectors is mentioned.

42 See in addition Matt. 5:46, where "Matthew the tax collector" is mentioned as a disciple of Jesus. The mention of the profession is unique, and it indicates that this person corrected his ways but maintained his professional identity. See also Matt. 11:19; 21:32, 33; and Luke 3:12–13. In Romans 13:7, the tax is legal and part of proper administration; however, it is unclear what Jesus's position was regarding the tax. See Marcus, *Mark 1–8*, 224–232.

43 Luke 18:13–14.

"Look, Lord! Here and now I give half of my possessions to the poor, and if I have cheated anybody out of anything, I will pay back four times the amount." Jesus said to him, "Today salvation has come to this house, because this man, too, is a son of Abraham; For the Son of Man came to seek and to save the lost."[44]

In this case, it is clearly stated that the tax collector is wealthy. Jesus proclaims that he achieved salvation because he was modest, gave half of his possessions to the poor, and offered fourfold compensation to anyone he had done wrong to in the past. The dichotomy between this story and the story of the rich person who would not give up all his money can be explained by the fact that in the latter case Jesus's group had congealed and he could allow himself to accept that not all people will leave everything to join him. There is value in what people like Zacchaeus are willing to do.

Luke also mentions a number of wealthy women that supported Jesus and his disciples and who were very close with him. He writes:

> The Twelve were with him and also some women who had been cured of evil spirits and diseases: Mary (called Magdalene) from whom seven demons had come out; Joanna the wife of Chuza, the manager of Herod's household; Susanna; and many others. These women were helping to support them out of their own means.[45]

These women "supported them out of their own means," which means that they were quite wealthy. The wealthiest was probably Joanna, whose husband ran Herod's household. On the other hand, it seems that she did not leave her husband to join Jesus; instead, she supported him while remaining in her own household. Jesus is willing to accept the support of these women despite their wealth.[46]

In the previous chapter of his work, Luke mentions an encounter between Jesus and a high-ranking soldier:

> There was a centurion's servant, whom his master valued highly, who was sick and about to die. The centurion heard of Jesus and sent some elders of the Jews to him, asking him to come and heal his servant.[47]

---

44 Ibid., 19:2–10.
45 Ibid., 8:2–3. In Luke 3:1, 19, Luke defines Herod as "tetrarch of Galilee."
46 Bovon, *Saint Luc*, 387–991.
47 Luke 7:2–9.

The encounter was concluded as follows: "When Jesus heard this, he was amazed at him, and turning to the crowd following him, he said, 'I tell you, I have not found such great faith even in Israel.'"[48] He praises the centurion who is wealthy and high-ranking in the Roman army. It seems that the reason for these ties with the wealthy and even people close to the Roman authorities was for the purpose of expanding his circle of influence and receiving financial support for the disciples who were now dependent on him.

In addition, Luke 15 (11–32) relates the Parable of the Prodigal Son, which is about a wealthy man who has two sons. One son is loyal to his father and is hard-working while the other is frivolous and wastes his money. The latter repents and the father accepts him back despite his sins and the protests of the former. This parable portrays the wealthy father as a positive figure even though he is bound by material possessions.

Luke 16 discusses the rich but has a complex message. The first part (1–13) is the Parable of the Shrewd Manager. It discusses a parable of a rich man whose manager cheated him. In this parable, the rich man is good and honest and the manager is evil. In the second part (14–18), the rich man accuses the Pharisees of loving money and prophesies that they will be punished for it. This accusation is similar to the way in which Luke describes the wealthy in other places, saying that in the future they will have nothing. The last portion from passage 19 and onward is about the wealthy man and Lazarus the poor man. The story shows how in the World to Come Lazarus is embraced in Heaven and the formerly wealthy man is humbled. This last account stands in contrast to the description of the rich man in the beginning of the chapter. The resolution is that the author of Luke is criticizing the rich man at the end of the chapter because he represents the kind of person who does not help the poor and therefore he is to suffer in the future.[49] Another reason to criticize the rich is their "love of money" for its own sake and not just as a means for other things. This is a criticism that is found all throughout the NT and in Christian writings of later authors.[50]

It seems that the early Christian attitude toward the rich and toward property is further mediated in the works ascribed to Paul and his disciples. In the "Pauline narrative," the rich are not mentioned as individuals or as a group of

---

48   Luke 7:9. In Luke 3:12–14, soldiers and tax collectors come to Jesus for guidance. See also John's Second Letter 2:16, "pride of property" and 3:17 "world property." On the rich in the Gospels, see Metzger, *Luke Consumption*, 63–182, 183–199.
49   Bauckham, *Apocalypses*, 97–118. On Luke's attitude toward the rich, see Lehtipuu, "Rich and Poor"; and Rosenfeld, "Rabbinic Attitudes."
50   On the issue of wealth that results in the love of money, see 2 Tim. 6:9, 10, 17.

people.[51] However, between the lines it can be seen that a rich man is a bad person when he uses his wealth in a negative way.

In Acts (10:1–2, 7) there is a story about Cornelius, a centurion of the Italian Cohort that resided in Caesarea, who invites Paul and who is convinced to believe in Jesus. He has a few slaves, which is an indication of wealth.

In another Pauline text from the 50s CE, Paul writes of the Jews in a letter to the Romans: "But if their transgression means riches for the world, and their loss means riches for the Gentiles, how much greater riches will their full inclusion bring!"[52] He is telling the Christians of Rome that success has been given to the Gentiles because the Jews did not fulfill their mission. It would be much better if the Jews joined them. Wealth as a symbol for religious accomplishment is a common motif in Paul's writings. Sometimes, it is in contrast to "poverty" used as a symbol for spiritual poverty.[53]

A similar attitude can be found in the letters attributed to Paul that represent a later stage in the development of Christianity, in which the Jewish communities outside Palestine grow and Christianity spreads throughout the Roman Empire.[54] The wealthy person represents the illusion of material pursuit that distracts the true believer from religious and spiritual devotion, for which one must make due with little. However, there is an effort to get close to the wealthy and influence them.[55] Still, in one source from this period the

---

51 A number of individuals mentioned in Acts may have been wealthy. Lydia, who is mentioned in Acts 16:14–15, was a dealer of purple cloth, which was a distinguished profession. In verse 16 (see also 19), there is a discussion of a (slave) girl who made her master a fortune because of her ability to see the future. In Acts 19:23–27, 38, Demetrius the silversmith generated a great deal of profit for his workers, and in Acts 28:7 the head of the island of Malta hosts Paul.

52 Rom. 11:12.

53 See, for example, Rom. 9:23 and 11:33 on the wealth of the honor of God, as well as Eph. 1:18, 2:7, 3:8, 16; Phil. 4:19, 22; Thess. 2:2; and Heb. 11:26. On poor people who are benevolent, see 2 Cor. 8:2; and John 5:12; 18:15–17.

54 On the geographic spread of Christianity in the second and third centuries, see, for example, Rhee, *Poor*, esp. 40–48.

55 See, for example, 1 Tim. 6:6–19, which is relatively late and attributed to the middle of the second century CE. The attitude to the rich man is negative because he is constantly chasing after wealth. However in verse 17, he calls on the rich to trust God, do good deeds, and give charity. This indicates that wealth in and of itself is not evil and that one can be wealthy and righteous at the same time. See Malherbe, "Wealth," esp. 395–398. See also John 2:9, 3:18, 5:12, 6:15, 13:16, 18:3, 15, 16, 19. This last chapter is a eulogy for a city that was destroyed and its wealth lost.

wealthy are described as evil people who use their wealth unjustly and who hurt the poor.[56]

4 Summary

The NT has various stages when it comes to the attitude it conveys toward the rich. The earliest sources are very critical of wealth itself, while the later ones are more accommodating of wealth if it is used properly. There is a consistent theme that wealth is not to be pursued and that one should make due with little on the material side and pursue spirituality. Altogether, it seems to be an ambivalent attitude toward the rich. However, the efforts to spread Christianity were directed toward all walks of life, including the rich. The fundamental recognition that the wealthy will always play an important role in society and that their abilities can be harnessed for good gradually enters the Christian texts. The average wealthy person was regarded as lustful and selfish, although there is increasingly more room for the righteous among the wealthy.

In the sources that describe Jesus's ministry, there is a categorical denouncement of wealth and the presentation of wealthy people as unsalvageable, but, on the other hand, there are wealthy people assisting Jesus on his way and supporting him and his disciples economically. Jesus's ideology involved renouncing worldly possessions and emphasizing complete devotion to lofty endeavors. Despite the acceptance of the rich and the cooperation with them that he developed, Jesus continued to portray the wealthy and wealth as a symbol for the injustice present in his society. His criticism was directed at the wealthy in general, but primarily at the common stereotype of the wealthy person who spends his life pursuing money, indulging in pleasures of this world, and not relating to the plight of the sick and poor. In Luke's writings, there are fewer negative images of wealthy individuals than in the earlier Gospels, though the critical sayings are still dominant. Paul shows consideration to the rich in his ideology and in his orations, as well as in practice and in the portrayal of wealthy members of various communities.

---

56 James 1:9–11, which is ascribed to the second century, addresses the Jewish-Christian community saying that the rich person is destined to leave the world quickly. The poor are called "rich in belief." The rich pursue their pleasure and mistreat the poor. See also James 4:13; and 5:1–6. See also Johnson, *James*, 184–191.

5   The Term "Wealthy" in Early Rabbinic Literature

The roots "*ashir*" ("עשיר") and "*osher*" ("עושר") describe the wealthy and wealth. These terms appear in Tannaitic literature 214 times.[57] In most of these sources, the terms are contrasted with "poor" and indicate someone with means beyond those necessary to supply their own basic needs. In some cases, the sources specify the amount of money that the "wealthy" are expected to possess or spend, which tends to be quite modest. "Wealthy" is not limited to the top percentiles of society, but rather describes someone who is simply not so destitute as to be considered poor. This principle can be illustrated by a number of representative examples.

One source deals with *arakhin* (ערכין). An *erekh* means an "evaluation" and is a type of vow in which a person "evaluates" another person (or himself), thereby vowing to contribute "my, his, [or her] value" to the Temple. According to the Torah, the amount one is obligated to give is a function of the age and gender of the person "evaluated" and is between 5 and 50 shekels.[58] The donor is required to give the sum to the Temple only if he can afford it; if not, he may give less according to his financial ability.[59]

The Mishnah relates to a case in which the donor was rich when he made his vow but subsequently became poor or vice versa.[60] It states:

> There is no [amount of money] in connection with valuations less than a *sela*, or more than 50 *sela*. How so? [If] one gave a *sela* and then became rich he gives nothing [more]. [If he gave] less than a *sela* and he became rich, he gives 50 *sela*. If he had 5 *sela*, Rabbi Meir says: "He gives only one [of them]." Some sages say: "He gives all of them."[61]

The source identifies the Torah's "holy shekel" with the *sela*, which was equivalent to four *denarii*. That means that the sages defined a man as "rich" who could afford to donate 200 *denarii* to the Temple, and a "poor" person was

---

57 The count is according to Bar-Ilan University's Responsa Project. For comparison, the terms "poor" and "poverty" appear 598 times, and the terms "homeowner" and "homeowners" appear 366 times.
58 Lev. 27:1–8. The highest sum is for a male adult and the lowest is for a baby.
59 Scholars analyzed the extensive discussion of the laws of purity in the Mishnah, which was redacted long after the destruction of the Temple. See Kraemer, "Mishnah," 310–313; Neusner, *Purity*, 72–76, 86–89, and *Purity in Rabbinic*, 34–50, 129–138; and Stemberger, "On Neusner Purities."
60 *M. Arakhin* 4:2.
61 Ibid., 2:1. Translation and transliteration follows Neusner ed., 811.

THE "RICH"

someone who did not have that sum of money.[62] The ability to pay 200 *denarii* was not limited to the very wealthy; the Mishnah states elsewhere that he who has 200 *denarii* may not collect tithes with the poor, implying that such a person was above the poverty line.[63] In short, this source is calling "rich" someone who is simply "not poor."

The above source also shows that the term *"osher"* is relative just like the term *"ashir."* Indeed, in many sources *osher* refers to plentiful property. For example: "Tithes are a fence for wealth," implying that the one who gives the tithes will be wealthy.[64] Nevertheless, according to the tosefta that discusses the above mishnah, Rabbi Judah says that one who was rich and became poor "reached *osher* at one time" and therefore must bring the evaluation mandated of the rich. This means that the noun *"osher"* was used to represent modest wealth as well.[65]

Sources concerning the sacrifices mandated of a healed leper (or someone afflicted with another type of scale disease) provide an additional perspective on the definition of the word "wealthy." The Book of Leviticus states that when a leper is cured he is to sacrifice three sheep to become pure.[66] It designates a less expensive offering for a leper who cannot afford three sheep.[67] The Sifra—the Tannaitic Midrash on Leviticus—calls the leper who can afford three sheep a "wealthy leper."[68] The cost of three sheep was nine *sela* (36 *denarii*) at a time when the price of sheep was high.[69] The use of the term "rich" to refer to someone who has 36 *denarii* to spend on sacrifices shows that in this text "rich" refers to someone who is not so poor as to be unable to spend this sum of money.[70]

---

62 This is in the case where the "evaluated" person was a male in the prime of his life. In other cases, the sum is lower.

63 M. Pe'ah 8:8 and M. Ketubbot 4:7 state that this was the sum that an average woman would be paid if she lost her husband through death or divorce. Rabbi Judah in T. Arakhin 2:14 defines the man who has 200 *denarii* as someone who rose to become "rich."

64 M. Avot 3:13, 4:9 (Neusner ed., 683); M. Kiddushin 4:14 (Neusner ed., 498); M. Eduyot 2:9 (Neusner ed., 645).

65 The term *"osher"* appears 24 times in Tannaitic literature according to a computer search in the Bar-Ilan University Responsa Project.

66 Lev. 14:10.

67 See Lev. 14:21–22.

68 Sifra, Metsora 4:4.

69 M. Shekalim 2:4 states that the price of a sheep for sacrifice was one *sela*, the equivalent of four *denarii*. See Sperber, *Money and Prices*, 105.

70 Similarly, in M. Shekalim 5:3, a sinner who can afford an animal offering is a "rich sinner." Sifra Metsora 4:4 states that someone who had lost half his fortune of 100,000 *zuz* was still "rich" and not "poor." This indicates that the source recognizes the relativity of wealth.

Another source demonstrates the relative meaning of the term "wealth" in rabbinic literature:

> "On condition that I am rich"—this does not mean that he has to be the richest of the rich but only as rich as people in his town generally regard as rich.[71]

This source rules that a man who proposes marriage to a woman "on condition that I am rich" fulfills his condition if he is rich relative to his neighbors. It clearly says he does not have to be objectively extremely wealthy to be considered rich.

In conclusion, when the sages use the term "*ashir*" it indicates one of two things: (a) someone who is not poor—he has at least 200 *zuz*; or (b) someone who is rich relative to his neighbors. According to both uses, the term could relate to an individual who is merely slightly above the poverty line and, alternatively, to someone who is relatively wealthy.

In light of the above, we would expect there to be additional terms used to describe very wealthy people, those who truly belong to the upper echelons of society. Above, the term "the rich of the rich" describes that segment of society. In the next section, it will be shown that there are various other terms in rabbinic literature that point to absolute wealth. The presence of these terms indicates that the rabbis were aware of people who were extremely wealthy beyond the relative wealth discussed above.

6 Terminology for Wealth

The Tannaim use specific words, phrases, and expressions when they wish to refer to extreme wealth, extremely wealthy people, or to the upper stratum of society. Examples are "rich of the rich"[72] (see above), "sons of kings,"[73]

When searching for an example of someone who lost a lot of money but is still clearly rich, it gives the example mentioned above.

71 *T. Kiddushin* 3:8 (Lieberman ed., 288). The text discusses a man who betroths a woman on the condition that he is rich. See Lieberman, *Tosefta Kifshuta*, Nashim, 948–949, lines 42–45 [in Hebrew].

72 Ibid.

73 *M. Berakhot* 1:2; *M. Shabbat* 6:9, 14:4. Rabbi Simon, who was active in the middle of the second century, states: "All of Israel are sons of kings." For this reason, he stated that all Jews should be allowed to use luxurious objects on the Sabbath and festivals.

THE "RICH"

"great of the generation,"[74] "proud" and "the proud,"[75] "great,"[76] "politicians,"[77] "honored,"[78] "wealth and property,"[79] "*hon*,"[80] and "*rebo*."[81] It is unclear how these terms compare with each other, but the use of these terms indicates that the word "rich" ("*ashir*") alone does not indicate membership in the "upper class," but includes all strata of society that are not considered poor.

The above terms can be divided into two groups. One is strictly financial, like ריבוא, עשיר שבעשירים (*ashir sheba'ashirim, rebo*): the rich of the rich, the 10,000. The other terms apply to the social and political aspects of wealth and are typically accompanied by mention of luxury items. "Sons of kings" (*bnei melakhim* or princes) use persimmon oil not only because of their extreme wealth but also because of their royal status, which differentiates them from average people.[82] *Politiqin* ("citizens" or "politicians") consumed delicate foods because of their Roman citizenship or involvement in local politics.[83] It seems

---

74 *T. Avoda Zarah* 4:4; Gibson, *Social Stratification*, 70, identified a similar word in the NT.
75 Sifra, Behukotai, 2:5, starting "I shall break." Alon, *Studies*, 1:313–320, maintains that the source refers to very wealthy members of Jewish society.
76 *T. Sanhedrin* 4:1, Sifra, Emor, 2:2. See also *JT. Hagigah* 2:1.
77 *M. Terumot* 2:5. In the Kaufman MS, *politiqim*, and in the Lowe MS, *polaktin*; if it is not miscellaneous, it is possible that it is a different word that indicates social status.
78 *T. Yoma* 2:7–8; *T. Sotah* 10:10; *M. Ketubbot* 5:8. See also *T. Sukkah* 4:6, which describes the wealth of Alexandrian Jewry as "the honor of Israel."
79 *M. Kiddushin* 4:14. See also *M. Avot* 2:5, "he who amasses property"; *M. Hagigah* 1:5: "much property"; and *M. Bava Batra* 9:1–2. See also Sifre, Deuteronomy, 11 and 52, which state that the prince uses up the money he was given but keeps the *nekhasim*, indicating that the term refers to real estate. However, in Mekhilta de-Rabbi Yishmael, Yitro, Bakhodesh 8, 235, and in Sifre, Numbers, 118, the term "*nekhasim*" refers to portable belongings as well.
80 Sifre, Deuteronomy, 355. Use of this term by the sages was rare, unlike in the Qumran literature and in the NT.
81 *M. Arakhin* 4:3: "*Ribbo sefinot*" ("ships"). See also *T. Yoma* 1:22; *T. Sukka* 4:6; Sifre, Deuteronomy, 306; and Midrash Tannaim, Devarim 32:2.
82 On the definition of luxury items, see Wallace-Hadrill, "Roman Luxury," 148–149.
83 Albeck, *Mishnah*, Zeraim, 184 explains the term as referring to the officials of the city that administer it. This explanation is logical based on the contrast to a previous term that was used, "*benei medina*," which refers to the common city dwellers. Krauss, *Lehnwörter* II, 425, and Jastrow, *Dictionary*, 1141b, translate "city people." Neusner, 96, translates this as "city people," but he adds "and therefore of higher quality," which indicates that they are consumed by the wealthy. Danby, *The Mishnah*, 55, translates this term as "better people." It is a unique form in the Mishnah and is probably taken from the Greek word πολίτης. Liddell and Scott, *Lexicon*, 1435a, translates it as "official." However, See Montanari, *Dictionary*, 1702, "πολιτικός." He states that the term can refer to city citizens or officials. As stated above, the latter translation is more likely because the Mishnah relates to citizens previously using a different term.

that "sons of kings" was a category wealthier and more powerful than the "rich of the rich," as will be shown below.

In summary, when the sages specifically discuss the extremely wealthy, they tend to add an additional adjective to the word "rich" to indicate that a man is "really" rich. Some of the terms relate to the amount of wealth such as "rich of rich," and others, like "son of kings," relate to the person's social status.

7 Rabbinic Attitudes toward the Rich and Powerful

When analyzing society according to economic factors, the Tannaitic sources divide society into "rich" and "poor." There is no mention of middling economic groups, although there is plenty of evidence that such groups actually existed.[84] The explanation is that the terms "rich" and "poor" are actually flexible according to the context in which they are used: there are various levels of wealth and poverty, and thus the terms actually cover all possible strata of society. "Poor" includes all groups of people who lack some basic necessities and who are entitled to collect the tithes left for the poor.[85] Whoever is financially independent is "rich," and there are additional terms to help determine the level of wealth.[86] Thus, most members of society were actually considered "rich."[87] The sources perceive social mobility from rich to poor and vice versa as plausible, and they extensively discuss the legal ramifications of such situations. If this was only a theoretical possibility, it would not be mentioned so often in rabbinic sources.[88]

There are numerous sources that show that the rabbis had a positive attitude toward wealth and the wealthy. Rabbinic law showed consideration for the wealthy by lessening the physical obligations of the wealthy person in comparison to the poor person.[89] One sage stated: "Wealth is not a result of one's choice of profession," which indicates that it is not bad to have wealth, but it

---

84   See Rosenfeld and Perlmutter, "Landowners."
85   See Rosenfeld and Perlmutter, "The Poor."
86   See, for example, *T. Kiddushin* 3:8; and Lieberman, *Tosefta Kifshuta*, Nashim, 949.
87   See Rosenfeld and Perlmutter, "Rich," and "Relatively Rich."
88   For examples, see *M. Ketubbot* 6:6; *M. Gittin* 3:7; *M. Kiddushin* 2:2; *M. Arakhin* 2:1; *M. Keritot* 6:8, *M. Negaim* 14:11; *T. Sabbath* 6:16, *T. Ketubbot* 5:9, *T. Kiddushin* 2:4, *T. Arakhin* 1:5, 2:14, *T. Keritot* 4:13–14, *T. Negaim* 9:8–9; Sifra, Chova, parsha 10, chapter 18; Sifra, Metzora, parsha 4; Sifre, Deuteronomy, 48; and Midrash Tannaim, Devarim 15:8 (Hoffman ed., 82).
89   *M. Bikurim* 3:8: the priests return the empty *bikurim* basket to the rich but not to the poor. In *M. Eruvin* 4:9 and *T. Eruvin* 3:17, the rich can send their *eruv* but the poor go to the place on foot. See also *T. Eduyot* 4:3; and *T. Shviit* 8:1. On the other hand, there is consideration regarding expecting the poor to fulfill commandments that require economic

THE "RICH"   159

is not dependent on the vocation chosen.⁹⁰ The Mishnah discusses a family, in which one son is rich and the other poor.⁹¹ The sources say that rich and poor should be treated equally. A judge should not extort from the rich man nor prefer him to the poor man.⁹² On the other hand, there are also demands upon the rich. The rich man should not avoid his religious responsibilities and must help others with his money and his efforts.⁹³ When a woman marries, her conditions in marriage and compensation in a case of divorce, or the death of her spouse, depend on her and her spouse's joint economic level: "She goes up with him but not down."⁹⁴ It states in the Torah that the judges should be *"anshei chayil"* ("powerful people"), and in an anonymous midrash that discusses the proper character for a judge, these words are seen as saying that *anshei chayil* are "rich, people with money."⁹⁵ This interpretation shows that rabbinic circles connected power and money, preferring a rich judge, who is not in need of bribes, to a poor one, who may be tempted to accept bribery. This idea was not merely theoretical. Rabbinic sources speak of *asara batlanim*—ten idle people who differentiate a town from a village:

> What is a large town? One in which there are ten men available at all times [to form a quorum], [if there are] fewer than this, lo, this is a village.⁹⁶

This group of "ten idle men" without which a city is not a city despite the large number of people residing in it should be interpreted as "ten men of leisure." These people do not have to work all day and are therefore available to handle city affairs as the unofficial municipal government of the city. Their presence is essential for defining the place as a city and not a village.⁹⁷ These people belong to the highest economic level in society. They have fields or business-

---

investment. See *T. Arakhin* 2:15–17. There were rules created to preserve the honor of the poor in *T. Niddah* 9:16.

90   *M. Kiddushin* 4:14. The statement is ascribed to the Sage Rabbi Meir, who was active in the middle of the second century CE. See also *JT. Berakhot* 9:1, 13b, which treats rich and poor equally.

91   *M. Bava Batra* 10:7; *T. Bava Batra* 11:12.

92   *M. Bava Metzia* 9:13, *T. Bava Metzia* 10:10. See, concerning the poor, *M. Arakhin* 4:1–2; *T. Pe'ah* 3:11; *T. Bava Metzia* 7:19; and *T. Sanhedrin* 1:8.

93   *M. Negaim* 14:11–12; *T. Nazir* 6:1, *T. Pe'ah* 4:19.

94   *T. Ketubbot* 4:9–10. See there that the *ketubba* of the woman is also a derivative of the economic level of the couple. See also *T. Ketubbot* 7:3.

95   Mekhilta de Rabbi Yishmael, Yitro, Amalek, parsha 2 (Horowitz ed., 198); Mekhilta de-Rabbi Shimeon bar Yohai, 18–21 (Epstein-Melamed ed., 133).

96   *M. Avot* 3:1 (Neusner ed., 317). See also *M. Megillah* 1:3.

97   See Safrai, *Economy*, 37, 38–50, 135.

es run by managers, and are free during the day in the same way the elite in Rome are.

At the same time that the rabbis attribute much value to the rich, they also state that the judge should not say: "How do I hurt the honor of the rich for a *denar*?"[98] In some sources, a link is mentioned between the priesthood and wealth: "Most priests are wealthy."[99] In one place, wealth is mentioned as something to be proud of.[100] One way to become wealthy is to save money slowly.[101] The wealth of a Gentile resident of the Land of Israel is attributed to his contact with the Jewish people.[102]

Indeed, there is also criticism of the wealthy. One source states that the wealthy will always have more even in the desert where all people were ostensibly equal; another source states that the rich acquire property at the expense of the poor.[103] The rich man feeds his children beef and fish and gives them good wine to drink.[104] He likes the company of people of similar wealth.[105]

One of the reasons that the general attitude toward the rich in rabbinic literature is positive is that there were prominent sages who were wealthy, though sages came from all economic levels in society.[106] The sages knew that they could not operate without help from the wealthy, and the poor needed the

---

98 Sifre, Deuteronomy, piska 17 (Finkelstein ed., 28–29). See Midrash Tannaim, Devarim 16:19 (Hoffman ed., 97); and Sifre, Devarim, piska 144 (Finkelstein ed., 198).

99 Ibid., 352 (Finkelstein ed., 409). There is a statement there that relates to the fact that many regular Jews lack bread. On the unique status of the priest even after the destruction of the Temple, see Stern, "Priesthood"; Goodman, *Ruling Class*, index, s.v. High Priest; Choi, *Jewish Leadership*, 130–167; Schwartz, *Jews*, esp. s.v. priest; Levine, *The Ancient Synagogue*, index, s.v. priests; Meyers and Strange, *Archaeology, Rabbis, Christianity*, 92–109; Strange, "Archaeology Judaism," esp. 664–667; and Irsai, "Priesthood."

100 Mekhilta de-Rabbi Shimeon bar Yohai 12: 36 (Epstein-Melamed ed., 31).

101 Sifre, Deuteronomy, piska 48 (Finkelstein ed., 108). See Midrash Tannaim, Devarim, 11:22 (Hoffman ed., 41).

102 Sifra, Behar, parsha 6, chapter 8 (Weiss ed., 110a).

103 Ibid., Mekhilta de-Rabbi Yishmael, Beshalach, Vayisa, parsha 4 (Horowitz ed., 167). The source is rare, as it serves as a voice for the poor that is usually absent in ancient literature, including ancient rabbinic literature.

104 See Sifre, Deuteronomy, piska 37 (Finkelstein ed., 71).

105 Sifre Zuta, Numbers, 35:25 (Horowitz ed., 334). Indeed, the rabbinic law states that when banishing a wealthy man for unintentional murder, it is impossible to consider his wish to be in the company of similar people.

106 There were rich sages in the first and second generations after the Temple was destroyed, such as Raban Gamaliel (85–115 CE), Rabbi Eliezer son of Hyrcanus (70–110 CE), Rabbi Tarfon (100–130 CE), and Rabbi Elazar son of Azariah (90–120 CE). See also Rosenfeld, *Torah Centers*, index.

wealthy to provide charity and work. Therefore, we find in Tannaitic sources much understanding for the rich.[107]

8   Summary

The sages divided society into two categories: those who have and those who do not. Those who do not have are entitled to benefit from the charitable assets designated by the Torah and community charity, as well as from economic leniency in the sacrifice of sin offerings and other religious obligations. Those who have must give to those who do not and fulfill all religious responsibilities. Among those who have, there are also groups of people who were very rich. The attitude of the rabbis toward those groups is positive. The rabbis were conservative. They did not support social revolution and collaborated with the wealthy members of society to supply the people with their needs. In judgments, the rabbis were instructed to disregard social status and treat all people equally. They criticized the wealthy when they exploited their situation to gain wealth unjustly.

Comparing the NT and rabbinic sources, it is possible to state that in principle the attitude to the rich in rabbinic sources is much more positive than in the NT, which has strong elements of social revolution in it. The criticism of the rich for doing unjust acts is similar but much sharper in NT sources. The NT does not see a legitimate tie between wealth and leadership, while rabbinic sources see this as an attribute because the rich are freer to resist bribery and judge everyone equally. Early Christian sources see wealth and material belongings as an obstacle to religious devotion and commitment to God, and convey the message that in order to become close to God one must renounce his wealth. However, there are sources that show that Jesus had rich people who were close to him. In the later generations of church leaders, the attitude to the rich mellowed, as Christian society became bigger and included a more varied social membership. The churches needed the support of the wealthy in order to take care of their congregations.

9   Subdivision of the Wealthy Stratum

Although the terminology of wealth does not reveal a clearly defined hierarchy of wealth, other sources do provide an economic calculation for various levels

---

107   On Roman writers' attitudes toward the rich and wealthy, see Morgan, *Morality*, 47, 90–94.

of wealth. In a statement ascribed to the first century CE sage Rabbi Elazar son of Azariah, quoted in the Tosefta, he recommends different lifestyles for people of various levels of wealth:[108]

> And so did R. Elazar b. Azariah say: "He who has ten *maneh* should get himself vegetables[109] in a pot every day. Twenty *maneh*—should get himself vegetables in a pot and a pan. Fifty *maneh* should eat a *litra* of meat from Friday to Friday; a hundred *maneh*, a *litra* of meat every day."[110]

R. Elazar ben Azariah mentions two foods whose consumption characterizes the rich: green vegetables (*yereq*) and meat. Another source attributes the consumption of green vegetables to the poor and the consumption of fish and meat to the rich.[111] Both sources show that one of the main distinctions between the rich and the poor was their diet. In addition, the source distinguishes four levels of wealth. The wealthiest level that the Tosefta mentions is where someone has capital of 100 *maneh*. The second wealthiest level is one at which a person has 50 *maneh* and he can eat meat once a week. The third level of wealth is one at which a person has 20 *maneh* and can eat greens in his skillet as well as in his pot. The lowest level is one at which a person only has 10 *maneh*—he may eat greens in his pot every day. These four levels can be divided into two: (1) greens eaters: 10–20 *maneh*; and (2) meat eaters: 50–100 *maneh*.[112]

The wealthiest level that the Tosefta mentions is one where a person has 1,000 *maneh* of capital. Given that 1 *maneh* = 100 *denarii*, this amounts to 10,000 *denarii*, which translates in Roman terms to 40,000 HS (*sestertii*). An additional Tannaitic source indicates that this sum was considered to define the very rich man.[113] However, this sum was very low compared to levels of wealth re-

---

108 Rabbi Elazar ben Azariah was considered very wealthy himself. See *M. Sotah* 9:15. See also below.
109 *T. 'Arakhin* 4:27 (Neusner ed., 5:204). The original word in the Mishnah is "*yereq*." *Yereq* refers to specifically green leaves that were rare and hard to obtain in the summer, while vegetables include also vegetables that were common all year-round and that were inexpensive.
110 In contrast, in the third century during the economic crisis in the Roman Empire that devaluated the currency (235–284 CE), the *Codex Hermogenianus* (295 CE; 4:48.210) defines "poor" as the state of having less than 50 *aurei*, which is equivalent to less than a pound of gold. See also Corbier, "Coinage," 430–431.
111 Sifri Devarim, Ekev, parsha 37. "Your father fed you greens and legumes and I feed you meat and wine."
112 For a comparison to the cost of living in the Roman Empire, see Frier, "Subsistence Annuities."
113 *T. Ketubbot* 15:1.

corded in Roman society, even in the smaller, provincial Roman towns. For the sake of comparison, in order to belong to the city council of the medium-sized port city of Puteoli in Italy one had to have an annual income (not capital) of 100,000 HS, which was the equivalent of 25,000 *denarii*.[114]

10 The Wealthy in Rabbinic Narrative

Rabbinic sources contain descriptions of events involving the wealthy. The Mishnah states that after Rabbi Elazar son of Azariah died there were no more wealthy sages.[115] According to Tosefta *Ketubbot* (5:1), Rabbi Tarfon, active 90–130 CE, betrothed 300 women in order to feed them priestly tithes during a drought year. Even if these numbers are exaggerated, they demonstrate the wealth of Rabbi Tarfon and the large quantity of tithes he received even in lean years. There is also a story about the daughter of Nakdimon son of Guryon, one of the wealthy in Jerusalem on the eve of the destruction of the Temple, who was allocated 500 gold pieces per day to purchase cosmetics and who subsequently complained that the sum was too low.[116] Tosefta *Moed Katan* mentions the golden ornaments worn by Rabban Gamaliel's (of Yavneh) two sons and the slaves who served them.[117] Another source states that the glory of the sages was their wealth.[118]

Rabbi Judah the Prince (Rabbi) serves as another example of a wealthy sage. The Tosefta states:

> R. Simeon b. Judah says in the name of R. Simeon: "Beauty, power, riches, long life, honor, glory and children for the righteous are a benefit to them and a benefit to the world." Simeon b. Menasiah says: "These are the seven virtues which sages listed for righteous men, and all of them have been realized in Rabbi and his sons."[119]

Sources in the Jerusalem Talmud (JT) relate incidental information concerning the wealth of Rabbi Judah the Prince.[120] The JT mentions strife between

---

114 Jones, *Bankers*, 37; Katsari, *Monetary System*, 169–171.
115 *M. Sotah* 9:15.
116 *T. Ketubbot* 5:8.
117 *T. Moed Katan* 2:8.
118 *T. Sotah* 15:3.
119 *T. Sanhedrin* 11:8 (Neusner ed., 233–234).
120 The probably is much exaggeration in this description, but it shows that the collective memory of the Jews attributes wealth to Rabbi Judah the Prince. On the Palestinian

Rabbi, who we can understand as Rabbi Judah the Prince, and Rabbi Pinkhas son of Ya'ir regarding the mules that Rabbi owned.[121] The Roman dignitary Antoninus gave Rabbi 2,000 fields to be cultivated by sharecroppers.[122] He purchased gourds for supplying the royal palace.[123] Rabbi's bulls were mated with those of the royal court.[124] He had a ship for transport of barrels of fish, indicating his involvement in import and export.[125] He had a *karon* ("wagon" or "cart") for land transport.[126] Another source mentions 24 *kerayot*—"cities"— or *keronot* that belonged to Rabbi.[127]

A large luxurious structure was found in Beit She'arim.[128] Some scholars are convinced that this house and its vicinity can be dated to the period of Rabbi Judah the Prince. They claim that the necropolis of Beit She'arim, full of graves of rich people from the Diaspora as well as local citizens, attracted the wealthy as a burial place because Rabbi Judah the Prince's headquarters were in the town. Of course, the identification is not definite. For our purposes, the excavations point to a wealthy Jewish population in Beit She'arim in this period. The house can be used to study the lifestyle of those wealthy individuals.[129]

11   Rich Individuals in Roman Palestine

Important, though sparse, historical information can be found in epigraphic sources concerning the levels of wealth of the upper strata of Jewish society in Roman Palestine. This information will be described in chronological order.

There is some evidence concerning Jews who were part of the local aristocracy prior to the third century CE. Tiberias and Sepphoris, both of which had a Jewish majority at the time, minted coins in the first century CE that mention members of the *boule*. In all provincial areas of the Roman Empire, the *boule*

Talmud as a historical source, see Millar, "Transformations," 154–155. On the wealth of Rabbi Judah the Prince, see Stern, "Rabbi," 207–210.

121   *JT. Demai* 1:3 (22:1).
122   *JT. Shviit* 6:1 (36:4).
123   *JT. Ma'aser Sheni* 4:1 (54:4).
124   *JT. Yevamot* 4:10 (6:1).
125   *JT. Avodah Zarah* 2:7 (42:2).
126   *JT. Shabbat* 17:1 (16:1). See also *JT. Avodah Zarah* 5:4 (44:4).
127   *JT. Sanhedrin* 1:2 (18:3). Regarding the proper reading of this source, see Lieberman, *Sifre Zuta*, 145–148; and Safrai, "The Localities," 3–4.
128   See below in the comparative table of houses, no. 4.
129   See Avigad and Mazar, "Beth She'arim," 239. For the scholars that identify the house as belonging to Rabbi Judah the Prince, see Tepper and Tepper, *Beit She'arim*, 73–75, 98–128; Levine, "Bet Shearim Patriarchal," 208–211, 218; and Weiss, "Burial Practices."

would have comprised wealthy individuals.¹³⁰ A sarcophagus of a man named Alexa was found in a cave in the Lydda area and was dated to the beginning of the second century CE. It had an inscription that read: Πυρίνου ν[εωτέ]ρο[υ] καὶ Μαλθάκης υἱῶν Ἀλκίου Σίμωνος Γωβάρ ("Belonging to Pyrinus the Younger and Malthace the Sons of Alkios [the Son?] of Simon Gobar [or Son of Gobar]").¹³¹ Inscriptions and decorations of graves are clear indicators of wealth.

In the third century, Ulpian reports that Septimius Severus and his son Antoninus (Caracalla) had decreed (sometime between 196 and 211 CE) that Jews could hold city offices (*honores*) and that functions could be imposed on them—but only such as did not offend their *superstitio*.¹³² This implies that there were observant Jews in the Empire, including Palestine, who were wealthy enough to hold city offices.

The Theodosian Code contains a law from 321 CE attributed to Constantine the Great that allowed for the inclusion of Jews on the town council—the *boule* or *curia*:¹³³

> IDEM A. Decurionibus Agrippinensibus Cuncctis ordinibus generali lege concedimus Iudaeos vocari ad curiam. Verum ut aliquid ipsis ad solacium pristinae observationis relinquatur, binos vel ternos privilegio perpeti patimur nullis nominationibus occupari.
>
> DAT. III ID. DEC. CRISPO II ET CONSTANTINO II CC. CONSS¹³⁴

> 11.12.321 The same Augustus to the Decurions of Colonia Agrippiniensis. We grant to all the *curias* in a general law that the Jews shall be nominated to the *curia*, but in order to leave them something of the ancient custom as a solace, we allow them in a perpetual privilege that two or three in every *curia* shall not be occupied through any nominations whatsoever. Given on the third day before the ides of December, in the consulate

---

130   Schürer, *History*, 2:172–176, 178–183; Katsari, *Monetary System*, 169–171. Numismatic findings confirm the existence of the *boule* of Tiberias. See Meshorer, *Coins Israel*, 34–37; Kindler and Stein, *City Coinage*, 230–248; Hirschfeld and Foerster, "Tiberias"; Meyers and Meyers, "Sepphoris"; Meshorer et al., *Coins*, 67–72; Rosenfeld and Weistuch, "Coinage"; and Syon, *Small Change*, 200–218, and s.v. Tiberias, Zippori. In the first centuries CE, Egyptian cities were not allowed to convene a *boule*. See Jones, *Cities Eastern*, 295–348; and Bowman and Rathbone, "Cities Egypt," 107–127.

131   Clermont-Ganneau, *Archaeological*, 2:266–267, 344–349; Klein, *Corpus Inscriptionum*, 58–59. Rosenfeld, "Gezer Boundary," 344, contains an extensive discussion of this inscription, its dating, and the names mentioned in it.

132   *Digest* l. 2.3.3; Linder, *Legislation Jews*, no. 2.

133   See Linder, *Legislation Jews*, no. 7, and "Legal Status."

134   See *Codex Theodosianus* 16.8.3. The date given was December 11, 321 CE.

of the Caesars, Crispus for the second time and Constantine for the second time.[135]

Indeed, it is recorded that Jews in the Diaspora served on a local *boule* as early as the third century CE. In the first two centuries CE, Roman law demanded possession of property worth 100,000 HS in order to be a member of the *boule* in the provinces. Hence, the presence of Jews who were members of this governing body is evidence that there were Jews who were wealthy, at least on a local level.[136]

A papyrus found in Oxyrinchus, Egypt, dating to 291 CE mentions a certain "βουλευτ[ο]υ" from the town of Ono in Roman Palestine, who was involved in redeeming a Jewish slave in conjunction with the local Jewish community.[137] From this inscription, we learn that there was a *boule* in the town of Ono in the third century CE, and that at least one Jew was a member of that *boule*. In addition, Levine mentions a synagogue in Tiberias dating to the beginning of the fourth century called the "Boule Synagogue," though it is unclear what this name meant.[138]

12   Archeology of Wealth

There are two complementary statements regarding determining levels of wealth through archeological finds. Balzaretti writes: "Indeed, determining the status of an individual through archaeology is difficult and connecting him to the discovery of his estate with any degree of certainty is a challenge."[139] On the other hand, Sodini writes: "It is certainly easier to detect wealth through

---

135   Translated by Linder, *Legislation Jews*, no. 2 (in the note).
136   See Trebilco, *Jewish Communities*, 60–66; Ameling, *Inscriptiones*, 362, no. 172. He mentions a Jewish member of the *boule* from Akmonia in Phrygia, Asia Minor. T. Flavius Alexandros, died in 243/4 CE, was βουλεύσας, a member in the city council, and also βουλαρχιά, the president of the city council. See also Ameling, ibid., c.v. Βουλευτής.
137   *P.Oxy.* 9:239–241.1205; Tcherikover et al., *CPJ*, 3:33–35, papyrus no. 473.
138   Levine, *The Ancient Synagogue*, 207; *JT. Shekalim* 7:3 (50, 3); *JT. Ta'anit* 1:2 (64, 1). He says it may be that members of the *boule* prayed there, but it may just indicate geographic proximity to the *boule*.
139   Balzaretti, "Curtis," 104. However, see Mouritsen, "Mobility," 63, on a patrician by the name of *A. Umbricius Scaurus* of Pompeii who was commemorated at death by inscriptions and a large *domus* (vii Ins. Occ. 25–35) that is thought to have belonged to him. Pompeii is a special case. There, the destruction was sudden and the site buried and preserved until excavated. See Allison, "Roman Households," 121–122. Compare Allison, *Pompeian Households*.

archaeology than to detect poverty.... The rich are visible: they possess land, houses, goods of every kind, even their dress indicates their social importance."[140] Nevertheless, our ability to trace the wealth of an individual through archeological excavation has been highly impaired due to reuse and theft over the course of history, making archeological findings partial at best.

For this reason, one must compare archeological findings with literary evidence—a complex task requiring much care and caution.[141] Because this study focuses on an entire stratum within society, not an individual, findings that indicate wealth are sufficient, even if it is not always possible to discover the owner of the wealth.

Four levels of wealth can be found in Tannaitic sources: (1) "not poor"; (2) "relatively wealthy"; (3) "extremely wealthy"; and (4) "royal." This division indicates the scarcity of people who had real aristocratic fortunes in Jewish society after the destruction of the Temple, further making it difficult to locate them in archeological remains. Below, the inquiry will answer the question of whether a similar division of wealth can be seen in archeological findings: are there various levels of wealth, or is there only a single type of wealth?

"Sons of kings" seems to be the term the rabbis used to describe the highest level of wealth with which they were familiar. This term could potentially refer to individuals such as the Roman governor, who was one of the wealthiest in the district if not the wealthiest. Archeologists have identified a palace discovered in Caesarea that they believe could be the governor's palace.[142]

Literary sources describing Jerusalem before the destruction of the Temple discuss the "rich of Jerusalem." Archeological finds have uncovered the homes of some of these extremely wealthy people. Excavations in the upper city of Jerusalem uncovered the "Burnt House," (110 sq. m.), the "Herodian House" (200 sq. m.), and the "Great Mansion" (600 sq. m.), all massive houses equipped with ritual baths and stone vessels, to allow for the observance of ritual purity, as well as other luxuries.[143] These findings were all from before the destruction of the Temple and Jerusalem in the year 70 CE.[144] In addition, examination of

---

140   Sodini, "Archaeology," 43–44, 52. Part of this quote was cited in the introduction to this volume.
141   On the difficulty of comparing archaeological findings to literary sources, see Smith, *Roman Villas*, 5–6.
142   See Netzer, "Caesarea Palace"; and Burrell, "Caesarea Palace."
143   Excavators suspect that the "Burnt House" extended beyond the area of excavation. See: H. Geva, "Chapter 1: Stratigraphy and Architecture," in H. Geva (ed.), *Jewish Quarter Excavation in the Old City of Jerusalem Conducted by N. Avigad 1969–1982, Vol. IV* (Jerusalem: The Israel Exploration Society, 2010), 33–34.
144   Avigad, *Jerusalem*, 84–94, 95–120, 120–139; Hirschfeld, *Dwelling*, 57–56; Meyers, "Gendered Space," 51–53.

the burial tombs from the first century CE in the Jerusalem necropolis that was used primarily until the destruction of the Temple shows that the Jerusalem elite invested much money in the burial of their family members, using expensive sarcophagi with decorations and inscriptions.[145]

After the destruction of the Temple in 70 CE, the spectrum of wealth that existed in Jewish society was probably limited. Below, a number of criteria that can be used to determine the level of wealth will be suggested. Fulfillment of even one of these criteria meant that one was a wealthy person. The quantity and quality of the find will indicate the extent of the owner's wealth.

Examining houses is one of the most obvious ways to detect wealth: what could the inhabitants afford to build? What did they possess? Marcus Vitruvius Pollio states that a Roman-style building has three important components that determine its grandeur: fine workmanship, magnificence, and architectural composition. When a building has a magnificent appearance, the expenditure of those who control it is praised. When the craftsmanship is good, the supervision of the works is approved, but when it has a graceful effect due to the symmetry of its proportions, the site is the glory of the architect.[146]

Ellis suggested the following criteria for identifying a house belonging to the wealthy:[147]

– A villa that dominates the surrounding area in its size and construction[148]
– The building demonstrates Roman influence in the presence of a dining area—*triclinium* of a large size—and if not, a reception area or large room for hosting
– The house could contain an *atrium* or peristyle[149]

---

145 See Peleg-Barkat, "Elite," and "Decoration."
146 Vitruvius, *De arch.* 6.8.9. He does not relate to size, as that varies according to urban and geographic constraints as will be explained below. Laurence, "Space and Text," 10, says of Vitruvius's work: "Vitruvius was creating a code from established forms yet interpreting those forms to reach an ideal formula."
147 Ellis, *Roman Housing*, esp. 6–9. On grading the worth of houses, see also Wallace-Hadrill, "Roman Luxury," 151–156. His criteria are similar to those of Ellis. His criteria are good for middling groups as well as the wealthy. In this chapter, the focus is on the wealthy.
148 On the size of homes as an indication of social status, see Wallace-Hadrill, "Roman Atrium," 222. We should clarify that the size of a rich man's city dwelling was constrained by the buildings surrounding it and was often smaller than village houses, though better decorated. On the other hand, in the country it was possible to build larger homes due to the availability of land. Vitruvius, *De arch.* 6.6:1, states that the size of the house in the rural context should be a factor of the size of the estate that surrounds it. In other words, the wealthier landlord builds a country house larger than his urban house.
149 Regarding the *triclinium*, see works cited by Uytterhoeven, "Housing in Late Antiquity," 50–53.

- The house would have decorations containing mosaics, stuccos, pillars, and other decorations[150]
- The house would have various luxuries such as a bathhouse, toilet, pools, running water,[151] and a separate kitchen[152]

Below are examples of wealthy dwellings of various levels and kinds that were likely to have been used by Jews during the period after the destruction.

In Sepphoris, a "large house" (200 sq. m.) was found on the western acropolis. Though previously identified as belonging to a Gentile, three ritual baths were found (though only two were in use simultaneously), and Jewish artifacts were found in an underground vault beneath the house. In addition, no pig bones were found in the house on the Roman level, while at the Byzantine level 20 percent of the faunal finds were from pigs. From the early Roman period, incense shovels and stone vessels were found, hinting at the possibility that the house was owned by priests.[153]

Also in Sepphoris, the "Dionysus House" is a large structure (300 sq. m.) surrounding an epistyle courtyard. The walls are decorated with frescoes and the floors are covered with mosaics containing scenes from the myths of Dionysus. A *mikveh* found in the house along with other pools and a private bathroom convinced Meyers and Nagy that the house was used by the local Jewish community.[154]

In lower Sepphoris, among dwellings of lesser quality that do not contain the amenities of the extremely wealthy dwellings described above, there were a number of structures that had one room "lavishly decorated with a mosaic floor."[155] These seem to belong to an "upper middle class group" that could

---

150   See Bopp, "Hauran," 63, diag. 1–2. Regarding the various kinds of decorations, see Bopp, *Culture Hauran*, 73–88, esp. 75–76.

151   Hales, *House and Social*, 229; and Uytterhoeven, "Housing in Late Antiquity," 54–56, posits that extremely wealthy Romans built private bathhouses within their homes in order to avoid mixing with Romans of lesser status in the public bathhouses. It is possible that in the east, where towns did not always have bathhouses, the wealthy would erect a private one because the city did not have one or the one that existed was of inferior quality. Smith, *Roman Villas*, 238–239, links the establishment of bathhouses in the provinces with Roman influence on city planning. Alston, "Houses in Roman Egypt," 31, also uses the bathhouse as an indication of a wealthy household.

152   Uytterhoeven, "Housing in Late Antiquity," 56.

153   Meyers, "Gendered Space," 51–53. However, as stated above, there is evidence of Jewish ownership of the house up until the Byzantine period. See also Meyers, "Sepphoris Pools."

154   Meyers, "Problems," 54–58. See also Nagy et al., *Sepphoris*, 198. Similar dwellings of the wealthy were found in Ramat Hanadiv. See Hirschfeld, *Ramat Hanadiv*, 16–85, and "Property versus Poverty."

155   See Weiss, "Dwellings Sepphoris."

afford some aspects of luxury but not all. This group corresponds to the "relatively rich" found in Jewish literature.

In Meiron, Meyers excavated two houses that belonged to a "well-to-do farmer or agriculturist." One he called "the Patrician House" and next door to it was the "Lintel House." The houses are relatively large and have many amenities compared to the average farmer's house found in Meiron and in other locations.[156]

A stark example of the difference between archeological remains left by a rich person and those left by a "very rich" person can be found in an excavation recently conducted in the Beit Guvrin area. The excavators found the remains of a house that originally was a simple "courtyard house" containing nine rooms, one of them a kitchen.[157] After the Bar Kokhba Revolt, it was remodeled to accommodate a luxurious Roman lifestyle. The area of the house was enlarged to 600 sq. m.; one of the rooms was changed so that it could accommodate a large *triclinium* with a mosaic floor; a latrine was added; the kitchen was moved and tiled; a bathhouse was constructed with pools and running water; and the whole area was surrounded by a wall.[158]

In recent excavations in Yodfat, Aviam mentions discovering a "working-class" district that contained modest-sized homes. On the same site, it may be possible to identify the "relatively rich," who can be categorized by the fact that most of the structures were similar in size and in construction materials, but two contained small ritual baths. These baths indicate not only the religious devotion of the inhabitants of these two houses but also the level of financial ability to build these baths and fill them with water. Next to it, the excavators mention a "small luxurious quarter" that contained "large mansions" with walls decorated with frescoes in the second Pompeian style as well as a floor decorated with a fresco whose presence indicates its belonging to the higher echelons of society.[159]

In order to make sure that the above-mentioned wealthy dwellings are indeed representative of the dwellings of the wealthy in Roman Palestine, we have analyzed and present to you below a comprehensive table of wealthy dwellings from the Roman period until the fourth century CE.

---

156 See Meyers, "Gendered Space." Compare this house to Hirschfeld's finding of a wealthy farmer's home: Hirschfeld, *Dead Sea Valley*, 135–139. On dwellings of the average farmer, see Yeivin, *Survey Settlements*, 154–183, and "Towns."
157 This house may have been owned by a Gentile prior to the Bar Kokhba Revolt as well. Nevertheless, it is a good example of a house of a very wealthy individual.
158 See Ganor et al., "Roman Villa."
159 Aviam, "First Century Galilee," 16–17.

THE "RICH"

Baruch compiled a list of houses in Roman Palestine and divided them into types.[160] The table below is based on his analysis but is expanded with details added to make it more comprehensive. The buildings that are in his inventory (chapter 2) include only buildings that were excavated and not those that were only surveyed. The reason for this was that the buildings surveyed dated from the "Roman-Byzantine" period and could not be clearly attributed to the Roman period. This excludes many houses that are mentioned in other scholarly research. The sites are arranged geographically from north to south. The largest and most decorated houses from each site are recorded in the table. The size of the actual house is sometimes hard to determine because the outer walls are measured and there may have been an inner courtyard.[161]

It is necessary to mention that some of the houses contain evidence that they were occupied by Jews, while others do not. The presence of a ritual bath (*mikveh*) in or under the house indicates that at least part of the time it was occupied by Jews. The existence of a ritual bath near the building also indicates the economic ability to dig and maintain the bath and is therefore included as one of the criteria in the table.

Nevertheless, even when Jewish ownership is in doubt, Jews of the period would have been aware of the existence of the varied levels of wealth that would have enabled the construction of dwellings of these types. This would explain the nuanced terminology used in rabbinic literature to describe various levels of wealth. The diversity of size and décor of the houses is compatible with the terms that the sages used to describe the relatively rich, the rich, and the "rich of the rich," as well as the other terms used to describe various kinds of wealth and relative wealth of the middle and upper-middle economic strata.

---

160   All sources for the table refer to the work of Baruch, *Dwelling House* unless otherwise indicated in the note. When a specific house is added to the table from a different source or information is added to the entry in the table from additional sources, it will be cited in the notes.

161   When available, the size of the courtyard is noted. When there is no inner courtyard, it will just say "built."

TABLE 6.1 Analysis of housing discovered in Roman Palestine and surroundings attributed to 0–300 CE

No.	ID.	Location	Type	Date	House size (sq. m.)	Court. (cm)	Width of wall (cm)	Misc.
1	Kfar Nasaj building 1700 area G[a]	Gamla	City	1st CE	145		550–110	2nd floor stucco arches
2	Fresco house Area XVI	Iotapata	City	Pre-67 CE	100[b]			2nd floor décor
3	M1 Meiron	Meiron	Town	2nd–4th CE	114/115[c]	335	66.5–85	2nd floor décor *mikveh*
4	M2 Patrician house	Meiron	Town	2nd–4th CE	140	222		2nd floor
5	Wealthy house	Meiron	Town	2nd–4th CE			1,120	2nd floor
6	M2 Lintel H.	Meiron	Town	2nd–4th CE	114/115	222		2nd floor impressive entrance
7	Fisherman's	Beit Saida-Kinneret	Village		486			2nd floor?
8	Beit Hakorem	Beit Saida	Village		291	153		
9	Kefar Nachum	Kefar Nachum	Village		670	Inner		2nd floor?
10	Arbel	Wadi Hamam[d]	Village	Early Roman	c. 400	"Wide courtyard"	0.60–0.80	2nd floor
11	Wealthy house[e]	Tiberius	City	3rd CE	1,000.	300 Peristyle	"Thick"	Stucco on walls and mosaic[a]

THE "RICH"

TABLE 6.1 Analysis of housing discovered in Roman Palestine (*cont.*)

No.	ID.	Location	Type	Date	House size (sq. m.)	Court. (cm)	Width of wall (cm)	Misc.
12	"Large house" (on top of palace of Herod Antipas?)	Villa		3rd CE	2,500	1/3 of the size of the house. Peristyle.		Fancy mosaica, geometric figurative
13	Sumaqa	Sumaqa (Mt. Carmel)	Village	Roman	655	66		
14	Nahal Ḥagit	Southern Mt. Carmel	Village	Middle Roman	Various sizes[f]	8,100[g]		Bath oil press mill
15	Hurvat Eqev	Ramat Hanadiv (Zichron Yakov)[h]	Farm	1st CE	560	2,800	30–50, 90.	2nd floor décor
16	Hurvat Aleq	Ramat Hanadiv	Farmstead	1st–3rd CE	600	4,800		2nd floor décor aqueduct decorated bathhouse
17	Hirbat Bureq[i]	Samaria (Shechem)	Village	1st–3rd CE	2,200		100	
18	Hirbat Basatin	Samaria	Villa or farm	3rd–5th CE		223 × 85	110	
19	Hirbat Deir Sam'an	Southern Samaria	Villa or farm	3rd–5th CE	114 × 52.5		50–100	
20	Southern building	Kalandia (Binyamin)	Farm	Pre-70 CE	2,208	11,200[j]		

TABLE 6.1   Analysis of housing discovered in Roman Palestine (*cont.*)

No.	ID.	Location	Type	Date	House size (sq. m.)	Court. (cm)	Width of wall (cm)	Misc.
21	Northern building	Kalandia (Binyamin)	Farm	Until 70 CE	4 units of 72[k]			
22	Beit Hamidot	Jerusalem	City	Pre-70 CE	600			Décor mikva'ot
23	The burnt house	Jerusalem	City	Pre-70 CE	64			2nd floor décor kitchen ovens
24	Ein Yael[l]	Jerusalem area	Villa	2nd–3rd CE[m]				2nd floor décor Tr/Pr/At bath
25	Bornet, area C[n]	Lod area	Village	2nd BCE–2nd CE	520		880	2nd floor Tr/Pr/At olive press
26	Roman manor	Lod	Villa/farm	2nd–3rd CE	300	Peristyle. 1/3 of the size of the house		Wall decorations, simple mosaica
27	Khirbet Baddisa[o] B1	Qiryat Sefer (Modiin)	Village	1st (Stage 1)	672 including an inner courtyard	Inner	50–60	*Mikveh* storage oil press
28	Khirbet Baddisa B2	Qiryat Sefer (Modiin)	Village	1st Stage 1st CE	286 including inner courtyard	Inner	50–60	*Mikveh* water supply

TABLE 6.1 Analysis of housing discovered in Roman Palestine (*cont.*)

No.	ID.	Location	Type	Date	House size (sq. m.)	Court. (cm)	Width of wall (cm)	Misc.
29	Khirbet Baddisa BIII	Qiryat Sefer (Modiin)	Village	1st stage 1st CE	137 including inner courtyard			
30	Khirbet Baddisa IV[p]	Qiryat Sefer (Modiin)	Village	1st stage 1st CE	95	No		*Mikveh* arches water supply
31	Khirbet Baddisa VII	Qiryat Sefer (Modiin)	Village	Early Roman	137	No		Pillars water supply
32	Hurvat Ethri[q]	Shfela (NW of Eleutheropolis-Beit Guvrin)	Village	Before and after 70 CE[r]	1,750		100 external wall	2nd floor cisterns mikveh storage hewed into the bedrock[s]
33	Urkhan El Khala[t]	Eleutheropolis (Beit Guvrin).	City–Polis	1st–3rd CE	600		Thick	Décor Tr/Pr/At fountain latrine bathhouse pool
34	Hilqiya's palace[u]	East of Eleutheropolis (Beit Guvrin)	Palace	1st CE	1,554		150	Décor Tr+Pr+At pillars, bathhouse, storage

TABLE 6.1 Analysis of housing discovered in Roman Palestine (*cont.*)

No.	ID.	Location	Type	Date	House size (sq. m.)	Court. (cm)	Width of wall (cm)	Misc.
35	Beit Hahkaluqim	Ein Gedi[v]	Village	Early Roman	80.75[w]	Inner and outer	60[x]	2nd floor cellar 6 ovens in courtyard + stove
36	House of keys	Ein Gedi	Village	Early Roman	99	Inner	60	2nd floor cellar
37	Northern house	Ein Gedi	Village	Early Roman	66		60	
38	Southern house	Ein Gedi	Village	Early Roman	117	Outer	60	Ovens, stovetop

a On this house, see Yavor, "Architecture (Gamla)," 78–85; see also ibid., 28–41, 61–110.
b See Aviam, *Galilee Second Temple*, 71–78. He says that there were four rooms, the largest of which was 27 sq. m. In the diagram of the houses, the other rooms are only slightly smaller, about 20 sq. m. each, and therefore, the entire house was approximately 100 sq. m. Décor was found on the walls and the floor. There was perhaps even a third floor. It was obviously the house of a wealthy man, but constrained in size because of surrounding buildings.
c The Meiron houses were excavated and recorded by Meyers et al., *Excavations*, 27–44. The Patrician House is discussed in ibid., 55–71; the Lintel House in discussed in ibid., 72–76.
d Leibner, "Wadi Hamam," "Areas B, C and F," esp. 195–217, 222–225, 234–238, 245, 247.
e Weiss, "Roman Antique Houses." He states that there were similar houses in Sepphoris from this period (ibid., 214–217).
f Seligman, "Architecture Nachal Hagit." There is a lengthy description of the rooms and facilities, but there is no mention of efforts to combine rooms into units that would house a family. However, the farmstead seemed to be owned by one person only (see summary on page 220). It was enclosed in one wall and planned meticulously, indicating that the owner was a very rich individual. Though the farm may have belonged to a Gentile, it was close enough to Jewish areas to have been known to contemporary Jews.
g Area enclosed by wall.
h For research on Ramat Hanadiv, see Hirschfeld, *Ramat Hanadiv*, 16–85.
i Dar, *Landscape and Pattern*, 1: 21–76, esp. 21–26 (*Hirbat Samarin*), and 73–76.
j Hirschfeld, *Dwelling*, 51–54.
k The apartments are part of an enormous 960 sq. m. building. In ancient times, an apartment of 72 sq. m. was comfortable but not luxurious. It would have belonged to the upper middle class, but not to the rich.

THE "RICH"

l A number of bricks were found there with the insignia of the Roman legion *Aelia* stamped on them. The villa was probably not owned by Jews based on the mythical scenes portrayed there. See Sartre, *Middle East*, 226.
m On this site, see also Edelstein, "Roman Villa," 32–42. He says that the villa may have covered an area of 32,000 sq. ft.
n Amit et al., "Horvat Bornat."
o Magen et al., "Qiryat Sefer," esp. 190–197.
p There is another building on the site, "building viii." It has an enormous courtyard of 16.30 × 20.30 m., and many buildings surround it. It seems to have belonged to multiple owners and therefore belonged to the lower class or lower middle class. It does not seem to have belonged to the rich or relatively rich (Magen et al., "Qiryat Sefer," 209–211), and therefore is not included in the above table.
q On this site, see Zissu and Ganor, "Horvat Ethri," 94–97.
r Stage 1 was destroyed in 70 CE. Stage 2 was built shortly thereafter. For information about these two stages, see Zissu and Ganor, "Horvat Ethri," 93–110.
s No decorations were found in this location, but architectural elements such as lintels, doorposts, and window frames were finely trimmed out of large *nari* blocks. Zissu and Ganor, "Horvat Ethri," 94–95.
t Regarding this house, see Ganor et al., "Roman Villa." See also Vincent, "Beit Djebrin."
u See Damati, "Hilkiya Palace." The name is found in a Greek inscription on one of the stones of the palace saying that Hilkiya son of Shimon wrote the inscription. It does not reveal who owned the palace but definitely fits the definition of "sons of kings" and has all the elements of a Roman palace. The presence of coins from the revolt in 67 CE indicates possible Jewish ownership.
v These houses were recorded by Hadas, "Ein Gedi," 41–43. There are a number of large houses at the site dating to the later Roman and Byzantine periods. See Hirschfeld, *En Gedi*, 52, who describes a home of 150 sq. m. On page 59, he describes a home of 240 sq. m. dated to somewhere between the fourth and seventh centuries CE.
w Scholars assume that the building contained two apartments of 45 sq. m. on the first floor. There was a cellar and a second floor, which indicates that the apartments were quite comfortable but did not belong to the very wealthy.
x In all the houses in Ein Gedi the external walls were manufactured from a mixture of mud and stone.

This table contains a comprehensive record of dwellings found in Roman Palestine that are ascribed to the period under discussion. The table analyzes aspects of wealth and convenience found in these houses including the size of the house, the size of the courtyard, the width of the walls, the existence of reception rooms, the number of floors, storage facilities, and bathing facilities that include ritual baths, and the decoration of floor or walls. It is similar to the criteria used by Wallace-Hadrill in his survey of Pompeian houses, differing in items that are specific to the conditions of the towns of Roman Palestine and the information available.[162] This analysis shows that the inhabitants of these houses had various levels of wealth. Some houses contain all the

---

162 Wallace-Hadrill, "Roman Luxury," 156–171.

indicators of wealth, while others were comfortable but with a limited amount of luxury items. This indicates a continuum of economic levels in society, from modest wealth stemming from a higher economic level than average, up to the extreme wealth manifested in enormous mansions with significant décor and comfort.[163] However, it must be emphasized that, compared to Roman housing, the houses described above, which were owned by the wealthy provincial elite, are modest in size and décor, thus making them equivalent to houses owned by the Roman middling group.[164]

13   Dwellings in the Vicinity of Roman Palestine: Southern Syria

The Golan and Hauran border the Galilee from the east. During part of the Roman period, they were ruled by the same local ruler (Herod Antipas), and in other times they were part of the same province. In the Golan, the Great Revolt brought about the destruction of the city of Gamla, and subsequently the Jewish population in Gamla was weakened. After the war, the population recovered, and there are archeological findings that can shed light on the issue of homes.

Sartre posits that the dwellings and settlements in southern Syria were similar to those in the Galilee in terms of the size and structure of the houses, methods of roofing, and organization of the villages. Isolated villas were not found in the Galilee as they were found in Judea and the coastal areas, and the most common form of settlement was the village.[165] In Syria as well, the majority of wealthy landowners lived in the cities, while dwellings in the villages that were larger and better decorated than the others likely belonged to managers of estates and local independent farmers. The houses were relatively limited in size, and the wealth of the owner was indicated by the planning and décor of the house. In the villages, it is possible to find vast villas larger than those found in the cities because there were fewer constraints due to neighboring properties, the price of land, and city planning. Bopp analyzes the houses of the wealthy found in the Hauran and shows that they were large and well-

---

163   This is also Wallace-Hadrill's conclusion concerning Pompeian houses—namely, that there was gradation in the economic status of the houses from those of the extremely wealthy to those of people who could only afford the bare necessities (ibid., 168).
164   This was also the conclusion of Andrea Berlin, who surveyed such sites of Roman Palestine. See Berlin, "Jewish Life," esp. 441–451, 456–458, 470. See also Berlin, "Land/Homeland" regarding the Second Temple and early Roman periods.
165   Sartre, *Middle East*, 226–227. The architecture in the Golan Heights and Southern Syria was similar. See Yavor, "Gamla Techniques"; and Peleg-Barkat, "Decoration."

decorated, but that there were significant discrepancies in size between different houses. The measurement of the size of the houses shows that there was a continuum: some were medium, between 220 sq. m. (Kefar Nasaj A) and 384 sq. m. (Kefar Shams 4), while some were much larger, up to 900 sq. m. (Umm iz Zetun, north of Jebel al Arab 6, Amrah, Djebel al Arab 7, Breiké, Ledja, Syrien House 1).[166] This, too, shows that there was a gradation in the levels of wealth in the Hauran.[167]

The spectrum of wealth corresponds with the analysis suggested above concerning Roman Palestine: when the rabbis mention a "wealthy" individual, it could be a reference to a local superintendent or to a successful independent farmer who is wealthy compared to the average villager. It could also relate to a local dignitary landowner who had a house in the city and property in the countryside.[168] Finally, it could also relate to a very wealthy individual, one with the ability to import goods and amass wealth similar to that associated with the upper classes of other cities of the Roman Empire.

14   Conclusion

There are primarily three levels of "wealthy" people found in literary descriptions of Jewish society in the first centuries CE. Anyone who has any economic means may be referred to as "rich" in contrast with the "poor." The second level has to do with someone who is relatively rich compared to his peers from the village or town. Finally, when wishing to describe the wealthy upper echelons of society, the sages would use additional terms such as "rich of rich." The fluid use of the term "wealthy" implies that when people spoke of the "rich" they were usually referring to people that would be considered middle or upper-middle class. This finding corresponds to a society that is complex, that has gradated economic levels, and that has a variety of forms of luxury.

Archeological findings from Roman Palestine and from southern Syria show that the large houses found in towns and villages were not uniform in size, shape, or décor. In some locations, there were houses that reflected all kinds of economic means, while in others some signifiers of wealth were found while others were lacking. Extremely wealthy individuals were a rare phenomenon

---

166   Bopp, *Hauran Culture*, 113–124. A special house is *Il Hayat*, house 1, north of Djebel al Arab. The size of the house is 25 × 25 × 9.5 m. It was very elaborately decorated.
167   Hirschfeld, *Dwelling*, 26, describes two Hauran structures.
168   Sartre, *Middle East*, 227, regarding the elegant houses found in the village of Refade in northern Syria.

in Jewish society after the destruction of the Temple, but nevertheless some evidence of this level of wealth can be found in the excavations in Sepphoris and in other locations. The houses of the "rich" were larger than others, were constructed with better materials, and were carefully planned, often according to Roman taste. In addition, they were decorated with mosaics and stucco and contained amenities such as a separate kitchen and private bathing facilities.

This study of the gradation of wealth in Jewish society in Roman Palestine can contribute, together with additional research, to the understanding of the various economic strata that existed in Roman society at that time. The lower middling groups considered the upper middling groups "rich," and in turn the upper middling groups would have considered the wealthy strata to be the unreachable "rich of the rich" or "sons of kings."[169]

Palestine was located at an important crossroads, as it was strategically located between the east and west and the north and south of the Roman Empire and because it was well connected with other regions of the Empire. Therefore, insight into the nature of Palestinian-Jewish society should shed light on the structure of the population in the Roman east, demonstrating that the levels of wealth in Roman society were gradated, varied, and more complex than previously assumed.

---

169   The term "middling class" rather than "middle class" is used in social studies to define the middle class of pre-industrial societies. See Verboven, "Associative Order," 861. In light of the comment of Wallace-Hadrill, "Trying," we prefer the term "middling groups."

Epilogue

The title of this research is indicative of the main contribution of this volume, which is the presentation of a comprehensive socioeconomic picture of the Jewish population in Roman Palestine during the first three centuries CE—an overview that is gleaned from the statements and definitions of the sages that lived in Palestine at that time. It defines boundaries for the various strata but shows that these boundaries were flexible and varied according to the perspective from which they were viewed. This structure is important for research into the Roman provinces in general. In addition, this study has provided many innovative insights into the philology of the economic concepts and terms used in the sources, has laid out the substratification inherent within the various strata, and has used material evidence to help clarify the nature of various economic and social situations. At the philological level, it has uncovered some of the deeper meanings of various socioeconomic words and expressions used in rabbinic literature, meanings that are not included in standard rabbinic philological dictionaries or in Modern Hebrew.

The above picture was enhanced by the study of the archeological finds of the period, primarily those regarding the regular person and his dwelling area, as well as the latter's level of décor and its production assets. The chapters of this volume are structured so as to describe the economic capabilities of the various strata in Jewish society in Roman Palestine. They start with the poor, who are at the bottom of the social pyramid: a position that holds throughout Roman society. They proceed to describe various middling groups and conclude with the wealthy. However, the wealthy described in rabbinic sources are by far less well-off than the wealthy of Rome, and as a group they can at most be compared with the provincial rich. Above that there are possibly individuals or families that are called in the sources "sons of kings," who may have had significant wealth in Roman terms though the size of their fortune is unknown. Consequently, this volume analyzes each of the three main social strata, determines the boundaries between them, and then divides them into gradated subgroups.

It is hard to glean from the sources the proportions and relative size of the three groups found: the poor, the middling groups, and the wealthy (that in Roman terms would be considered "upper middling groups"). However, there is an implication from the way the groups are described that the middling groups formed a considerable part of Palestinian-Jewish society. The sources indicate that the amount of poor who lived off of charity was relatively small, though there were probably a lot of working people who would be considered poor from the perspective of Roman society as a whole. This can also be seen in archeological sources. The structure and layout of the villages and towns as attested to by various surveys show us that all populated areas in the villages belonged to the middle class or to their fields, leaving little living space for additional destitute persons. No dwelling areas were uncovered on the outskirts of the villages or in the fields, though it is possible that there were temporary structures that did not leave a trace in the record. This indicates that the village poor were a minority of the population, and that they did not occupy much space.

The middling groups are portrayed as the backbone of society and receive the most attention. This fact has led to a suggested estimate of 50 percent for the segment of society that had more than 200 *zuz*. However, as pointed out above, this poverty line was a line that was measured in real time and many people probably lived above the line some of the time and lived under it some of the time. One day or for a given week, a man could be regarded as "poor" and at another time, when working, he could be called a "laborer." Regarding the wealthy, it was found that, when the sages say of someone that he is "wealthy," it merely means that he is "not poor." Only if they say more than that, "rich of the rich" or "politicians," do they actually mean to indicate that a person had significant wealth.

In the area of substratification, there were at least four levels of poverty defined by the sources for the purpose of the allocation of public and private assistance. Regarding the middling groups, there were various levels including unskilled workers, skilled workers, small landowners, and entrepreneurs. The *ba'al habayit*—landowner—was a distinct category and the landowners comprised a group in society that had a common identity and a mutual support system. The term represents the small landowners, who were the backbone of the Jewish population in the villages and small towns.

Specifically, the day laborer, *po'el*, was better off than the "poor" man, but he was on the lowest level of the working class, though he may be financially close to the poverty line, either just above it or just below it. Above him are the professionals, such as the craftsmen. The professionals are gradated according to the size of their enterprise, the craft in which they work, and whether they employ workers.

The sources represent primarily small towns and villages of Roman Palestine and reflect the large cities—the *poleis*—less often. This is true also concerning the large variety of dwelling places found in Palestine that show a continuum of economic means from paltry to sizeable. These findings too originate from the towns and villages.

EPILOGUE

Therefore, it can be concluded that there is a need to place greater emphasis on the middling groups when calculating the population of Roman Palestine and how it was divided socioeconomically. This may indicate that a similar situation was true regarding the Roman Empire in general, excluding the big cities for which there is evidence of large areas in which the poor and destitute lived.

Our research concludes with the rich. As shown above, the word "rich" in the sources indicates someone who is "not poor," including all levels of the population above the poverty line. When wishing to refer to someone who belongs to the elite upper strata of society, the rabbis added words to show that the person was very wealthy. One example is the term "rich of rich," which is found in the Mishnah. However, it seems that even the wealthiest Jews mentioned in the sources were merely "provincially rich" and could not compare at all to the rich of the city of Rome.

It seems that there has not yet been research that systematically gradates the various groups in society from poor to rich by breaking down the general categories into subcategories based on contemporaneous sources. This model can be implemented in future research into other societies in the Roman Empire and will likely draw interest from Roman social and economic historians. Similarly, since Palestine was part of the Roman economy and the Roman market, it is possible that linguistic insights into words that have hidden socioeconomic meanings, such as the notion that "rich" actually means "not poor," can be examined in the context of other contemporaneous societies to see whether there is hidden meaning in these terms in those societies as well.

Finally, the vast amount of material compiled in this volume indicates that the economy of Roman Palestine was complex and versatile, with many professions, enterprises, and markets.[1] It included groups of people of various economic means and among which there was sophisticated self-knowledge of the stratification of the economy. Economic means was a function of ownership of revenue-providing property and professional expertise. These factors show that the economy was far from primitive, as stated by Finley, and that it was quite advanced compared to the economies that preceded it. Many products were manufactured and marketed, and many professions existed. There were wealthy people who consumed luxury items and others who had no more than the necessities. This leads to the conclusion that Roman society can compare favorably to other societies of the late pre-industrial world.

The following figure summarizes the findings of this study. All the segments are equally divided. It does not show the relative size of each stratum, just the

---

1 Regarding markets, see Rosenfeld and Menirav, *Markets and Marketing*.

hierarchy of the various strata uncovered in rabbinic literature. Again, it should be emphasized that, excluding "sons of kings," all the levels of wealth described here would fall into the middling groups of the city of Rome and possibly the upper classes of the provinces.

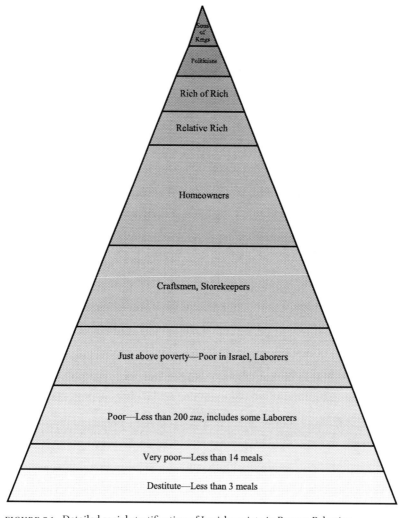

FIGURE 7.1 Detailed social stratification of Jewish society in Roman Palestine

Bibliography

Ancient Sources: Translations

Neusner, The Mishnah = J. Neusner, *The Mishnah*. New Haven—London: Yale University Press, 1988.
Neusner, The Tosefta = J. Neusner, *The Tosefta*, 6 Vols. New York: Ktav, 1981.
Neusner, The Talmud = J. Neusner, *The Talmud of the Land of Israel*. Atlanta: Scholars Press, 1996.
Epstein, The Babylonian Talmud = I. Epstein, *The Babylonian Talmud*. London: Soncino Press, 1979.

Ancient Works: Translations

Ben Sira (English), Skehan and Di Lella—See Modern Works.
Ben Sira (Heb.), Segal ed.—See Modern Works.
Ben Sira—Academy of the Hebrew Language = *The Historical Dictionary of the Hebrew Language: The Book of Ben Sira, Text, Concordance and an Analysis of the Vocabulary*. Jerusalem: The Academy of the Hebrew Language and the Shrine of the Book, 1973.
Bible—New Revised Standard Version. Grand Rapids, MI: Zondervan, 2008.
Bible 2—The Jewish Study Bible (2nd Ed.). Ed. Adele Berlin and Marc Zvi Brettler. Oxford: Oxford University Press, 2014.
New Testament (default)—New International Version. New York: Biblica, 1983.
New Testament (comparison)—The Anchor Bible. New York: Doubleday, 1985.

Modern Works

Aarts, "Coins and Money" = J. Aarts, "Coins, Money and Exchange in the Roman World: A Cultural-Economic Perspective," *Archaeological Dialogues* 12, no. 1 (2005): 1–28.
Aberbach, *Work and Crafts* = M. Aberbach, *Labor Crafts and Commerce in Ancient Israel*. Jerusalem: Magnes Press, 1994.
Adams, *Rome, Elite, and Suburbs* = G.W. Adams, *Rome and the Social Role of Elite Villas in its Suburbs*. Oxford: Archaeopress, 2008.
Adams, "Poverty and Otherness" = S.L. Adams, "Poverty and Otherness in Second Temple Instructions," in D.C. Harlow, Mathew Goff, Karina Martin Hogna, and Joel S. Kaminsky (eds.), *The "Other" in Second Temple Judaism: Essays in Honor of John J. Collins*, Grand Rapids, MI: Eerdmans, 2010, 189–203.

Adams, *Social and Economic* = S.L. Adams, *Social and Economic Life in Second Temple Judea*. Louisville, KY: Westminster John Knox Press, 2014.

Adan-Bayewitz, *Pottery Galilee* = D. Adan-Bayewitz, *Common Pottery in Roman Galilee: A Study of Local Trade*. Ramat Gan: Bar-Ilan University Press, 1993.

Adan-Bayewitz and Aviam, "Iotapata" = D. Adan-Bayewitz and M. Aviam, "Iotapata, Josephus, and the Siege of 67: Preliminary Report on the 1992–94 Seasons," *JRA* 10 (1997): 131–165.

Albeck, *Mishnah* = H. Albeck and H. Yalon, *The Six Orders of the Mishnah*, 6 Vols. Jerusalem: Devir, 1957–1959 [in Hebrew].

Albright and Mann, *Matthew* = W.F. Albright and C.S. Mann, *Matthew*. New York: Doubleday, 1971.

Alcock, *Understanding Poverty* = P. Alcock, *Understanding Poverty*. Basingstoke, UK: Macmillan Education, 1993.

Alexander, "Rabbinic Literature" = P.S. Alexander, "Using Rabbinic Literature as a Source for the History of Late Roman Palestine: Problems and Issues," in M. Goodman and P.S. Alexander (eds.), *Rabbinic Texts and the History of Late Roman Palestine*. Oxford: The British Academy, 2011, 7–24.

Alföldy, *Roman Society* = G. Alföldy, *Die Römische Gesellschaft: Ausgewählte Beiträge*. Stuttgart: Franz Steiner Verlag, 1984.

Alföldy, *Social History* = G. Alföldy, *The Social History of Rome*. Trans. D. Braund and F. Pollack. Baltimore: Johns Hopkins University Press, 1988.

Allegro, *Qumran Cave 4* = J.M. Allegro, *Qumran Cave 4, i (4q158–4q186)*. Oxford: Oxford University Press, 1968.

Allen, "Prosperous Romans" = R.C. Allen, "How Prosperous Were the Romans? Evidence from Diocletian's Price Edict (301 AD)," in A.K. Bowman and A. Wilson (eds.), *Quantifying the Roman Economy: Methods and Problems*. Oxford: Oxford University Press, 2009, 327–345.

Allison, "Roman Households" = P.M. Allison, "Roman Households: An Archaeological Perspective," in H.M. Parkins (ed.), *Roman Urbanism: Beyond the Consumer City*. London: Routledge, 1997, 112–146.

Allison, *Pompeian Households* = P.M. Allison, *Pompeian Households: An Analysis of the Material Culture*. Los Angeles: Cotsen Institute of Archaeology Press, 2004.

Alon, *History* = G. Alon, *History of the Jews in the Land of Israel in the Period of the Mishnah and Talmud*, 2 Vols. Tel Aviv: Hakibbutz Hameuchad, 1977.

Alon, *Studies* = G. Alon, *Studies in Jewish History*, 2 Vols. Tel Aviv: Hakibbutz Hameuchad, 1978 [in Hebrew].

Alon, *The Jews* = G. Alon, *The Jews in their Land in the Talmudic Age*, 2 Vols. Jerusalem: Magnes Press, 1980–1984.

Alston, "Houses in Roman Egypt" = R. Alston, "Houses and Households in Roman Egypt," in Laurence and Wallace-Hadrill, *Domestic Space*, 25–39.

Ameling, *Inscriptiones* = W. Ameling, *Inscriptiones Judaicae Orientis II*. Tübingen: Mohr Siebeck, 2004.

Amit, "Bread Stamps" = D. Amit, "Jewish Bread Stamps and Wine and Oil Seals from the Late Second Temple, Mishnaic, and Talmudic Period," in E. Eshel and Y. Levine (eds.), *"See, I Will Bring a Scroll Recounting What Befell Me" (Ps 40:8): Epigraphy and Daily Life from the Bible to the Talmud, Dedicated to the Memory of Professor Hanan Eshel*. Göttingen: Vandenhoeck & Ruprecht, 2014, 159–174.

Amit et al., "Horvat Bornat" = D. Amit, H. Torgü, and P. Gendelman, "Horvat Bornat; A Jewish Village in the Lod Shefelah during the Hellenistic and Roman Periods," *Kadmoniyot* 41 (2008): 96–107 [in Hebrew].

Anderson, *Architecture and Society* = J.C. Anderson, *Roman Architecture and Society*. Baltimore: Johns Hopkins University Press, 1997.

Applebaum, *Work* = H. Applebaum, *The Concept of Work: Ancient, Medieval, and Modern*. New York: State University of New York Press, 1992.

Applebaum, "Economic Life" = S.S. Applebaum, "Economic Life in Palestine," in S. Safrai, M. Stern, D. Flusser, and W.C. Van Unnik (eds.), *The Jewish People in the First Century*. Assen: Van Gorcum, 1976, 631–701.

Applebaum, "Agrarian Situation" = S.S. Applebaum, "The Agrarian Situation after the Destruction of the Second Temple," in A. Oppenheimer and U. Rappaport (eds.), *Bar Kochba Revolt—New Research*. Jerusalem: Yad Yitzhak Ben Zvi, 1984, 147–152 [Hebrew with English summary].

Arjava, "Paternal Power" = A. Arjava, "Paternal Power in Late Antiquity," *JRS* 88 (1998): 1–10.

Arnaoutoglou, "Collegia Asia Minor" = I.N. Arnaoutoglou, "Roman Law and Collegia in Asia Minor," *Revue Internationale des droits de l'Antiquité* 49 (2002): 27–44.

Arnaoutoglou, "Craftsman Associations" = I.N. Arnaoutoglou, "Craftsmen Associations in Roman Lydia: A Tale of Two Cities?" *Ancient Society* 41 (2011): 257–290.

ASBS, *Peshitta* = The Aramaic Scriptures Research Society in Israel, *The New Covenant Peshitta Aramaic Text with a Hebrew Translation*. Jerusalem: The Bible Society, 1986.

Ascough et al., *Associations* = R.S. Ascough, P.A. Harland, and J.S. Kloppenborg, *Associations in the Greco-Roman World: A Sourcebook*. Berlin: De Gruyter, 2012.

Aubert, "Workshop Managers" = J.J. Aubert, "Workshop Managers," in W.V. Harris (ed.), *The Inscribed Economy: Production and Distribution in the Roman Empire in the Light of Instrumentum Domesticum*. Ann Arbor: University of Michigan Press, 1993, 171–181.

Aubert, "Production" = J.J. Aubert, "Managing Non-Agricultural Production in the Roman World," in D.J. Mattingly and J. Salmon (eds.), *Economies beyond Agriculture in the Classical World*. London: Routledge, 2001, 90–111.

Aubert, "Conclusion" = J.J. Aubert, "Conclusion: A Historian's Point of View," in Aubert and Sirks, *Roman Law*, 185–187.

Aubert and Sirks, *Roman Law* = J.J. Aubert and B. Sirks, eds., *Speculum Iuris: Roman Law as a Reflection of Social and Economic Life in Antiquity*. Ann Arbor: University of Michigan Press, 2002.

Avery Peck, "Agriculture" = A.J. Avery-Peck, "Scripture and Mishnah: The Case of the Mishnaic Division of Agriculture," *JJS* 38, no. 1 (1987): 56–71.

Avi-Yonah, *Rome and Byzantium* = M. Avi-Yonah, *Geschichte der Juden im Zeitalter des Talmud. In den Tagen von Rom und Byzanz*. Berlin: De Gruyter, 1962.

Avi-Yonah, *Political History* = M. Avi-Yonah, *The Jews of Palestine: A Political History from the Bar Kokhba War to the Arab Conquest*. Jerusalem: Magnes Press, 1976.

Avi-Yonah, "Jews under Roman" =

Aviam, "First Century Galilee" = M. Aviam, "First Century Jewish Galilee: An Archaeological Perspective," in D.R. Edwards (ed.), *Religion and Society in Roman Palestine: Old Questions New Approaches*. New York: Routledge, 2004, 7–27.

Aviam, *Galilee Second Temple* = M. Aviam, *A Case Study in the Development of the Jewish Settlement in the Galilee during the Second Temple Period*. PhD Diss., Bar-Ilan University, 2006 [in Hebrew].

Aviam, "Socio-Economic" = M. Aviam, "Socio-Economic Hierarchy and Its Economic Foundations in First-Century Galilee: The Evidence from Yodfat and Gamla," in J. Pastor, P. Stern, and M. Mor (eds.), *Flavius Josephus: Interpretation and History*. Leiden: Brill, 2011, 29–38.

Avigad, *Jerusalem* = N. Avigad, *Discovering Jerusalem*. Nashville, TN: T. Nelson, 1983.

Avigad and Mazar, "Beth She'arim" = N. Avigad and B. Mazar, "Beth She'arim," in E. Stern (ed.), *The New Encyclopedia of Archaeological Excavations in the Holy Land*, Vol. 1, Jerusalem: Carta, 1993, 236–248.

Ayali, *Laborer* = M. Ayali, *The Status of the Laborer and the Relationship between Employers and Employees in the Talmudic and Midrashic Literature*. Jerusalem: M. Ayali, 1980 [in Hebrew].

Ayali, *Workers* = M. Ayali, *Workers and Artisans: Their Work and Status in Rabbinic Literature*. Givatayim: Masada, 1987 [in Hebrew].

Bagnall, *Egypt* = R.S. Bagnall, *Egypt in Late Antiquity*. Princeton, NJ: Princeton University Press, 1985.

Bagnall, *Papyrology* = R.S. Bagnall, ed., *The Oxford Handbook of Papyrology*. Oxford: Oxford University Press, 2009.

Bagnall and Frier, *Demography* = R.S. Bagnall and B.W. Frier, *The Demography of Roman Egypt*. Cambridge: Cambridge University Press, 1994.

Bagnall et al., *Encyclopedia* = R.S. Bagnall, K. Brodersen, C.B. Chapion, A. Erskine, and S.R. Huebner, eds., *The Encyclopedia of Ancient History*, Vol. 3. Chichester, UK: Wiley-Blackwell, 2013.

Balch, "Rich and Poor" = D.L. Balch, "Rich and Poor, Proud and Humble in Luke–Acts," in L.M. White and O.L. Yarbrough (eds.), *The Social World of the First Christians: Essays in Honor of Wayne A. Meeks*. Minneapolis: Fortress Press, 1995, 214–233.

Balzaretti, "Curtis" = R. Balzaretti, "The Curtis: The Archaeology of Sites of Power," in R. Francovich and G. Noye (eds.), *La Storia dell'alto Meidoevo Italiano (vi–x Secolo) Alla Luce Dell'archeologia*. Firenze: All'Insegna Del Giglio, 1994, 99–108.

Bammel, "πτωχός" = E. Bammel, "πτωχός," *TDNT*, 6, 885–915.

Banerjee and Duflo, "Middle Class" = A. Banerjee and E. Duflo, "What Is Middle Class about the Middle Classes around the World?" *Journal of Economic Perspectives* 22, no. 2 (2008): 3–28.

Bang, "Trade and Economy" = P.F. Bang, "Trade and Empire: In Search of Organizing Concepts for the Roman Economy," *Past and Present* 195, no. 1 (2007): 3–54.

Bang, "Grain Market" = P.F. Bang, "P. Erdkamp: The Grain Market in the Roman Empire. A Social, Political and Economic Study," *The Classical Review (New Series)* 58, no. 1 (2008): 228–230.

Bang, *Roman Markets* = P.F. Bang, *The Roman Bazaar: A Comparative Study of Trade and Markets in a Tributary Empire*. Cambridge: Cambridge University Press, 2008.

Bar, "Third Century" = D. Bar, "The Third Century Crisis in the Roman Empire and Its Relevance to Palestine during the Late Roman Period," *Zion* 66 (2001): 143–170 [Hebrew with English summary].

Bar-Asher, "Mishnaic Hebrew" = M. Bar-Asher, "Mishnaic Hebrew: An Introductory Survey," *CHJ* 4 (2006), 369–403.

Bar-Asher, *Studies* = M. Bar-Asher, *Studies in Mishnaic Hebrew, Vol. 1: Introduction and Linguistic Investigations*. Jerusalem: Bialik Institution, 2009 [in Hebrew].

Barclay, "Poverty Pauline" = J. Barclay, "Poverty in Pauline Studies: A Response to Steven Friesen," *JSNT* 26, no. 3 (2004): 363–366.

Bar Ilan, "Patrimonial Burial" = M. Bar Ilan, "Patrimonial Burial Practices in Israel in the Ancient Period," in I. Singer (ed.), *Graves and Burial Practices in Israel in the Ancient Period*. Jerusalem: Yad Yitzhak Ben Zvi, 1994, 212–229 [in Hebrew].

Barker, Lloyd, and Webley, "Landscape" = G. Barker, J. Lloyd, and D. Webley, "A Classical Landscape in Molise," *PBSR* 46 (1978): 35–51.

Barton, *Ethics* = J. Barton, *Ethics in Ancient Israel*. Oxford: Oxford University Press, 2014.

Baruch, *Dwelling House* = E. Baruch, *The Dwelling House in the Land of Israel during the Roman Period: Material Culture and Social Structure* (PhD Diss., Bar-Ilan University, 2008).

Basser and Cohen, *Matthew* = H.W. Basser with M.B. Cohen, *The Gospel of Matthew*. Leiden: Brill, 2015.

Bauckham, *Apocalypses* = R. Bauckham, *The Fate of the Dead: Studies on the Jewish and Christian Apocalypses*. Leiden: Brill, 1998.

Bauckham, "Lazarus" = R.J. Bauckham, "The Rich Man and Lazarus: The Parable and the Parallels," in R.J. Bauckham, *The Fate of the Dead: Studies on the Jewish and Christian Apocalypses*. Leiden: Brill, 1998, 97–118.

Beechey, "Rethinking Work" = V. Beechey, "Rethinking the Definition of Work: Gender and Work," in J. Jenson, E. Hagen, and C. Reddy (eds.), *Feminization of the Labour Force: Paradoxes and Promises*. New York: Oxford University Press, 1988, 45–62.

Ben Iehuda, *Dictionary* = E. Ben Iehuda, *A Complete Dictionary of Ancient and Modern Hebrew*. Jerusalem: La'am Publishing, 1949.

Ben Shalom, *Beit Shammai* = I. Ben Shalom, *The School of Shammai and the Zealots: Struggle against Rome*. Jerusalem: Yad Yitzhak Ben Zvi, 1993 [in Hebrew].

Berlin, "Jewish Life" = A. Berlin, "Jewish Life before the Revolt: The Archaeological Evidence," *JSJ* 36, no. 4 (2005): 417–470.

Berlin, "Household Judaism" = A. Berlin, "Household Judaism," in D.A. Fiensy and J.R. Strange (eds.), *Galilee in the Late Second Temple and Mishnaic Periods*. Minneapolis: Fortress Press, 2014, 208–215.

Berlin, "Land/Homeland" = A. Berlin, "Land/Homeland, Story/History: The Social Landscapes of the Southern Levant from Alexander to Augustus," in Yasur-Landau, E.H. Cline, and Y.M. Rowan (eds.), *The Social Archaeology of the Levant: From Prehistory to the Present*. Cambridge: Cambridge University Press, 2019, 410–437.

Bintliff, "Protocapitalist" = J. Bintliff, "The Hellenistic to Roman Mediterranean: A Protocapitalist Revolution?" in T. Kerig, and A. Zimmermann (eds.), *Economic Archaeology: From Structure to Performance in European Archaeology*. Bonn: Habelt, 2013, 285–292.

Birdsall, "Middle Class" = N. Birdsall, "The (Indispensable) Middle Class in Developing Countries," in R. Kanbur and M. Spence (eds.), *Equity and Growth in a Globalizing World*. Washington, DC: World Bank, 2010, 157–188.

Birkelund, "Class Future" = G.E. Birkelund, "A Class Analysis for the Future," *Acta Sociologica* 45, no. 3 (2001): 217–221.

Birks, "Dominium" = P. Birks, "The Roman Law Concept of Dominium and the Idea of Absolute Ownership," *Acta Juridica* 1 (1985): 1–37.

Blau, *Approaches* = P.M. Blau, *Approaches to the Study of Social Structure*. London: Collier Macmillan, 1975.

Bopp, "Hauran" = E.M. Bopp, "Die Bauornamentik in den Antiken Wohnhäusern des Hauran," in K.S. Freyberger, A. Henning, and H. Von Hesberg (eds.), *Kulturkonflikte im Vorderen; Orient an der Wende Vom Hellenismus zur Römischen Kaiserzeit*. Rahden, Germany: German Archaeological Institute, 2003, 47–63.

Bopp, *Culture Hauran* = E.M. Bopp, *Die Antieke Wohnkultur des Hauran in Syrien*. Rahden, Germany: Marie Leidorf, 2006.

BIBLIOGRAPHY

Bouquet, *Everyday Life* = A.C. Bouquet, *Everyday Life in New Testament Times*. London: Bastford, 1970.

Bovon, *Saint Luc* = F. Bovon, *L'évangile selon Saint Luc*, 3 Vols. Geneva: Labor et Fides, 1991.

Bowman and Rathbone, "Cities Egypt" = A.D. Bowman and D. Rathbone, "Cities and Administration in Roman Egypt," *JRS* 82 (1992): 107–127.

Bowman and Wilson, "Roman Agriculture" = A.K. Bowman and A. Wilson, "Introduction: Quantifying Roman Agriculture," in A.K. Bowman and A. Wilson (eds.), *The Roman Agricultural Economy: Organization, Investment, and Production*. Oxford: Oxford University Press, 2013, 1–32.

Boyarin, *Carnal Israel* = D. Boyarin, *Carnal Israel: Reading Sex in Talmudic Culture*. Berkeley: University of California Press, 1993.

Brabec, "Laborers–Citizens" = M. Brabec, "Recognition of Laborers as Citizens: First Worker Democracy versus Liberal Capitalist Democracy," *Perspectives on Global Development and Technology* 15, no. 1–2 (2016): 157–165.

Breuer, "Aramaic" = Y. Breuer, "Aramaic in Late Antiquity," *CHJ* 4 (2006): 457–491.

Broshi, "Diet" = M. Broshi, "The Diet of Palestine in the Roman Period—Introductory Notes," *The Israel Museum Journal* 5 (1986): 41–56.

Broshi, *Bread, Wine, Scrolls* = M. Broshi, *Bread, Wine, Walls, and Scrolls*. London: Sheffield Academic Press, 2001.

Brown, *New Testament Theology* = C. Brown, ed., *New International Dictionary of New Testament Theology*, Vol. 2. Grand Rapids, MI: Zondervan, 1979.

Brown, *Poverty and Leadership* = P. Brown, *Poverty and Leadership in the Later Roman Empire*. Hanover, NH: University Press of New England, 2002.

Brun, "French Approach" = J.P. Brun, "The Archaeology of the Roman Urban Workshops: A French Approach?" in A. Wilson and M. Flohr, *Urban Craftsmen and Traders in the Roman World*. Oxford: Oxford University Press, 77–95.

Brunt, *Italian Manpower* = P.A. Brunt, *Italian Manpower 225 BC–AD 14*. Oxford: Clarendon Press, 1987.

Brunt, "Labour" = P.A. Brunt, "Labour," in J. Wacher (ed.), *The Roman World*, 2 Vols. London: Routledge, 1990, II: 701–716.

Burford, *Craftsmen* = A. Burford, *Craftsmen in Greek and Roman Society*. Ithaca, NY: Cornell University Press, 1972.

Burke, *History and Social* = P. Burke, *History and Social Theory*, 2nd ed. Ithaca, NY: Cornell University Press, 2005.

Burrell, "Caesarea Palace" = B. Burrell, "Palace to Praetorium: The Romanization of Caesarea," in A. Raban and K.G. Holum (eds.), *Caesarea Maritima: A Retrospective after Two Millennia*. Leiden: Brill, 1996, 228–247.

Butcher, *Roman Syria* = K. Butcher, *Roman Syria and the Near East*. London: The British Museum, 2003.

Cain, "Marxian Economic" = M. Cain, "Marxian Economic Thought," in N.J. Smelser and P.B. Baltes (eds.), *International Encyclopedia of the Social and Behavioral Sciences*, vol. 14, Oxford: Elsevier, 2001, 9286–9295.

Carandini, *Peasants* = A. Carandini, *Schiavi in Italia: gli strumenti pensanti dei Romani fra tarda repubblica e medio impero*. Rome: La Nuova Italia Scientifica, 1988.

Cardman, "Early Christian" = F. Cardman, "Early Christian Ethics," in S. Ashbrook Harvey and D.G. Hunter (eds.), *The Oxford Handbook of Early Christian Studies*. Oxford: Oxford University Press, 2008, 932–956.

Cartledge, Cohen, and Foxhall, *Money Labour and Land* = P. Cartledge, E.E. Cohen, and L. Foxhall (eds.), *Money Labour and Land: Approaches to the Economies of Ancient Greece*. London: Routledge, 2002.

Cashell, "Middle Class" = B.M. Cashell, "Who Are the 'Middle Class?'" *CRS Report for the Congress*. Ithaca: Cornell University School of Industrial and Labor Relations, March 20, 2007.

Chancey, *Culture, Galilee* = M.A. Chancey, *Greco-Roman Culture and the Galilee of Jesus*. Cambridge: Cambridge University Press, 2005.

Charlesworth, "Suffering" = J.H. Charlesworth, "Suffering," in Schiffman and VanderKam, *Dead Sea Scrolls* 2:900.

Chayanov, *Peasant Economy* = A.V. Chayanov, *The Theory of the Peasant Economy*. Ed. D.B. Thorner, B. Kerblay, and R.E.F. Smith. Homewood, IL: R.D. Irwin, 1966.

Chilton, "James" = B. Chilton, "James and the Christian Pharisees," in A.J. Avery-Peck, D. Harrington, and J. Neusner (eds.), *When Judaism and Christianity Began: Essays in Memory of Anthony J. Saldarini*, vol. 1. Leiden: Brill, 2004, 19–47.

Choi, *Jewish Leadership* = J. Choi, *Jewish Leadership in Roman Palestine from 70 CE to 135 CE*. Leiden: Brill, 2013.

Choi, "Interaction" = A. Choi, "Never the Two Shall Meet? Urban–Rural Interaction in Lower Galilee," in D.A. Fiensy and J.R. Strange (eds.), *Galilee in the Late Second Temple and Mishnaic Periods*. Minneapolis: Fortress Press, 2014, 297–311.

Christ, "Roman Social" = K. Christ, "Grundfragen der römischen Sozialstruktur," in W. Eck, H. Galstrerer, and H. Wolff (eds.), *Studien zur antiken Sozialgeschichte: Festschrift Friedrich Vittinghoff*. Cologne: Bohlau, 1980, 197–228.

Clement and Myles, *Class and Gender* = W. Clement and J. Myles, *Relations of Ruling: Class and Gender in Postindustrial Societies*. Montreal: McGill–Queens University Press, 1994.

Clermont-Ganneau, *Archaeological* = C. Clermont-Ganneau, *Archaeological Researches in Palestine during the Years 1873–74*, 2 Vols. Trans. J. Macfarlane. London: Palestine Exploration Fund, 1896.

Clines, *Hebrew Dictionary* = D.J.A. Clines (ed.), *The Dictionary of Classical Hebrew*, Vol. 2. Sheffield: Sheffield Academic Press, 1995.

Cohen, *Economy* = E.E. Cohen, *Athenian Economy and Society: A Banking Perspective*. Princeton, NJ: Princeton University Press, 1992.

Cohen, *Athenian Nation* = E.E. Cohen, *The Athenian Nation*. Princeton, NJ: Princeton University Press, 2000.

Cohen, "Unprofitable Masculinity" = E.E. Cohen, "An Unprofitable Masculinity," in Cartledge, Cohen, and Foxhall, *Money, Labour and Land*, 100–112.

Cohen, "Rabbi" = S.J.D. Cohen, "The Rabbi in Second-Century Jewish Society," *CHJ* 3 (1999), 922–990.

Cohen, *Yavneh* = S.J.D. Cohen, *The Significance of Yavneh and Other Essays in Jewish Hellenism*. Tübingen: Mohr Siebeck, 2010.

Cohon, "Tools" = R. Cohon, "Tools of the Trade: A Rare, Ancient Roman Builder's Funerary Plaque," *Antike Kunst* 53 (2010): 94–100.

Cole, "Conception Middle Class" = G.D.H. Cole, "The Conception of the Middle Class," *BJS* 1, no. 4 (1950): 275–290.

Collins, "Wisdom Apocalypticism" = J.J. Collins, "Wisdom, Apocalypticism, and Generic Compatibility," in L.G. Perdue et al. (eds.), *In Search of Wisdom: Essays in Memory of John G. Gammie*. Louisville, KY: John Knox, 1993, 165–185.

Collins, "Wisdom" = J.J. Collins, "Wisdom Reconsidered in Light of the Scrolls," *DSD* 4 (1997): 265–281.

Cooper, "Roman Households" = K. Cooper, "Closely Watched Households: Visibility, Exposure, and Private Power in the Roman Domus," *Past and Present* 197, no. 1 (2007): 3–33.

Corbier, "Coinage" = M. Corbier, "Coinage, Society and Economy," *CAH* 12 (2005), 327–392.

Corbo, *Cafarnao I* = V.C. Corbo, *Cafarnao I Gli Edifici Della Citta*. Jerusalem: Franciscan Printing Press, 1975.

Cornelius, "haras" = I. Cornelius, "haras," in VanGemeren, *Dictionary*, 2:298–300.

Cornelius, "hoseb" = I. Cornelius, "hoseb," in VanGemeren, *Dictionary*, 2:310–311.

Cornelius, "umman" = I. Cornelius, "umman," in VanGemeren, *Dictionary*, 1:433–434.

Costin, "Craft and Social" = C.L. Costin, "Introduction: Craft and Social Identity," in C.L. Costin and R.P. Wright (eds.), *Craft and Social Inquiry*. London: Wiley-Blackwell, 1998, 1–13.

Cotter, "The Collegia" = W. Cotter, "The Collegia and Roman Law: State Restrictions on Voluntary Associations, 64 BCE–200 CE," in J.S. Kloppenborg and S.G. Wilson (eds.), *Voluntary Associations in the Graeco-Roman World*. London: Routledge, 1996, 74–89.

Cotton, "Ein Gedi" = H.M. Cotton, "Ein Gedi between the Two Revolts," *SCI* 20 (2001): 139–154.

Cotton, "Language Gaps" = H.M. Cotton, "Language Gaps in Roman Palestine and the Roman Near East," in Ch. Frevel (ed.), *Medien im antiken Palastina*. Tübingen: Mohr Siebeck, 2005, 151–169.

Cotton and Yardeni, *Nahal Hever* = H.M. Cotton and A. Yardeni, *Aramaic, Hebrew and Greek Documentary Texts from Nahal Hever and Other Sites: With an Appendix Containing Alleged Qmran Texts (The Seiyal Collection II)*, DJD 27. Oxford: Oxford University Press, 1997.

Cox, *Household Interests* = C.A. Cox, *Household Interests: Property, Marriage Strategies, and Family Dynamics in Ancient Athens*. Princeton, NJ: Princeton University Press, 1998.

Crompton, *Class* = R. Crompton, *Class and Stratification*, 3rd ed. Cambridge: Cambridge University Press, 2008.

Crossan, "Relationship" = J.D. Crossan, "The Relationship between Galilean Archaeology and Historical Jesus Research," in D.R. Edwards and C.T. McCollough (eds.), *Archaeology and the Galilee: Texts and Contexts in the Graeco Roman and Byzantine Periods*. Atlanta: Scholars Press, 1997, 151–162.

Curchin, "Labour" = L.A. Curchin, "Non-Slave Labour in Roman Spain," *Gerión* 4 (1986): 177–187.

Dahms, "Weberian Marxism" = H.F. Dahms, "Theory in Weberian Marxism: Patterns of Critical Social Theory in Lukács and Habermas," *Sociological Theory* 15, no. 3 (1997): 182–217.

Dalton, *Tribal and Peasant* = G. Dalton (ed.), *Tribal and Peasant Economies*. Austin: University of Texas Press, 1967.

Daly and Wilson, "Keeping Up" = M. Daly and D. Wilson, "Keeping Up with the Joneses and Staying Ahead of the Smiths: Evidence from Suicide Data," *Federal Reserve Bank of San Francisco Working Paper*, 2006, 1–41.

Damati, "Hilkiya Palace" = E. Damati, "The Palace of Hilkiya," *Kadmoniot* 15 (1982): 117–120 [in Hebrew].

D'Ambra, "Smith's Tomb" = E. D'Ambra, "A Myth for a Smith: A Meleager Sarcophagus from a Tomb in Ostia," *AJA* 92, no. 1 (1988): 85–99.

Dan, *The City* = Y. Dan, *Life in The City in Eretz-Israel During the Late Ancient Period*, Jerusalem: Yad Yitzhak Ben Zvi, 1984 [in Hebrew].

Danby, *The Mishnah* = H. Danby, *The Mishnah Translated from the Hebrew*. Peabody, MA: Hendrickson, 2011 [1933].

Danker, *Dictionary* = F.W. Danker, *Greek–English Lexicon of the New Testament and Other Early Christian Literature*. Chicago: University of Chicago Press, 2000.

Dar, *Landscape and Pattern* = S. Dar, *Landscape and Pattern: An Archeological Survey of Samaria 800 BCE–636 CE*. Oxford: Biblical Archaeological Review, 1986.

Dar, *Sumaqa* = S. Dar, *Sumaqa: A Roman and Byzantine Jewish Village on Mount Carmel, Israel*. Oxford: Archaeopress, 1999.

Dar, *Mount Carmel* = S. Dar, *Rural Settlements on Mount Carmel in Antiquity*. Oxford: Archaeopress, 2014.

Dar et al., *Um Rihan* = S. Dar, Z. Safrai, and Y. Tepper, *Um Rihan: A Village of the Mishnah*. Tel Aviv: Hakibbutz Hameuchad, 1987 [in Hebrew].

Dark, *Theoretical Archeology* = K.R. Dark, *Theoretical Archeology*. Ithaca, NY: Cornell University Press, 1995.

D'Arms, *Commerce Standing* = J.H. D'Arms, *Commerce and Social Standing in Ancient Rome*. Cambridge, MA: Harvard University Press, 1981.

Davies, "Wealth" = J. Davies, "Wealth, attitudes to," in *OCD*, 1571–1572.

Davies, "Work and Slavery" = M. Davies, "Work and Slavery in the New Testament: Impoverishments of Traditions," in John W. Rogerson, M. Davies, and M.D. Carroll (eds.), *The Bible in Ethics*. Sheffield, UK: Sheffield Academic Press, 1995, 315–347.

De Ligt, "Peasantry" = L. De Ligt, "Demand, Supply, Distribution: The Roman Peasantry between Town and Countryside: Rural Monetization and Peasant Demand," *MBAH* 9, no. 2 (1990): 24–56.

De Ligt, *Markets* = L. De Ligt, *Fairs and Markets in the Roman Empire: Economic and Social Aspects of Periodic Trade in a Pre-Industrial Society*. Amsterdam: Gieben, 1993.

De Ligt, *Peasants* = L. De Ligt, *Peasants, Citizens and Soldiers: Studies in the Demographic History of Roman Italy 225 BC–AD 100*. Cambridge: Cambridge University Press, 2012.

Delitzsch, *Hebrew NT* = F. Delitzsch, *The Hebrew New Testament of the British and Foreign Bible Society*. Leipzig: Dörffling & Franke, 1883.

De Ste Croix, *Class Struggle* = G.E.M. De Ste Croix, *The Class Struggle in the Ancient Greek World: From the Archaic Age to the Arab Conquest*. London: Duckworth, 1981.

Derret, *Law* = F.D.M. Derret, *Law in the New Testament*. Eugene, OR: Wipf and Stock, 2005.

Dessau, *ILS* = H. Dessau, *Inscriptiones Latinae Selectae*, II. Berlin: Weidmann, 1962.

Destro and Pesce, "Householders" = A. Destro and M. Pesce, "Fathers and Householders in the Jesus Movement: The Perspective of the Gospel of Luke," *Bible Interpretation* 11, no. 2 (2003): 211–238.

De-Vaan, *Dictionary Latin* = M. De-Vaan, *Etymological Dictionary of Latin and the other Italic Languages*. Leiden: Brill, 2008.

Devine, *Social Class* = F. Devine, *Social Class in America and Britain*. Edinburgh: Edinburgh University Press, 1997.

Dixon, *Roman Family* = S. Dixon, *The Roman Family*. Baltimore: Johns Hopkins University Press, 1992.

Domeris, "asir" = W.R. Domeris, "*asir*," Van Gemeren, *Dictionary*, 3:558–560.

Domeris, "dk'" = W.R. Domeris, "dk'," in VanGemeren, *Dictionary*, 1:943–946.

Domeris, "ebion" = W.R. Domeris, "ebion," in VanGemeren, *Dictionary*, 1:228–232.

Domeris, "hon" = W.R. Domeris, "*hon*," in VanGemeren, *Dictionary*, 1:1020–1021.

Domeris, "misken" = W.R. Domeris, "misken," in VanGemeren, *Dictionary*, 2:1001–1002.

Domeris, "mwk" = W.R. Domeris, "mwk," in VanGemeren, *Dictionary*, 2:868.

Domeris, "rws" = W.R. Domeris, "rws," in VanGemeren, *Dictionary*, 3:1085–1087.

Drexhage, Konen, and Ruffing, *Wirtschaft* = H.-J. Drexhage, H. Konen, and K. Ruffing, *Die Wirtschaft des römischen Reiches (1.–3. Jahrhundert), Eine Enführung*. Berlin: Akademie Verlag, 2002.

Dumbrell, "anaw, ani" = W.J. Dumbrell, "anaw, ani," in VanGemeren, *Dictionary*, 3:454–464.

Duncan-Jones, *Economy* = R. Duncan-Jones, *The Economy of the Roman Empire: Quantitative Studies*. Cambridge: Cambridge University Press, 1982.

Duncan-Jones, *Structure* = R. Duncan-Jones, *Structure and Scale in the Roman Economy*. Cambridge: Cambridge University Press, 1990.

Duncan-Jones, *Money* = R. Duncan-Jones, *Money and Government in the Roman Empire*. Cambridge: Cambridge University Press, 1994.

Dyson, "Settlement Patterns" = S. Dyson, "Settlement Patterns in the Ager Cosanus," *Journal of Field Archaeology* 5, no. 3 (1978): 68–251.

Dyson, *Community and Society* = S. Dyson, *Community and Society in Roman Italy*. Baltimore: Johns Hopkins University Press, 1992.

Edelstein, "Roman Villa" = G. Edelstein, "What's a Roman Villa Doing outside Jerusalem?" *BAR* 16 (1990): 32–42.

Edgell, *Class* = S. Edgell, *Class*. London: Routledge, 1993.

Edwards, "Jotapata" = D.R. Edwards, "Jotapata," *OEANE* 3 (1997): 251–252.

Edwards, "Khirbet Qana" = D.R. Edwards, "Khirbet Qana: From Jewish Village to Christian Pilgrim Site," in J.H. Humphrey (ed.), *The Roman and Byzantine Near East 3*. Ann Arbor, MI: Cushing Malloy, 2002, 101–132.

Edwards and Eshel, "Language and Writing" = D.R. Edwards and E. Eshel, "Language and Writing in Early Roman Galilee: Social Location of a Potter's Abecedary from Khirbet Qana," in D.R. Edwards (ed.), *Religion and Society in Roman Palestine: Old Questions, New Approaches*. London: Routledge, 2004, 49–55.

Ellis, *Roman Housing* = S.P. Ellis, *Roman Housing*. London: Duckworth, 2000.

Ellis, "Middle Class Houses" = S.P. Ellis, "Middle Class Houses in Late Antiquity," in W. Bowden, A. Gutteridge, and C. Machado (eds.), *Social and Political Life in Late Antiquity*. Leiden: Brill, 2006, 413–437.

Elman, "Orality" = Y. Elman, "Orality and the Redaction of the Babylonian Talmud," *Oral Tradition* 14, no. 1 (1999): 52–99.

Elman, "Response" = Y. Elman, "How Should a Talmudic Intellectual History Be Written? A Response to David Kraemer's Responses," *JQR* 89 (1999): 361–386.

Epstein, *Introduction Mishnah* = J.N. Epstein, *Introduction to the Mishnaic Text*. Jerusalem: Magnes Press, 2001 [in Hebrew].

Erdkamp, *Grain Market* = P. Erdkamp, *The Grain Market in the Roman Empire: A Social, Political and Economic Study*. Cambridge: Cambridge University Press, 2005.

Erdkamp, "Economic Growth" = P. Erdkamp, "Economic Growth in the Roman Mediterranean World: An Early Goodbye to Malthus?" *Explorations in Roman Economic History* 60 (2016), 1–20.

Eshel, "Aramaic Ostraca" = E. Eshel, "Aramaic Ostraca from Areas W and X-2," in H. Geva (ed.), *Jewish Quarter Excavations in the Old City of Jerusalem: Conducted by Nahman Avigad, 1969–1982*, Vol. 2: *The Finds from Area A, W and X-2*. Jerusalem: Israel Exploration Society, 2003, 401–404.

Eshel, "Bar Kochba" = H. Eshel, "The Bar Kochba Revolt, 132–135," in *CHJ* 4 (2006), 105–127.

Even-Shoshan, *Dictionary* = A. Even-Shoshan, *Hamilon Hechadash*. Jerusalem: Kiryat Sefer, 1998 [in Hebrew].

Ewherido, *Matthew* = A.O. Ewherido, *Matthew's Gospel and Judaism in the Late First Century CE: The Evidence from Matthew's Chapter on Parables (Matthew 13:1–52)*. New York: Peter Lang, 2006.

Fagan, "Social Structure" = G.G. Fagan, "Social Structure and Mobility: Greece and Rome," in Bagnall et al., *Encyclopedia* 11, 6299–6303.

Faust and Safrai, "Salvage Excavations" = A. Faust and Z. Safrai, "Salvage Excavations as a Source for Reconstructing Settlement History in Ancient Israel," *Palestine Exploration Quarterly* 137, no. 2 (2005): 139–158.

Fiensy, *Social History* = D.A. Fiensy, *The Social History of Palestine in the Herodian Period: The Land Is Mine*. Lewiston, NY: E. Mellen, 1991.

Fiensy, "Leaders" = D. Fiensy, "Leaders of Mass Movements and the Leader of the Jesus Movement," *JSNT* 21, no. 74 (1999): 3–27.

Fiensy, "Galilean House" = D.A. Fiensy, "The Galilean House in the Late Second Temple and Mishnaic Periods," in D.A. Fiensy and J.R. Strange (eds.), *Galilee in the Late Second Temple and Mishnaic Periods*. Minneapolis: Fortress Press, 2014, 216–241.

Fiensy, "Villages" = D.A. Fiensy, "The Galilean Village in the Late Second Temple and Mishnaic Periods," in D.A. Fiensy and J.R. Strange (eds.), *Galilee in the Late Second Temple and Mishnaic Periods*. Minneapolis: Fortress Press, 2014, 177–207.

Fine, "Marxist Social" = R. Fine, "Marxist Social Thought, History of," in N.J. Smelser and P.B. Baltes (eds.), *International Encyclopedia of the Social and Behavioral Sciences*, vol. 14, Oxford: Elsevier, 2001, 9311–9317.

Fine, *Art and Judaism* = S. Fine, *Art and Judaism in the Greco-Roman World: Toward a New Jewish Archaeology*. Cambridge: Cambridge University Press, 2005.

Fine, "Reading Sources" = S. Fine, "Archaeology and the Interpretation of Rabbinic Literature: Some Thoughts," in M. Kraus (ed.), *How Should Rabbinic Literature Be Read in the Modern World?* Piscataway, NJ: Gorgias Press, 2006, 199–217.

Finkelstein, *Pharisees* = L. Finkelstein, *The Pharisees: The Sociological Background of their Faith*, Philadelphia: Jewish Publication Society of America, 1962.

Finley, *Ancient Economy* = M.I. Finley, *The Ancient Economy*, 2nd ed. London: Chatto and Windus, 1985. [And with addendum and update, *The Ancient Economy*, update ed. with forward by Ian Morris, Berkeley: University of California Press, 1999].

Fitzmyer, *Luke I–IX* = J.A. Fitzmyer, *The Gospel According to Luke I–IX: Introduction, Translation, and Notes*. New York: Doubleday, 1985.

Fitzmyer, *The Acts of the Apostles* = J.A. Fitzmyer, *The Acts of the Apostles—A New Translation with Introduction and Commentary*. New York: Doubleday, 1998.

Flohr and Wilson, "Craftsmen" = M. Flohr and A. Wilson, "Roman Craftsmen and Traders: Toward an Intellectual History," in A. Wilson and M. Flohr (eds.), *Urban Craftsmen and Traders in the Roman World*. Oxford: Oxford University Press, 2016, 23–54.

Foster, "Relative Poverty" = J.E. Foster, "Absolute Versus Relative Poverty," *The American Economic Review* 88, no. 2 (1998): 335–341.

Foxhall, "Dependent Tenant" = L. Foxhall, "The Dependent Tenant, Land Leasing and Labor in Italy and Greece," *JRS* 80 (1990): 97–114.

Foy, "Glass" = D. Foy, "An Overview of the Circulation of Glass in Antiquity," in A. Wilson and A. Bowman (eds.), *Trade, Commerce and the State in the Roman World*. Oxford: Oxford University Press, 2018, 265–300.

Fraade, "Local Leadership" = S.D. Fraade, "Local Jewish Leadership in Roman Palestine: The Case of the 'Parnas' in Early Rabbinic Sources in Light of Extra-Rabbinic Evidence," in A.I. Baumgarten et al. (eds.), *Halakhah in Light of Epigraphy*. Göttingen: Vandenhoeck & Ruprecht, 2011, 155–173.

Fraade, "Language" = S.D. Fraade, "Language Mix and Multilingualism in Ancient Palestine: Literary and Inscriptional Evidence," *Jewish Studies* 48 (2012): 1–40.

Fraade, "Innovation" = S.D. Fraade, "The Innovation of Nominalized Verbs in Mishnaic Hebrew as Marking an Innovation of Concept," in A. Elitzur, S. Bar-Asher, and A.J. Koller (eds.), *Studies in Mishnaic Hebrew and Related Fields—Proceedings of the Yale Symposium on Mishnaic Hebrew*. Jerusalem: Ben Yehuda Center for the History of the Hebrew Language, The Hebrew University of Jerusalem, 2017, 129–148.

Frank, *Economic History* = T. Frank, *An Economic History of Rome: To the End of the Republic*. Baltimore: Johns Hopkins University Press, 1920.

Freu, "Labour Status" = C. Freu, "Labour Status and Economic Stratification in the Roman World: The Hierarchy of Wages in Egypt," *JRA* 18 (2015): 161–177.

Freyne, *Jesus Galilee* = S. Freyne, *Jesus, a Jewish Galilean: A New Reading of the Jesus Story*. London: Bloomsbury, 2004.

Friedman, *Marriage* = M.A. Friedman, *Jewish Marriage in Palestine: A Cairo Geniza Study*. Tel Aviv: Tel Aviv University, 1980.

Friedman, *Tosefta Atiqta* = S. Friedman, *Tosefta Atiqta Pesah Rishon*. Ramat Gan: Bar-Ilan University Press, 2002.

Friedman, "Yevamot" = S. Friedman, "A Critical Study of Yevamot X with a Methodological Introduction," in *Texts and Studies*. New York: Ktav, 1974, 275–441.

Friedrichsen, "The Temple" = T.A. Friedrichsen, "The Temple, a Pharisee, a Tax Collector, and the Kingdom of God: Rereading a Jesus Parable (Luke 18:10–14A)," *JBL* 129 (2005): 89–119.

Frier, "Subsistence Annuities" = B. Frier, "Subsistence Annuities and Per Capita Income in the Early Roman Empire," in *Classical Philology* 88, no. 3 (1993): 222–230.

Frier and Kehoe, "Law and Institutions" = B.W. Frier and D.P. Kehoe, "Law and Economic Institutions," in W. Scheidel, I. Morris, and R. Saller (eds.), *The Cambridge Economic History of the Greco-Roman World*. Cambridge: Cambridge University Press, 2007, 113–143.

Friesen, "Poverty Pauline" = S.J. Friesen, "Poverty in Pauline Studies," *JSNT* 26, no. 3 (2004): 323–361.

Gabba, "History" = E. Gabba, "The Social, Economic and Political History of Palestine 63 BCE–CE 70," *CHJ* 3 (1999), 94–167.

Gafni, "Rabbinic Historiography" = I. Gafni, "Rabbinic Historiography and Representations of the Past," in C.E. Fonrobert and M.S. Jaffee (eds.), *The Cambridge Companion to the Talmud and Rabbinic Literature*, Cambridge: Cambridge University Press, 2007, 295–312.

Galinsky, "Augustan Programme" = K. Galinsky, "Augustan Programme," in Jacobson and Kokkinos, *Herod and Augustus*, 29–42.

Galor, "Domestic Architecture" = K. Galor, "Domestic Architecture," in C. Hezser (ed.), *The Oxford Handbook of Jewish Daily Life in Roman Palestine*. Oxford: Oxford University Press, 2010, 420–439.

Gane, "Weber" = N. Gane, "Max Weber as Social Theorist: 'Class, Status, Party,'" *European Journal of Social Theory* 8, no. 2 (2005): 211–226.

Ganor et al., "Roman Villa" = A. Ganor, A. Klein, S. Ganor, and E. Klein, (eds.), "A Roman Villa at Urkan el Khala Northwest of Eleutheropolis," *Kadmoniyot* 139 (2010): 26–30 [in Hebrew].

Gardner, Organized Charity = G.E. Gardner, *The Origins of Organized Charity in Rabbinic Judaism*. Cambridge: Cambridge University Press, 2015.

Garnsey, "Legal Privilege" = P. Garnsey, "Legal Privilege in the Roman Empire," *Past and Present* 41 (1968): 324.

Garnsey, "Introduction" = P. Garnsey, "Introduction," in P. Garnsey, (ed.), *Non-Slave Labor in the Greco-Roman World*. Cambridge: Cambridge Philological Society, 1980, 1–5.

Garnsey, *Famine* = P. Garnsey, *Famine and Food Supply in the Graeco-Roman World*. Cambridge: Cambridge University Press, 1988.

Garnsey, "Veyne" = P. Garnsey, "The Generosity of Veyne," *JRS* 81 (1991): 164–168.

Garnsey, "Mass Diet" = P. Garnsey, "Mass Diet and Nutrition in the City of Rome," in P. Garnsey and W. Scheidel (eds.), *Cities, Peasants and Food in Classical Antiquity*. Cambridge: Cambridge University Press, 1998, 226–252.

Garnsey, "Peasants" = P. Garnsey, "Peasants in Ancient Roman Society," in P. Garnsey and W. Scheidel, (eds.), *Cities, Peasants and Food in Classical Antiquity*. Cambridge: Cambridge University Press, 1998, 91–106.

Garnsey, *Food* = P. Garnsey, *Food and Society in Classical Antiquity*. Cambridge: Cambridge University Press, 1999.

Garnsey, "The Land" = P. Garnsey, "The Land," *CAH* 11 (2000): 679–709.

Garnsey and Saller, *Economy and Society* = P. Garnsey and R. Saller, *The Roman Empire: Economy, Society and Culture*. London: Duckworth, 1987.

Garrison, *Redemptive Almsgiving* = R. Garrison, *Redemptive Almsgiving in Early Christianity*. Sheffield: JSOT Press, 1993.

Giardina, *The Romans* = A. Giardina, ed., *The Romans*. Trans. L.G. Cochrane. Chicago: University of Chicago Press, 1993.

Gibbs, "Collegia" = M. Gibbs, "Collegia," in Bagnall et al., *Encyclopedia*, 3:1649–1652.

Gibson, *Social Stratification* = G.S. Gibson, *The Social Stratification of Jewish Palestine in the First Century of the Christian Era*, PhD Diss., University College, London, 1976.

Giddens, *Class Structure* = A. Giddens, *The Class Structure of the Advanced Societies*. New York: Harper and Row, 1981 [1973].

Giddens, *Sociology* = A. Giddens, *Sociology*. Cambridge: Polity Press, 1993.

Giddens and Held, "Introduction" = A. Giddens and D. Held, "Introduction," in A. Giddens and D. Held (eds.), *Classes, Power and Conflict: Classical and Contemporary Debates*. Berkeley: University of California Press, 1982, 3–11.

Giddens et al., *Introduction* = A. Giddens, M. Duneier, R.P. Applebaum, and D. Carr, *Introduction to Sociology*, 9th ed. New York: Norton and Company, 2013.

Glare, *Latin Dictionary* = P.G.W. Glare, *Oxford Latin Dictionary*. Oxford: Oxford University Press, 1983.

Gluska, *Hebrew and Aramaic* = I. Gluska, *Hebrew and Aramaic in Contact during the Tannaitic Period: A Sociolinguistic Approach*. Tel Aviv: Papirus, 1999 [in Hebrew].

Goldberg, "Mishnah" = A. Goldberg, "The Mishnah—A Study Book of Halakha," in Safrai, *The Literature*, 1: 211–262.

Goldberg, "Tosefta" = A. Goldberg, "The Tosefta: Companion to the Mishnah," in Safrai, *The Literature*, 1: 283–302.

Goldthorpe and Marshall, "Promising Future" = J.H. Goldthorpe and G. Marshall, "The Promising Future of Class Analysis: A Response to Recent Critiques," *Sociology* 26, no. 3 (1992): 381–400.

Goodblatt, "Rehabilitation" = D. Goodblatt, "Towards a Rehabilitation of the Talmudic History," in B.M. Bokser (ed.), *History of Judaism: The Next Ten Years*. Chico, CA: Scholars Press, 1980, 31–44.

Goodblatt, *Monarchic Principle* = D. Goodblatt, *The Monarchic Principle: Studies in Jewish Self-Government in Antiquity*. Tübingen: Mohr Siebeck, 1994.

Goodblatt, "History" = D. Goodblatt, "The Political and Social History of the Jewish Community in the Land of Israel, c. 235–638," *CHJ* 4 (2006), 404–430.

Goodman, *Ruling Class* = M. Goodman, *The Ruling Class of Judaea: The Origins of the Jewish Revolt against Rome, AD 66–70*. Cambridge: Cambridge University Press, 1987.

Goodman, *Roman Galilee* = M. Goodman, *State and Society in Roman Galilee AD 132–212*, 2nd Ed. London: Vallentine Mitchell, 2000.

Gorin-Rosen, "Ancient Glass" = Y. Gorin-Rosen, "The Ancient Glass Industry in Israel: Summary of the Finds and New Discoveries," *Travaux de la Maison de l'Orient méditerranéen* 33 (2000): 49–63.

Gorin-Rosen, "Glass" = Y. Gorin-Rosen, "The Ancient Glass Industry in Eretz-Israel: A Brief Summary," *Michmanim* 16 (2002): 7–18.

Grantham, "The Butchers of Sepphoris" = B. Grantham, "The Butchers of Sepphoris: Archaeological Evidence of Ethnic Variability," in D.R. Edwards and C.T. McCollough (eds.), *Archaeology and the Galilee: Texts and Contexts in the Graeco Roman and Byzantine Periods*, Atlanta: Scholars Press, 1997, 279–289.

Gray, "Formally Wealthy" = A.M. Gray, "The Formally Wealthy Poor: From Empathy to Ambivalence in Rabbinic Literature of Late Antiquity," *AJS* 33, no. 1 (2009): 101–133.

Gray, "Redemptive Almsgiving" = A.M. Gray, "Redemptive Almsgiving and the Rabbis of Late Antiquity," *JSQ* 18, no. 2 (2011): 144–184.

Greene, *Archaeology* = K. Greene, *The Archaeology of the Roman Economy*. London: Batsford, 1986.

Greene, "Technological Innovation" = K. Greene, "Technological Innovation and Economic Progress in the Ancient World: M.I. Finley Re-Considered," *Economic History Review* 53, no. 1 (2000): 29–50.

Grey, "Colonatus" = C. Grey, "Contextualizing Colonatus: The Origo of the Late Roman Empire," *JRS* 97 (2007): 165–170.

Grusky, "Social Stratification" = D.B. Grusky, "Introduction: The Contours of Social Stratification," in D.B. Grusky (ed.), *Social Stratification: Class, Race, and Gender in Sociological Perspective*. Boulder, CO: Westview Press, 1994, 1–18.

Guijarro, "Family Galilee" = S. Guijarro, "La familia en la Galilea del siglo primero," *Estudios Bíblicos* 53, no. 4 (1995): 461–488.

Guijarro, "Family First Century" = S. Guijarro, "The Family in First-Century Galilee," in H. Moxnes (ed.), *Constructing Early Christian Families*. London: Routledge, 1997, 42–65.

Guijarro, "Home and Family" = S. Guijarro, "Domestic Space, Family Relationships and the Social Location of the Q People," *JSNT* 27, no. 1 (2004): 69–81.

Hadas, "Ein Gedi" = G. Hadas, "The Second Temple Period Village at the *Ein Gedi* Oasis," *Kadmoniot* 44 (2011): 41–43 [in Hebrew].

Hales, *House and Social* = S. Hales, *The Roman House and Social Identity*. Cambridge: Cambridge University Press, 2003.

Halivni, "Methods" = D.W. Halivni, "Contemporary Methods of the Study of Talmud," *JJS* 30, no. 2 (1979): 192–201.

Hall, "Reworking" = J.R. Hall, "The Reworking of Class Analysis," J.R. Hall (ed.), *Reworking Class*. Ithaca, NY: Cornell University Press, 1997, 1–37.

Hamel, *Poverty* = G. Hamel, *Poverty and Charity in Roman Palestine*. Berkeley, University of California Press, 1990.

Hamel, "Poverty and Charity" = G. Hamel, "Poverty and Charity," in C. Hezser (ed.), *The Oxford Handbook of Jewish Daily Life in Roman Palestine*. Oxford: Oxford University Press, 2010, 308–324.

Hands, *Charities* = A.R. Hands, *Charities and Social Aid in Greece and Rome*. London: Thames and Hudson, 1968.

Hanson and Oakman, *Palestine Jesus* = K.C. Hanson and D.E. Oakman, *Palestine in the Time of Jesus: Social Structures and Social Conflicts*. Minneapolis: Fortress Press, 1998.

Harries, *Cicero* = J. Harries, *Cicero and the Jurists: From Citizens' Law to the Lawful State*, London: Bristol Classical Press, 2006.

Harries, *Law and Crime* = J. Harries, *Law and Crime in the Roman World*. Cambridge: Cambridge University Press, 2007.

Harris, "Workshop" = E.M. Harris, "Workshop, Marketplace and Household," in P. Cartledge, E. Cohen, and L. Foxhall (eds.), *Money Labor and Land: Approaches to the Economies of Ancient Greece*. London: Routledge, 2001, 67–99.

Harris, "Midrash Halakhah" = J.M. Harris, "Midrash Halakhah," *CHJ* 4 (2006), 336–368.

Harris, *Imperial Economy* = W.V. Harris, *Rome's Imperial Economy: Twelve Essays*. Oxford: Oxford University Press, 2011.

Harris, "Wood" = W.V. Harris, "The Indispensible Commodity: Notes on the Economy of Wood in the Roman Mediterranean," in A. Wilson and A. Bowman (eds.), *Trade, Commerce and State in the Roman World*. Oxford: Oxford University Press, 2018, 211–236.

Hatch and Redpath, *Concordance Septuagint* = E. Hatch and H.A. Redpath, *A Concordance to the Septuagint*. Grand Rapids, MI: Baker Books, 1998.

Hauck, πένης = F. Hauck, πένης, in Kittel, *TDNT*, 6:37–40.

Hauck and Kasch, πλοῦτος, πλούσιος πλουτέω, πλουτίζω = F. Hauck and W. Kasch, πλοῦτος, πλούσιος πλουτέω, πλουτίζω, in Kittel, *TDNT*, 6: 318–332.

Hawkins, *Artisans* = C. Hawkins, *Roman Artisans and the Urban Economy*. Cambridge: Cambridge University Press, 2016.

Heichelheim, *Roman Syria* = F.M. Heichelheim, *Roman Syria*. Baltimore: Johns Hopkins University Press.

Hezser, *Social Structure* = C. Hezser, *The Social Structure of the Rabbinic Movement in Roman Palestine*. Tübingen: Mohr Siebeck, 1997.

Hicks, "Markan Discipleship" = R. Hicks, "Markan Discipleship according to Malachi: The Significance of μὴ ἀποστερήσῃς in the Story of the Rich Man (Mark 10:17–22)," *JBL* 132, no. 1 (2013): 179–199.

Hirschfeld, *Dwelling* = Y. Hirschfeld, *The Palestinian Dwelling in the Roman–Byzantine Period*. Jerusalem: Israel Exploration Society, 1995.

Hirschfeld, *Dead Sea Valley* = Y. Hirschfeld, *Hakmihah el Hamidbar: Bikat Yam Hamelakh Bitkufat Habayit Hasheni*. Tel Aviv: Yediot Aharonot, 2000.

Hirschfeld, *Ramat Hanadiv* = Y. Hirschfeld, *Ramat Hanadiv Excavations: Final Report of the 1984–1998 Seasons*. Jerusalem: IEA, 2000.

Hirschfeld, "Property versus Poverty" = Y. Hirschfeld, "Ramat Hanadiv and Ein Gedi: Property versus Poverty in Judea before 70," in J.H. Charlesworth (ed.), *Jesus in Archaeology*. Grand Rapids, MI: Eerdmans, 2006, 384–392.

Hirschfeld, "En Gedi" = Y. Hirschfeld, "En Gedi: 'A Very Large Village of Jews'—Summary and Conclusions," in Y. Hirschfeld, *En Gedi Excavations II Final Report (1996–2002)*. Jerusalem: Israel Exploration Society, 2007, 641–653.

Hirschfeld and Foerster, "Tiberias" = Y. Hirschfeld and G. Foerster, "Tiberias," in E. Stern (ed.), *NEAEHL* 4:1464–1473.

Hock, *Social Paul* = R. Hock, *The Social Context of Paul's Ministry*. Philadelphia: Fortress Press, 1980.

Hogeterp, "Luke Wisdom" = A.L.A. Hogeterp, "Immaterial Wealth in Luke between Wisdom and Apocalypticism: Luke's Jesus Tradition in Light of 4QInstruction," *Early Christianity* 4, no. 1 (2013): 41–63.

Holleran, *Shopping* = C. Holleran, *Shopping in Ancient Rome: The Retail Trade in the Late Republic and the Principate*. Oxford: Oxford University Press, 2012.

Hope, *Song of Songs* = M.H. Hope, *Song of Songs*. New York: Doubleday, 1977.

Hope, "Roman Identity" = V.M. Hope, "Constructing Roman Identity: Funerary Monuments and Social Structure in the Roman World," *Mortality* 2, no. 2 (1997): 103–121.

Hopkins, "City Region" = I.W.J. Hopkins, "The City Region in Roman Palestine," *PEQ* 112 (1980): 19–32.

Hopkins, *Conquerors and Slaves* = K. Hopkins, *Conquerors and Slaves*. Cambridge: Cambridge University Press, 1978.

Hopkins, "Economic Growth" = K. Hopkins, "Economic Growth and Towns in Classical Antiquity," in P. Abrahams and E.A. Wrigley (eds.), *Towns in Societies: Essays in Economic History and Historic Sociology*. Cambridge: Cambridge University Press, 1978, 35–77.

Hopkins, "Taxes" = K. Hopkins, "Taxes and Trade in the Roman Empire (200 BC–AD 400)," *JRS* 70 (1980): 101–125.

Hopkins, "Rome Taxes" = K. Hopkins, "Rome, Taxes, Rents and Trade," in W. Scheidel and S. Von Reden (eds.), *The Ancient Economy*. Edinburgh: Edinburgh University Press, 2002, 190–230.

Horbury, *Trajan and Hadrian* = W. Horbury, *Jewish War under Trajan and Hadrian*. Cambridge: Cambridge University Press, 2014.

Horden and Purcell, *The Corrupting Sea* = P. Horden and N. Purcell, *The Corrupting Sea: A Study of Mediterranean History*. Oxford: Wiley-Blackwell, 2000.

Horrell, *Social* = D.G. Horrell, *Social Scientific Approaches to New Testament Interpretation*. Edinburgh: T&T Clark, 1999.

Horrell, "Meetings" = D.G. Horrell, "Domestic Space and Christian Meetings at Corinth: Imagining New Contexts and the Buildings East of the Theatre," *New Testament Studies* 50, no. 3 (2004): 349–369.

Howgego, "Use of Money" = C. Howgego, "The Supply and Use of Money in the Roman World, 200 BC to AD 300," *JRS* 82 (1992): 1–31.

Iacono, "Pottery Trade" = F. Iacono, "Pottery Trade," in Bagnall et al., *Encyclopedia*, 10: 5489–5491.

Irsai, "Priesthood" = O. Irsai, "The Role of the Priesthood in the Jewish Community in Late Antiquity: A Christian Model?" in C. Cluse, A. Havercamp, and I.J. Yuval (eds.), *Jüdische Gemeinden und ihr christlicher Kontext in kulturräumlich vergleichender Betrachtung, von der Spätantike bis zum 18. Jahrhundert*. Hannover: Hahn, 2003, 75–85.

Israelowich, *Patient and Healers* = I. Israelowich, *Patient and Healers in the High Roman Empire*. Baltimore: Johns Hopkins University Press, 2015.

Jackson, "Ketubah" = B.S. Jackson, "Problems in the Development of the Ketubah Payment: The Shimon ben Shetah Tradition," in C. Hezser (ed.), *Rabbinic Law in its Roman and Near Eastern Context*. Tübingen: Mohr Siebeck, 2003, 199–225.

Jackson, *Doctors* = R. Jackson, *Doctors and Diseases in the Roman Empire*. Norman: University of Oklahoma Press, 1988.

Jacobson and Kokkinos, *Herod and Augustus* = D.M. Jacobson and N. Kokkinos (eds.), *Herod and Augustus: Papers Prsented at the IJS Conference June 21–23, 2005*. Leiden: Brill, 2008.

Jastrow, Dictionary = M. Jastrow, *Dictionary of the Targumim, The Talmud Babli and Yerushami, and the Midrashic Literature*, 2 Vols. New York: Pardes, 1950.

John, *Social Standing* = H.D. John, *Commerce and Social Standing in Ancient Rome*. Cambridge, MA: Harvard University Press, 1981.

Johnson, James = L. Timothy Johnson, *The Letter of James: A New Translation with Introduction and Commentary*. New York: Doubleday, 2010.

Johnston, *Roman Law* = D. Johnston, *Roman Law in Context*. Cambridge: Cambridge University Press, 1999.

Jones, "Urbanization" = A.H.M. Jones, "The Urbanization of Palestine," *JRS* 21 (1931): 78–85.

Jones, *Later Empire* = A.H.M. Jones, *The Later Roman Empire 284–602 CE*, Vols. 1–2. Oxford: Blackwell, 1964.

Jones, *Cities Eastern* = A.H.M. Jones, *The Cities of the Eastern Roman Provinces*. Oxford: Oxford University Press, 1971.

Jones, Economy = A.H.M. Jones, *The Roman Economy*. Ed. P.A. Brunt. Oxford: Blackwell, 1974.

Jones, Bankers = D. Jones, *The Bankers of Puteoli: Finance, Trade, Industry in the Roman World*. Glaucestershire, UK: Tempus, 2006.

Jongkind, "Corinth and Class" = D. Jongkind, "Corinth in the First Century AD: The Search for Another Class," *Tynbul* 52 (2001): 139–148.

Jongman, *Pompeii Society* = W. Jongman, *The Economy and Society of Pompeii*. Amsterdam: J.C. Gieben, 1988.

Jongman, "Hunger and Power" = W. Jongman, "Hunger and Power: Theories, Models and Methods in Roman Economic History," in H. Bongenaar (ed.), *Interdependency of Institutions and Private Entrepreneurs: Proceedings of the Second MOS Symposium*. Leiden: Nederlands Historisch-Archaeologische Instituut, 1998, 259–284.

Joshel, *Work Identity* = S.R. Joshel, *Work Identity and Legal Status in Rome*. Norman: University of Oklahoma Press, 1992.

Kahana, "Halakhic Midrashim" = M.I. Kahana, "The Halakhic Midrashim," in Safrai, *The Literature*, 3–105.

Kalmin, "Problems Talmud" = R.L. Kalmin, "Problems in the Use of the Babylonian Talmud for the History of Late-Roman Palestine: The Example of Astrology," in M. Goodman and P. Alexander (eds.), *Rabbinic Texts and the History of Late-Roman Palestine*. Oxford: Oxford University Press, 2010, 165–183.

Kalmin, "Royal Family" = R.L. Kalmin, "The Adiabenian Royal Family in Rabbinic Literature of Late Antiquity," in J. Roth, M. Schmeltzer, and Y. Francus (eds.), *Tiferet leYisrael: Jubilee Volume in Honor of Israel Francus*. New York: JTS, 2010, 61–77.

Kasher, *Jews in Egypt* = A. Kasher, *The Jews in Hellenistic and Roman Egypt: The Struggle for Equal Rights*. Tübingen: Mohr Siebeck, 1985.

Kasher, *Cities* = A. Kasher, *Jews and Hellenistic Cities in Eretz-Israel: Relations of the Jews in Eretz-Israel with the Hellenistic Cities during the Second Temple Period (332 BCE–70 CE)*. Tübingen: Mohr Siebeck, 1990.

Katsari, *Monetary System* = C. Katsari, *The Roman Monetary System—The Eastern Provinces from the First to Third Century AD*. Cambridge: Cambridge University Press, 2011.

Kay, *Economic Revolution* = P. Kay, *Rome's Economic Revolution*. Oxford: Oxford University Press, 2014.

Keel, *Song of Songs* = O. Keel, *The Song of Songs: A Continental Commentary*. Trans. F.J. Gaiser. Minneapolis: Fortress Press, 1994.

Kehoe, *Economy Agriculture* = D.P. Kehoe, *The Economics of Agriculture on Roman Estates in North Africa*. Göttingen: Vandenhoeck and Ruprecht, 1988.

Kehoe, *Profit Tenancy* = D.P. Kehoe, *Investment, Profit and Tenancy: The Jurists and the Roman Agrarian Economy*. Ann Arbor: University of Michigan Press, 1997.

Kehoe, *Law Rural Economy* = D.P. Kehoe, *Law and Rural Economy in the Roman Empire*. Ann Arbor: University of Michigan Press, 2007.

Kehoe, "State and Production" = D. Kehoe, "The State and Production in the Roman Agrarian Economy," in A.K. Bowman and A. Wilson (eds.), *The Roman Agricultural Economy: Organization, Investment, and Production*. Oxford: Oxford University Press, 2013, 33–54.

Kelly, *Petitions* = B. Kelly, *Petitions, Litigation, and Social Control in Roman Egypt*. Oxford: Oxford University Press, 2011.

Kenny, "Past Poor" = C. Kenny, "Were People in the Past Poor and Miserable?" *Kyklos* 59, no. 2 (2006): 275–306.

Kerbo, *Social Stratification* = H.R. Kerbo, *Social Stratification and Inequality: Class Conflict in Historical, Comparative, and Global Perspective*. New York: McGraw-Hill, 2012.

Kharas and Gertz, "New Global Middle Class" = H. Kharas and G. Gertz, "The New Global Middle Class: A Cross-Over from East to West," in C. Li (ed.), *China's Emerging Middle Class: Beyond Economic Transformation*. Washington, DC: Brookings Institution Press, 2010, 32–51.

Killebrew, "Village" = A.K. Killebrew, "Village and Countryside," in C. Hezser (ed.), *The Oxford Handbook of Jewish Daily Life in Roman Palestine*. Oxford: Oxford University Press, 2010, 189–210.

Kindler and Stein, *City Coinage* = A. Kindler and A. Stein, *A Bibliography of the City Coinage of Palestine: from the 2nd Century B.C. to the 3rd Century A.D.* Oxford: BAR International, 1987.

Kittel, *TDNT* = G. Kittel and G. Friedrich (eds.), *Theological Dictionary of the New Testament*, Trans. G.W. Bromile, 10 Vols. Grand Rapids, MI: Eerdmans, 1964–1976.

Klein, *Corpus Inscriptionum* = S. Klein, *Jüdisch Palästinisches Corpus Inscriptionum*, 2 Vols. Vienna: R. Löwit, 1920.

Kloft, *Wirtschaft* = H. Kloft, *Die Wirtschaft der Griechisch-Roemischen Welt*. Darmstadt: Wissenschaftliche Buchgesellschaft, 1992.

Kloppenborg, "Tenancy" = J.S. Kloppenborg, "The Growth and Impact of Agricultural Tenancy in Jewish Palestine (III BCE–I CE)," *JESHO* 51 (2008): 31–66.

Kloppenborg and Ascough, *Associations* = J.S. Kloppenborg and R.S. Ascough, *Greco-Roman Associations: Texts, Translation, and Commentary*, Vol. 1: *Attica, Central Greece, Macedonia, Thrace*. Berlin: Walter de Gruyter, 2011.

Knapp, *Invisible* = R. Knapp, *Invisible Romans*. Cambridge, MA: Harvard University Press, 2011.

Koehler and Baumgartner, *Lexicon OT* = L. Koehler and W. Baumgartner (eds.), *The Hebrew and Aramaic Lexicon of the Old Testament*. Leiden: Brill, 1996.

Kokkinos, *Herodian Dynasty* = N. Kokkinos, *The Herodian Dynasty: Origins, Role in Society and Eclipse*. Sheffield: Sheffield Academic Press, 1998.

Kolakowski, *Currents of Marxism* = L. Kolakowski, *Main Currents of Marxism: Its Origins, Growth, and Dissolution*. Oxford: Oxford University Press, 2004.

Kolendo, "Peasants" = J. Kolendo, "The Peasants," in A. Giardina (ed.), L.G. Cochrane, (trans.), *The Romans*. Chicago: University of Chicago Press, 1993, 199–213.

Koopmans, "Ba'al" = W.I. Koopmans, "Ba'al" (b'l), in VanGemeren, *Dictionary*, 1:682.

Kraemer, "Mishnah" = D. Kraemer, "The Mishnah," *CHJ* 4 (2006), 299–315.

Krauss, *Lehnwörter* = S. Krauss, *Griechische and Lateinische Lehnwörteer in Talmud, Midrasch und Targum*, 2 Vols. Hildesheim, Germany: Georg Olms Verlagsbuchhandlung, 1964.

Kron, "Housing and Distribution" = G. Kron, "Comparative Evidence and the Reconstruction of the Ancient Economy: Greco–Roman Housing and the Level and Distribution of Wealth and Income," in F. De Callataÿ (ed.), *Quantifying the Greco-Roman Economy and Beyond*. Edipuglia, Italy: Bari, 123–146.

Lampe, *Patrisic Greek Lexicon* = C.W.H. Lampe, *A Patristic Greek Lexicon*. Oxford: Clarendon Press, 1961.

Lapin, *Law and History* = H. Lapin, *Early Rabbinic Civil Law and the Social History of Roman Galilee: A Study of Mishna Tractate Baba' Mesi'a'*. Atlanta: Scholars Press, 1995.

Laurence, "Space and Text" = R. Laurence, "Space and Text," in Laurence and Wallace-Hadrill, *Domestic Space*, 7–14.

Laurence and Wallace-Hadrill, *Domestic Space* = R. Laurence and A. Wallace-Hadrill (eds.), *Domestic Space in the Roman World: Pompeii and Beyond*. Portsmouth, RI: *JRA*, 1997.

Lee, "Class Theories" = D.J. Lee, "Weak Class Theories or Strong Sociology?" in D.J. Lee and B.S. Turner (eds.), *Conflicts about Class: Debating Inequality in Late Industrialism*. London: Longman, 1996, 245–253.

Légasse, *Du riche* = S. Légasse, *L'Appel du riche (Marc 10, 17–31 et parallèles): Contribution à l'étude des fondements scripturaires de l'état religieux*. Paris: Beauchesne, 1966.

Légasse, *Marc* = S. Légasse, *L'évangile de Marc*, Paris: Éditions du Cerf, 1997.

Lehtipuu, "Rich and Poor" = O. Lehtipuu, "The Rich, the Poor, and the Promise of an Eschatological Reward in the Gospel of Luke," in T. Nicklas, J. Verheyden, E. Eynikel, and F. Garcia Martinez (eds.), *Other Worlds and their Relation to this World: Early Jewish and Ancient Christian Traditions*. Leiden: Brill, 2010, 229–246.

Leibner, "Arts" = U. Leibner, "Arts and Crafts, Manufacture and Production," in C. Hezser (ed.), *The Oxford Handbook of Jewish Daily Life in Roman Palestine*. Oxford: Oxford University Press, 2010, 264–296.

Leibner, "Wadi Hamam" = U. Leibner, "Excavations at Khirbet Wadi Hamam (Lower Galilee): The Synagogue and the Settlement," *JRA* 23 (2010): 220–237.

Leibner, "Areas B, C and F" = U. Leibner, "Areas B, C and F: Stratigraphy and Architecture," in U. Leibner (ed.), *Khirbet Wadi Hamam: A Roman-Period Village and Synagogue in the Lower Galilee*. Qedem Reports 13. Jerusalem: The Hebrew University of Jerusalem, 2018, 195–254.

Lenski, *Power and Privilege* = G. Lenski, *Power and Privilege: A Theory of Social Stratification*. Chapel Hill: University of North Carolina Press, 1966.

Lenski and Lenski, *Human Societies* = G. Lenski and J. Lenski, *Human Societies: An Introduction to Macrosociology*. New York: McGraw-Hill, 1982.

Levine, "The Third Century" = L.I. Levine, "Palestine in the Third Century CE," in Z. Baras, S. Safrai, Y. Tsafrir, and M. Stern (eds.), *Eretz Yisrael from the Destruction of the Second Temple to the Muslim Conquest*, Vol. 1. Jerusalem: Yad Yitzhak Ben Zvi, 1982, 119–143 [in Hebrew].

Levine, *Rabbinic Class* = L.I. Levine, *The Rabbinic Class of Roman Palestine in Late Antiquity*. Jerusalem: Yad Yitzhak Ben Zvi, 1989.

Levine, "Bet Shearim Patriarchal" = L.I. Levine, "Bet Shearim in its Patriarchal Context," in M. Perani (ed.), *The Words of a Wise Man's Mouth Are Gracious*. Berlin: Walter de Gruyter, 2005, 197–225.

Levine, *The Ancient Synagogue* = L.I. Levine, *The Ancient Synagogue: The First Thousand Years*. New Haven, CT: Yale University Press, 2005.

Lewis and Short, *Latin Dictionary* = C.T. Lewis and C. Short, *A Latin Dictionary*. Oxford: Oxford University Press, 1966.

Lewis et al., *Cave of Letters* = N. Lewis, Y. Yadin, and J.C. Greenfield (eds.), *The Documents from the Bar Kokhba Period in the Cave of Letters*. Jerusalem: Israel Exploration Society, 1989.

Liddell and Scott, *Greek Lexicon* = H.G. Liddell and R. Scott, *A Greek-English Lexicon*, 9th edition. Oxford: Oxford University Press, 1996.

Lieberman, *The Tosefta* = S. Lieberman, *The Tosefta*, 8 Vols. New York: JTS, 1955–1988 [in Hebrew].

Lieberman, *Tosefta Kifshuta* = S. Lieberman, *Tosefta Kifshuta: A Comprehensive Commentary on the Tosefta*, Order *Zeraim*. New York: JTS, 1955; Order *Moed*, New

York: JTS, 1962; Order *Nashim*, New York: JTS, 1967–1968; Order *Neziqin*, New York: JTS, 1988 [in Hebrew].

Lieberman, *Sifre Zuta* = S. Lieberman, *Sifre Zuta: Midrashah Shel Lod*. New York: JTS, 1968.

Lieberman, *Studies* = S. Lieberman, *Studies in Palestinian Talmudic Literature*. Ed. D. Rosenthal. Jerusalem: Magnes Press, 1991 [in Hebrew].

Linder, *Legislation Jews* = A. Linder, *The Jews in Roman Imperial Legislation*. Detroit: Wayne State University Press, 1987.

Linder, "Legal Status" = A. Linder, "The Legal Status of the Jews in the Roman Empire," *CHJ* (2006), 4:128–173.

Ling, *Poor* = T.J.M. Ling, *The Judean Poor and the Fourth Gospel*. Cambridge: Cambridge University Press, 2006.

Lippold, *Vatican Sculptures* = G. Lippold, *De Skulpturen des Vatikanischen Museums Bd. III.2*, Berlin: Walter de Gruyter, 1956.

Lis and Soly, *Worthy Efforts* = C. Lis and H. Soly, *Worthy Efforts: Attitudes to Work and Workers in Pre-Industrial Europe*. Boston: Brill, 2012.

Liu, *Collegia* = J. Liu, *Collegia Centonariorum: The Guilds of Textile Dealers in the Roman West*. Leiden: Brill, 2009.

Loane, *Industry* = H.J. Loane, *Industry and Commerce of the City of Rome (50 BC–200 AD)*. Baltimore: Johns Hopkins University Press, 1938.

Lo Cascio, "Roman State" = E. Lo Cascio, "The Early Roman Empire: The State and the Economy," in W. Scheidel, I. Morris, and R. Saller (eds.), *The Cambridge Economic History of the Greco-Roman World*. Cambridge: Cambridge University Press, 2007, 619–647.

Loewe, "Structure and Practice" = M. Loewe, "The Structure and Practice of Government," in D. Twitchett and M. Loewe (eds.), *The Cambridge History of China 1: The Ch'in and Han Empires 221 BC–AD 220*. Cambridge: Cambridge University Press, 1986, 463–490.

Loewenberg, *Charity* = F.M. Loewenberg, *From Charity to Social Justice*. New Brunswick, NJ: Transaction, 2001.

Loewenstamm, "Neshech ve'Tarbit" = S.E. Loewenstamm, "Neshech ve'Tarbit," *Encyclopedia Biblica* (1968): 5:929–930.

Longenecker, "Economic Middle" = B.W. Longenecker, "Exposing the Economic Middle: A Revised Economy Scale for the Study of Early Urban Christianity," *JSNT* 31, no. 3 (2009): 243–278.

Longman, *OT Commentary* = T. Longman, *The Old Testament: New International Commentary*. Grand Rapids, MI: Eerdmans, 2001.

López-Calva and Ortiz-Juarez, "Vulnerability" = L.F. López-Calva and E. Ortiz-Juarez, "A Vulnerability Approach to the Definition of the Middle Classes," *Journal of Economic Inequality* 12, no. 1 (2014): 23–47.

Louw and Nida, *Lexicon* = J.P. Louw and F.A. Nida, *Greek-English Lexicon of the New Testament: Based on Semitic Domains*. New York: United Bible Societies, 1988–1989.

Love, *Antiquity Capitalism* = J.R. Love, *Antiquity and Capitalism: Max Weber and the Sociological Foundation of Roman Civilization*. London: Routledge, 1991.

Luhmann, *Law* = N. Luhmann, *Law as a Social System*. Trans. Klaus Ziegert, Ed. R. Nobles, David Schiff, and Rosamund Ziegert. Oxford: Oxford University Press, 2004.

Lukács, *HCC* = G. Lukács, *History and Class Consciousness: Studies in Marxist Dialectics*. Trans. Rodney Livingston. Cambridge, MA: MIT Press, 1971.

Luomanen, "Rich Man" = P. Luomanen, "Where Did another Rich Man Come From? The Jewish-Christian Profile of the A Story about a Rich Man in the 'Gospel of the Hebrews' (Origen, *Comm. In Matt*, 15.14)," *Vigiliae Christianae* 57, no. 3 (2003): 243–275.

Mackensy, "Pay Differentials" = D.C. Mackensy, "Pay Differentials in the Early Empire," *Classical World* 75, no. 6 (1983): 267–273.

MacMullen, *Social Relations* = R. MacMullen, *Roman Social Relations*, 50 BC to AD 284. New Haven: Yale University Press, 1974.

Magen et al., "Qiryat Sefer" = Y. Magen, Y. Tzionit, and O. Sirkis, "Hirbet Badd Isa–Qiryat Sefer," in Y. Magen et al. (eds.), *The Land of Benjamin*. Jerusalem: Israel Antiquities Authority, 2004, 179–241 [in Hebrew].

Magness, "Synagogues" = J. Magness, "Synagogues in Ancient Palestine: Problems of Typology and Chronology," in L.I. Levine (ed.), *Continuity and Renewal: Jews and Judaism in Byzantine Christian Palestine*. Jerusalem: Dinur Center for Research in Jewish History, 2004, 507–525.

Magness, Stone and Dung = J. Magness, *Stone and Dung Oil and Spit: Jewish Daily Life in the Time of Jesus*, Grand Rapids: Eerdmans, 2011.

Malherbe, "Wealth" = A.J. Malherbe, "Godliness, Self-Sufficiency, Greed, and the Enjoyment of Wealth in 1 Timothy 6: 3–19, Part 1," *Novum Testamentum* 52, no. 4 (2010): 376–405.

Mandel, "Tosefta" = P. Mandel, "The Tosefta," *CHJ* (2006), 4:316–335.

Manza and Brooks, "Class Analysis" = J. Manza and C. Brooks, "Does Class Analysis Have Anything to Contribute to the Study of Politics?" *Theory and Society* 25, no. 5 (1996): 717–724.

Marcus, *Mark 1–8* = J. Marcus, *Mark 1–8*. New Haven, CT: Yale University Press, 1999.

Marcus, *Mark 8–16* = J. Marcus, *Mark 8–16*. New Haven, CT: Yale University Press, 1999.

Marshall, *Repositioning* = G. Marshall, *Repositioning Class: Social Inequality in Industrial Societies*. London: Sage, 1997.

Mattila, "Inner Village" = S.L. Mattila, "Inner Village Life in Galilee: A Diverse and Complex Phenomenon," in D.A. Fiensy and J.R. Strange, *Galilee in the Late Second Temple and Mishnaic Periods*. Minneapolis: Fortress Press, 2014, 311–345.

Mayer, "Lower Middle Class" = A.J. Mayer, "The Lower Middle Class as a Historical Problem," *Journal of Modern Society* 47, no. 3 (1975): 409–436.

Mayer, *Middle Classes* = E. Mayer, *The Ancient Middle Classes: Urban Life and Aesthetics in the Roman Empire 100 BCE–250 CE*. Cambridge, MA: Harvard University Press, 2012.

Meeks, *Social Paul* = W.A. Meeks, *The First Urban Christians: The Social World of the Apostle Paul*. New Haven, CT: Yale University Press, 1983.

Meeks, "Social" = W.A. Meeks, "Social and Ecclesiastical Life of the Earliest Christians," *CHC* (2006), 1:145–173.

Meggitt, *Poverty* = J.J. Meggitt, *Paul, Poverty and Survival*. Edinburgh: T&T Clark, 1998.

Meikle, "Modernism" = S. Meikle, "Modernism, Economics and the Ancient Economy," in Scheidel and Von Reden, *Economy*, 233–250.

Meshorer, *Coins Israel* = Y. Meshorer, *City Coins of Eretz Yisrael and the Decapolis in the Roman Period*. Jerusalem: The Israel Museum, 1985.

Meshorer et al., *Coins* = Y. Meshorer, with G. Bijovsky and W. Fischer-Bossert, *Coins of the Holy Land*, in D. Hendin and A. Meadows (eds.), *The Abraham and Marion Sofaer Collection at the American Numismatic Society and The Israel Museum*. New York: American Numismatic Society, 2013.

Metzger, *Luke Consumption* = J.A. Metzger, *Consumption and Wealth in Luke's Travel Narrative*. Leiden: Brill, 2007.

Meyers, "Sepphoris Pools" = E.M. Meyers, "The Pools of Sepphoris—Ritual Baths or Bathtubs?" *BAR Review* 26, no. 4 (2000): 46–60.

Meyers, "Gendered Space" = E.M. Meyers, "The Problem of Gendered Space in Syro-Palestinian Domestic Architecture: The Case of Roman-Period Galilee," in D.L. Balch and C. Osiek (eds.), *Early Christian Families in Context*. Grand Rapids, MI: Erdmans, 2003, 44–69.

Meyers and Meyers, "Sepphoris" = C.L. Meyers and E.M. Meyers, "Sepphoris," in E.M. Meyers (ed.), *The Oxford Encyclopedia of Archaeology in the Near East*, 5 Vols. Oxford: Oxford University Press, 1997, 4:527–536.

Meyers and Strange, *Archaeology, Rabbis, Christianity* = E.M. Meyers and J.F. Strange, *Archaeology, The Rabbis, and Early Christianity*. Nashville, TN: Abingdon, 1981.

Meyers et al., *Excavations* = E.M. Meyers, J.F. Strange, C.L. Meyers, *Excavations at Ancient Meiron: Upper Galilee Israel, 1971–1972, 1974–1975, 1977*. Cambridge, MA: American Schools of Oriental Research, 1981.

Milanovic and Yitzhaki, "Middle Class" = B. Milanovic and S. Yitzhaki, "Decomposing World Income Distribution: Does the World Have a Middle Class?" *Review of Income and Wealth* 48, no. 2 (2002): 155–178.

Miliband, *Class Struggle* = R. Miliband, *Divided Societies: Class Struggle in Contemporary Capitalism*. Oxford: Clarendon Press, 1989.

Milikowsky, "Status" = C. Milikowsky, "The Status Quaestionis of Research in Rabbinic Literature," *JJS* 39, no. 2 (1988): 201–211.

Millar, *Near East* = F. Millar, *The Roman Near East (31 BC–AD 337)*. Cambridge, MA: Harvard University Press, 1993.

Millar, "Transformations" = F. Millar, "Transformations of Judaism under Graeco-Roman Rule: Responses to Seth Schwartz's *Imperialism and Jewish Society* [2001]," *JJS* 57 (2006): 139–158.

Miller, *Commoners* = S.S. Miller, *Sages and Commoners in Late Antique 'Erez Israel: A Philological Inquiry into Local Traditions in Talmud Yerushalmi*. Tübingen: Mohr Siebeck, 2006.

Miller, *Texts and Materials* = S.S. Miller, *At the Intersection of Texts and Material Finds: Stepped Pools, Stone Vessels, and Ritual Purity among the Jews of Roman Galilee: From Roman Galilee to Nineteenth-Century Chesterfield, Connecticut*. Gottingen: Vandenhoeck and Ruprecht, 2015.

Millett, *Lending in Athens* = P. Millett, *Lending and Borrowing in Ancient Athens*. Cambridge: Cambridge University Press, 1991.

Moatti, "Translation" = C. Moatti, "Translation, Migration and Communication in the Roman Empire: Three Aspects of Movement in History," *Classical Antiquity* 25, no. 1 (2006): 109–140.

Montanari, *Dictionary* = F. Montanari, *The Brill Dictionary of Ancient Greek*. Leiden: Brill, 2015.

Monteix, "Pompeian Bakeries" = N. Monteix, "Contextualizing the Operational Sequence: Pompeian Bakeries as a Case Study," in A. Wilson and M. Flohr (eds.), *Urban Craftsmen and Traders in the Roman World*. Oxford: Oxford University Press, 2016, 153–182.

Mor, "Bar Kokhba Revolt" = M. Mor, "The Geographical Scope of the Bar Kokhba Revolt," in P. Schäfer (ed.), *The Bar Kokhba War Reconsidered: New Perspectives on the Second Jewish Revolt against Rome*. Tübingen: Mohr Siebeck, 2003, 107–131.

Mor, *Bar Kokhba* = M. Mor, *The Second Jewish Revolt: The Bar Kokhba War 132–136 CE*. Leiden: Brill, 2016.

Morazé, *Middle Classes* = C. Morazé, *The Triumph of the Middle Classes*. London: Anchor Books, 1966.

Moreland, "Galilean Response" = M. Moreland, "Galilean Response to Earliest Christianity," in D.R. Edwards (ed.), *Religion and Society in Roman Palestine: Old Questions, New Approaches*. London: Routledge, 2004, 37–49.

Morgan, *Morality* = T. Morgan, *Popular Morality in the Early Roman Empire*. Cambridge: Cambridge University Press, 2007.

Morley, "Poor Rome" = N. Morley, "The Poor in the City of Rome," in M. Atkins and R. Osborne (eds.), *Poverty in the Roman World*. Cambridge: Cambridge University Press, 2006, 21–39.

Morley, *Antiquity* = N. Morley, *Antiquity and Modernity*. Chichester, UK: Wiley-Blackwell, 2009.

Mossé, *Ancient Work* = C. Mossé, *The Ancient World at Work*. Trans. Janet Lloyd. London: Chatto & Windus, 1969.

Mouritsen, "Mobility" = H. Mouritsen, "Mobility and Social Change in Italian Towns during the Principate," in H.M. Parkins (ed.), *Roman Urbanism: Beyond the Consumer City*. London: Routledge, 1997, 59–82.

Moxnes, "Patron Client" = H. Moxnes, "Patron-Client Relations and the New Community in Luke-Acts," in J.H. Neyrey (ed.), *The Social World of Luke-Acts*. Peabody, MA: Hendrickson, 1991, 241–268.

Murphy, *Wealth* = C.M. Murphy, *Wealth in the Dead Sea Scrolls*. Leiden: Brill, 2002.

Nagy et al., *Sepphoris* = R.M. Nagy, E.M. Meyers, Z. Weiss, and C.I. Meyers (eds.), *Sepphoris in Galilee: Crosscurrents of Culture*. Raleigh, NC: Museum of Art, 1996.

Najman, *Losing the Temple* = H. Najman, *Losing the Temple and Recovering in the Future: An Analysis of 4 Ezra*. Cambridge: Cambridge University Press, 2014.

Naveh, "Hebrew versus Aramaic 1" = Y. Naveh, "Hebrew versus Aramaic in Epigraphic Findings during the Second Temple Period until 135 CE," *Leshoneinu* 56, no. 4 (1993): 301–316 [in Hebrew].

Naveh, "Hebrew versus Aramaic 2" = Y. Naveh, "Hebrew versus Aramaic in Epigraphic Findings during the Second Temple Period until 135 CE," *Leshoneinu* 57, no. 1 (1994): 17–38 [in Hebrew].

Netzer, "Caesarea Palace" = E. Netzer, "The Promontory Palace," in A. Raban and K.G. Holum (eds.), *Caesarea Maritima: A Retrospective after Two Millennia*. Leiden: Brill, 1996, 193–208.

Neudecker, *Moses Interpreted* = R. Neudecker, *Moses Interpreted by the Pharisees and Jesus: Matthew's Antitheses in the Light of Early Rabbinic Literature*. Rome: Gregorian and Biblical Press, 2012.

Neusner, *Purity* = J. Neusner, *The Idea of Purity in Ancient Judaism*. Leiden: Brill, 1973.

Neusner, "Aristotle" = J. Neusner, "Aristotle's Economics and the Mishnah's Economics: The Matter of Wealth and Usury," *JSJ* 21, no. 1 (1990): 41–59.

Neusner, *Economics* = J. Neusner, *The Economics of the Mishnah*. Chicago: University of Chicago Press, 1990.

Neusner, *Introduction* = J. Neusner, *Introduction to Rabbinic Literature*. New York: Doubleday, 1994.

Neusner, *Purity in Rabbinic* = J. Neusner, *Purity in Rabbinic Judaism: A Systematic Account*. Atlanta: Scholars Press, 1994.

Neusner, "Rabbinic Sources" = J. Neusner, "Rabbinic Sources for Historical Study—A Debate with Ze'ev Safrai," in J. Neusner and A. Avery-Peck (eds.), *Judaism in Late Antiquity: Where We Stand: Issues and Debates in Ancient Judaism*, Vol. 3, Issue 1, Leiden: Brill, 1999, 123–142.

Nicholas, *Law* = B. Nicholas, *An Introduction to Roman Law*. Oxford: Clarendon Press, 1962.

Nicolet, "The Citizen" = C. Nicolet, "The Citizen; The Political Man," in Giardina, *The Romans*, 16–54.

Nishijima, "Han History" = S. Nishijima, "The Economic and Social History of Former Han," in D. Twitchett and M. Loewe (eds.), *The Cambridge History of China 1: The Ch'in and Han Empires 221 BC–AD 220*. Cambridge: Cambridge University Press, 1986, 551–607.

Nolte, "Social Inequality" = P. Nolte, "Social Inequality in History (Social Stratification and Classes)," in N.J. Smelser and P.B. Baltes (eds.), *International Encyclopedia of the Social and Behavioral Sciences*, Vol. 21. Oxford: Elsevier, 2001, 14313–14320.

Nutton, "Archiatri" = V. Nutton, "Archiatri and the Medical Profession in Antiquity," *PBSR* 45 (1977): 191–226.

Nutton, *Ancient Medicine* = V. Nutton, *Ancient Medicine*, 2nd Ed. London: Routledge, 2013.

Oakes, "Constructing Poverty" = P. Oakes, "Constructing Poverty Scales for Graeco-Roman Society: A Response to Steven Friesen's 'Poverty in Pauline Studies,'" *JSNT* 26, no. 3 (2004): 367–371.

Oakman, "Agrarian Palestine" = D.E. Oakman, "Jesus and Agrarian Palestine: The Factor of Debt," in J.H. Neyrey and E.C. Stewart (eds.), *The Social World of the New Testament: Insights and Models*. Peabody, MA: Hendrickson, 2008, 62–85.

Oakman, "Jesus Peasant" = D.E. Oakman, "Was Jesus a Peasant? Implications for Reading the Jesus Tradition," in J.H. Neyrey and E.C. Stewart (eds.), *The Social World of the New Testament: Insights and Models*. Peabody, MA: Hendrickson, 2008, 125–140.

O'Boyle, "Middle Class" = L. O'Boyle, "The Middle Class in Western Europe," *American Historical Review* 71, no. 3 (1966): 826–845.

Öğüş, "Sarcophagi" = E. Öğüş, "Columnar Sarcophagi from Aphrodisias: Elite Emulation in the Greek East," *American Journal of Archaeology* 118, no. 1 (2014): 113–136.

Oppenheimer, *Between Rome and Babylon* = A. Oppenheimer, *Between Rome and Babylon: Studies in Jewish Leadership and Society*. Tübingen: Mohr Siebeck, 2005.

Osborne, *Roman Society* = R. Osborne, ed., *Studies in Ancient Greek and Roman Society*. Cambridge: Cambridge University Press, 2004.

Osborne, "Roman Poverty" = R. Osborne, "Introduction: Roman Poverty in Context," in M. Atkins and R. Osborne (eds.), *Poverty in the Roman World*. Cambridge: Cambridge University Press, 2006, 1–21.

Owens, *The City* = E.J. Owens, *The City in the Greek and Roman World*. London: Routledge, 1991.

Palme, "Texts" = B. Palme, "The Range of Documentary Texts: Types and Categories," in Bagnall, *Papyrology*, 358–394.

Park and Maxey, *Two Studies* = M.E. Park and M. Maxey, *Two Studies on the Roman Lower Classes*. New York: Amo Press, 1975.

Parkin and Pomeroy, *Social History* = T.G. Parkin and A.J. Pomeroy, *Roman Social History: A Sourcebook*. New York: Routledge, 2007.

Pastor, *Land and Economy* = J. Pastor, *Land and Economy in Ancient Palestine*. London: Routledge, 1997.

Paterson, "Production" = J. Paterson, "Production and Consumption," in P. Jones and K. Sidwell (eds.), *The World of Rome*. Cambridge: Cambridge University Press, 1997, 181–207.

Peleg-Barkat, "Decoration" = O. Peleg-Barkat, "Architectural Decoration," in D. Sion and Z. Yavor (eds.), *Gamla II: The Architecture: The Shmarya Gutmann Excavations 1976–1988*. Jerusalem: Israel Antiquities Authority, 2010, 159–174.

Peleg-Barkat, "Elite" = O. Peleg-Barkat, "The Relative Chronology of Tomb Façades in Early Roman Jerusalem and Power Displays by the Élite," *JRA* 25 (2012): 403–418.

Pennycook, "Incommensurable Discourses" = A. Pennycook, "Incommensurable Discourses?" *Applied Linguistics* 15, no. 2 (1994): 115–138.

Philipson, "Securities" = D. Philipson, "Development of Roman Law of Debt Security," *SLR* 20, no. 6 (1968): 1230–1248.

Poblome, "Production" = J. Poblome, "Comparing Ordinary Craft Production: Textile and Pottery Production in Roman Asia Minor," *JESHO* 47, no. 4 (2004): 491–506.

Poblome et al., "Pottery Roman Empire" = J. Poblome, D. Malfitana, and J. Lund, "Pottery, Roman Empire," in Bagnall et al., *Encyclopedia*, 10: 5482–5489.

Pope, Song of Songs = M.H. Pope, *Song of Songs*. New York: Doubleday, 1977.

Portes, "Resilient Class" = A. Portes, "The Resilient Importance of Class: A Nominalist Interpretation," *Political Power and Social Theory* 14 (2000): 249–284.

Powell, *Labor* = M.A. Powell, ed., *Labor in the Near East*. New Haven, CT: American Oriental Society, 1987.

Prell, *Sozialökonomische* = M. Prell, *Sozialökonomische Untersuchungen zur Armut im antiken Rom: Von den Gracchen bis Kaiser Diokletian*. Stuttgart: Franz Steiner Verlag, 1997.

Purcell, "Plebs Urbana" = N. Purcell, "The City of Rome and the Plebs Urbana in the Late Republic," *CAH* 9 (1994): 644–688.

Radner, "Hired Labor" = K. Radner, "Hired Labour in the Neo-Assyrian Empire," *State Archives of Assyria Bulletin* 16 (2006): 185–226.

Rathbone, *Economic Rationalism* = D. Rathbone, *Economic Rationalism and Rural Society in 3rd Century A.D. Egypt*. Cambridge: Cambridge University Press, 1991.

Ravallion, "Middle Class" = M. Ravallion, "The Developing World's Bulging (but Vulnerable) Middle Class," *World Development* 38, no. 4 (2010): 445–454.

Rawson, "Family and Society" = B. Rawson, "Family and Society," in A. Barchiesi and W. Scheidel, eds., *The Oxford Handbook of Roman Studies*. Oxford: Oxford University Press, 2010, 610–623.

Rengstorf, *Concordance Josephus* = K.H. Rengstorf (ed.), *A Complete Concordance to Flavius Josephus*, 5 Vols. Brill: Leiden, 1975.

Resnick and Wolff, *Marxian Critique* = S. Resnick and R.D. Wolff, *Knowledge and Class: A Marxian Critique of Political Economy*. Chicago: University of Chicago Press, 1987.

Reumann, *Philippians* = J. Reumann, *Philippians: A New Translation with Introduction and Commentary*. New Haven, CT: Yale University Press, 2008.

Rhee, *Poor* = H. Rhee, *Loving the Poor, Saving the Rich: Wealth, Poverty, and Early Christian Formation*. Grand Rapids, MI: Eerdmans, 2013.

Rhodes, "boule" = P.J. Rhodes, "boule," *NP*, 2: 739–742.

Richardson, "Typology of Houses" = P. Richardson, "Towards a Typology of Levantine-Palestinian Houses," *JSNT* 27, no. 1 (2004): 55–61.

Rilinger, *Humiliores–Honestiores* = G.R. Rilinger, *Humiliores–Honestiores: Zu einer sozialen Dichotomie im Strafrecht der römischen Kaiserzeit*. Munich: Oldenbourg, 1988.

Rilinger, "Ordo" = R. Rilinger, "Ordo und dignitas als soziale Kategorien der römischen Republik," in M. Hettling and Hans-Ulrich Wehler (eds.), *Was ist Gesellschaftsgeschichte? Positionen, Themen, Analysen*. Munich: Beck, 1991, 81–90.

Rilinger, "Domus" = R. Rilinger, "Domus und res publica: Die politisch-soziale Bedeutung des aristokratischen 'Hauses' in der späten römischen Republik," in A. Winterling (ed.), *Zwischen "Haus" und "Staat": Antike Höfe im Vergleich*. Munich: Oldenbourg, 1997, 73–89.

Rilinger, "Collegia" = R. Rilinger, "Moderne und zeitgenössische Vorstellungen von der Gesellschaftsordnung der römischen Kaiserzeit," in R. Rilinger, *Ordo und Dignitas: Beiträge zur römischen Verfassungs und Sozialgeschichte*. Stuttgart: Steiner, 2007, 152–179.

Rindge, *Rich Fool* = M.S. Rindge, *Jesus' Parable of the Rich Fool: Luke 12: 13–34 among Ancient Conversations on Death and Possessions*. Atlanta: Society of Biblical Literature, 2011.

Ro, "Piety" = J.U. Ro, "Piety of the Poor in the Community of Qumran and its Historical Origins," in J.U. Ro (ed.), *From Judah to Judaea: Socio-Economic Structures and Processes in the Persian Period*. Sheffield: Sheffield Phoenix Press, 2012, 54–85.

Robinson, *Roman Law* = O.F. Robinson, *The Sources of Roman Law: Problems and Methods for Ancient Historians*. London: Routledge, 1997.

Rodas, "Dal II" = M.D.C. Rodas, "dal II," in VanGemeren, *Dictionary*, 1:951–954.

Rodd, *Old Testament Ethics* = C.S. Rodd, *Glimpses of a Strange Land: Studies in Old Testament Ethics*. London: Bloomsbury, 2001.

Rodewald, *Money Tiberius* = C. Rodewald, *Money in the Age of Tiberius*. Manchester: Manchester University Press, 1967.

Rosenfeld, "Gezer Boundary" = B.Z. Rosenfeld, "The Boundary of Gezer Inscriptions and the History of Gezer at the End of the Period of the Second Temple," in *IEJ* 38 (1989): 235–245.

Rosenfeld, "Innkeeping" = B.Z. Rosenfeld, "Innkeeping in Jewish Society in Roman Palestine," *JESHO* 41, no. 2 (1998): 133–158.

Rosenfeld, "Galilean Valleys" = B.Z. Rosenfeld, "The Galilean Valleys (Beq'aoth) from the Bible to the Talmud," *Revue Biblique* 109, no. 1 (2002): 6–100.

Rosenfeld, "Rich" = B.Z. Rosenfeld, "The Wealthy Members of Jewish Society in Roman Palestine," *Materia Giudaica* 8 (2005): 381–387.

Rosenfeld, *Torah Centers* = B.Z. Rosenfeld, *Torah Centers and Rabbinic Activity in Palestine 70–400 C.E.* Leiden: Brill, 2010.

Rosenfeld, "Linen" = B.Z. Rosenfeld, "Linen Production and Trade in Roman Palestine Due to the Roman East: 0–400 CE," *ARAM* 27 (2015): 97–103.

Rosenfeld, "Rabbinic Attitudes" = B.Z. Rosenfeld, "The Attitudes of Rabbinic and Christian Literature to the Poor," in Jean-Marie Salamito and J. Cornilon (eds.), *L'argent des dieux: Religions et richesses en Méditerranée dans l'Antiquité et au Moyen Âge*. Paris: Forthcoming.

Rosenfeld and Menirav, "Synagogue" = B.Z. Rosenfeld and J. Menirav, "The Ancient Synagogue as an Economic Center," *JNES* 58, no. 4 (1999): 259–276.

Rosenfeld and Menirav, *Markets and Marketing* = B.Z. Rosenfeld and J. Menirav, *Markets and Marketing in Roman Palestine*. Leiden: Brill, 2005.

Rosenfeld and Perlmutter, "Landowners" = B.Z. Rosenfeld and H. Perlmutter, "Landowners in Roman Palestine: A Distinct Social Group," *JAJ* 2, no. 3 (2011): 327–352.

Rosenfeld and Perlmutter, "The Poor" = B.Z. Rosenfeld and H. Perlmutter, "The Poor as a Stratum of Jewish Society in Roman Palestine 70–250 CE: An Analysis," *Historia* 60, no. 3 (2011): 273–300.

Rosenfeld and Perlmutter, "Craftsmen" = B.Z. Rosenfeld and H. Perlmutter, "The Social Context of Craftsmen in Roman Palestine 70–250 CE," *Journal Asiatique* 303, no. 1 (2015): 87–100.

Rosenfeld and Perlmutter, "Rich" = "Who Is Rich?—The Rich in Jewish Society of Roman Palestine 70–250 CE," *Journal of Ancient Judaism* 6, no. 2 (2015): 275–299.

Rosenfeld and Perlmutter, "Relatively Rich" = B.Z. Rosenfeld and H. Perlmutter, "Rich and Relatively Rich in Roman Palestine 70–250 CE," *Journal of Ancient Judaism* (Forthcoming).

Rosenfeld and Weistuch, "Coinage" = B.Z. Rosenfeld and Y. Weistuch, "Tosefta Ma'aser Sheni 1:4—The Rabbis and Roman Civic Coinage in Late Antiquity," in S. Fine and

A. Koller (eds.), *Talmuda de'Eretz Israel: Archaeology and the Rabbis in Late Antique Palestine*. Berlin: De Gruyter, 2014, 53–61.

Rostovtzeff, *Roman Empire* = M. Rostovtzeff, *The Social and Economic History of the Roman Empire*. Oxford: Clarendon Press, 1957.

Rowlandson, *Landowners* = J. Rowlandson, *Landowners and Tenants in Roman Egypt: The Social Relations*, Oxford: Clarendon Press, 1996.

Rubin, "Mourning" = N. Rubin, "For Whom Does One Mourn? A Sociological Analysis of Talmudical Sources," *Bar Ilan* 10 (1972): 111–122 [in Hebrew].

Rubin, *End of Life* = N. Rubin, *The End of the Life: Rites of Mourning and Burial in the Talmud and Midrash*. Tel Aviv: Hakibbutz Hameuchad, 1997 [in Hebrew].

Rubin, *Time* = N. Rubin, *Time and Life Cycle in Talmud and Midrash*. Boston: Academic Studies Press, 2008.

Ruffing, "Specialization" = K. Ruffing, "Driving Forces for Specialization: Market, Local Factors, Productivity Improvements," in A. Wilson and M. Flohr (eds.), *Urban Craftsmen and Traders in the Roman World*. Oxford: Oxford University Press, 2016, 115–131.

Runciman, "Capitalism Rome" = W.C. Runciman, "Capitalism without Classes: The Case of Classical Rome," *BJS* 34, no. 2 (1983): 157–181.

Saddington, "Armies under Augustus" = D.B. Saddington, "Armies under Augustus: The Case of Herod," in Jacobson and Kokkinos, *Herod and Augustus*, 303–323.

Safrai, "Sikrikon" = S. Safrai, "Sikrikon," *Zion* 17 (1957): 56–64 [in Hebrew].

Safrai, "Sabbatical Year" = S. Safrai, "The Practical Implementation of the Sabbatical Year after the Destruction of the Second Temple," *Tarbiz* 35 (1965/66): 304–328 and 36 (1966/67): 1–21 [Hebrew with English summary].

Safrai, "The Localities" = S. Safrai, "The Localities of the Sanctification of Lunar Months and the Intercalation of Years in Palestine after 70 C.E.," *Tarbiz* 35 (1966): 27–38 [in Hebrew with English summary].

Safrai, *The Literature* = S. Safrai (ed.), *The Literature of the Sages*, Part 1. Assen, The Netherlands: Van Gorcum, 1987.

Safrai, *The Literature* = S. Safrai, (ed.), *The Literature of the Sages*, Part 2. Assen, The Netherlands: Van Gorcum, 2007.

Safrai, "Family Structure" = Z. Safrai, "Structure of the Family in the Period of the Mishna and Talmud," *Millet* 1 (1983): 129–156 [in Hebrew].

Safrai, *Economy* = Z. Safrai, *The Economy of Roman Palestine*. London: Routledge, 1994.

Safrai, "Rabbinic Sources" = Z. Safrai, "Rabbinic Sources as Historical: A Response to Professor Neusner," in J. Neusner and A. Avery-Peck (eds.), *Judaism in Late Antiquity: Where We Stand: Issues and Debates in Ancient Judaism*, Vol. 3, Issue 1. Leiden: Brill, 1999, 143–167.

Safrai, "Agrarian Structure" = Z. Safrai, "The Agrarian Structure in Palestine in the Time of the Second Temple, Mishnah and Talmud: Rural Landscape," in A.M. Maeir,

S. Dar, Z. Safrai (eds.), *The Rural Landscape of Ancient Israel*. Oxford: Archaeopress, 2003, 105–125.

Safrai, "Judaean Desert" = Z. Safrai, "Halakhic Observance in the Judaean Desert Documents," in R. Katzoff and D. Schaps (eds.), *Law in the Documents of the Judaean Desert*. Leiden: Brill, 2005, 205–236.

Safrai, "Socio-Economic" = Z. Safrai, "Socio-Economic and Cultural Developments in the Galilee from the Late First to the Early Third Century," in P.J. Tomson and J. Schwartz (eds.), *Jews and Christians in the First and Second Centuries: How to Write Their History*. Leiden: Brill, 2014, 278–310.

Safrai, "Urbanization and Industry" = Z. Safrai, "Urbanization and Industry in Mishnaic Galilee," in D.A. Fiensy and J.R. Strange (eds.), *Galilee in the Late Second Temple and Mishnaic Periods*. Minneapolis: Fortress Press, 2014, 263–271.

Saldarini, *Pharisees and Sadducees* = A.J. Saldarini, *Pharisees, Scribes, and Sadducees in Palestinian Society*. Grand Rapids, MI: Eerdmans, 1988.

Saller, *Patronage* = R.P. Saller, *Personal Patronage under the Early Empire*. Cambridge: Cambridge University Press, 1982.

Saller, "Family" = R.P. Saller, "Familia, Domus and the Roman Conception of the Family," *Phoenix* 38, no. 4 (1984): 336–355.

Saller, "Status and Patronage" = R.P. Saller, "Status and Patronage," *CAH* 11 (2000), 822–838.

Saller, "Ancient Economy" = R.P. Saller, "Framing the Debate over Growth in the Ancient Economy," in Scheidel and Von Reden (eds.), *Economy*, 251–269.

Salvaterra and Cristofori, "Italian Scholarship" = C. Salvaterra and A. Cristofori, "Twentieth-Century Italian Scholarship on Roman Craftsmen, Traders and their Professional Organizations," in A. Wilson and M. Flohr (eds.), *Urban Craftsmen and Traders in the Roman World*. Oxford: Oxford University Press, 2016, 55–76.

Samson, *Social Houses* = R. Samson, *The Social Archaeology of Houses*. Edinburgh: Edinburgh University Press, 1991.

Sartre, *L'orient Romain* = M. Sartre, *L'orient Romain: Provinces et Sociétés Provinciales en Méditerranée Orientale d'Auguste aux Sévères* (31 avant j-c.–235 après j-c.). Paris: Seuil, 1991.

Sartre, "Syria and Arabia" = M. Sartre, "Syria and Arabia," *CAH* 11 (2000), 635–663.

Sartre, *Middle East* = M. Sartre, *The Middle East under Rome*. Trans. C. Porter and E. Rawlings. Cambridge, MA: Harvard University Press, 2005.

Satlow, "Rabbinic Views" = M.L. Satlow, "Rabbinic Views on Marriage, Sexuality, and the Family," *CHJ* 4 (2006), 612–626.

Satlow, "Charity" = M.L. Satlow, "'Fruit and Fruit of Fruit': Charity and Piety among Jews in Late Antique Palestine," *JQR* 100 (2010): 244–277.

Sauer, *Jesus Sirach* = G. Sauer, *Jesus Sirach (Ben Sira)*. Gütersloh: Gerd Mohn, 1981.

Scarborough, *Roman Medicine* = J. Scarborough, *Roman Medicine*. London: Thames and Hudson, 1969.

Schäfer, "Rabbinic Literature" = P. Schäfer, "Research into Rabbinic Literature: An Attempt to Define the Status Quaestionis," *JJS* 37, no. 2 (1986): 139–152.

Schäfer, *History* = P. Schäfer, *The History of the Jews in the Greco-Roman World*. London: Routledge, 2003.

Schäfer and Milikowsky, "Current Views" = P. Schäfer and C. Milikowsky, "Current Views on the Editing of the Rabbinic Texts of Late Antiquity: Reflections on a Debate after Twenty Years," in M. Goodman and P. Alexander (eds.), *Rabbinic Texts and the History of Late-Roman Palestine*. Oxford: Oxford University Press, 2010, 79–88.

Schalit, *König Herodes* = A. Schalit, *König Herodes: Der Mann und sein Werk*. Trans. Jehoschua Amir. Berlin: De Gruyter, 1969.

Schanbacher, "Dominium, Dominus" = D. Schanbacher, "Dominium, Dominus," *NP* 4 (2004): 631–633.

Scheidel, "Libertina" = W. Scheidel, "Libertina's Bitter Grains: Seasonal Mortality and Endemic Disease in the Ancient City of Rome," *Ancient Society* 25 (1994): 151–175.

Scheidel, "Human Mobility" = W. Scheidel, "Human Mobility in Roman Italy, 1: The Free Population," *JRS* 94 (2004): 1–26.

Scheidel, "Stratification" = W. Scheidel, "Stratification, Deprivation, and Quality of Life," in M. Atkins and R. Osborne (eds.), *Poverty in the Roman World*. Cambridge: Cambridge University Press, 2006, 40–59.

Scheidel, "Economic Growth" = W. Scheidel, "In Search of Roman Economic Growth," *JRA* 22 (2009): 46–71.

Scheidel, "Population" = W. Scheidel, "Population and Demography," in A. Erskine (ed.), *A Companion to Ancient History*. New York: Wiley, 2009, 134–145.

Scheidel, "Economy and Quality" = W. Scheidel, "Economy and Quality of Life," in A. Barchiesi and W. Scheidel (eds.), *The Oxford Handbook of Roman Studies*. Oxford: Oxford University Press, 2010, 593–609.

Scheidel, "Real Wages" = W. Scheidel, "Real Wages in Early Economies: Evidence for Living Standards from 1800 BC to 1300 CE," *JESHO* 53, no. 3 (2010): 425–462.

Scheidel, "Roman Economy" = W. Scheidel, "Approaching the Roman Economy," in W. Scheidel (ed.), *The Cambridge Companion to the Roman Economy*. Cambridge: Cambridge University Press, 2012, 1–23.

Scheidel and Friesen, "Size Economy" = W. Scheidel and S.J. Friesen, "The Size of the Economy and the Distribution of Income in the Roman Empire," *JRS* 99 (2009), 61–91.

Scheidel and Von Reden, *Economy* = W. Scheidel and S. Von Reden (eds.), *The Ancient Economy*. Edinburgh: Edinburgh University Press, 2002.

Schiffman, "Scrolls and Rabbinic" = L.H. Schiffman, "The Dead Sea Scrolls and Rabbinic Halakhah," in J.R. Davila (ed.), *The Dead Sea Scrolls as Background to*

BIBLIOGRAPHY

Postbiblical Judaism and Early Christianity: Papers from an International Conference at St. Andrews in 2001. Leiden: Brill, 2003, 3–24.

Schiffman, "Temple" = L.H. Schiffman, "The Importance of the Temple for Ancient Jews," in J.H. Charlesworth (ed.), *Jesus and the Temple: Textual and Archaeological Explorations.* Minneapolis: Fortress Press, 2014, 75–93.

Schiffman and VanderKam, *Dead Sea Scrolls* = L.H. Schiffman and J.C. VanderKam (eds.), *Encyclopedia of the Dead Sea Scrolls,* 2 Vols. Oxford: Oxford University Press, 2000.

Schortman and Urban, "Craft Economy" = E.M. Schortman and P.A. Urban, "Modeling the Roles of Craft Production in Ancient Political Economies," *Journal of Archaeological Research* 12, no. 2 (2005): 185–226.

Schultz, *Conquering* = B. Schultz. *Conquering the World: The War Scroll (1QM) Reconsidered.* Leiden: Brill, 2009.

Schulz, *Roman Law* = F. Schulz, *Classical Roman Law.* Oxford: Clarendon Press, 1969.

Schürer, *History* = E. Schürer, *The History of the Jewish People in the Age of Jesus Christ,* 4 Vols. Ed. F. Millar and G. Vermes. Edinburgh: T&T Clark Int., 1973–1986.

Schwartz, *Judaea* = J. Schwartz, *Jewish Settlement in Judaea after the Bar Kochba War until the Arab Conquest 135 CE–640 CE.* Jerusalem: Shazar Center, 1986 [in Hebrew].

Schwartz, "Material Culture" = J. Schwartz, "Material Culture and Rabbinic Literature in the Land of Israel at the End of the Ancient Period: Beds, Bedding and Sleeping Practices," in Y. Levine (ed.), *Continuity and Change: Jews and Judaism in the Land of Israel under Christian–Byzantine Rule.* Jerusalem: Yad Yitzhak Ben Zvi, 2004, 197–209 [in Hebrew].

Schwartz, "Material Culture" = J. Schwartz, "Material Culture and Rabbinic Literature in the Land of Israel at the End of the Ancient Period: Beds, Bedding and Sleeping Practices," in Y. Levine (ed.), *Continuity and Change: Jews and Judaism in the Land of Israel under Christian–Byzantine Rule.* Jerusalem: Dinur Center, 2004, 197–209 [in Hebrew].

Schwartz, "Yavne Revisited" = J. Schwartz, "Yavne Revisited: Jewish 'Survival' in the Wake of the War of Destruction," in Tomson and Schwartz, *Jews and Christians,* 238–252.

Schwartz, "Economic Life" = S. Schwartz, "Political, Social and Economic Life in the Land of Israel 66–235 CE," *CHJ* 4 (2006), 23–52.

Schwartz, "Political Geography" = S. Schwartz, "The Political Geography of Rabbinic Texts," in C.E. Fonrobert and M.S. Jaffee (eds.), *The Cambridge Companion to the Talmud and Rabbinic Literature.* Cambridge: Cambridge University Press, 2007, 75–96.

Schwartz, *Jews* = S. Schwartz, *Were the Jews a Mediterranean Society? Reciprocity and Solidarity in Ancient Judaism.* Princeton, NJ: Princeton University Press, 2010.

Segal, "Mišnaic Hebrew" = H.M. Segal, "Mišnaic Hebrew and Its Relation to Biblical Hebrew and to Aramaic," *JQR* 20, no. 4 (1908): 647–737.

Segal, *Ben Sira* = M.H. Segal, *Sefer Ben Sira Complete Edition*. Jerusalem: Academy for Hebrew Language, 1973 [in Hebrew].

Seligman, "Architecture Nachal Hagit" = J. Seligman, "The Architecture and Stratigraphy," in J. Seligman (ed.), *Nahal Ḥagit: A Roman and Mamluk Farmstead in the Southern Carmel*. Jerusalem: Israel Antiquities Authority, 2010, 11–97.

Severy, *Augustus* = B. Severy, *Augustus and the Family at the Birth of the Roman Empire*. London: Routledge, 2003.

Shanin, *Peasants* = T. Shanin, *Peasants and Peasant Societies: Selected Readings*, 2nd Ed. New York: Blackwell, 1987.

Shatzman, *The Armies* = I. Shatzman, *The Armies of the Hamonaeans and Herod: From Hellenistic to Roman Frameworks*. Tübingen: Mohr Siebeck, 1991.

Shaw, "Family Late Antiquity" = B.D. Shaw, "The Family in Late Antiquity: The Experience of Augustine," *Past and Present* 115, no. 1 (1987): 3–51.

Silver, "Hired Workers" = M. Silver, "Slaves versus Free Hired Workers in Ancient Greece," *Historia: Zeitschrift für Alte Geschichte* 55, no. 3 (2003): 257–263.

Silver, "Roman Economic Growth" = M. Silver, "Roman Economic Growth and Living Standards: Perceptions versus Evidence," *Ancient Society* 37 (2007): 191–252.

Silver, "Roman Bazaar" = M. Silver, "Historical Otherness, *The Roman Bazaar* and Primitivism: P.F. Bang on the Roman Economy," *JRA* 22 (2009): 421–443.

Simon, "Marc 12" = L. Simon, "Le sous de la veuve: Marc 12, 41–44," *Études théologiques et religieuses* 44 (1969): 115–126.

Sirks, "Law" = B. Sirks, "Law, Commerce and Finance in the Roman Empire," in A. Wilson and A. Bowman (eds.), *Trade, Commerce and State in the Roman World*. Oxford: Oxford University Press, 2018, 53–116.

Sivan, *Palestine Late Antiquity* = H. Sivan, *Palestine in Late Antiquity*. Oxford: Oxford University Press, 2008.

Skehan and Di Lella, *Ben Sira* = P.W. Skehan and A.A. Di Lella (eds.), *The Wisdom of Ben Sira*. New York: Doubleday, 1987.

Smallwood, *The Jews* = M.E. Smallwood, *The Jews under Roman Rule: From Pompey to Diocletian*, 2nd ed. Leiden: Brill, 1981.

Smith, *Roman Villas* = T.J. Smith, *Roman Villas: A Study in Social Structure*. London: Routledge, 1997.

Sneider, "Technology" = H. Sneider, "Technology," in W. Scheidel, and I. Morris, R. Saller (eds.), *The Cambridge Economic History of the Greco-Roman World*. Cambridge: Cambridge University Press, 2007, 144–171.

Sodini, "Archaeology" = J.P. Sodini, "Archaeology and Late Antique Social Structures," in L. Lavan and W. Bowden (eds.), *Theory and Practice in Late Antique Archaeology*. Leiden: Brill, 2005, 25–56.

BIBLIOGRAPHY

Sørensen, "Sounder Basis" = A.B. Sørensen, "Toward a Sounder Basis for Class Analysis," *American Journal of Sociology* 105, no. 6 (2000): 1523–1558.

Southern, *Roman Empire* = P. Southern, *The Roman Empire from Severus to Constantine*. London: Routledge, 2004.

Sperber, "The Third Century" = D. Sperber, "On Social and Economic Conditions in 3rd Century Palestine," *Archív Orientální* 38 (1970): 1–25.

Sperber, *Money and Prices* = D. Sperber, *Roman Palestine 200–400: Money and Prices*, 2nd Ed. with Supplement. Ramat Gan: Bar-Ilan University Press, 1991 [1974].

Sperber, *Land* = D. Sperber, *Roman Palestine 200–400: The Land*. Ramat-Gan: Bar-Ilan University Press, 1978.

Sperber, *Material Culture* = D. Sperber, *Material Culture in Eretz-Israel during the Talmudic Period*, 2 Vols. Jerusalem: Yad Yitzhak Ben Zvi, [1993] 2005 [in Hebrew].

Sperber, *The City* = D. Sperber, *The City in Roman Palestine*. New York: Oxford University Press, 1998.

Stearns, "Middle Class" = P.N. Stearns, "The Middle Class: Toward a Precise Definition," *Comparative Studies in Society and History* 21, no. 3 (1979): 377–396.

Stemberger, "On Neusner Purities" = G. Stemberger, "On Jacob Neusner: *A History of the Mishnaic Law of Purities*, Parts 21 & 22," *Kairos* 20 (1978): 311–313.

Stemberger, "Rabbinic Sources" = G. Stemberger, "Rabbinic Sources for Historical Study," in J. Neusner and A. Avery-Peck (eds.), *Judaism in Late Antiquity: Where We Stand: Issues and Debates in Ancient Judaism*, Vol. 3, Issue 1. Leiden: Brill, 1999, 169–186.

Stern, "Herod" = M. Stern, "The Reign of Herod and the Herodian Dynasty," in: S. Safrai and M. Stern (eds.), *The Jewish People in the First Century*, Vol. I, Issue 1. Assen, The Netherlands: Van Gorcum, 1974, 216–307.

Stern, "Priesthood" = M. Stern, "Aspects of Jewish Society: The Priesthood and Other Classes," in S. Safrai and M. Stern (eds.), *The Jewish People in the First Century*. Assen: Van Gorcum, 1976, 561–630.

Stern, *Greek and Latin Authors* = M. Stern, *Greek and Latin Authors on Jews and Judaism*, vol. 2. Jerusalem: Israel Academy of Sciences and Humanities, 1980.

Stern, "Attribution and Authorship" = S. Stern, "Attribution and Authorship in the Babylonian Talmud," *JJS* 45, no. 1 (1994): 28–51.

Stern, *Jewish Identity* = S. Stern, *Jewish Identity in Early Rabbinic Writings*. Leiden: Brill, 1994.

Stern, "Authorship" = S. Stern, "The Concept of Authorship in the Babylonian Talmud," *JJS* 46 (1995), 183–195.

Stern, "Rabbi" = S. Stern, "Rabbi and the Origins of the Patriarchate," *JJS* 54 (2003): 192–215.

Stewart, *Roman Art* = P. Stewart, *The Social History of Roman Art*. Cambridge: Cambridge University Press, 2008.

Strack and Stemberger, *Introduction* = H.L. Strack, *Introduction to Talmud and Midrash*. Ed. G. Stemberger and Trans. M. Bockmuehl. Minneapolis: Fortress Press, 1992.

Strange, "Archaeology Judaism" = J.F. Strange, "Archaeology and the Religion of Judaism in Palestine," in *Aufstieg und Niedergang der Römischen Welt*. Berlin: Walter de Gruyter, 1979, II, 19.2, 646–685.

Strong, *Bible Dictionary* = J. Strong, *The New Strong's Complete Dictionary of Bible Words*. Nashville, TN: Thomas Nelson, 1996.

Strugnell et al., *Qumran Cave 4* = J. Strugnell et al. (eds.), *Qumran Cave 4 XXIV: Sapiential Texts, Part 2, 4Q415, DJD* 34. Oxford: Clarendon Press, 1999.

Stuart Jones, *Sculptures* = H. Stuart Jones, *A Catalogue of Ancient Sculptures Preserved in the Municipal Collections of Rome: The Sculptures of the Museo Capitolino*, Oxford: Oxford University Press, 2012.

Sussman, *Jewish Oil Lamps* = V. Sussman, *Ornamented Jewish Oil-Lamps: From the Destruction of the Second Temple through the Bar-Kokhba Revolt*. Warminster, UK: Aris & Phillips, 1982.

Sussman, *Roman Period Oil Lamps* = V. Sussman, *Roman Period Oil Lamps in the Holy Land: Collection of the Israel Antiquities Authority*. Oxford: British Archaeological Reports, 2012.

Syon, *Small Change* = D. Syon, *Small Change in Hellenistic-Roman Galilee*. Jerusalem: Israel Numismatic Society, 2015.

Tabory, "Table" = J. Tabory, "The Household Table in Rabbinic Palestine," *AJS Review* 4 (1979): 211–215.

Tabory, "Paschal Meal" = J. Tabory, "Towards a History of the Paschal Meal," in P.F. Bradshaw and L.A. Hoffman (eds.), *Passover and Easter: Origin and History to Modern Times*. Notre Dame, IN: University of Notre Dame Press, 1999, 62–80.

Tchalenko, *Syrian Villages* = G. Tchalenko, *Villages Antiques de la Syrie du nord 1*. Paris: P. Geuthner, 1953.

Tcherikover et al., *CPJ* = V.A. Tcherikover et al. (eds.), *Corpus Papyrorum Judaicarum*. Cambridge, MA: Harvard University Press, 1964, 3 Vols.

Tchernia, *The Romans* = A. Tchernia, *The Romans and Trade*. Oxford: Oxford University Press, 2016.

Temin, "Market Economy" = P. Temin, "A Market Economy in the Early Roman Empire," *JRS* 91 (2001): 169–181.

Temin, "Labor Market" = P. Temin, "The Labor Market of the Early Roman Empire," *Journal of Interdisciplinary History* 34, no. 4 (2004): 513–538.

Temin, "Economy" = P. Temin, "The Economy of the Early Roman Empire," *JEP* 20, no. 1 (2006): 133–151.

Temin, *Roman Market Economy* = P. Temin, *The Roman Market Economy*. Princeton, NJ: Princeton University Press, 2013.

Tepper and Tepper, *Beit She'arim* = Y. Tepper and Y. Tepper, *Beth She'arim: The Village and Nearby Burials*. Tel Aviv: Hakibbutz Hameuchad, 2004 [in Hebrew].

Therborn, "Class Perspectives" = G. Therborn, "Class Perspectives: Shrink or Widen?" *Acta Sociologica* 45, no. 3 (2002): 221–225.

Tigchelaar, "Aramaic Texts" = E.J.C. Tigchelaar, "Aramaic Texts from Qumran and the Authoritativeness of Hebrew Scriptures, Preliminary Observations," in M. Popović (ed.), *Authoritative Scriptures in Ancient Judaism*. Leiden: Brill, 2010, 155–171.

Todd, *Lysias* = S.C. Todd, *Lysias: A Translation*. Austin: University of Texas Press, 2000.

Tomson and Schwartz, *Jews and Christians* = P.J. Tomson, and J. Schwartz (eds.), *Jews and Christians in the First and Second Centuries: How to Write Their History*. Leiden: Brill, 2014.

Toner, *Rethinking Roman* = J.P. Toner, *Rethinking Roman History*. Cambridge: Oleander Press, 2002.

Trebilco, *Jewish Communities* = P.R. Trebilco, *Jewish Communities in Asia Minor*. Cambridge, Cambridge University Press, 1991.

Tsafrir, *Israel Archaeology* = Y. Tsafrir, *Eretz Israel from the Destruction of the Second Temple to the Muslim Conquest*, Vol. 2: *Archaeology and Art*. Jerusalem: Yad Yitzhak Ben Zvi, 1984 [in Hebrew].

Tsafrir, "Synagogues" = Y. Tsafrir, "The Synagogues at Capernaum and Meroth and the Dating of the Galilean Synagogue," in J.H. Humphrey (ed.), *The Roman and Byzantine Near East*. Ann Arbor: University of Michigan Press, 1995, 151–161.

Tsafrir et al., *Tabula Iudaea* = Y. Tsafrir, L. Di Segni, and J. Green (eds.), *Tabula Imperii Romani, Iudaea, Palaestina: Maps and Gazetteer*. Jerusalem: The Israel Academy of Sciences and Humanities, 1994.

Udoh, *Taxes Palestine* = F.E. Udoh, *To Caesar What Is Caesar's: Tribute, Taxes, and Imperial Administration in Early Roman Palestine 63 BCE.–70 CE*. Providence, RI: Brown Judaic Studies, 2005.

Ulrich, "Artisans" = R.B. Ulrich, "Artisans," in Bagnall et al., *Encyclopedia*, 2:802–804.

Urbach, "Idolatry" = E.E. Urbach, "The Rabbinical Laws of Idolatry in the Second and Third Centuries in the Light of Archaeological and Historical Facts," *IEJ* 9 (1959): 149–165, 229–245 [= E.E. Urbach, *Collected Writings in Jewish Studies*. Ed. R. Brody and M.D. Herr. Jerusalem: Magnes Press, 1999, 151–194].

Urbach, "Slavery" = E.E. Urbach, "The Laws Regarding Slavery as a Source for Social History of the Period of the Second Temple, the Mishnah and Talmud," in E.E. Urbach, *Collected Writings in Jewish Studies*. Jerusalem, Magnes Press, 1999, 56–150.

Uytterhoeven, "Housing in Late Antiquity" = I. Uytterhoeven, "Housing in Late Antiquity: Thematic Perspectives," in L. Lavan, L. Özgenel, and A. Sarantis (eds.), *Housing in Late Antiquity: From Palaces to Shops*. Brill: Leiden, 2007, 25–66.

VanGemeren, *Dictionary* = W.A. VanGemeren (ed.), *New International Dictionary Of Old Testament Theology and Exegesis*, 5 Vols. Grand Rapids, MI: Zondervan, 1997.

Van Henten, "Judean Antiquities" = J.W. Van Henten, *Judean Antiquities 15* = Vol. 7b of S. Mason (ed.), *Flavius Josephus—Translation and Commentary*. Leiden: Brill, 2014.

Van Minnen, "Agriculture" = P. Van Minnen, "Agriculture, and the 'Taxes-and-Trade' Model in Roman Egypt," *ZPE* 133 (2000): 205–220.

Van Minnen, "Money and Credit" = P. van Minnen, "Money and Credit in Roman Egypt," in W.V. Harris (ed.), *The Monetary System of the Greeks and Romans*. Oxford: Oxford University Press, 2008, 226–241.

Van Nijf, *Associations* = O.M. Van Nijf, *The Civic World of Professional Associations in the Roman East*. Amsterdam: J.C. Gibben, 1997.

Varner, "Replications" = E.R. Varner, "Reading Replications: Roman Rhetoric and Greek Quotations," *Art History* 29, no. 2 (2006): 280–303.

Verboven, "Associative Order" = K. Verboven, "The Associative Order: Status and Ethos among Roman Businessmen in the Late Republic and Early Empire," *Athenaeum* 95, no. 2 (2007): 861–893.

Verhagen, "Pignus" = H.L.E. Verhagen, "The Evolution of Pignus in Classical Roman Law *ius honorarium* and *ius novum*," *The Legal History Review* 81 (2013): 51–79.

Veyne, *Bread and Circuses* = P. Veyne, *Bread and Circuses*. London: Penguin, 1990.

Vincent, "Beit Djebrin" = L.H. Vincent, "Une Villa Gréco Romain á Beit Djebrin," *Revue Biblique* 31 (1922): 259–281.

Vine, *Matthew Audience* = C.E.W. Vine, *The Audience of Matthew*. London: T&T Clark, 2014.

Virlouvet, *Tessera* = C. Virlouvet, *Tessera frumentaria: Les procédures de distribution du blé public'a Rome'a la fin de la République et au début de l'Empire*. Rome: Bibliothéque des écoles françaises d'Athènes et de Rome, 1995.

Vittinghoff, "Gesellschaft" = F. Vittinghoff, "Gesellschaft," in F. Vittinghoff (ed.), *Handbuch der Eurpäische Wirtschafts und Sozialgeschichte in der Römischen Kaiserzeit*. Stuttgart: Stuttgart University Press, 1990, 161–369.

Vittinghoff, "Social Structure" = F. Vittinghoff, "Sociale Stuktr und politiches System in der hohen römischen Kaiserzeit," in F. Vittinghoff, *Civitas Romana: Stadt und politisch-soziale Integration im Imperium Romanum der Kaiserzeit*. Stuttgart: Klett-Cotta, 1994, 253–271.

Vyhmeister, "Rich Man" = N.J. Vyhmeister, "The Rich Man in James 2: Does Ancient Patronage Illumine the Text?" *Andrews University Seminary Studies* 33, no. 1 (1995): 265–283.

Wallace-Hadrill, "Roman Luxury" = A. Wallace-Hadrill, "The Social Spread Of Roman Luxury: Sampling Pompeii and Herculaneum," *Papers of the British School at Rome* 58 (1990): 145–192.

Wallace-Hadrill, *Houses and Society* = A. Wallace-Hadrill, *Houses and Society in Pompeii and Herculaneum*. Princeton, NJ: Princeton University Press, 1994.

Wallace-Hadrill, "Roman Atrium" = A. Wallace-Hadrill, "Rethinking the Roman Atrium House," in Laurence and Wallace-Hadrill, *Domestic Space*, 219–240.

Wallace-Hadrill, "Trying" = A. Wallace-Hadrill, "Trying to Define and Identify the Roman 'Middle Classes,'" *JRA* 26 (2013): 605–609.

Watson, *Roman Law* = A. Watson, *Roman Law and Comparative Law*. Athens: University of Georgia Press, 1991.

Watson, *Spirit* = A. Watson, *The Spirit of Roman Law*. Athens: University of Georgia Press, 1995.

Weber, *Economy and Society* = M. Weber, *Economy and Society: An Outline of Interpretive Sociology*, 2 Vols. Ed. G. Roth and C. Wittich. Berkeley: University of California Press, 1978 [1922].

Weiss, "Dwellings Sepphoris" = Z. Weiss, "Private Architecture in the Public Sphere: Urban Dwellings in Roman and Byzantine Sepphoris," in K. Galor and T. Waliszewska (eds.), *From Antioch to Alexandria: Recent Studies in Domestic Architecture*. Warsaw: Institute of Archaeology of the University of Warsaw, 2007, 125–136.

Weiss, "Burial Practices" = Z. Weiss, "Burial Practices in Beth She'arim and the Question of Dating the Patriarchal Necropolis," in Z. Weiss et al. (eds.), *Follow the Wise: Studies in Jewish History and Culture in Honor of Lee I. Levine*. Winona Lake, IN: Eisenbrauns, 2010, 213–225.

Weiss, "Roman Antique Houses" = Z. Weiss, "Houses of the Wealthy in Roman and Late Antique Tiberias," in J. Patrich, O. Peleg-Barkat, and E. Ben Yosef (eds.), *Arise, Walk through the Land: Studies in the Archaeology and History of the Land of Israel*. Jerusalem: Israel Exploration Society, 2016, 211–220 [in Hebrew].

Welborn, "The Polis and the Poor" = L.L. Welborn, "The Polis and the Poor: Reconstructing Social Relations from Different Genres of Evidence," in J.R. Harrison and L.L. Welborn (eds.), *The First Urban Churches 1: Methodological Foundations*. Atlanta: SBL Press, 2015, 189–243.

White, "Technology Expansion" = L. White, "The Expansion of Technology 500–1500," in C.M. Cipolla (ed.), *The Fontana Economic History of Europe: The Middle Ages*. London: Collins/Fontana, 1993, 143–174.

Whittaker, "The Poor" = C.R. Whittaker, "The Poor in the City of Rome," in C.R. Whittaker, *Land, City and Trade in the Roman Empire*. Aldershot, UK: Variorum, 1993, 1–25 [= C.R. Whittaker, "The Poor," in A. Giardina (ed.), *The Romans*. Chicago: University of Chicago Press, 1993, 272–299].

Wieacker, *Römische Rechtsgeschichte* = F. Wieacker, *Römische Rechtsgeschichte: Quellenkunde, Rechtsbildung, Jurisprudenz und Rechtsliteratur*. Munich: Beck, 2006 [1988].

Wiedemann, "Patron" = T. Wiedemann, "The Patron as Banker," in K. Lomas and T. Cornell (eds.), *Bread and Circuses: Euergetism and Municipal Patronage in Roman Italy*. London: Routledge, 2003, 12–27.

Wilson, "Growth Indicators" = A. Wilson, "Indicators for Roman Economic Growth: A Response to Walter Scheidel," *JRA* 22 (2009): 71–82.

Wilson and Bowman, "Introduction" = A. Wilson and A. Bowman, "Introduction," in A. Wilson and A. Bowman (eds.), *Trade, Commerce and the State in the Roman World*. Oxford: Oxford University Press, 2018.

Wilson and Flohr, "Introduction" = A. Wilson and M. Flohr, "Introduction," in A. Wilson and M. Flohr (eds.), *Urban Craftsmen and Traders in the Roman World*. Oxford: Oxford University Press, 2016, 1–22.

Winterling, *Politics* = A. Winterling, *Politics and Society in Imperial Rome*. Chichester, UK: Wiley-Blackwell, 2009.

Witcher, "Agrarian" = R. Witcher, "Agrarian Spaces in Roman Italy: Society, Economy and Mediterranean Agriculture," *Arqueología espacial (Paisajes agrarios)* 26 (2006): 341–359.

Wolf, "Europe" = E.R. Wolf, "Introduction to Europe and the People without History," in H.L. Moore and T. Sanders (eds.), *Anthropology in Theory: A Reader*. Oxford: Blackwell, 2006, 367–382.

Wolff, "Wealth Distribution" = E.N. Wolff, "Wealth Distribution," in N.J. Smelser and P.B. Baltes (eds.), *International Encyclopedia of the Social Behavioral Sciences*. Oxford: Elesvier, 2001, 16394–16401.

Wood, "Class Relations" = E.M. Wood, "Landlords and Peasants, Masters and Slaves: Class Relations in Greek and Roman Antiquity," *Historical Materialism* 10, no. 3 (2002): 17–69.

Woolf, "Food Poverty" = G. Woolf, "Food, Poverty and Patronage: The Significance of the Epigraphy of the Alimentary Schemes in Early Imperial Italy," *PBSR* 58 (1990): 197–228.

Woolf, *Becoming Roman* = G. Woolf, *Becoming Roman: The Origins of Provincial Civilization in Gaul*. Cambridge: Cambridge University Press, 1998.

Woolf, "Writing Poverty" = G. Woolf, "Writing Poverty in Rome," in M. Atkins and R. Osborne (eds.), *Poverty in the Roman World*. Cambridge: Cambridge University Press, 2006, 83–99.

Wright, "Rich and Poor" = B.G. Wright, "The Categories of Rich and Poor in the Qumran Sapiential Literature," in J.J. Collins, G.E. Sterling, and R.A. Clements (eds.), *Sapiential Perspectives: Wisdom Literature in Light of the Dead Sea Scrolls: Proceedings of the Sixth International Symposium of the Orion Center 2001*. Leiden: Brill, 2004, 101–123.

Wright and Camp, "Ben Sira's Discourse" = B.G. Wright and C.V. Camp, "'Who Has Been Tested by Gold and Found Perfect?' Ben Sira's Discourse of Riches and Poverty," *Henoch* 23 (2001): 153–174.

Wright, *Classes* = E.O. Wright, *Classes*. London: Verso, 1985.

Wright, "Continuing Relevance" = E.O. Wright, "The Continuing Relevance of Class Analysis," *Theory and Society* 25, no. 5 (1996): 697–716.

Wright, "Rethinking" = E.O. Wright, "Rethinking the Concept of Class Structure," in E.O. Wright (ed.), *The Debate on Classes*. New York: Verso, 1998, 269–348.

Yadin, *The War* = Y. Yadin, *The Scroll of the War of the Sons of Light against the Sons of Darkness*. Oxford: Oxford University Press, 1962.

Yavor, "Architecture (Gamla)" = Z. Yavor, "The Architecture and Stratigraphy of the Eastern and Western Quarters," in D. Sion and Z. Yavor (eds.), *Gamla II: The Architecture: The Shmarya Gutmann Excavations 1976–1988*. Jerusalem: Israel Antiquities Authority, 2010, 13–112.

Yavor, "Gamla Techniques" = Z. Yavor, "Building Techniques and Urban Planning," in D. Sion and Z. Yavor (eds.), *Gamla II: The Architecture: The Shmarya Gutmann Excavations 1976–1988*. Jerusalem: Israel Antiquities Authority, 2010, 153–157.

Yeivin, *Survey Settlements* = Z. Yeivin, *Survey of Settlements in Galilee and the Golan from the Period of the Mishna in Light of the Sources*. PhD Diss., The Hebrew University, Jerusalem, 1971 [in Hebrew].

Yeivin, "Towns" = Z. Yeivin, "Haayarot Habeinoniyot," *Eretz Yisrael* 19 (1987), 59–81 [Hebrew, with English summary].

Zaccagnini, "Mobility" = C. Zaccagnini, "Patterns of Mobility among Ancient Near Eastern Craftsmen," *JNES* 42, no. 4 (1983): 245–264.

Zanker, *Images* = P. Zanker, *The Power of Images in the Age of Augustus*. Ann Arbor, University of Michigan Press, 1990.

Zangenberg and Van den Zande, "Urbanization" = J.K. Zangenberg and D. Van de Zande, "Urbanization," in C. Hezser (ed.), *The Oxford Handbook of Jewish Daily Life in Roman Palestine*. Oxford: Oxford University Press, 2010, 165–188.

Zimmer, *Occupations* = G. Zimmer, *Römische Berufsdarstellungen*. Berlin: Deutsches Archäologisches Institute, 1982.

Zissu and Ganor, "Horvat Ethri" = B. Zissu and A. Ganor, "Horvat Ethri: A Jewish Village from the Second Temple Period and the Bar Kokhba Revolt in the Judean Foothills," *JJS* 60, no. 1 (2009): 90–136.

Index of Modern Authors

Aberbach 94n17, 100n51, 106, 185n87
Adan-Bayewitz 98
Albeck 23, 40n87, 47n116, n119, 62n186, 76n41, 80n71, n73, 83n88, 84n91, 113n121, 128n57, 157n83
Alföldy 1n1, 12n3–4, 16–19, 52, 130n62, 141n2
Aviam 11n33 and 35, 98n39, 99n43, 170, 176b
Ayali 68n6, 73n21g, 83–87, 94n17, 100n53, 106

Bagnall 116n4, 135n83, 138
Balzaretti 166
Baruch 171
Beechey 4n12, 97
Bopp 169n150, 178, 179n66
Brown 1n1, 25n2, 40n92, 48n122, 51, 118n11

Cole 4n12, 5n14, 16n49, 18

Dar 11n35, 48n122, 116n2, 133–134, 176i
Dark 11n35

Ellis 11n35, 131, 133, 142n7, 168
Epstein 32n49, 73n23, 79n68, 107, 114n47, 159n95, 160n100

Fine R. 15n46
Fine S. 9n24, 11n33, 104
Finley 13, 14n42–44, 34n60, 43n100, 103n73, 183
Freyne 18
Friesen 3n7, 4n11, 19–21, 40n91, 43n99, 52, 91n4, 94n15, 130n62, 141n4

Garnsey 1, 2, 6, 14, 15, 25, 51, 53, 90, 92, 116n3, 118n13, 121n25, 128n56, 135n83, 136n85, 138n95
Gluska 100n51, 101n56, 106

Hamel 4n9, 19n63, 25n5, 26n10, 34n58, 46, 127n53
Harris E.M. 91n4, 92n7, 94, 110n108
Harris J.M. 8n20
Harris W.V. 14n44, 99n44

Heichelheim 84–86
Hezser 9
Hirschfeld 26n7, 132, 133n72–73, 165n130, 167n144, 169n154, 170n156, 176h-j, 177v, 179n167
Hock 93n10, 105

Jongkind 53, 205

Kehoe 10n31, 14n42, 16n48, 49n123, 73n22, 97, 98n34, 118n14, 138n92
Knapp 4n10, 14n43, 20c–d, 26, 42n97, 51n128, 115n141, 117n5, 119n19
Lenski 6n17, 15n45, 19n63, 92, 115n139
Lieberman 9n24, 23, 32n51, 33n53, 39n81, 40n87–88–90, 41n95, 43n102, 44n103, 46n113, 48n120, 57n163, 58n154–157, 60n176, 61n179–182, 62n186, 72n15–18, 73n20, 74n24–32, 75n38–40, 76n44–46, 77n49–52, 78n53, 78n60–61, 79n62–63, 79n66, 80n75–77, 81n78, 82n82, 83n90, 85, 86n101, 86n105, 107n95, 112n120, 113n121n127n133, 114n136, 123n38, 124n39–40, 125n43, 127n54, 129n61, 130n64, 156n71, 158n86, 164n127
Loane 14n44, 96
Longenecker 3n7, 17n54, 18n58, 19–20, 34n62, 52, 94n15, 142n6

MacMullen 1n1, 3n7, 19n61n63, 21, 130n62, 135n83
Marx 15
Meggitt 19
Meyers E.M. 98, 160n99, 165n130, 167n144, 169n153–154, 170, 176c
Meyers C.L. 165n130

Nagy 169
Neusner 8, 23, 38n80, 39n84–85, 41n94, 42n96n98, 44n105, 45n109–110, 47n116–117, 48n120, 72n15n18–19, 74n37, 75n38, 77n49–50, 81n78, 83n85, 86n104, 111n112, 123n34, 154n59n61, 155n64, 157n83, 159n96, 162n109, 163n119

INDEX OF MODERN AUTHORS

Oakes   1n1, 20a, 21, 52, 214
Oğuş   97

Richardson   53
Rostovtzeff   13, 14
Rowlandson   137–138
Ruffing   2n6, 25n5, 93n13, 95

Safrai S.   9n25, 25n47, 128n56
Safrai Z.   8n23, 16n48, 48n122, 92n5, 94n17, 98n38, 112n118, 114n138, 116n2, 118n12, 132n70, 134, 159n97, 164n127
Saller   1n1, 2n6, 14n42n44, 18n55, 21, 92n5, 118n12, 120n23, 135n83, 138n93, 141n3
Sartre   2n2, 11n36, 137n87, 142n6–7, 177n1, 178, 179n168
Scheidel   1n1, 2n3, 3n7, 4n11, 14n42n44, 19n61n64, 20b, 21, 40n91, 43n99, 45n108, 52n133, 83, 89n110, 91n4, 93n13, 94n15, 108n102, 136n85, 141n4, 142n6
Sodini   11n35, 93n11, 95n21, 141n4, 166, 167n140
Stewart   93n11, 96, 97, 101n55

Tepper   134, 164n129

Uytterhoeven   26, 131n66–67, 132n70, 168n49, 169n151–152

Verboven   2n1, 18, 141n4, 142n6, 180n169

Wallace-Hadrill   3, 4, 15, 53, 131n65–67, 157n82, 168n147–148, 177, 178n183, 180n169
Weber   5n12, 15, 104n75, 194
Whittaker   20e–f, 25, 26n6
Winterling   2n1, 17, 18n57, 141n2, 142n6
Woolf   19n63, 26n6, 51, 52n133n135, 122n33
Wright   15n46–47, 29n32, 30, 31n44

Yeivin   11n35, 16n50, 112n118, 131, 132n68, 170n156

Zaccagini   94, 113n132
Zuckermandel   23

General Index

Abba Saul (Sage)   38
Agriculture, Agricultural (see also: farming)   8, 14n43–44, 37n75, 67,69, 71, 78, 83n87, 87, 89, 91, 92, 115n139, 131, 132n68, 138n92, 187, 188, 191, 206, 226, 228
Amrah (site)   179
Apocrypha, Apocryphal   29, 117
Antoninus   111n115, 164, 165
Aqiva, Aqiba, Akiva   56, 60, 63, 84, 111, 114n137
Aramaic   49n124, 100n51, 101, 106, 107n90, 115, 187, 191, 194, 197, 200, 207, 213, 222, 225
Arbel   99, 134, 172
Archaeology, Archaeological   26, 166–167
Asia Minor   35, 53, 93, 95n21, 97, 136n85, 137, 139, 166n136
Artisan (see also: craftsman)   90–113, 115, 131
Atrium   53, 168
Augustus   12, 135n83, 165

Bailiff   51, 77, 88, 126, 136, 137
Baker (Nahtom)   83, 99
Balsam   99
Bank, banker   43, 80, 113
Barley   38, 45, 46, 74n25, 82
Bath, bathouse   98, 112n17, 167, 169–171, 173–175, 177, 180
Ben Sira   29–30, 68n6, 101, 102n60–61, 106, 143
Beit Guvrin (Eleutheropolis)   12, 170, 175
Beit Saida (Bethseda)   172
Beit She'arim   164
Bible   23, 27–28, 31, 44, 55, 68, 102, 103n69, 117n6n8, 119n16, 123, 143
Blacksmith   108, 112
Ben tovim, Bnei – Tovim   32, 59–60
Border(s)   22, 40, 42, 44, 52, 90, 91, 92n5, 114, 178
Bornet (excavation).   174
Boule   141, 164–166
Breiké (excavation)   179
Burnt House   167, 174
Byzantine   x, 7, 11, 133, 169, 171, 177v

Caesar,   18, 20, 51, 111n115, 141, 166

Caesarea   152, 167
Caracalla   165
Center(s)   8, 16n50, 98, 100, 110
Charity   26n10, 27–32, 38n76, 40–41, 44, 47n116, 49, 56–61, 63, 64, 66, 67, 140, 152n55, 161, 181
Christian(s), Christianity   x, 7, 13, 35, 47n118, 105, 122n34, 136n54, 145, 151–153, , 161
Chronological, Chronology   11, 164
City (Cities)   10, 12, 14, 16, 17–18, 19n61, 20–21, 32, 40, 42n97, 52, 53, 59, 69, 75, 87, 89, 91n4, 92n7n9, 93n10, 95, 99, 109, 111–112, 138, 141–142, 152–153, 157n83, 159, 163, 164, 165m 166n136, 167, 168n148, 169n151, 172, 174, 175, 178, 179, 182, 183, 184
City Council   163, 166n136
Class (Classes)   2–5, 6n16, 13, 15, 19–20, 23–24, 45n108, 84, 86, 88, 89, 91–97, 100n47, 104n74, 105, 108, 115–117, 120, 128,130–131, 134, 137, 140–142, 144n22, 145, 157–159, 168–170, 177p, 180n169, 182, 184
Class, Lower   2, 6n17, 44, 45n108, 84, 104n74, 105, 134
Class, Middle – Middling groups   3n7, 4–6, 13, 15–20, 23, 45n108, 84, 86, 88–91–97, 100n47, 104n74, 105, 108, 115–117, 120, 128, 130- 131 142n6, 144n22, 145, 157, 169–170, 170, 176, 177p, 179, 180n169, 182, 184
Class, Upper (also: High Society)   2, 5, 15–20, 23, 89, 97, 120, 130–131, 141–142, 144n22, 145, 158–160, 168–170, 176, 177p, 179, 184
Coastal   178
Codex   162n110, 165n134.
Coins   11, 26, 34, 164, 177u
Colonia   165
Commandment(s)   3, 28, 58, 79, 145, 146n28, 158n89
Commerce, Commercial   10n29, 12–14, 24, 37, 44, 93, 95, 100, 132n68, 138
Community   5, 21, 26n10, 33, 38, 40, 42, 44, 46, 49, 51, 58–63, 66, 72, 82, 102, 105, 149, 153n56, 161, 166, 169
Constantine the Great   165–166

GENERAL INDEX

Corinth 53
Countryside 17, 46, 69, 133, 135
Court 82, 110, 164
Courtyard 111, 130–131, 133–134, 169, 170–177
Craft 12, 91, 92n9, 93, 94–97, 99–106, 112–115, 182
Craftsmen 1, 4n10, 14, 20, 22, 67n1, 69, 73, 88, 89, chapter 4, 182
Culture 6, 8n23, 9, 11, 12, 55n148, 100n47, 105n80, 122n34, 132n68
Culture - Material 8–9, 55n148
Curia 141, 165

Damage(s) 43n103, 62, 66, 76n47, 123
Date(s) (fruit) 38, 46, 123
Date(d) (time unit) 32, 89n109, 133, 164–165, 171, 172–177
Dead Sea 31, 68–69, 143
Decoration 96, 165, 168, 169n150, 174, 177s, 178
Decurion(s), 18, 20, 165
Damascus
  Document 30
  city 105n84
Denar, Denarii, Denarius 35n68, 42n97, 43, 45, 52n136, 70–72, 81–86, 88, 90, 119, 154–155, 160, 162–163
Destitute 15, 18–22, 28, 30, 31n44, 33–37, 41, 47, 49, 50–56, 65, 68n4, 91, 120n20, 132, 154, 182–183
Diaspora 164, 166
Dionysus 169
Disciple 35–36, 56, 104–105, 111, 120n21, 127n52, 144n23, 145–151, 153
Djebel al Arab 179
Dock Workers 90
Doctor 105, 110–112, 149
Donkey 64
  Donkey drivers 124n40–42
Dosa, Rabbi 81
Dye 98, 107
Dynasty
  Hamonean 11
  Han 25
  Severan 97
  Herodian 142f

Economy (Economic) 1, 7, 12–14, 34n97, 99, 135n82, 183
Ein Gedi 132, 133n72–73, 176
Ein Yael 174
Elazar, 58, 62, 63, 82n84, 114n137, 160n106, 162–163
Empire, Roman 1–3, 6–7, 9, 12–16, 17n54, 21–22, 26, 74, 83, 86, 87, 89, 93- 99, 103–104, 110–111, 112, 115–116, 121–122, 129–131, 135n83, 136, 139, 140, 141, 145, 152, 162n110, 164, 165, 179–180, 183
  Commerce 13–14, 16, 92–93, 104
  Economic Crisis 12, 45n108, 86n102, 162n110
  Economy 7
  Geography 2, 179–180
  Labor and Crafts 83, 87, 89, 95–98, 99n35, 103n73, 104, 112, 115
  Population and Demography 21, 135n83, 136
  Pottery 98n35
  Standard of living 17n54, 26, 48n122, 74, 83, 116, 136, 162n112
  Stratification 22, 50–54, 129–131, 136, 139–145, 164, 183
  Taxation 121–122
Essenes 31
Evyon 31, 55

Family (Families) 5, 18, 20, 22, 32–33, 42, 44n106, 48, 49, 53, 57, 58, 59, 67, 78, 83–85, 87–88, 96, 118, 122n29, 123, 127n53, 131–139, 168, 176f, 181
  Caesar's 18, 20
  Herodian 22
  Income 5, 44n106, 83–85, 87–88, 127n53, 131
  Nuclear 48–49, 53, 87n108, 122n29
Fruit (s) 38, 45–46, 59, 72, 78, 82, 85, 88, 109, 119n19, 123–124, 130n62
Frumentatio (grain dole) 51

Galilee 8, 12, 16, 98–99, 126n49, 131–132, 142n7, 145, 150n45, 178
Gamaliel Rabban 59, 62, 78, 105n84, 114, 160n106, 163
Gamla 172, 176, 178

Gentile   12, 152, 160, 169, 170n157, 176f
Geography   2n2, 10
Glass   96, 99
Golan Heights   12, 131, 132n68, 178
Gospels   33, 36–37, 104, 139, 145–146, 151n48, 153
Grain   21, 38, 51, 64, 81, 146–147
Grave(s), gravestones   93, 148, 164–165
Greek   11–12, 14n42, 34, 43, 52–53, 69n9, 92n9, 96, 102–103, 106, 117–118, 119n19, 120–122, 132, 139, 143, 157n83, 177u
Groups, social: see class
Halakha, halakhic   3, 7–8, 23, 27, 39, 54, 56, 59, 62, 66, 72, 116n1
Hauran   178–179, 190
Hebrew   24, 62n186, 68–69, 73, 101, 106, 115–118, 122, 139, 181
Helena (Queen)   57
Hermopolite   137
Herod, Herodian   11–12n36, 19n63, 22, 32, 52, 69, 103–104, 142, 150, 167, 173, 178
Herod Antipas   173, 178
Hillel   32
Hilqiya's Palace   175
Hirbat Bureq   173
Hirbat Basatin   173
Hirbat Deir Sam'an   173
History, Historical   1–3, 6, 7n18, 8–10, 13, 16, 41, 48, 60–61, 68, 73, 87, 96, 100, 112, 114, 116–117, 130, 135–136, 164, 167
   Cultural   x
   Economic   6–7
   Jewish   3
   Material   1
   Political   6–7
   Social   1, 6–7
Holy   119, 154
Home(s)   11, 15, 19n62, 34, 36, 39, 40n88, 46, 53, 57, 73, 88, 107, 109, 118, 121, 122n29, 125, 127, 130–135, 139, 149, 168, 169n151, 170, 177v, 178
Homeowner   1, 19n62, 39n81, 57, 72, 77, 82, 88, 115–119, 122–123, 124n42, 136, 139, 144–145
House(s)   10, 21, 29, 39–41, 42n96, 45n110, 46n112, 47, 49–50, 53, 105, 108–110, 116–122, 124–127, 130–136, 142n7, 148–150, 164, 167–180

Household (householder)   5n14, 40, 47, 49, 70, 72, 74n32, 77, 81, 92n7, 101, 110, 120–122, 125, 130, 133, 136, 139, 150, 169n151
Hurvat Aleq   173
Hurvat Eqev   173
Hurvat Ethri   175

Imperial   138, 141–142
Industry   95, 96n23, 101, 105–106
Inscription(s)   6, 14, 53, 89n109, 93, 96, 110, 115, 142, 165–166, 168, 177u
Iotapata   98n39, 172
Italy   6, 90, 92n6, 163

Jerusalem   12, 33, 58, 64, 69, 99–100, 103, 109, 145, 163, 167–168, 174
Jewish Society   x, 1, 3, 5, 8, 11, 12, 16, 19n63, 21–22, 25–26, 33, 36, 40, 48, 58, 66, 87, 93, 94n17, 113, 116, 130, 134–136, 145, 149, 157n74, 164, 167–168, 179–181, 184
Jose, Joseph   69, 104, 148
Josephus   31, 57, 58n164, 68–69, 71, 87, 92n5, 102–104, 106, 117–118
Joshua   142
Jotapata: See: Iotapata
Judah   8, 59n171, 113n127, 114, 125, 128, 155, 163–164
Judea, Judean   8, 12, 25n5, 99, 114, 120, 132n68, 142n8, 148, 178
Judean Desert   30, 98, 122
Judean Hills, Plain   8
Judge(s), Judged   2, 8, 10, 32n42, 73, 102n60, 142, 147, 159–161
Juvenal   50

Kalandia   173–174
Karanis   138
Kfar Hanania   98
Kefar Nahum   132, 172
Kefar Nasaj   172, 179
Kefar Shams   179
Kefar Shikhin   98
Kefar Tabya   110
Kefar Yavor   98
Kfar Qana   99
Kerayot   164
Kibbutz Lavi   134

GENERAL INDEX

Khirbet Baddisa   174–175
Khirbet Mishkena   134
Kinneret   172
Kitchen, Kitchenware   44n106, 169–170, 174, 180

Land   12–13, 16n48, 17, 19, 23, 25n3, 29, 46, 48, 49, 50, 62, 73, 77, 87- 92, 96, 105, 114–121, 126–128, 131–139, 143, 160, 164, 167, 168n148, 178
Landowner, landed   12n37, 13, 18, 19n63, 23, 42, 45, 48, 49n123, 88, 115n140, 116–118, 121–130, 132, 134–140, 144, 158, 178, 179, 182
Law   1–2, 10, 18, 37, 39, 41, 43n100, 44n104, 78n54, 86, 88–89, 96, 99n40, 108, 112, 115, 121–122, 128, 137, 148, 154n59, 158, 160n105, 165, 166
Lazarus   33–34, 145n26, 151
Ledja   179
Levi, Levite   36n70, 78n54, 123n38, 124, 126, 148
Life, Lifestyle   12, 26n9, 31, 36, 43, 60, 90, 93n10, 130, 141, 143n17, 144, 146–147, 153, 155n62, 162–164, 170
   Day to day   1, 10–11, 17–18, 25, 34n61, 117
Literature   2, 5, 6, 28, 53, 94–96, 99, 115–116, 170
   Biblical   31n40, 39, 101
   Greek   52–53, 117
   Rabbinic and Tannaitic   x, 3–4, 7–13, 16, 18, 21, 26, 31n40, 32, 37, 49, 52n136, 54n144, 55n151, 58–61, 67, 72, 75, 106–107, 112, 120n22, 123, 126, 128n55, 129, 133, 139, 154, 155n65, 156, 160, 171, 181, 184
   Roman   2n5, 15, 26n6, 50–51, 91n4, 101, 104, 116n1, 141
   Second Temple   29–30, 68, 87, 99–100, 101–102, 107, 117, 122, 142–144, 157n80
Livelihood   67, 71, 87n108, 88, 92, 114, 121, 122n29, 134, 138–139
Lod (Lydda)   8, 12, 110, 111, 165, 174
Lycia   53

Malthace   165
Mansion   167, 170, 178
Manufacture   13–14, 95, 98–99, 101, 105, 108–110, 112–113, 115, 177x, 183

Map   16, 23
Maritime   90
Market(s)   10, 14, 43n99, 44, 70, 75, 95–96, 98, 103n73, 112, 120, 124, 130, 135n82, 183
Marxism   16n47
Master   76n47, 91, 103, 116–117, 120–122, 150, 152n51
Maximus   50
Mediterranean   92n5, 100
Meir   38, 65, 114, 125, 154, 159n90
Meiron, Meron   98, 132n68, 170, 172, 176c
Merchandise   41, 44, 49, 73, 80n71, 124n40
Merit   63n191, 64–66, 94n16
Midrash   7–8, 23, 27, 44n103, 48n121, 55, 57, 59, 64, 65, 72, 107, 114, 116n1, 155, 157n81, 158n88, 159, 160n98
Mikve (ritual bath)   98, 167, 169–172, 170, 174–175
Money   5, 18, 19n63, 22, 28, 30, 32–33, 35–36, 41–44, 46, 48, 50- 51, 53, 55, 57, 61, 63–64, 65n205, 71n12, 73, 75, 76n41, 78–80, 83–86, 94n14, 97, 127, 141, 142n8, 143, 146, 148, 150–151, 153–155, 156n70, 157n79, 159–160, 168
Monobases (King)   57–58
Month   61, 75, 83n86
Mosaic   169–170, 172, 174, 180
Mt. Carmel   133–134, 173

Nahal Hagit   173
Nakdimon son of Guryon   64, 163
Nazareth   99, 104n75
Nehemiah   29
Network   13, 137
Neusner, Jacob   8, 23, 39n84, 41n94, 42n96, 45n110, 47n116, 48n120, 72n15, 74n37, 75n38, 86n104, 123n37, 154n59–61, 157n83, 159, 162n109
New Testament, NT   23, 33–37, 53, 68–69, 71, 87, 92n5, 99, 104–106, 118, 120, 122–123, 130, 132, 136, 139, 144–145, 151, 153, 157n74, 157n80, 161
Nonagricultural   67, 69, 87, 91, 104–105, 107n91, 112n118
Non Biblical   26, 29, 101
Non-Jewish   23–24, 48n122, 76, 95
Non Skilled   20, 45n108

Oil   35n68, 36, 38, 45–46, 84, 99, 157, 173–174
Olives   38, 77, 127, 133, 174
Oral   Agreements   88
   Tradition   122
Oxyrhynchite   138

Peasant   26, 73, 89, 92n5–6, 97, 108n98, 112n116, 115n139, 116–117, 118n12, 121n25, 132, 134, 136n85, 137n87, 138
Peristyle   131, 168, 172–174
Pharisees   33n54, 35, 148, 151
Philo   31, 102, 106, 142
Philology, Philological   x, 1, 4, 7, 181
Philosophy, Philosophical, Philosopher   31, 64, 96, 102, 121, 181
Pilgrim(s)   109
Pillar(s)   169, 175
Pious,   31, 57
Politics, Political, Politician   6–7, 11–12, 18, 25, 118, 121, 135, 141, 145, 157, 182
Poor   x, 3–6, 10, 11n35, 12n37, 15–67, 68n4, 72, 76, 78n60, 82, 84, 86–89, 92n7, 116, 118, 120, 123, 126–127, 129–134, 136–143, 145–148, 150–160, 162, 167, 179, 181–183
Potter   101, 107
Pottery   98, 99, 101n57, 107
Poverty, Poverty Line   1–2, 4n9, 5, 18–38, 40–46, 48–56, 60, 62–67, 88, 97, 119n19, 152, 154–156, 158, 167, 169n154, 182–183
Price(s)   39, 43n99, 44n104, 83, 85, 86n102, 155, 178
Prince   8, 23, 56, 114n136, 128, 157, 163–164
Profession(al)   x, 4, 18n59, 20, 36, 43, 62, 65, 66–67, 68n6, 69, 73, 91–115, 149n42, 152n51, 158, 182–183
Province, Provincial   1–2, 6–7, 12n38, 20–22, 92n6, 97, 116n3, 121–122, 125, 136, 139–141, 163–164, 166, 169n151, 178, 181, 183–184
Public   5, 10, 18, 25n3, 34–35, 39–40, 43, 47, 71, 72n17, 82, 102, 147, 169n151, 182
Purity   154n59, 167
Puteoli   19n61, 163

Qiryat Sefer (Modiin)   174–175
Qumran   28n21, 30–31, 102, 117n8, 157n80

Rabban Gamaliel   59, 62, 78, 114, 163
Rabbi Avardimos son of Rabbi Yossi   58
Rabbi Akiva   60, 63, 84, 111, 114, 115

Rabbi Elazar son of Azariah,   62, 63n193, 114n137, 160n106, 162, 163
Rabbi Elazar son of Hizma   82n84
Rabbi Elazar son of Rabbi Yossi   58
Rabbi Joshua son of Korha   58
Rabbi Judah the Prince   8, 114n136, 128, 163–164
Rabbi Judah son of Ilai   59n171, 113n127, 114, 125, 155
Rabbi Meir   38, 65, 98, 114, 125, 154, 159n90
Rabbi Simeon (Bar Yohai)   32, 56, 84, 114n137, 126, 163
Rabbi Simeon Shezuri   126n49
Rabbi Simeon son of Judah   163
Rabbi Simeon b. Menasiah   163
Rabbi Tarfon   76n48, 160n106, 163
Rabbi Yohanan son of Zakai   64, 74, 127n52
Rabbi Yohanan son of Broqa   84n91
R. Yohanan son of Matya   74, 84
Rabbi Yonatan   63
Rabbi Yossi   58, 62
   The Galilean   114n137
Rabbinic   x, 1, 8–11, 16, 23, 37, 39, 41, 48, 53–56, 59–62, 65–67, 71, 87, 94, 98, 99, 108, 112, 113, 115, 126, 128–130, 145, 151, 158–161, 163, 181
Rabbinic Literature   3–10, 18, 26, 31, 32, 49, 54, 58–61, 63, 72, 87, 91, 101, 106, 107, 112, 117, 120, 128, 129, 139, 154, 156, 160, 171, 181, 184
Ramat Hanadiv (Zikhron Yaacov)   169n154, 173, 176h
Ramathaim   148
Rash   31, 55
Rent, Renter, Rentee   77, 79, 117, 119, 120n20, 134, 137, 138n93
Revolt, Revolts   48, 87, 126n49, 128, 135
   Bar Kokhba Revolt   8, 12, 48, 62n187, 99, 114–115, 125n46, 128, 132n68, 135, 142, 170
   Great Revolt   12, 48, 58n164, 116n2, 128, 135, 142, 177u, 178
   Hasmonean   32, 135 142, 170, 177, 178
Rich   1, 3–6, 15, 17–18, 20a, 22–25, 27, 29–31, 33–35, 37, 40, 48n121, 51–54, 56–57, 60, 63n191, 64–66, 84n91, 92n7, 112, 116, 120–121, 126, 129–130, 132–134, 136, 138–148, 150–165, 167, 168n148, 170–171, 176f,k, 177p, 179–183

GENERAL INDEX

Roman(s) (People)   2, 4n10, 18, 19n61, 45n108, 51, 152, 169n151
Roman Roman (period)   x, 1–3, 6–7, 8n23, 9–11, 16, 18, 21, 25–27, 36–37, 45n108, 48, 53–54, 70, 73, 86–87, 93, 94, 96, 98, 100, 103, 110–112, 115, 116, 130, 135, 139, 140–142, 164, 166, 170–183
Roman Army   11, 12n36, 43n100, 98, 151
Roman Empire (World)   x, 2, 3, 6–7, 9–11, 12–14, 16, 17n54, 21, 22, 25n3, 26, 34, 48, 50, 51n132, 53–54, 58n164, 69, 74, 83, 86n102, 93–97, 98n35, 99n45, 103n73, 104, 110, 112, 115–116, 121, 122n31–32, 129–131, 135n83, 136, 139–141, 145, 152, 162n110n112, 164
Rome (city)   6, 18, 19n61, 21, 43n99, 46n111, 51–52, 69, 83, 92n6, 93, 95, 96, 141–142, 152, 160, 181, 183–184
Rural   16, 18, 89, 91n4, 100, 104n75, 105n80, 112, 131–132, 135, 137–139, 168n148

Sabbath   39n82, 40n93, 41, 43, 46, 74–75, 83, 156n73
Sabbatical (year)   27, 38, 59n171, 82, 85, 107–108, 126
Samaria   133–134, 173
Scribe(s)   102, 105, 112n117
Scythopolis   98
Sea   31, 68, 69, 92n5, 143
Second Temple   3, 8, 26, 29, 32, 48, 53, 58, 60, 61n184, 66, 68, 73, 99, 101, 104, 107, 117, 142, 178n164
Sepphoris   8, 110, 164, 169, 176e, 180
Septimius Severus   165
Septuagint   101n54, 102, 117, 121n28, 143–144
Settlement(s)   131–132, 135, 138, 143, 170, 178
Shammai (Beit Shammai)   39n82
Sharecropper   19n63, 22–23, 36, 73, 117, 119n19, 122n32, 126, 131, 132, 135, 137–139, 164
Shfela   8, 175
Shikhin   98
Ship(s)   164
Shoe, Shoemaker   45–46, 101, 112, 115
Shop, workshop   12, 20, 73, 92n7, 95–96, 98, 99, 107–110, 113, 121
Simeon, Shimon
    Father of Hilkiya   177u
    Rabbi   56, 84, 114n137, 163

Rabbi, Shezuri   126n49
Rebel Leader   69
The Righteous   32
Simon Gobar   165
Slave(s)   17, 19, 20, 28n23, 29, 50–51, 60, 62, 76, 86n102, 89, 90, 92n7–9, 93n10, 118–119, 120n20, 122n29, 123, 130–131, 135n82, 136–137, 152, 163, 166
Social, Sociology, Society   x, 1–28, 30–37, 40–42, 43n99, 46, 48–58, 60, 64, 66, 67, 72, 77, 79, 88, 91–95, 97, 101n60, 103–104, 106–107, 109, 110–113, 115–118, 120–123, 125, 126–131, 133–143, 145, 149, 153–161, 163–164, 167–168, 170, 178–184
Store, storekeeper (see also: shop)   20, 72–73, 74n33, 80, 86, 91, 98, 109, 119, 121, 124n40
Strata, Stratum, Stratification   x, 1–6, 10–11, 13, 15–26, 49, 50–53, 56n153, 77, 94n15, 97, 107n92, 113, 115, 120, 125, 129n60, 131n66, 133–136, 138, 139, 141, 142n8, 145, 156–158, 161, 164, 167, 171, 180–184
Stucco   172, 180
Synagogue   39n82, 110–111, 160
Sumaqa   134, 173
Syria   53, 136n85, 137, 139, 142n7, 178–179

Tanna, Tannaitic, Tannaim   3, 7–8, 13, 16, 21, 26, 48, 55n149, 71, 72, 75, 106–107, 113–115, 116n1, 123, 125–126, 133, 136, 154–156, 158, 161–162, 167
Tax, taxation   2, 25n3, 36, 43n103, 44, 92n6, 111, 117, 121–122, 134–137, 139, 148-151
Teacher   147–148
Temple   3, 4n9, 8, 12, 26–27, 29, 32–33, 35–37, 39n82, 48–49, 53–54, 58–66, 68–69, 73, 99–101, 103–104, 105n85, 107, 108n101, 109, 113–115, 117, 118n12, 128–129, 142, 147, 149, 154, 160n99, 163, 167–168, 178n164, 180
Tenant   26, 119, 137
Theodosian Code   165
Threshing Floor   38–39
Tiberius   164, 165n130, 166, 172
Tithes   27–28, 33, 37n75, 38–39, 42, 46, 49, 50, 56, 58, 59, 63, 67, 72, 76, 78n54, 79, 82, 84, 88, 123–127, 129, 130n63, 155, 158, 163
Tomb, tombstone   89n109, 95–96, 115, 168

Torah   27, 28, 30, 43, 57–58, 62–65, 78–79, 85, 90, 102, 146n28, 154, 159, 161
Town(s) (See also: Cities, Villages).   6, 10, 16, 18, 40n93, 82, 91n4, 92n7, 97, 99, 110, 112, 129, 131, 132n68, 134–135, 137, 156, 159, 163–166, 169n151, 170, 172, 177, 179, 182
Trade   4, 12, 15, 17, 35n68, 62n186, 90–91, 94n16, 95–96, 99–100, 109–110, 112, 114–115, 132n68, 138
Triclinium   168, 170

Umm Iz Zetun   179
Urban   16–18, 92n6, 100n47, 104n75, 105n80, 115n141, 137, 168n146
Urbanization   16, 87, 95, 97, 112
Urkhan El Khala   175
Usha   8, 132n68

Vegetables   74, 162
Vessel, Vessels   11, 56, 99, 103, 167, 169
Village(s), villager   10, 16–17, 39, 83n87, 87, 91n4, 97, 105, 112, 115n141, 129–135, 138, 139, 142, 159, 168n148, 172–176, 178, 179, 182
Vitruvius   93n11, 96, 168

Wadi Hamam   172
Wealthy   x, 3, 8n23, 12n37, 15, 18, 20, 22, 26n7, 31–33, 40, 49, 55, 59, 60, 63–65, 74, 82n80, 88, 93, 116, 119–120, 124, 126n49, 129, 130, 132, 134, 136–137, 139, 141–170, 172, 176–183
Wheat   27, 38–39, 40n87, 45–46, 51–52, 58, 76, 81–84, 89n109, 119, 130n63
Wine, winepress   38, 40n90, 41n93, 46n113, 47–48, 50, 56, 84, 85n100, 99, 119, 133, 160, 162n111
Women (Woman)   34, 35n68, 42, 43, 46, 47n118, 56, 60, 62, 74, 97, 105, 112n116, 129n61, 150, 155n63, 156, 159, 163
Workshop   12, 20, 73, 92n7, 95–96, 98, 99, 105, 108–109, 110n108, 121
Wood   96, 99, 101, 113

Yavneh   8, 62n186, 111, 114, 163
Yishmael   48n121, 54, 55n150, 58n165, 59n174, 64n199, 65, 83n85, 114n137, 157n79, 159n95, 160n103
Yodfat   170
Yosi ben Yohanan   32